Lauren St John is golf correspondent to *The Sunday Times* and has also written for *The Financial Times*, *Golf World* and *Today's Golfer*. Her first book, *Shooting at Clouds: Inside the PGA European Tour*, was published in 1991 to great critical acclaim and her latest book, *Out of Bounds*, was shortlisted for The William Hill Sports Book of the Year Award.

SEVE

Lauren St John

CORGI BOOKS

For my sister, Lisa, to whom I can only return
the best advice in the world:
Accept nothing less than everything.

SEVE
A CORGI BOOK : 0 552 145882

Originally published in Great Britain by Partridge Press,
a division of Transworld Publishers Ltd

PRINTING HISTORY
Partridge Press edition published 1993
Corgi edition published 1994
Corgi edition reprinted 1996
Corgi edition reissued 1997

Set in 10½/12pt Linotype Plantin by
Falcon Oast Graphic Art

Corgi Books are published by Transworld Publishers Ltd,
61–63 Uxbridge Road, London W5 5SA,
in Australia by Transworld Publishers (Australia) Pty Ltd,
15–25 Helles Avenue, Moorebank, NSW 2170,
and in New Zealand by Transworld Publishers (NZ) Ltd,
3 William Pickering Drive, Albany, Auckland.

Printed and bound in Great Britain by
Cox & Wyman Ltd, Reading, Berkshire.

Acknowledgements

I am eternally grateful to Dudley Doust, not only for being good enough to speak to me but also for the breadth of understanding and knowledge he brought to *Seve: the Young Champion*, which helped considerably in the research for this book. Also to everyone at Partridge Press, especially Debbie Beckerman, my publisher, who has seemingly infinite reserves of patience, energy and good humour; and to my agent, Sara Menguc at Murray Pollinger, for always knowing what's best for me.

Thanks to all members of the Association of Golf Writers, particularly John Hopkins, Chris Plumridge, Renton Laidlaw, Michael Williams and Liz Kahn, all of whom have helped me more than they know; to Joe Collet, Ballesteros's manager, for giving so generously of his time; to Robert Green for allowing me access to *Golf World*'s library; to the players and caddies of the European Tour, especially Tony Jacklin and Dave Musgrove; to Ben Crenshaw, whose love for the game is an inspiration to anyone who meets him; to Frances Simpson for a million things, but particularly for the garret with the carpet; to Lynne Warnick for the supply of Lion bars and Greek yoghurt; and lastly, but most importantly, thanks to my mom and dad, to whom I owe everything.

'There are many good players but they are not champions in their hearts. To be a champion it has to be inside. Some people they have that naturally and other people they don't. That's why they don't become champions.'

Severiano Ballesteros, March 1990

Contents

Introduction

When the passage of time takes the lustre off the game's brightest careers, only greatness endures, its acid test being that the player is respected as much by his peers as by the public, that, through artistry, skill and passion, he adds a dimension to the sport that was never previously there, and that his last shot is as important as his first.

Few players have had an impact on golf at every stage of their career the way that Severiano Ballesteros has: first as prodigy, reinventing the game; then as angry young man, black-eyed and emotional; later as gracious major champion, handsome and brave; and finally, as an elder statesman, humbled by his flaws. In his early years, Ballesteros was world golf's hurricane. From the moment he executed that butterfly-light miracle chip in the last green at Royal Birkdale to finish runner-up to Johnny Miller as a teenager in the 1976 British Open, he has never stopped amazing us, and, in two decades of drama – of conflicts and glorious victories, legal battles and theatrical escapes – his intelligence, honesty, kindness and humour have shown him to be worthy of a place in our hearts, not just the record books.

At thirty-nine, Ballesteros's five major championship victories (the 1979, 1984 and 1988 British Opens, and 1980 and 1983 Masters) and five World Match Play titles stand out as his greatest achievements, but it is the Ryder Cup that might eventually come to define his career. There is scarcely a match that Ballesteros has participated in that has not been unforgettable and there is no finer testimony to his bravery and heart than that he was as inspiring in his darkest hour, the singles match he lost to Tom Lehman in the 1995 Ryder Cup at Oak Hill, as he has been in his strongest. When agonizing back problems threatened to keep him out of the matches in 1993, Payne Stewart voiced what everyone else thought: 'It wouldn't be the Ryder Cup as I know it if Seve wasn't playing.'

11

Ballesteros's latest manifestation, as captain of the European team at the 1997 Ryder Cup in Valderrama, Spain, may be his most awe-inspiring role yet.

Over the years, tour policies on both sides of the Atlantic, petty bureaucracies and homesickness have prevented the Spaniard from playing in the United States as much as he would have liked to, but the Ryder Cup has brought his gifts and his charisma to a wider audience. 'Ballesteros has been the most influential non-American golfer since Harry Vardon,' *Golf World* (US) reported in 1996. 'His performances in America in the late Seventies and early Eighties convinced other international players that the US was not an impregnable fortress.'

But Tom Callahan showed another side to the story in *Golf Digest*. 'A great failure of the American sporting press is that it has not communicated Ballesteros adequately to the people of the United States,' he said. 'American golf fans know that he is great and that he won two US Masters and three British Opens. But they think of him as "their Palmer" when he might have been our Seve, too.'

Nick Price, who duelled with Ballesteros in the 1988 Open at Lytham, said that even now Ballesteros is the only player he would go out onto the course to watch. 'Seve can shoot sixty-four a hundred different ways. Faldo can do it only one way: down the middle, on the green, one or two putts.'

Nowadays, Ballesteros has more frailties than he perhaps had when he dominated the game throughout the Eighties. Family life has become more important to him, and has made him a more rounded person, a more compassionate person. Once golf was his whole world; now he says that if he only had one hour to live, he would spend it talking to his sons. But he still has the capacity to astonish us with his gift on the course. He still has grace, power and charisma. He still has presence, he still has genius. Most importantly, he still inspires love as well as admiration.

Years ago, Ballesteros said that when his career was over he only wanted to be remembered as 'someone who did what he did with honour.'

He'll be remembered as all of that and more.

1

The Seeds of Greatness

When I was small, I never think about winning. I never even was thinking about the majors. I was just thinking about being a champion. I was thinking, I'd like to be the best.

Severiano Ballesteros, March 1990

It was almost midnight when Severiano Ballesteros, aged nine, stirred, stretched and cautiously pushed back the covers. For hours he had lain in the darkness, feigning sleep, until he heard his brother Vicente, with whom he shared a single bed and the windowless room they called 'the dungeon', come quietly through the door, and his parents' muffled tread on the stairs. Now he listened. When there was no sound save Vicente's rhythmic breathing and the low roar of the distant sea, he dressed silently, felt for his precious golf club and went out into the balmy night air. A cool and dusty track led the way from the farmhouse. Wraithlike, he slipped down the hill to the Real Club de Golf de Pedreña – built in 1929 at the behest of King Alfonso XIII of Spain, and strictly out of bounds to small peasant farmers' sons – and there, alone but for the swaying shadows of the pines, he hit a hundred or more balls at the benign silver moon. 'I could not see them but I could tell how good and how straight I hit them by the feel in the hands and the sand.'

Most nights he practised on the second hole, a 198-yard

par three named La Rivera, measuring his progress over the seasons by the club he took to reach the green. 'My ambition was to be able to use an iron. I would ask, "When will I be big enough?" And my brothers would answer, "Soon, soon." ' He also played golf along the seashore, or stood in the backyard and hit balls over the high trees and onto the second green – a distance of 150 yards. These stolen hours, ghostly and filled with dreams, remain with him still. 'My *best* memories are of sneaking onto the golf course and playing when it was dark.' At last, cold and exhausted, he would return to the sleeping house. But when dawn broke he would be out again, searching for the lost balls and occasionally playing. Day in and day out Ballesteros did this, in sunshine and in snow. Then he would walk along the dirt road to the golf club where he caddied, often arriving shivering, muddy and bedraggled, to wait for the first amateurs to drive up.

Years later, long after he had become the best golfer in the world, he could still remember the jeers of the other boys and feel the sharp sting of injured pride. 'All the other caddies they laugh at me – and the more when it rained and I come in in the morning and they say I am the drowning rat.' But their taunts goaded him, strengthened him, made the desire burn more fiercely in his heart; and in 1984, when he won the Open Championship for the second time, he could say with quiet assurance:

'No, they have not laughed now for some years.'

Severiano Ballesteros was born on 9 April 1957, in a stone farmhouse overlooking the Bay of Santander in the village of Pedreña, northern Spain. The youngest son of Baldomero Ballesteros Presmanes and Carmen Sota Ocejo, he grew up in the shadow of the Cantabrian mountains, not far from the Bay of Biscay, running barefoot and free over the hills. He had three brothers: Baldomero Jnr, nicknamed Merin (pronounced Marine), who was ten years older than he was, Manuel and Vicente who were, respectively, seven and five years older. A fourth brother, the first-born, had died at the age of two from a wasp sting.

The house in which Ballesteros spent the first sixteen

years of his life, and to which he returns still for it now belongs to Manuel and his family, was a quaint white-washed double-storey, with an uneven red-tiled roof, red-brick sides, jade-green doors and railings and an adjoining half-painted extension of delightfully home-made appearance. Built by his great-grandparents in 1882, it once belonged to his mother's uncle. She took care of him in the last days of his life and he left it to her when he died. At the back of the house were some stables, where the family kept several dairy cows, a few chickens, a donkey and some rabbits, all of which had names and were tended to by Severiano and his father. The basement of the house was lit by the cosy glow of an elderly wood stove. Here, Ballesteros used to practise on the harshest winter days, smashing balls interminably into a heavy canvas cloth hung from the rafters. From there, a shadowy staircase led to the living quarters. There were four bedrooms. The two older brothers each had their own, but Severiano shared a narrow bed with Vicente until he was ten and the dark cell-like room where they slept until he was fourteen. His earliest memory is of his mother coming in to wake him up for school and finding him on the floor, Vicente having pushed him there when he was sleeping. Outside was a well which provided water for the house.

The Ballesteros family lived simply and toiled hard, subsisting off the land where they could. They milked their cows, gathered eggs from their chickens and grew vegetables. As a family friend observes, 'They didn't just go down to the supermarket to buy the butter, they had to churn it.' One's impression is that they epitomized village life and hard times in rural Spain in the Fifties and Sixties, and that they were essentially peasant farmers. But Dudley Doust, former sports correspondent for *The Sunday Times* and author of Ballesteros's early biography, *Seve: the Young Champion*, maintains that, although 'the illustion is cast of a small-holding, struggling family, actually, the Ballesteroses, even before the youngest son achieved fame and fortune, had accumulated untold [acres] of land. If not wealthy, the family is near to it.'

Later, he talks of the characteristics of the Montañeses,

the people of the Cantabrian mountains and coastline around Santander, among whom are the Ballesteros and Sota families, describing them as brave, resourceful, suspicious, superstitious and thrifty to the point of meanness. Ballesteros himself has been richly endowed with these qualities. The *Encyclopedia Britannica* has it that their forebears, the Cantabri, an Iberian tribe which occupied the region until the first century AD, 'were regarded as the fiercest people in the peninsula'. They were children of their environment, for La Montana, as the land of the Montañeses is popularly known, is wild and mysterious. It was on the cliffs near Pedreña, so it is said, that bonfires were once lit and ships lured onto the rocks so that their cargoes could be pillaged and sold; it was men from the Cantabrian coast – navigators, cartographers and traders carrying wool, flour and eucalyptus wood – who took a ship for the New World, returning as wealthy men; and it was into this bleak and beautiful landscape, where legend and reality are intertwined, that one of the most gifted golfers the world has ever seen was born.

The picture Ballesteros paints of his boyhood is one of perfect contentment. He can only ever remember it as being idyllic. 'I was very happy. We have always been a happy family. It was tough, of course, as well, but that also helped me.' Warm-hearted and sunny by nature, with dark hair, laughing brown eyes and an impish grin, he was adored by his close-knit family. 'My parents spoilt me but I had to do everything for my brothers,' he told *The Times*. 'I shopped for them. I was the one who, every Sunday, had to clean all their shoes. For that I got five pesetas, which was enough to go to the cinema.'

Sundays were special days in the Ballesteros household. While Severiano helped his father in the cowshed, his mother would prepare a three-course lunch. 'She would put it on the fire to cook and then we would walk to church, which was five minutes away. My father would go for an aperitif with his friends, come home for lunch and then he would go and caddie . . . He fished, too, for clams – for us to eat and also to sell . . . It seemed he was always working and so was my mother . . . One thing I still find hard to take in is how hard my mother worked for all of us. She would go to the super-market to buy the food, she would cook, she would clean the house and then she would help my father with the cows. She never seemed to stop working . . . This is one thing together that they transmit to me. I have never forgotten how tough life can be and how hard you must work to achieve all you want.'

When he was seven years old Ballesteros was given his first golf club – the rusting head of an ancient three-iron. It became his pride and joy. He scrubbed it and scoured it and polished it till it shone, and afterwards went out and searched for sticks for its shafts. These slender pieces of wood, carefully chosen for durability, he hid from his brothers. Whenever one broke, which they did almost daily, he would go through the slow process of cutting a new 'shaft' to length, whittling it to a point, fitting it into the hosel and then soaking it overnight in a bucket of water so that the wood swelled to fill the narrow neck of the club. Time and time again he did this, and always lovingly, without impatience. With golf balls he had to be equally resourceful for his brothers wouldn't give him theirs. He roamed the beach hunting for pebbles of their approximate size and, when he found them, would stuff them in his pockets and spirit them away to his cache. His golf courses were the illicit fairways of Club de Golf de Pedreña by night, and those of his own invention on the beach and around the farm – with twigs for pins and paper for flags – by day.

His devotion to the game was absolute. He lived it, breathed it and slept it; thoughts of it occupied his every waking hour. And while that in itself is not uncommon, obsessions of one kind or the other (usually fleeting and directionless) being an integral part of childhood, what is rare is to find a boy as young as Ballesteros pursuing his goal with such enduring fervour and single-mindedness.

'Seve had a love of golf you could almost touch,' Manuel once observed. 'Without a golf club in his hand, he was like a man with no legs. It was part of him. You never saw him without a golf club.'

At the age of eight Ballesteros began caddying at Club de

Golf de Pedreña, where Ramon Sota, his famous uncle, was and still is the professional, for the equivalent of twenty-five pence a day. He earned forty pesetas for the first bag he ever carried and gave it all to his mother. Not long afterwards he was given his first real golf club – another three-iron – by Manuel, and it was at that point that his competitive nature truly began to assert itself. In the summers Ballesteros spent most of his time down at the course, lounging about with an assortment of dark-eyed vagabond caddies. These boys occupied themselves with games of ferocious intensity and infinite variety. Every conceivable competition, within the limits of the resources available to them, was devised by them, a favourite being the egg and spoon races they had up and down the beach using golf balls and clubs. Ballesteros, his gambling instincts quickly aroused, reached the stage where he would wager virtually every peseta he made on his ability to triumph in any contest the other caddies could name. 'I would bet more than I could afford to lose to make myself win.'

The first trophy he ever won was for running rather than golf. He swept to victory in the regional 1,500 metre championship by some 16 seconds. 'My friend, Javier, couldn't keep up with me even on a bicycle,' he recalled proudly. That tiny cup, shaped like a thimble, still has a special place in his trophy cabinet. Running, at that age, was his passion and the sport he feels he would have been most successful at if he had not chosen golf. 'Like everybody, I played soccer, but I was bad. I remember I was quite fast but I had no real ability. It was not my game. I was a good runner – running 1,500 metres. I think if I had gone that way instead of playing golf, maybe I'd have been easily as good as Sebastian Coe or Steve Ovett.'

Slowly his incredible talent for golf began to manifest itself. When he was nine, he stole round the 6,315-yard Pedreña course in an hour. A year later, playing in his first caddie tournament, he made 10 on the opening hole, and when he finished fifth with a total of 51 was inconsolable. At eleven, he was runner-up in the same event with a score of 42. But when he was twelve and it became an eighteen-hole tournament, he won with a nine over par 79, wearing his first pair of golf shoes – an oversized pair given to him by a club member. By the end of the year he was playing to the equivalent of a scratch handicap and, not long afterwards, beat his tournament professional brother, Manuel, for the first time. There are no records to prove it, but it seems probable that Ballesteros was one of the most advanced players for his age in the history of the game.

The bane of young Severiano's life was the National Primary School in Pedreña. He played truant at every opportunity and paid no attention either to the teachers or his mother, who told him that he would not make a career out of golf. Already that streak of defiance, which makes him strive for and achieve undreamt of heights in the face of adversity or opposition and which he was to use to such great effect later on in life, was inherent in him, and rather than working harder at his algebra he simply thought more determinedly of winning tournaments – 'Every one in the world and by twenty strokes.'

When he was twelve years old he became drunk for the first and last time. 'My father and mother had gone fishing,' he recalls. 'My lunch had been left and there was a bottle of wine, so I took a drink. I had four glasses. I was drunk when I got back to school. I slapped the woman teacher and I was suspended. It was revenge because she had smacked me across the hand with a ruler because I was talking in class.' Two years later he gave up attending school altogether and vowed never to touch another glass of alcohol. 'I used to have white wine at lunch. It never affected me. I smoked a little, too, but I saw that all the good players didn't drink or smoke. So I said to myself: "Seve, if you want to be a good player, you stop." So I stop.'

On the afternoons when he wasn't playing sport Ballesteros's favourite form of amusement was television. At that time in Pedreña, which had a population of little more than 3,000, there was only one of these in existence and that was to be found in a village bar. He whiled away many enjoyable hours in the jovial and smoky atmosphere of that tavern, gazing with rapt attention at American programmes like *Bonanza* and *The Fugitive* dubbed in Spanish. 'There was no golf on TV in Spain in those days,' he

19

remembers. 'I never saw golf on television until I was sixteen.'

In this instance, at least, there can be little doubt that fortune smiled upon Ballesteros – as it did when it handed him one club instead of fourteen. Instead of spending his youth trying to learn from the example of tournament professionals of unexceptional talent, with staid and conservative golf games, and gradually, through no fault of his own, becoming inured to the fact that golf should not be a great adventure but should be approached methodically, like chess, by selecting the appropriate club for the appropriate distance and playing down the centre of the fairway, Ballesteros learned by imitation and thought of nothing else but getting the ball in the hole from the tee. With his three-iron he could play any shot that had ever been invented, and a whole lot more besides. And it was by playing with one ambition, and one ambition only, to be the best golfer in the world, that he developed all the flair, strength, fire, individuality and originality which eventually helped him realize his dream and made him the most exciting and charismatic player in the modern era.

'Today the biggest mistake that a person could make with a youngster is to give him a full set of golf clubs,' says Lee Trevino, who taught himself the game with only a five-iron. 'Because he says, "This nine-iron goes 120 yards, the eight goes 135," and they hit the shot that is called for instead of standing there and imagining some type of a shot with a seven-iron that you only have to hit 50 yards, or you might have to duck-hook it and hit it 190 yards.'

'I don't think there's any question about that,' agrees Ben Crenshaw, the 1984 US Masters Champion and one of golf's most popular and respected players. 'You can certainly see that with Seve, who played every shot with that three-iron. He played on the beach, around the greens and everywhere. He learned to be more inventive . . . and inventiveness is a great part of the game because it cultivates imagination.'

Ballesteros's desire to be the best did not stop at golf. He was a natural athlete and, like Nick Faldo, the current world No. 1, who had the same deep and abiding affection for sport when he was a boy, wanted to excel at everything. Thus he spent his days running, swimming, cycling, playing football and boxing. His love of competition was jointly inherited from the two men who were to influence him most: his father, Baldomero Ballesteros, and his mother's brother, Ramon Sota.

Baldomero Snr was a tall, lean, soft-spoken man, with strong arms and huge hands. On the heel of his left hand was a scar which had been incurred during the Spanish Civil War. An ardent Franco supporter, he had been recruited into the Republican Army in 1937 and had shot himself through the hand in protest. He was court-martialled, convicted of self-mutilation and sentenced to twenty years in prison. But a fate worse than death was spared him when Santander fell to Franco's troops not long after he had emerged from hospital, and he fought alongside the Franquistas until the end of the war. On his return home, Baldomero married Carmen Sota Ocejo and took over the dairy farm bequeathed to him by his father. His wife was of agricultural stock. Her family had farmed the valley of the River Cubas in Pedreña for generations and it was her father who, in 1928, sold the land that eventually became part of the first, fourth and sixth holes of the Real Club de Golf de Pedreña. Baldomero was the great-grandson of an acclaimed bell-founder whose own son had learned the trade but had exchanged it for dairy farming upon his father's death. After the war, he threw himself whole-heartedly not only into the agricultural business but also into training for the Regata de Traineras, an annual three-mile race around Santander Bay which dates back to the early eighteenth century. Five times he helped row the Pedreña boat to victory, and in 1946 he and his thirteen fellow *remeros* (oarsmen) set a record that stands to this day. He was well respected in the local community and had a great number of friends, and his courage as an oarsman was renowned throughout the region. A close associate of the Ballesteroses describes him as, 'beloved by all the family and a real father-figure'.

Certainly Baldomero Snr was a larger than life figure, and his standing as a local hero in the village was a hard act for his sons to follow. Baldomero, the eldest, did not attempt to. He was a quiet, pensive man who always seemed rather intimidated by the sheer magnetism of his father's presence

21

and by his physical strength. Manuel was tougher and more independent. He was also very motivated and, but for his selfless devotion to the nurturing of Severiano's incredible talent, would almost certainly have achieved much more as a Tour player than he did. Vicente, the second youngest, was a silent, almost secretive young man. In later life he became an excellent teacher but remained, nevertheless, an enigma, flitting about as shadowy as a moth on the edges of his brother's brilliant career. All the brothers were talented and special enough in their own way, but it was his youngest son who was the apple of Baldomero Snr's eye. From the very first moment Severiano picked up a golf club, he made it his life's work to encourage him and build up his confidence, and for that the boy loved him completely and without reserve. 'I have to say that my father was always very optimistic,' he was to remark years later. 'He always believed in me. My mother was always very nice, very loving, but she has always been very pessimistic, fatalistic.'

Doubtless that is true, but Doust has a theory that 'great sportsmen very often come from a matriarchy rather than a patriarchy. I mean, that it's the mother that worships them.' A Spanish-speaker, he knew Severiano long before the draw-bridge of fame came down between them and, as such, was able to get much closer to the heart of the Ballesteros family than anyone else has subsequently managed to. Severiano's mother speaks no English at all and Baldomero Jnr and Vicente have but a smattering. Even Manuel is by no means fluent.

When Ballesteros was nineteen and the darling of all the golf world, Doust, then in the employ of *The Sunday Times*, went out to Pedreña to write a feature on him, along with sports photographer Chris Smith. '[We] were sitting around the house and they were having little arguments: who's the most handsome? who's so and so. All the brothers and the father. And they deferred always to Seve. And he was a youngster. And the mother would bring him milk – the others would be drinking the hard stuff – and she would just kind of run around at his heels. So he was spoilt hollow. But like many spoilt people, he expects the best. I think that's part of it, too [his success], being spoilt; and if you've got a pretty strong nature and you're spoilt you're better off still, because you're never satisfied because you've always just got what you've wanted. And he always got what he wanted and he was tough enough to get what he wanted when he played golf.

'That day,' remembers Doust, '[his mother] was sitting in the kitchen with a tea-cosy on – it wasn't a tea-cosy but it looked like one – and I went out to speak with her and she said: "He'll be the greatest golfer in the world." And, I mean, it wasn't vain, it wasn't anything. It was just a statement of fact. And I think he thought so himself. And it was true.'

The role of his father and of his brothers who, by the time he was in his mid-teens, were all professional golfers, in the shaping of his career, is frequently talked of by Ballesteros. He seems more reluctant to acknowledge the assistance of Ramon Sota: 'When I was a caddie, Ramon was playing outside and when Ramon retired, I was just starting. So I never have a chance to play with him too much.'

Long before Ballesteros hit his first golf ball, Sota had been recognized as one of the most talented players ever to emerge from Spain, a nation which did not at that time have a long history of tournament golf. The first Spanish golf course, Club de Golf de Las Palmas in the Canary Islands, was not built until 1891, and it was 1904 before the game moved to the mainland. Twenty years later Spain produced the first of many gifted tournament professionals, namely Angel and Sebastian Miguel, sons of a poverty-stricken labourer and caddies at Puerta de Hierro in Madrid. The former won three tournaments in Britain, two Spanish Opens, was fourth in the 1957 Open at St Andrews, played five times in the US Masters and won the individual World Cup (then the Canada Cup) title in 1958. Sota came next. John Jacobs, the eminent British golf teacher, remembers coaching both Sota and his nephews when he began giving clinics to golf professionals and teams in Spain around 1970.

'I feel – people may not agree with me – that I've had a tremendous influence on Spanish golf,' says Jacobs, 'because I feel that the game has been taught better in Spain than anywhere else in the world . . . Apparently Seve was one of the youngsters [I taught], but I couldn't tell you. It's only been pointed out to me that he was. But I'm not making any claims to have made Seve great. He was hugely gifted . . . But Ramon used to come and listen to me saying how the game should be taught . . . and put himself in front of me for me to teach him, which was tremendously good for me in front of all those pros. Ramon, I get on ever so well with. But they're *very strong* characters all of them [the Sotas and the Ballesteroses]. They're not easy characters. I don't mean I dislike them – in fact, I'd much rather have that sort than the person who everyone likes and then there's probably something up with them – but they could be very difficult.'

Physically, there was little resemblance between Severiano and his uncle. Sota was a short, stocky figure with an unlovely but effective swing, which assisted him to victory in the Spanish, Portuguese, Dutch, Italian and Brazilian Opens. He, too, had learnt golf by caddying, and it was he who enforced the bar against caddies on the course at Club de Golf de Pedreña. One wonders, possibly completely erroneously, whether Ballesteros didn't hold this against him. Michael McDonnell of the *Daily Mail* once described him as, 'a repressive figure who never seems happy with the efforts of his nephews', then later said that his attitude towards them was 'disparaging, perhaps intentionally so, because he knew how difficult it could be to sustain a lifestyle as a playing professional and how much heartbreak was involved.' 'Seve is far more sophisticated than Ramon, as a person,' says Mark Wilson, a former correspondent for the *Daily Express*. 'Ramon – nice fellow – was a very basic man. Seve is a different person altogether. Were their games at all similar? No, not at all. Nothing's similar to Seve, is it? Surely Seve's got the best golf swing in the world? No, Ramon stayed with the caddie swing and very effective it was, too.'

'I play a bit with Ramon,' remembers Vicente Fernandez, the little Argentinian who was to become one of Ballesteros's most loyal and trusted friends. 'He was a great player, too. Fantastic. But his game wasn't like Seve's. I don't think Ramon had the courage that Seve has. The difference is that

' he art. I'm not saying that Ramon didn't have
bout as more.'
d it, had little to offer his small nephew from
that of view, he did do one essential thing: he
On t a boy from a poor village in the north of
are but into the world and win.
the

the was fourteen the extent of Severiano Balles-
nal us talent was becoming apparent. He could
osc Manuel, himself a strong, experienced golfer
ave d in several international teams and who ulti-
or ed his own career for the sake of his brother's,
d I the Club Caddies' Championship by sixteen
ng e was he of his own ability that, when he had
ne is brother at the Spanish Under-25s Champion-
ur vious year and watched Manuel perform badly,
or ped the golf bag on the green, screamed at him
le incompetent and said arrogantly: 'I could have
se myself.' Meanwhile, his reputation as a prodigy
e ng like wildfire. Fernandez can recall Manuel tell-
hree years before Ballesteros played his first Tour
g he had a young brother who was going to be great,
e no, who played with Sota in South America in the
s says that: 'He told me he had a nephew who was
o be a helluva player. I knew about him way before he
out on Tour.'
ust, too, can remember talking to the Spanish golfers
he Continental Tour as far back as 1971 about how many
d players were starting to emerge from Spain, and being
ld: '"Well, there's this kid up in Pedreña who's better than
iny of us." He was about fourteen then. And they all knew
him and worshipped him. And he was absolutely special.'

The speed at which Ballesteros developed as a player is
commonly held to be due to the aforementioned influences:
his father, his brothers, Sota and, obviously, his unique gift.
But he himself feels that his environment played an equal part
– the proximity of his home to a golf course, the relative penury
of his childhood and the instilling in him of the work ethic.
Fernandez believes he is right. 'I don't think [Seve] could

have taken to golf the way he took to it if he was rich[says. 'Because first you have to love the small things the game itself. You have to appreciate it and understar and you are mentally open to learn because you know you don't have a choice to go and learn somewhere else the one hand, you get your experiences from books [if you wealthy], and on the other, you have to live them. That's hardest way but it's the way that will stay with you.'

Manuel Piñero who, like Ballesteros, came through Spanish caddie system that has produced such exceptic players over the years, agrees. 'I think, especially in tl days, we were hungry to get money because we didn't h any. For us, golf was everything. Either we became good we were nothing. It was our only chance to survive. And think, when you have such a great difficulty to do somethi in life, and if you come through it, you will have such discipli and a strong mentality that you can beat anybody. Also, background was very low but the people we were caddying were very high class and we wanted to prove to those peop that we can do very well. I don't say this as revenge to tho people, no, no, no. It's just something that we had to prov to ourselves and to those people.'

Ballesteros, for his part, was prevented from becomin an actual member of the Pedreña course by the 'rigid cast system of Spanish society', and therefore concentrated all hi efforts on escaping from that world to pursue his goals. Once when he was asked how a young boy from a remote fishing village achieved those ambitions, he replied: 'Well, in order to be successful, whether you play golf or you do any other thing, there's two things that you need. You have to work very hard. That's No. 1. And No. 2, you need a tremendous amount of discipline. If you have those two things, I think whatever you want you will get.'

In 1973 Ballesteros effectively lost his amateur status by accepting a set of promotional golf clubs from an American army officer stationed near Zaragoza, where Vicente was working as a club professional. The inscription on them was 'Super'. On New Year's Day the following year, having satisfactorily met the requirements of entry into the Spanish

Professional Golfers' Association by passing a written test on the Rules of Golf, returning correct and legible scorecards and paying a membership fee of 5,000 pesetas, Ballesteros was awarded his player's card and became, at sixteen years, eight months and twenty-one days, the youngest accredited professional tournament player in the history of Spanish golf.

And so it was that on the first day of the following April, with a $1,000 loan in his pocket – given to him to cover his expenses for the Portuguese, Spanish, Madrid and French Opens by Santander-born Dr Cesar Campuzano, a wealthy Madrid radiologist whose golf holidays were spent in Pedreña – Severiano Ballesteros shook hands with his father, hugged his weeping mother, waved to a crowd of well-wishers and set off down the dirt track with his golf clubs over his shoulder. From Pedreña, he took a bus to Santander and then an overnight train through the mountains to Madrid. Alone, nervous and excited, but full of hope for what the future might bring, he made his way through the city to the airport and boarded a flight to Portugal. In this manner, he left Spain for the first time.

2

Rebel with a Cause

When I was younger I used to be difficult.

Severiano Ballesteros, Royal Lytham, July 1988

October 1974, Madrid, Spain. At the end of his first season as a tournament professional, Severiano Ballesteros was bound, once again, for Lisbon. When his flight was called he followed Gary Player, Tony Jacklin and his brother Manuel aboard the aircraft, where he sat in his seat and stared despondently out of the window, dwelling on bureaucracy and opportunities lost. All things considered it had not been a good week. Ibergolf, a course construction company, had invited nine players to compete in a thirty-six hole event at Las Lomas el Bosque, near Madrid. In the first round, erratic driving had cost Ballesteros dearly on the heavily wooded, water-traversed course, and he had returned the worst score of the competition, a 79. But he had pulled himself together determinedly and had shot a 69 on the second day, finishing in fifth place behind Player, the eventual winner. Curiously enough, the mere fact that he had finished fifth was responsible for his melancholy air. Instead of congratulating himself on his achievement, which would have been a wholly natural and acceptable reaction in a player so young, he was remonstrating with himself for allowing victory to escape him. 79, 69 he thought with disgust. What a way to end his first season on the European Tour. And now there was this problem of the visa. Nobody had told him he would need a visa to enter South Africa; or if they had he'd forgotten. Of course, Player had assured him that he would use his influence to obtain the necessary documentation immediately the embassy opened the following morning, but the delay would mean that the Ballesteros brothers would miss their connecting flight and arrive in Johannesburg only hours before the South African PGA Championship was due to begin. Ballesteros glared out into the night. How could anyone be expected to play golf under such conditions?

'My brother,' said Manuel confidentially to Player and Jacklin when Ballesteros's attention was thus diverted, 'best young player in the world.'

'Oh, Manuel,' said Player in a kindly but rather patronizing way, 'I don't think so.'

But Manuel persisted. 'You should see my brother play,' he told Jacklin. 'My brother is fantastic. My brother is better than all the players in Spain. You should see him hit the ball. My brother can win many tournaments. He . . .'

'Yeah, yeah, we know,' interrupted Jacklin in a bored tone.

Manuel gave him an exasperated look. 'You will see,' he said stubbornly. 'You will see. One day my brother will be the best player in the world.'

Ballesteros had played the first round of his first professional tournament outside of Spain on 9 April 1974, the day he turned seventeen. The Portuguese Open was held at Estoril that year, on the grey Atlantic coast, and Ballesteros was encouraged by the fact that on the two practice days, playing with Manuel and the genial Argentinian Vicente (Chino) Fernandez, he had hit the ball well enough to score under par. But when the gun went off in the pre-qualifying round, it all fell to pieces. That morning he visited every bunker, pine thicket, shrubbery and rockery on the 5,656-yard course, going out in 43 and coming back in 46 to finish at twenty over par. Later he was to admit that he had tried to put the ball in the hole off every tee.

'Seve, what did you shoot?' asked Fernandez that afternoon, coming upon the young Spaniard practising.

'Eighty-nine,' said Ballesteros with a break in his voice, and when he looked at Fernandez there were tears in his eyes.

'Don't worry, Sev,' said the Argentinian gently, touched at the boy's distress. 'Take it easy. It's only your first tournament.' And he took Ballesteros aside and talked to him for a long time about golf and about his attitude to the game. They were friends from that moment on.

'He was very disappointed,' recalls Fernandez, 'but already he showed his temperament because he kept on practising harder and harder. He was so strong it was unbelievable. So long. He always went for everything, no matter what kind of shot he had. And his short game was fantastic. Probably the best part of his game at that time. With his driver he could be two fairways away, but his short game was fantastic.'

A fortnight earlier, Ballesteros had played in the Spanish PGA Championship at Club de Golf de San Cugat in Barcelona, his first actual tournament as a professional. There, too, he had lived up to all of his own expectations in practice, scoring an astonishing 27 on the front nine on the opening day, but had crashed and burned when it counted. At the end of the final round he signed his scorecard with shaking hands and rushed to look at the leaderboard. He was twentieth in the 110-man field and would only earn £15. What had gone wrong? In his heart of hearts he had believed he could win – had *expected* to win, but somehow the gods had conspired to prevent it. Worst of all, he had let Manuel and Dr Campuzano down. Choking with fury and humiliation, Ballesteros ran for the solitude of the locker room; Manuel Piñero found him there hours later, his head in his hands, sobbing.

'I think what surprised some of us was how angry he was with himself for not doing better,' says Piñero, who sat with his young compatriot, comforting him, until he calmed down. 'He was so angry and cross. I remember thinking at the time, "This boy could be a very, very good player." '

From Portugal Ballesteros flew to La Manga for the start of the Spanish Open. He had already dismissed his fears of failure as groundless, recovered his high spirits, and was contemplating the tournament ahead with enthusiasm.

The field was a strong one; Player, who had won the US Masters in April, Maurice Bembridge and Jerry Heard were all entered. Ballesteros relished the fresh challenge. This week, he felt sure, he would show people what he was made of. He boosted his hopes still further on practice days and in the pre-qualifying, where he recorded a one under par 71 on the long and treacherous course, and felt more confident than he had at any time since leaving Pedreña. But when the tournament began, he succumbed once again – not meekly, mind you, but fighting like a wildcat – to the pressure.

For the most part, pressure in professional golf is self-inflicted. Ballesteros had that in common with the majority, but there the similarity ended. He didn't, as so often happens with Tour rookies, regard the halfway cut with increasing dread as the weeks went by, or allow it to assume such gargantuan proportions in his mind that he ended up being unable to think of tournaments as four-round events and simply went out at the start of each one with an eye fixed firmly on the thirty-six hole score where the axe was likely to fall. He thought only of the finish line. From the very first hole of every tournament, he threw himself heart, body and soul into trying to win, clawing and scratching at the unyielding golf course in a furious attempt to gain birdies, eagles and even albatrosses, and getting scratched and bitten as often as not in return.

La Manga lulled him into a false sense of security. When he reached the 586-yard ninth in the opening round, he had already made eight straight pars and was beginning to think that he could take advantage of her forgiving nature. He stood on the tee and looked boldly down the fairway. Here was his chance to capitalize on his length and make a 4 or even a 3. He set up over the ball and struck it with such force that his follow-through ended in a kind of high twirl. It flew away in a magnificent banana-shaped curve and vanished into oblivion. He teed up again. This time the ball went right, slicing smoothly out of bounds and out of sight. His third attempt (and fifth stroke) was on the fairway. Ballesteros by now was virtually apoplectic with rage. He slammed his club viciously into the golf bag and set off in pursuit of the miscreant ball, cursing and scowling and denouncing the world in Spanish. The golfing gods took a dim view of his behaviour. They saw to it that his sixth shot homed in, as if by magnet, on a water hazard. Ballesteros dropped miserably out under penalty, played a poor chip into a bunker, found the green in 9 and two-putted for an 11. He scored 83 that day and 78 the next to miss the cut by a shot.

It was during this low period in his first season that subtle distinctions between Ballesteros and his colleagues began to emerge. For a start, he held himself aloof from the crowd, preferring his own company or that of a handful of Spanish friends to the social gatherings integral to the Tour. His lack of English distanced him still further. He was obsessed with the game to the exclusion of all else and thus had an acceptance of, and even a love for, its vagaries, a quality rare among young golfers. While others grew dejected or self-pitying when confronted with the harsh reality of life on the European Tour, Ballesteros became angry or tearful, then used those emotions to fuel his desire. He set himself a punishing practice regime and disciplined himself to adhere religiously to it. Not a day went by when he didn't stand on the range until dark. Where Ballesteros was particularly unusual, however, was in his zest for watching great players work on their games. Most golfers, having failed to qualify for a tournament, will do anything short of walk on water to put as much distance between themselves and the scene of their misfortune as possible. Ballesteros was just the opposite. He would stay on at the golf course for the weekend, just so that he could see Player practise bunker shots, Heard hit iron shots or Peter Oosterhuis putt.

All this had little effect on his scoring. Absorbed in the contemplation of good golf swings, Ballesteros lost sight of the importance of the finer art of course management. He could not think in terms of percentages or see the advantages of tempering his game. He could not express himself but through towering drives, freakish iron play, miraculous recoveries and audacious chip shots. His sole aim was to win every tournament he played in and win it by twenty shots. Caution was not in his vocabulary. As a consequence, he shot

84, 79 to miss the thirty-six hole cut in the Madrid Open at Puerto de Hierro by a comfortable margin, and 76, 75, 74 to miss the fifty-four hole cut in the French Open at Chantilly.

When the Tour went to Britain the following week, it left without Ballesteros. Manuel had persuaded him to go home. Heartsore and travel weary, he returned to Pedreña to face the inevitable questions and enquiring glances of his friends. He felt strongly that he had let down the people who believed in him, but saw no immediate way of remedying the situation other than through hard work and grind on the practice range. He could no more consider a life of monotony, regimentation and toil as a factory worker, bank clerk or farm labourer than he could cut off a limb. Golf filled his dreams and his every waking hour. Without it there was nothing – only emptiness. Nevertheless, he had to find some way of recouping his lost earnings. To date, the young Spaniard had earned the grand total of £40 on the Tour. His travel expenses had come to rather more than that and his funds from Dr Campuzano had almost dried up as a result. With no alternative on the horizon, Ballesteros resorted once more to caddying, for twenty-five pence a round.

Salvation came in the shape of the National Under 25's Championship, held at Pedreña. Ballesteros had recovered all his old self-esteem and was now certain he would soon be the best player in the world. When the tournament began he set about proving it, attacking his home course with cavalier flair and determination and, driven by pride and aided by local knowledge, swept to his first professional victory. He was overjoyed. Not only was the title a salve on all the hurts and humiliations he had suffered since surrendering his amateur status, but it had earned him £500. Ballesteros felt ten feet tall. He finished runner-up in the next tournament, the Santander Open, also played at Pedreña, and a week later took top honours at Bilbao in the Vizcaya Open, beating Manuel and Vicente into second and third place.

In October, having regained the physical and emotional resources necessary to cope with day-to-day life on the professional circuit, Ballesteros took a flight to Venice, where the Italian Open was being held. On practice days he played with his brother Manuel and Piñero, who marvelled at his prodigious length off the tee. 'He was so young that it was impossible to say how far he would go in his career, but it was obvious he had a fantastic talent for the game. Fantastic talent.'

Exactly how gifted he was, Ballesteros demonstrated when the tournament started. After nine holes of the first round he was three under par and sharing the lead with Johnny Miller, the golden boy of American golf, and Oosterhuis, the player who dominated the European Tour at that time. But in the afternoon fog rose like steam from the languid green canals, and play was suspended then halted for the day. Ballesteros whiled away the hours on the putting green, working on his stroke and smiling at Manuel's discomfiture as players came up to him and commented on his score. 'It's not me, it's Seve, my little brother,' Manuel would say without rancour. For as long as he could remember, he had been preparing himself for the time when he would have to take a back seat to young Severiano at a golf tournament. Now that that day was at hand, he felt nothing but pride.

As the week progressed and Ballesteros maintained his position on the upper rungs of the leaderboard, scoring 75, 73, 73 to finish five shots adrift of Oosterhuis, the winner, Piñero was struck by his assurance and calm bearing when faced with competition of the calibre of the Englishman and the American. 'He was not intimidated by playing with Johnny Miller or anybody. Normally when you see a young player like him play with top players, they are very nervous. And Seve had no fear. When he was young he watched people to learn, not to see how good they were. He was thinking: "I'm going to beat him; I'm going to be better than him," which is a positive attitude.'

Miller has no recollection of the gauche Spanish boy who came fifth in the Italian Open that week. He can't recall practising under that dark and envious gaze, or taking note of the power with which the youth propelled balls down the range. Engrossed in the study of his own graceful, rhythmical swing, he was oblivious to everyone and everything around him, and remained blissfully unaware that in less than two

34

years, the seventeen-year-old caddie from Pedreña would have come close to denying him victory in the Open Championship and would have changed the course of golfing history for ever.

The last official tournament of the year was the El Paraiso Open in the south of Spain. Traditionally, the final event of the season is the one where those golfers who are on the borderline between success – meaning that they will be able to continue to pursue their quest for fame and fortune on the golf tour to the detriment of families, bank balances and sanity; and failure – meaning that they may at last have to look for a proper job – make a last ditch stand to keep their playing card. Ballesteros was in the happy position of not being one of their number, due to his fine performances in his national events. Roddy Carr, son of the famous amateur, Joe, was not so fortunate. He had to make the cut in order to finish in the top sixty on the money list. If he didn't, then he, like so many of those who follow golf's uncertain dream, would find himself washed up on the stony beach of life. Then what would he do? Carr quashed an uncomfortable uprising of butterflies at the thought, and drove shakily off the first tee. His playing partner was a moody Spanish teenager, whom Carr supposed to be related to Manuel Ballesteros. He watched him unleash himself on his tee shot and hurry after it, muttering under his breath. Next, the youngster hit a five-iron to 20 feet and was so dissatisfied with the result that he beat his club repeatedly against the ground.

'Jesus,' thought Carr, eyeing him narrowly. 'Does he expect to hole it?'

They walked to the green, whereupon Ballesteros missed his putt, lost his temper and kicked his golf bag into the air.

Carr was annoyed. 'My God Almighty,' he fumed silently, 'who does this kid think he is? Does he not know that this is golf and that you can't hole every forty-five footer and you can't hit every five-iron into two feet?'

This pattern continued on the second hole and on the third. Indeed every time Ballesteros hit a poor shot – by his standards, that is, which would not necessarily have been those of anyone else – he would throw a tantrum, displaying a total disregard for Carr who was trying desperately to concentrate. At the end of the round, an angry and disappointed Carr went looking for Severiano's brother to complain to him about the boy's conduct. 'Manuel,' he said sternly when he found him, 'if it was anybody else I would have reported him. Somebody's got to tell this kid that he can't hole every shot he hits.'

'Oh, I'll speak to him, I'll speak to him,' Manuel assured him nervously, and thanked Carr for not taking it any further. Little did the Irishman realize how much that small kindness would be repaid in later years.

'The thing I'll always remember about Seve,' grins Carr, 'is how he couldn't understand why he couldn't hole these putts. Literally. And I kept saying, "This guy must be loco." But, of course, it's part of his absolute genius that he did expect to hole everything. That's how good he was.'

Since golf is a game without equal in sport when it comes to sheer frustration, it is hardly surprising that it has a long and entertaining history of great players who have yielded to the temptation, having been tried beyond endurance, to violate its sacred codes by systematically destroying the tools of their trade. These men are outlaws who quickly become legends, though few quicker than Tommy Bolt, the mercurial 1958 US Open Champion.

Jacklin has a tale he tells about Bolt at a tournament in Santiago, California, in which the American, who had had a bad start to his round and whose temperature gauge was already in the red zone, hooked his tee shot over a cliff at the fifth hole. Smoke was coming out of his ears as he and his caddie disappeared over the brink and down the steps to look for his ball. Jacklin waited for him to reappear. Nothing happened. Silence reigned.

'He never came back up again,' recalls Jacklin with a grin. 'I didn't see him till the next week. I said, "Tom, did you ever find that ball down there?" He said, "No, but I found the Eastern Airlines ticket counter." '

Nevertheless, there is a big distinction between a player like Bolt, who was incredibly hot-headed and explosive, and one like Ballesteros, who was simply youthful and impetuous and desperate to prove his worth.

'He didn't lose his temper when he played with me,' insists Simon Hobday, who has always been one of the game's most volatile players as well as one of its finest ball strikers, 'and he had reason to at times. He was wild off the tee. He hit the ball all over the bloody place. He didn't get too fazed at all. I thought his temperament was pretty damned good.' He laughs wickedly. 'Mind you, when you compare it to Hobday's temper . . . !'

'I think with most champion golfers you'll find that in their youth they were fiery,' says Ben Crenshaw. 'Bobby Jones was that way [so were Palmer, Norman, Nicklaus and so on]. He was an awful club-thrower. Really had a helluva burning temper about him. That's what [Bernard] Darwin always spoke about. He said that if a fellow who has a fiery temperament learns to bottle it, he's going to be a dangerous fellow later on. You know, you can get angry for a few holes and that will cost you, but the more mature you get the more you start trying to treat tournaments as a whole. It's a difficult thing to do. But these are the things that, when you have the ability of Seve, save maybe four or five shots a week, which may be the difference between winning and losing.'

How much of a difference Ballesteros's temperament made to his overall results in 1974, no-one will ever know, but with £275 earned for his seventeenth place finish at El Paraiso and £1,440 for his performance at the Ibergolf Trophy at Las Lomas el Bosque, his first season as a tournament professional drew to a close. In Spain he had had two victories and two second places and was ninth on the money list; on the Continental Order of Merit he was thirteenth; and on the European rankings (British Order of Merit), he was one hundred and thirteenth, having played in just five tournaments. His stroke average was a poor 74.76 and his combined earnings amounted to some £5,000. But these achievements were nothing when compared to the rookie years of players such as Jacklin and Player, and it was for that reason, more than any other, that those two gentlemen were so sceptical when they heard Manuel Ballesteros declare his brother Severiano to be the 'best young player in the world'.

May 1975, PGA Championship, Sandwich, Kent. When Ballesteros had first been woken by the terrible sound of crashing keys, followed by a fortissimo performance of Beethoven's finest works with the odd dance-hall favourite thrown in, he had leapt from his bed as if shot. Now, however, he had grown used to it so the shock was not so great and, when the owner of the house he was staying in attacked the piano at two o'clock in the morning, it only served to enhance his impression that Royal St George's or, more particularly, links golf, was the golfing equivalent of Hieronymus Bosch's most fevered vision of hell.

The PGA Championship was Ballesteros's British début. He had never set foot on these Isles before and thus far it had been a baptism of fire. Soon after his arrival at Royal St George's, Manuel, who had been looking forward to introducing his young brother to the pleasures of links golf, had led him proudly to the front of the clubhouse and swept an arm over the bleak, unremarkable landscape. Ballesteros followed the direction of his gaze. It was late afternoon, and the sun setting on the dull day had made the mounds and hollows tawny with shadow. Pale grasses waved, the grey sea shimmered and, to the accustomed eye, the scene had a harshness and simplicity that was beautiful to behold. Severiano's eye was not accustomed.

'Where is the golf course?' he asked in some bewilderment.

Manuel laughed. 'Oh, it's out there somewhere,' he said vaguely.

'It was horrible,' recalls Ballesteros who, to this day, has never been able to find a place in his heart for Royal St George's. 'So cold, so much wind, so much different from any other course I had ever known. Especially I didn't like the fact that there were no trees for my eyes to get reference . . . I tell you, by the time I had played one round I didn't like *anything* about Sandwich.'

His impression of its worthlessness was cemented when a Dunlop representative came up to him on the practice ground, handed him three golf balls and told him that if he made the cut he would be given another three. 'I saw the rough was about one and a half metres high and I thought, "These will last me about six holes," ' recalls Ballesteros. As it turned out, Sandwich had as little regard for him as he had for it and sent him on his way after only two rounds, following scores of 79 and 84. Manuel, on the other hand, led the field for most of the tournament and eventually finished fifth to Arnold Palmer on a day when electrical storms turned the golf course into a nightmare.

It was a relieved Ballesteros who quit the home of the demented musician and the hostile shores of Kent for the warmer climes of his native land. Almost at once he began to establish himself as the dominant player on the Spanish circuit. He successfully defended his National Under 25's title at Sotogrande, finished runner-up in the El Maresme Open and in the Spanish Professionals Championship, and was third in two other events. By the time July came, his experiences at Sandwich had receded into a distant corner of his memory and he was optimistic about his chances in the Open Championship at Carnoustie. But a week before the tournament he injured his foot while practising on the beach in Pedreña, and, his balance and rhythm destroyed, shot 79, 80 to miss the cut by a comfortable margin. The capriciousness of links golf had defeated him once again.

Elsewhere Ballesteros had begun to demonstrate his potential. He had finished joint sixth with Manuel in the first event of the season, the Portuguese Open – also known as the 'Impossible Open' because political unrest had threatened to put a stop to it – and joint sixth in the second, the Spanish Open at La Manga. There is no finer example of how rapidly the young Spaniard was progressing than his figures there, 73, 72, 70, 72, compared with the scores he had returned in the same tournament and on the same course in 1974, when he had shot 83, 76 and failed to qualify. In the Madrid Open, his third event of the season, he shared eighth place, and he was twenty-sixth in France.

At last people started to sit up and take notice of him.

'Severiano Ballesteros has become the foremost of the Spanish young,' wrote Pat Ward-Thomas. 'Like many Spaniards,
he has great flair. His swing is not absolutely firm at the top
but he attacks the ball with great confidence and appears to
have a good head.'

'I thought he was a bit wild,' admits Sandy Lyle, who
can recall playing in a pro-am with him as an amateur. 'But
obviously there's a bit of magic and a bit of fire. If he got a
run going, he could really tear the golf course up.'

'I think he was seen very early on to be something
special,' says Christy O'Connor Jnr. 'He was very dedicated,
that he certainly was, and of course he wanted it more than
anything else in the world. He would spend hours and hours
on the practice ground. He hit the ball so hard he would
almost run after it. Totally fearless. Wonderful short game,
too, he pitched and putted incredibly well, but really he just
hit such good golf shots. He was so exciting. A breath of fresh
air, like a young John Daly without the control.'

The intensity of Ballesteros's desire manifested itself in
several ways. One, as we have already seen, was his temper,
another was the amount of time he spent on the range, and
yet another was his fits of pique or depression. After a day
in which he had struggled on the greens, Dudley Doust can
recall him punishing himself by not allowing himself dinner.
'He had a bad putting round at some rinky-dink tournament
– didn't matter – and then he putted for about an hour and
a half on the putting green and went back and wouldn't let
himself eat.'

Dave Musgrove saw him do the same thing on a number
of occasions once he started caddying for him. In the PGA
Championship at Royal St George's in 1976, for instance,
Ballesteros shot 71, 72 in the opening rounds and 76 in
the third and then just went back to his room and locked
himself away until morning. 'He went to bed in the afternoon
and wouldn't get up to eat or anything,' says Musgrove, who
had been staying in the same boarding house as the Spaniard.
'Just lay in bed. I remember that vividly because we all kept
going and asking if he was coming out. "No!" he said. "*No!*" '

Where Ballesteros was fortunate was that he was surrounded

by a small circle of close friends and relatives, who supported him through these periods. When Manuel was on Tour he acted as translator, mentor, travel agent, protector and coach to his young brother and, when he wasn't, his friends Piñero and Fernandez took over. 'Seve was Manuel's baby brother,' remembers Bill Longmuir, 'and was sort of molly-coddled a bit around the Spanish players because he was so young. Everyone used to sort of look out for Seve.'

This hot-house environment of nurture and encouragement did wonders for Ballesteros's confidence, which was growing daily, and his golf game benefited as a result. His best finishes in the second half of the year were joint eighth in the Swiss Open, third in the Lancome Trophy and twelfth in the Italian Open. By the end of the season he was the No. 1 player on both the Spanish and Continental Orders of Merit, and was twenty-sixth on the British money list with earnings of £4,118. Manuel was twenty-fifth. He also had an improved stroke average of 73.91 and was the only golfer in Europe to have been placed in all the Continental Opens.

'I had seen many good players for the first time in my life,' he said later. 'I thought to myself, "Seve, you can beat them all." '

There are two wonderfully revealing stories about Ballesteros at that age, one of which is told by Peter Ryde, a former *Times* golf correspondent, and the other by Fernandez. In the first, Ballesteros was playing in a golf tournament in Spain. Crossing from one hole to the next, he stopped at a stand to get a drink. The vendor eyed him shyly.

'Mr Ballesteros, I have the same name as you,' he told the tall, broad-shouldered young man at his counter.

Ballesteros looked at him. 'How old are you?' he asked.

'Twenty-six,' answered the surprised vendor.

'I am eighteen,' said Ballesteros, 'therefore it is I who have the same name as you.'

For Fernandez, one memory stands out more clearly in his mind than all the rest: a summer's day at Fulford Golf Club in York.

Ballesteros had produced a round of near flawless golf in the first round of the Benson and Hedges Festival. Most of his approach shots had been hit within easy two-putt range, and though he had been bunkered twice he had got up and down each time. Only once did he seem in danger of being over par, but disaster was averted with a long putt at the twelfth hole and his score of 64 equalled that of Fernandez and was a shot off the pace at the end of the day. In the second round, however, his touch seemed to desert him. He slipped back into the pack with a three over par 75 and, despite following it with rounds of 72 and 71, was left trailing in thirty-sixth place when perfect conditions led to record scoring.

Fernandez, meanwhile, had taken advantage of the fine weather to make his move on the trophy and was occupying a seemingly invincible position at the top of the leaderboard, four shots clear of Maurice Bembridge, when he reached the fifteenth hole on the final day. There, inexplicably, he hooked out of bounds and took a seven, while Bembridge holed a long putt to draw level with him. It was a familiar scenario and one in which the hunter usually becomes the hunted. Fernandez is a man of steely resolve, and he birdied the next to reassert his authority, but surrendered it again on the seventeenth when he drove into the bushes and three-putted.

As he teed up on the final hole, a tense young face watched him from the gallery. It turned as Fernandez drove the ball down the centre of the fairway and it followed the flight of his three-iron to the heart of the green. Fernandez, small, wiry and eager, carefully studied his line. His first putt ran by the hole but his second dropped for a birdie, a four-round total of 266 and victory. Hardly had the ball touched the cup when Ballesteros, black hair flying, arms outstretched, was over the ropes and racing across the green towards his friend while the gallery exploded into tumultuous applause.

'He was the first person to run and congratulate me,' says Fernandez emotionally. 'He took me from behind, jumping in the air. He was crying like a baby. He was in *tears*.

'And that's the kind of person that lives inside of Seve.'

3

Rites of Passage

When you're young you can only see the top and you just want to get there.

Bill Longmuir, Mallorca, March 1992

One bright morning in the summer of 1976 an untidy procession of red vans and blue ones and odd coloured trucks and men on bicycles or walking came bumping slowly over the narrow roads that wander through the dunes of Royal Birkdale. A dust plume charted their progress. Halting, they disbanded and threw down their loads, and with hammering and laughter soon drove away the sound of silence. The day was an infinite, azure blue. As the sun climbed higher it blazed with a fiery intensity and the air began to burn and grew languorous with the weight of humidity. Defenceless, the vast undulating greens were quickly scarred, while the rough grew dry and brittle and was bleached to the colour of pale straw. The scattered men worked on tirelessly. White rivulets of sweat ran down their brown cheerful faces, as they erected steel skeletons, carted signs about and forced the hard earth to admit ungainly wooden legs.

Towards evening, a cooling wind blew in from the sea. Salt and the smell of cut grass caught the breeze and drifted across the tented expanse. Greenkeepers gathered the bright pins; the hum of mowers ceased. As the final crossbar was being bolted onto the grandstand facing the great yellow leaderboard, Jimmy Dickinson, a caddie, prepared to go forth into the sunset to measure the course for Jack Nicklaus. Then, as sprinklers hissed and a solitary night bird called, the caravan filed slowly down the drive, transporting the weary men. Above the quiet links the canvas village flapped, snapped and billowed like a giant sail, and the flags of thirty nations streamed.

The 105th Open Championship had begun.

Monday, 5 July 1976, Southport, Lancashire. The far end of the practice range at Royal Birkdale resounded with the crack of wood meeting golf ball with unrestrained force. Several players glanced up. Severiano Ballesteros, the nineteen-year-old executant of the shot, watched it pass the 250-yard marker on the fly and disappear over the boundary fence before turning to his gathered admirers with a toss of his black hair and a grin. Manuel nodded approvingly. The other Spanish onlookers conferred among themselves and added their comments. Ballesteros considered their appraisal momentarily, rapped his club smartly against his golf shoe to clean the blade and, with uninhibited energy and enthusiasm, launched another attack on the ball.

Walking by, Christy O'Connor Jnr received an impression of youth, strength, wildness, long hair and flares. A year earlier Dave Musgrove, the dry-humoured, razor-tongued Midlander who was to become Ballesteros's regular caddie, had been struck on first sight of the young Spaniard by the length of his legs and by his large hands. To defending champion Tom Watson, pausing in practice to see him hit the ball, Ballesteros's strength was nothing less than awesome. 'I remember how hard he swung at the ball – how he just lashed at it, hit it with all his might.'

The Ballesteros brothers had already spent several days at Royal Birkdale. On the Saturday before the tournament Severiano had caddied for Manuel in the thirty-six hole Open Qualifying at Southport & Ainsdale, where he was among 650 players on five courses attempting to gain entry to the greatest tournament in the world. Manuel had played well

44

enough to get into the play-off but was then unfortunately beaten, whereupon his young brother had abandoned him without a word and marched disgustedly back to the club-house, Manuel trailing miserably in his wake. 'You ought to have seen [Seve's] face,' says Musgrove laughing. 'One mile long it was. Stamping and swearing.'

But it was not the Spaniards who made news the following morning. As Pat Ward-Thomas remarked in the *Guardian*: 'Whether or not Nicklaus, Palmer, Watson, Miller and the rest had arrived at Birkdale for the Open Championship seemed for a while to be of little account when the extraordinary story of Maurice Flitcroft, a crane driver at Vickers in Barrow-in-Furness who had entered as a pro, came to light. In the first qualifying round at Formby, he fashioned a matchless score of 121.' Flitcroft, it transpired, much to the embarrassment of the Royal and Ancient [R&A], the inestimable controlling body of golf, had never played eighteen holes in his life before but had somehow slipped through their net of entry restrictions. The game up, they dispatched the culprit speedily, with a flea in his ear.

The weather throughout had been hot and close, as though a thunderstorm lurked beneath the horizon and might reveal itself at any time. Nobody would have been distraught if it had. Inevitably, the conditions had baked the fairways of Birkdale to the consistency of concrete and it was playing far shorter than it otherwise would, but even if it remained so, the quality of the tournament would be unlikely to be diminished. Nicklaus observed that there would not be a fluke winner of the Open Championship – nor has there ever been.

Late afternoon Johnny Miller arrived for a practice round. Seeing Ballesteros in the locker room, gazing enviously at the clubs and clothes of other players with his dark, expressive eyes, he greeted him cordially, for they shared a manager, and cast an amused glance at the young man's Johnny Miller-endorsed trousers. The American's Open record was astonishing: a second place, a tenth and a third in the preceding three years. In 1975 at Carnoustie he had hit his tee shot into a fairway bunker on the final hole, heard the gallery on the seventeenth roar and assumed, incorrectly, that either

Watson or Jack Newton had birdied the hole and that he would need a birdie at the last to tie. He took a five-iron out of the bunker, left the ball in the trap and missed the play-off by a shot. As far as he was concerned, he had come to Royal Birkdale to fulfil a date with destiny: 'I've paid my dues. This year it's going to be my turn.'

Tuesday, 6 July 1976. The British golf writers, cowed, like British golfers, by years of American domination, were all doom and despondency as to the tournament's eventual outcome. 'It would be stretching optimism to its limits to say that a British victory is likely,' said the *Guardian* pessimistically, and other papers followed suit. However, only two European players had won the Open Championship since the early Fifties – Max Faulkner in 1951 at Royal Portrush and Tony Jacklin in 1969 at Royal Lytham and St Annes, and in the interim honours had been divided between Argentina (once), South Africa (five times), Australasia (seven times) and the United States (ten times). No Continental player had triumphed in the Open since Arnaud Massy lifted the claret jug at Hoylake in 1907 with a score of 312.

It had never been an obsession of Ballesteros's to become the first Spaniard to end the European drought. As a boy he did not, as other golfers claim they have, dream of becoming Open Champion and occupy a fantasy world where he regularly putted for victory at St Andrews. He simply wanted to be the best. Now that the time had come for him to prove that he could be, he didn't shy away from it, but looked forward to it with a singular relish. Having devoted the morning to altering the loft and lie of his golf clubs to suit the conditions at Birkdale, he spent the afternoon playing a practice round with Manuel and the Argentinians Roberto de Vicenzo and Vicente Fernandez in the shadow of the thunderheads, testing the brisk wind and the smooth shining greens, and watching how the ball flew from the saddle of one mound but rolled through the valley of another, until at last he felt that he would come to love and understand links golf the way he did the courses of his native Spain. Thus prepared, Ballesteros scorned the conventional European attitude – which said that all American players were superior beings whose right to the Open trophy was preordained – and turned squarely to face the dangers which the morrow would surely bring.

Wednesday, 7 July 1976. The long breathless days and indigo skies had brought Royal Birkdale to the point of spontaneous combustion. At midday it succumbed to the inevitable: beside the first tee, a bush burst into flames. Spectators were evacuated, fire engines wailed, Howard Clark, Bob Shearer and Guy Hunt ran for their lives with towels over their heads, and the opening round was held up for 30 minutes while the small conflagration was subdued. There was an air of comic absurdity about the scene, rather in the manner of a P.G. Wodehouse novel, and for an hour or two the general attention of the public, and of a few players, was concerned with things apart from golf. It was then that two unknown names appeared on the leaderboard and made their way inexorably to the top. Joining Irishman Christy O'Connor Jnr, who had returned a three under par 69 to finish leader in the clubhouse, were Norio Suzuki, the diminutive Japanese player, and Ballesteros.

They say that fortune favours the brave. The previous afternoon, US Open Champion Jerry Pate had emphasized the importance of precise tee shots, especially for long hitters, because of the risk of running out of fairway. Wilfully, and because he had never played any other way, Ballesteros took his driver from the bag on the very first hole and, with joyous abandon, smashed it as far as he possibly could – carelessly disregarding the out of bounds which protected the right side of the fairway. On the next tee he again lashed at the ball with his wide, free swing and again lost nothing to par. At the third, his aggression was rewarded. Fine attacking iron play won him a birdie three there and a two at the 150-yard seventh. Before long the record galleries began to drift from the failing greats to take up with the young Spaniard. He responded by flirting with peril more outrageously at the eighth. By the time he had reached number nine, they were fast warming to his ready smile and devil-may-care golf game, and were sorry to see him take three putts to turn in 33.

There is an element of caprice in the nature of every links course which is subtly influenced by, and at the mercy of, the wind. A stretch of holes that is no more threatening than an aged spaniel during a south-westerly will be transformed into the Hound of the Baskervilles by the slightest shift in the direction of the breeze. So it is in the case of Royal Birkdale. When from the ocean the wind helps the thirteenth, seventeenth and eighteenth, respectively 504, 526 and 513 yards, and they can play too short for genuine par fives. Now it became a sirocco and gusted around the easternmost holes of the course, so that the drives were more exacting and the greens out of range for all but the strong. Ballesteros continued to boldly court disaster. His freedom of spirit was infectious; the gallery were carried along by it and derived a certain vicarious pleasure from his adventures. They delighted with him at the twelfth, where he secured a birdie after holing a monster putt, and at the thirteenth, where he was home in two with a one-iron, but were as downcast as the Spaniard himself when he dropped a shot at the next par three, taking two to recover from a greenside trap. A stiff breeze made the closing holes especially difficult, and it is a measure of his strength that he was green high with a one-iron at the last, and could get up and down for a birdie four and a back nine of 36. His score of 69 brought him level with O'Connor Jnr and Suzuki at the end of the first day of play. Brian Barnes, Tom Kite and Jack Newton were a shot further back, with Gary Player and Johnny Miller on level par.

Afterwards, Ballesteros was disarmingly unaffected and cheerful. 'If I play like this I have very good chancc. My driving is very good. Maybe I win. But if the wind blows I make eighty tomorrow, perhaps.'

Thursday, 8 July 1976. A gambling man would not have placed money on Ballesteros to retain his position at the top of the leaderboard after two rounds. It is traditional for the first day of the Open Championship to be dominated by the heroics of journeymen and pretenders to the throne; this is their moment of glory and no-one denies it to them. After that, the established stars will usually pull up their shirt sleeves and set to work, then it is business as usual on the links. Not so at Royal Birkdale. Miller, a charismatic figure with flying gold hair and a tall slender frame, had taken the early lead after Ballesteros dropped two strokes to par on his outward half. The American played the front nine in 36, but took full advantage of the back nine which had been made benign by a sudden change of wind. At fifteen, the longest par five, he pulled his tee shot into heavy rough and could do no more than hack the ball out sideways with a wedge. With 240 yards to go, he hit a long-iron to the heart of the green and sank a 14-foot putt for birdie. Prudent use of the one-iron – which he used ten times, six from the tee – netted him birdies at the fourteenth, seventeenth and eighteenth holes, so he was four under par for the last seven holes and ended with a 68 and a total of 140.

Now Ballesteros entered the fray. His gallery was growing larger by the hour, drawn to the pervading atmosphere of gay drama that surrounded his match. They crowded quickly after him, as he struck fearlessly off the tee, ran to follow the flight of his ball as it departed the fairway for the dunes, then strode through the rough like a beagle on the scent with an alert and confident stride. 'A Spaniard in Lancashire,' remarked a watching commentator. 'Everyone enjoying him and waiting for him to vanish from the leaderboard.' Ballesteros, of course, had no intention of obliging. Gathering himself for the finish, he began to fire at the pins with crisp and powerful iron shots. At the eleventh he was rewarded with his first birdie and earned another two holes later. The fifteenth, seventeenth and eighteenth were reached with a one-iron, three-iron and five-iron respectively for his second shots. At the close of play his score of 69, for an aggregate of 138, six under par, gave him a two-stroke lead over Miller; with O'Connor Jnr and Ken Brown next, followed by Barnes, Tommy Horton and Raymond Floyd.

At all of Ballesteros's post-round interviews, Manuel acted as translator. His brother's broken English was not yet equal to the demands of press conference dialogue and in this, as with everything, Manuel liked to be by his side to protect him from harassment and unnecessary pressure. Bilingual debates at golf tournaments tend to degenerate fairly rapidly into mini-circuses, and Thursday's was no exception. Eventually, Ballesteros gave one Spanish reporter a reply that was so convoluted it went on for five minutes, and provoked much hilarity among the Latin contingent of golf writers.

'What did he say?' a member of the British press said impatiently to Manuel when Severiano finally came to a stop.

'Well,' replied Manuel seriously, 'he said: "No."' And brought the house down.

The Ballesteros brothers had found accommodation at a small guesthouse in Southport. Neither of them could drive, and it was before the days of courtesy cars (without which one can hardly imagine life on Tour these days), so they relied upon Musgrove and his friend, Constable Dick Draper, to fetch and carry them from the golf course. Musgrove, who later became famous as Sandy Lyle's caddie and co-author with John Hopkins of the book *Life with Lyle*, had worked on a casual basis for Ballesteros since 1975 but, because he traditionally carried Roberto de Vicenzo's bag in the Open, he had suggested to the young Spaniard that Draper, a five handicapper from his home town of Kirkby with previous experience of caddying in the Open, work for him at Birkdale. Ballesteros agreed straight away; like most Spanish players, he revered Vicenzo, the 1967 Open Champion. The respect was mutual. Later in the week the Argentinian remarked to Musgrove that in his opinion there were only three golfers in the world that mattered: Johnny Miller, Tom Weiskopf and Severiano Ballesteros. 'They are in a different class to the rest of us.'

Friday, 9 July 1976. The third round brought rain, heavy and disagreeable, drenching the rainbow gallery and transforming the narrow footpaths into twisting rusty streams. When it cleared the wind had moved for the first time to the south-west, the true direction for the course and, in doing so, had induced a schizophrenic change in the character of several key holes.

Ballesteros and Miller were the last of the field to tee off. At his press conference on Thursday evening, the Spaniard had been asked whether or not it would bother him to play with a golfer of the Californian's repute. 'Where is Johnny Miller?' demanded Ballesteros. 'Come, you tell him we can go and play now.' This morning as he drove from the first, he was no less assured, but with his spontaneous smile, canary yellow shirt and sky-blue waterproofs brought a welcome ray of sunshine to the air of prevailing gloom. Two holes later, he was looking slightly crestfallen. His eagerness to make Royal Birkdale conform to the way he wanted to play the game, rather than to try and adapt his golf to suit the course, had resulted in a clash of wills in which Birkdale came out on top. It was Miller's turn to suffer at the next, where he took a bogey five. But he retaliated with a tee shot to 4 inches at the 206-yard fourth, while Ballesteros missed the green and became entangled in heavy grass. On close inspection of the lie a lesser player might have written the hole off as lost, but young Severiano never hesitated as he lofted the ball smoothly and easily to 2 inches for a par, grinning at his caddie's astonished face as he did so. The period of grace was not a long one. A par at the fifth was followed by further punishment at the sixth and seventh, so that when he reached the ninth hole Ballesteros was four over par and Miller was leading the tournament.

Then the wheel of fortune began to turn in the young Spaniard's favour. He persisted in lashing away from the tee, but with remarkable recoveries survived the consequences of his wildness. At the eleventh, where he fired his drive so far left that it vanished over a sandhill, a double-bogey or even quadruple seemed imminent. There was no need for concern. Ballesteros disappeared into the undergrowth and disbelieving fans heard a crack and saw the ball rise towards the green. Miller was not amused. His own approach from a good lie had finished short and left and he took three more to get down. Ballesteros required only two putts for his par. On the short twelfth the Spaniard again explored uncharted territory when his tee shot flew over the dunes. Miller waited smugly on the putting surface for him to reappear. Over the hill came another ball; Ballesteros was still fighting and put his recovery close enough to get an impudent three. Even for a player of Miller's experience the sight of these Houdini-like endeavours was disconcerting. 'It was very frustrating,' he later admitted. 'It would not have been so upsetting if we had both got a share of the luck, but he seemed to have got both our rations.'

Witness the fifteenth. Miller's tee shot on the 542-yard par five rivalled Ballesteros's for waywardness, and they both played provisional balls. But where Miller was forced to drop out under penalty and so notched up a bogey six, the irrepressible Spaniard escaped unharmed, holing a 12-foot putt for par to increase his lead to two shots. At the next, the pattern continued. Miller, who was on the fairway, hit his approach to 20 feet with a high and beautiful swing. Ballesteros, who wasn't, missed the green altogether, but took a putter from the short rough and almost holed it for birdie. Then Miller's ball lipped out for par. As the *Daily Mail* recorded, 'One of the most delightful sights of this championship was that of Miller, one of the world's highest paid sporting superstars, kicking his hat in disgust by the sixteenth green, then throwing his ball angrily into the bushes because it had refused to drop for a birdie . . . What maddened Miller more was that every time Severiano pulled off one of his escapades, he smiled apologetically and with reverence at the man he acknowledges as one of the golf masters.'

At the seventeenth, Ballesteros added insult to injury, making eagle from the rough to increase his lead to five under par. Miller closed with two birdies but the Spaniard's score at the end of the day, a 73 for an aggregate of 211, left him two strokes ahead of his playing companion, four ahead of Horton and five ahead of Nicklaus and Floyd. Watson's hopes died with an uninspired 80, while Pate shot a fifteen over par 87.

All the golfing world now wondered whether Ballesteros could become the youngest player since Tom Morris a century before to win the Open Championship. Whatever the outcome of the tournament, however, one thing was for certain, Ballesteros's simple charm off the course and appealing dash and flair on it had earned him lasting respect and admiration. 'Seve was almost made to entertain people through golf,' said Miller. 'He is a very unique player. He is a genius. He has got charisma, he's got power, he's got flair and he has a passion which people can feel.'

Nevertheless, it was almost impossible to believe that Ballesteros would continue to elude capture if he persisted in employing the same strong-arm tactics he had used all week on the final day. Miller drew parallels between their two golf games: 'Seve had a big swing, swung hard, went for the pins and had a lot of emotions – *I* had a lot of emotions on the golf course. I could relate to him and I think he could relate to me, and I respected his game and he really respected mine.' Miller also said that Ballesteros only had one shot in his bag: the hard hit. 'You need patience over here,' he commented to reporters. 'You can't throw everything at the pin.'

Ballesteros scoffed at the Californian's cautionary words. 'I am still young,' he declared. 'When I am older there will be time to be careful.'

Ever since Ballesteros had arrived at Royal Birkdale, he had played golf every day, practised when he had come off the course, slept for a couple of hours, then behaved like any other teenager in the evening. He and his brother did the rounds of most of the nightclubs in Southport that week, and he can still recall walking through the town and laughing as passers-by congratulated Manuel on his marvellous performance in the Open.

How, Manuel was asked in an interview on the eve of the fourth round, was his brother planning to prepare himself for the most important day of his young life?

'Well,' he replied, 'first, we'll have dinner and then he will go dancing for an hour or two. It is OK if he is in bed between twelve and one o'clock. He will have no nerves.'

Was Severiano very excited at the prospect of vying with the best players in the world for the Open trophy, a reporter wanted to know.

'I am not excited and I am not nervous,' said Ballesteros with calm authority. 'I will play to win and, if I have a three-foot putt to win the Open Championship, I will know that anyone can put it in and anyone can miss it.'

Saturday, 10 July 1976. Severiano Ballesteros stood on the tee at Royal Birkdale in the final round of the Open Championship looking as exuberant and happy as a boy at his first funfair. The pressure that had been talked about at length since the start of the tournament had failed to touch him and, as he smashed the ball from the tee and trotted joyfully down the fairway after it, it seemed that he had rarely enjoyed himself more. 'The nicest smile that I ever saw in golf,' recalls Puerto Rican Chi Chi Rodriguez. 'He was very colourful. I don't say handsome, because I never have seen a handsome man or an ugly woman, but I really liked what I saw, you know – strong guy, Spanish, the smile, the drive, the way he walked. He walked like a champion.'

Miller, by contrast, was preoccupied with the task before him. He watched Ballesteros's tussle with the rough and subsequent shots to the green expressionlessly. His own ball was 4 feet from the pin and waiting to be tapped in for par. When the young Spaniard came striding onto the putting surface, he simply lined up his putt from both sides of the hole and stroked it in from 20 feet for a four. Miller's face registered utter disbelief. He walked to his ball like a man in a dream and missed the short putt for bogey.

But on the next it became apparent that Ballesteros's luck had run out on him. He hooked wildly from the tee into the willow scrub that grew along the sandhills, put his recovery into a bunker some 45 yards short of the green, splashed out to 15 feet and made bogey; Miller sank his putt for birdie and claimed two shots back in one hole. Nicklaus and Floyd, too, were closing in on the lead. They had had two birdies apiece in the first five holes when they reached the 468-yard sixth – a notorious dog-leg par four that had already cost O'Connor Jnr a seven, Graham Marsh a six and Horton a five. There, their hopes were dashed. In trying to avoid the cross-bunkers, Nicklaus hit a one-iron close to a fairway trap in the dunes crossing the fairway. He then faced a 220-yard second shot to the flag but proceeded to block it into the willow scrub and, after playing a provisional, failed to find his first ball. When he walked off the green he had a six on his card. Ballesteros visited the bushes Nicklaus had just vacated. Having located the ball, he could do little more than nudge it out with a putter, whereupon it caught the top of a bunker and fell in. He took a double-bogey from 7 feet, while Miller made par from four. Two holes later he was in trouble once again, after hitting a reckless tee shot into the dunes. His ball was nestled snugly against the trunk of a small bush and his only option was to move it further along the sandhills – which he did, then pitched to 20 feet. By now he was tried beyond endurance and his shoulders were bowed with the weight of despair. When he missed the putt and saw Miller go three ahead, he was near to tears. He passed a hand across his eyes and trailed miserably after the confident Californian.

Disaster followed disaster. On the eleventh he lost heavily in yet another encounter with the dunes, and took a treble-bogey seven. At the short twelfth, he was forced to drop out and made a bogey four, while Miller hit a four-iron to 10 feet for birdie. But still Ballesteros refused to compromise. At every tee he swung at the ball so furiously that he actually walked after it. Then he would search for it among the hills and scrub and, having found it, would try to hole it. As Roberto de Vicenzo said, 'Maybe Seve will hit the ball left or maybe he will hit one right, but he'll *hit* it. It won't be a duff shot. It won't be a half shot. He won't miss the shot. Wherever it goes, he's hit it. Hard.'

Miller put an arm around the boy's shoulders as they walked to the thirteenth. 'I said: "Seve why don't you put on a real strong finish and see if you can finish in second place?". I didn't really mean to make a big deal of it, but I genuinely knew I had the tournament won. It's easy to be nice when you've got a six-shot lead. I was feeling bad because he was struggling. He's such a pusher, you know, he's so competitive. And I was basically just saying, "Why don't you regroup and get it together?" '

At the fourteenth Ballesteros began to fight back, hitting his third shot from the rough to 2 inches and making his second consecutive birdie. Then Miller chipped into the hole for eagle, after missing the fairway from the tee, and his partner's name slid even further down the leaderboard. 'After such a promising beginning,' a commentator said sorrowfully, 'now destined to finish among the also-rans.' Proof positive that nothing was further from the young Spaniard's mind, and that he was once more relaxed and focused on the challenge before him, was provided at the next hole. Finding himself in trouble off the tee, he paused, bent down to inhale the scent of a flowering bush of yellow bracken, and only then considered his lie.

'I don't think he was old enough to realize how important it all was,' says Draper, 'or how big the Open Championship was. He was playing it as though it was the monthly medal at his golf club. It was important to him, but it wasn't the end of the world. I think he knew how good he was and that his time would come eventually.'

In the waning afternoon the sky had cleared to a brilliant cobalt blue. A fresh wind blew silvery waves through the pale grass, whipping at the clothes of the excited gallery as it surged over the sandhills and deserted fairways like a swarm of marauding locusts. Nicklaus had finished leader in the clubhouse on 285. Aware that something approaching a miracle was needed if he was to lift himself clear of the chasing pack, Ballesteros sank a 25-foot putt for eagle on the seventeenth with great spirit and determination and found that now he needed only a birdie to tie Nicklaus. He had regained his eagerness and cheerful demeanour, and responded to Miller's handshake as they walked to the final tee with a sudden smile of pure pleasure.

For the last time at Royal Birkdale, Ballesteros unleashed himself on a drive. He had hit only three fairways from the tee all day and the eighteenth, unfortunately, wasn't one of them. As Miller said: 'He was so bold but his driver killed him.' The Californian's approach was perfect. When he had played it he stood in the centre of the fairway, arms raised heavenwards, as the crowd acknowledged him as Open Champion.

The Spaniard's second shot flew into the left rough and finished just short of the putting surface. He threw up his hands in a typically Latin gesture of annoyance at his mistake and the gallery flocked around him, racing to jostle for position by the green. With some difficulty, he and Draper fought their way forward through the throng. The ball was resting in trampled yellow grass, some 15 yards away from where a hard path rode the crest of two bunkers and ran up to the green. Draper gave the matter but a minute's consideration. To him, only one shot was even remotely possible: a sand-iron over the bunkers. After weeks of continuous sunshine, the putting surface bore an uncanny resemblance to a downhill section of motorway – in pace as well as appearance – and the ball, once struck, might bounce in an infinite variety of directions, at an infinite variety of speeds, possibly running through the green altogether and possibly ending in the bunkers. Ballesteros was not so hasty. In his mind he was trying to envisage a shot so perfect that it would flit as lightly as a feather over the scorched and rumpled earth, neatly evade the hazards and run smoothly into the hole for eagle.

The atmosphere was rigid with tension. Only the low whine of the wind and the creaking of the great stands as the gallery craned expectantly over the railings broke the cathedral-like silence of the eighteenth green. Ballesteros put out his hand for the nine-iron. Draper handed it to him and moved away, the golf bag scraping on the ground. Then, with scarcely a pause, the young Spaniard stepped forward and played one of the lightest, most delicate little chip shots conceivable. Years on, he still considers it to be one of the most important of his life. The risks attached to it were considerable. If he had caught it too heavily, he would have left it in the rough and taken bogey; if he had put it in the trap, he would have taken a five or worse; and if it had run right over the green, he might have lost everything. Instead, he banished every negative thought from his head and committed himself to the shot. The ball bounced onto the path, skipped gaily up to the peak of a mound and over the other side, rolled smoothly along the green and finished 4 feet from the pin.

John Jacobs, who was watching it on television in Hampshire, leapt to his feet and said: 'This boy is a genius. If he ever learns to play, he will be unbeatable.' Lee Trevino, recovering from a back injury in Texas, laughed out loud at the audacity of it. 'I thought he might have won that golf tournament if he'd had a little bit more experience. He took too many chances. He was going at the flag all the time . . . But what a wonderful short game he had. He could do anything he wanted with a golf ball. That's the greatest thing in the world about Seve; he's got imagination. It's great to have imagination if you can execute the shot.'

Miller's first putt shaved the hole, but he was sporting enough to tap it in for victory and a nine under par score of 279, thereby allowing Ballesteros to play the last stroke, an honour usually reserved for the champion. The Spaniard sank his birdie putt with aplomb; then he threw his ball as high as he could into the grandstand, lifted his hands to the acclaim and beamed up at the people who had taken him into their hearts. Afterwards, Draper recalls Ballesteros being very calm, collected and contented, but not in the least bit emotional. He had finished tied with Nicklaus for second place, while Floyd was third and Mark James, who recorded a course record 66, was joint fourth. He knew what an achievement it was, but still said to himself: 'I should have won this championship.'

In his press conference Miller was generous in his praise of the young Spaniard, and admitted that if Ballesteros had used a one-iron off the tee he would probably have won. 'Don't get me wrong,' he said, 'but I think it was a good thing for Seve that he didn't win. Day in, day out he wouldn't have been able to back it up. He might have been swamped by the resulting pressures. Now lots of lovely things can happen to him just because he's come second. Just like me: best thing that happened to me was not winning the Masters in 1971. It gave me time to prepare myself for winning a big one . . . No, the best thing for his career was to finish second. His day will come.'

4

Fame and Misfortune

He was a bit like the Kennedy family: you were either for
him or against him.

> Doust on Ballesteros's first years on Tour, July, 1992

At the time the Ballesteros brothers embarked upon their
journey to the Southern hemisphere in 1974, the interests of
all South African pro golfers and many foreign players were
watched over by George Blumberg, a gentle and benevolent
man. Blumberg, or Uncle George, as he was universally
known, was a retired paper millionaire whose consuming
passion was golf. He travelled the fairways of the world in
search of new talent and, when he found it, would nurture it
until it yielded up its potential. This he did both for his own
pleasure and for International Management Group (IMG), on
whose board of directors he sat and for whom he recruited
likely champions. A Churchillian figure who puffed great
cigars, he gave freely and generously of his time and money
and it is said that he was almost single-handedly responsible
for the financial support of some of the finest players ever to
emerge from his country – including Gary Player (although
there is some dispute about this), Dale Hayes, Bobby Cole
and the Henning brothers – as well as several British players,
such as Clive Clark and Warren Humphries.

The golfers whom Blumberg helped returned his love and

admiration a hundredfold. They advised him on prospective winners, assisted him with his management choices and, in general, tried to give back to him a little of what he had given to them. In the autumn of his years, they made him an honorary member of the South African PGA, and it was in this capacity that he first encountered Ballesteros. He was collecting score-cards during the Toro Classic at Glendower Golf Club, near Johannesburg (so the story goes), when he came across those of Severiano Ballesteros; who had recorded identical sub-par totals on all four days. Observing to himself that the unknown Spaniard must be the very model of consistency, Blumberg ran his finger down the numbers. There was hardly a par to be seen. There were flocks of birdies, aviaries full of eagles and an arresting number of bogeys, double-bogeys and triple-bogeys, but few pars (regulation ones, anyway). Blumberg could not believe the evidence of his own eyes. Further enquiries into the boy's background convinced him he was not mistaken. It was obvious that here was a player of rare and wonderful gift – a player bold enough to go for the ultimate shot, confident enough to take the consequences and skilful enough to reap the benefits.

Shortly afterwards, Blumberg sent an impassioned letter to the directors of IMG in London. 'I have seen what I consider to be the most exciting prospect in the world for the next ten to fifteen years,' he wrote.

When the answer came back it was simply: 'We're not interested.'

From time to time one hears of record companies, film studios, publishers, talent agencies and like institutions making monumental blunders. This one turned down the Beatles, so and so rejected Elvis and Dunkin' Donuts sacked Madonna. With Ballesteros, IMG made theirs. Eighteen years on they are still paying for it. Repeated attempts to lure him away from his various managers have resulted in only one reply: 'I'm not interested.' Somewhere along the line Ballesteros found out that IMG had rejected him and his pride has never allowed him to forgive them.

In September 1975 Ballesteros played in the Double Diamond

International at Turnberry in conditions scarcely fit for polar bears. When the full fury of the gale hit the tournament on the final day, tents were ripped from their moorings, hats were torn from the heads of spectators, and rain hailed down upon the golfers without mercy. Ballesteros was in the Rest-of-the-World side that week, along with Player, Hayes, Jack Newton and Bob Charles. Incredibly, given that he still had relatively little experience of playing golf in unplayable weather, he managed to beat Guy Hunt 3 & 2 and Craig Defoy 5 & 4, only losing 3 & 2 to American Jim Colbert. His performance was so outstanding that it attracted the notice of Roberto de Vicenzo, the 1967 Open Champion and winner of more than 170 tournaments worldwide. Vicenzo, who was and still is the hero of every Spanish pro golfer in the world, thought highly enough of Ballesteros as a player to take the trouble to call his own manager, an American by the name of Ed Barner, with a testimonial.

'I am going to tell you something important,' Vicenzo told Barner earnestly. 'This Spanish boy, Ballesteros, he can hit the ball. He will be a great player. You should keep an eye on him.'

Barner was never slow to pursue a lead on a possible client and he immediately asked Billy Casper to play a practice round with Ballesteros at the Lancome Trophy the following week. Casper duly obliged. Ballesteros then went on to win the pre-tournament long-hitting contest, with a drive of 293 yards, and finish third behind Player in the main event. Casper, one of the most talented players in the game in his day, was unstinting in his praise of the young Spaniard. 'Severiano is not only a gorilla off the tee,' he enthused to Barner, 'he also has the finest short game I have ever seen in my life.'

This from a man who had seen the very best.

Billy Casper had in fact been one of the founder members of Uni-Managers International (UMI), along with Barner, a former show-business promoter. Until the US PGA Tour required him to divest himself of all his interests in the company – for it was considered ethically unsound and a conflict of interests for one professional golfer to represent another playing in the same event – Casper assisted Barner in the recruitment of players and the running of the business. When he left UMI in 1972, he sold his shares to a law firm in Los Angeles; whereupon Brent Turley, an attorney with that firm, joined UMI as general counsel and director, and Barner took up the reins of the company. UMI had already built up a strong client base. Both Barner and Casper were Mormons (or Latter Day Saints), which had been an incentive for Johnny Miller, who was born and raised in the Church, to join them in 1970, and Miller had brought in several of his friends – players like Jerry Heard, Lanny Wadkins, J.C. Snead and Dave Hill. Sam Snead, Vicenzo and the 1969 US Open champion, Orville Moody, had been with UMI from the outset.

Barner now became intent on signing up the prodigiously talented Ballesteros. At St Nom la Breteche, where the Lancome Trophy is held, he approached Severiano and Manuel with a proposition. He would pay their airfares to Como for the Italian Open and cover the cost of their accommodation; organize invitations for them both to play in the Walt Disney World National Team Championship in Florida; pay for their travel and living expenses while they were in America; and give them return tickets to Spain. He would do all of these things with no strings attached, provided Severiano would go to the US PGA Tour Qualifying School and attempt to win his card. After that, well, maybe then they'd talk about him representing them.

A fortnight later the Ballesteroses flew to America for the first time. As soon as they had found their bearings they made their way out to the Lake Buena Vista course, where they were told they had missed their tee-off time. Indeed, it was only through the intervention of Jim Colbert, an eventual winner with Dean Refram, that they were allowed to play at all. Both failed to qualify. Barner, meanwhile, had drawn up a contract for Severiano but not for Manuel (the latter's role in America was purely one of translator·and companion, did he but know it). He arranged a meeting with them. Five hours after the pre-arranged time, he was still waiting. The brothers had fallen into conversation with Moody, a Spanish speaker, who was giving them chapter and verse on the iniquities of managers as a species and on his own unhappy dealings with Barner. When they finally knocked on Barner's door they were in mutinous frame of mind. They wanted him to prove that he would be able to make Severiano the kind of money he claimed he could and obtain the contracts he promised. If not, they weren't interested.

'Look,' said Barner, struggling to control his temper. 'Nobody here has ever heard of Severiano Ballesteros. One day, maybe, everybody will have, but right now I can only make money if *you* play well. I can't sell a loser.'

There is no question that Barner was talking from a position of strength. He had a great deal of personal charm and a pleasantly reassuring manner and – aided by the obvious advantages that a professional salesman has over two naïve Spaniards in a foreign land with little English and hardly any business acumen between them – easily won them round. He readily agreed to them taking the five-year contract back to Spain to be vetted by a local attorney. Severiano, his guard lowered, then agreed to sign on the dotted line, but not until he had mulled over his alternatives. Johnny Miller is positive that when he did so, he brought Miller into the equation.

'I really believe that Seve admired me a lot,' observes Miller with an arrogance so natural that he'd be stunned if you pointed it out to him. 'I know that he watched me at the World Cup in 'seventy-three at Nueva Andalucia, Spain. I was a young, sort of dashing player, swung hard, and I won the individual title. I'm not saying that I was his idol, but I took him a little bit by storm. I wasn't just a guy he'd read about; he had actually seen me in person. So when I met him, he knew what kind of player I was . . . I think I had an impact on him because we've always had a very special relationship. There was always a bond between Seve and I. Maybe it was because he was so young and I was in my prime . . . but it's always been there, to this day. We've always been close. Not close in that we go out *per se*, but when he went to UMI I really believe that he went with UMI because I was with UMI. *One* reason. Not all the reasons. But one good reason was, "Geez, if it's good enough for Johnny Miller, maybe it's good enough for me." And Ed Barner was great at selling himself. He was a *genius* at selling himself.'

From Florida, Ballesteros went to the US PGA Tour Qualifying School to try for his card. There is not much difference between it and the PGA European Tour Players' School now, in terms of actual degree of difficulty, but seventeen years ago it was unrivalled as the most gruelling academy of skill and nerve in sport. Held over six days, its sole purpose was, and still is, to determine which players are most likely to survive the competition on the Tour. Thus, around 400 golfers fight for twenty-five or thirty spots.

Ballesteros, who had negligible working knowledge of American courses and conditions, found himself hurled into this maelstrom without warning. He shot 77 and 75 in the opening rounds before finding his feet. On the sixth day he came within a hair's breadth of winning his player's card; but inexperience got the better of him and, after an outward 33, he took 40 over the back nine and missed qualifying by four strokes. When it was over, he was exhausted and homesick and anxious to return to Europe. Barner had other plans for him. He wanted Severiano to return to California with him, where UMI would begin grooming him for stardom. Reluctantly, Ballesteros complied. They travelled to Los Angeles, where Ballesteros was to spend nearly two months in total at the home of Barner and his wife, studying English and playing the great Californian courses.

'It was a tough time for Seve,' admitted Barner later. 'I think he is still uncomfortable remembering those days at our house, alone and without his family.'

When the news came that Franco had died, Ballesteros, who was a Franquista, locked himself in his room and cried as if his heart would break.

Brent Turley, who accompanied Ballesteros to Japan in November that year, where he tied seventeenth in the Dunlop Phoenix, remembers him as being very young and very lonely. 'He kept his own counsel. Very impressive in a sense of his talent, although maybe he did not know then how good he was or how difficult it was . . . Nice kid. He was apprehensive about things around him. His brother Manuel was very much involved in his life, helping him make certain adjustments, but he wasn't with him in Japan and he wasn't with him for a good period of time when Ed had him in Los Angeles learning English and doing all these things to help him bridge the cultural and language gap.'

When UMI had signed Miller who, as a nineteen-year-old university student, had rocked the golfing establishment by finishing eighth behind Casper in the 1966 US Open, Barner's first action had been to alter Miller's name. John, he maintained, was bland and boring, while Johnny had an appealing boy-next-door quality about it. Miller was opposed to the change. Barner persuaded him to accept it by explaining to him the potential commercial benefits of such a decision, but to this day Miller, in conscious or subconscious rebellion, still signs his name 'John ny', leaving a space between the two n's.

Now Barner turned his attention to the Spaniard. He had already decided that something had to be done about the boy's name. S-e-v-e-r-i-a-n-o B-a-l-l-e-s-t-e-r-o-s, spelt out, added up to twenty characters. 'How could they get that in a headline?' he reasoned. 'How could they fit it on the head of a golf club? How many sports commentators would manage to say it?'

'What do they call you at home?' he asked the boy.

'Seve,' replied Ballesteros, only he pronounced it the Spanish way – 'Sebbay.'

'Sevvy,' mused Barner. 'And what was your mother's maiden name?'

'Sota.'

'What do you think about using Sevvy Sota?'

Ballesteros saw red. He refused point blank to even contemplate such a thing. Sevvy, or Seve, he would go along with but as for Sota . . . ? Pfff. The very idea was anathema to him. So Seve Ballesteros it became; and Barner adopted the same, peculiarly proprietary interest in the young Spaniard as he had in Miller.

5 August 1976, Dutch Open, Holland. 'The name Severiano Ballesteros is beginning to take on an ominous ring. It does not yet carry the same charge of awe as, say, Walter Hagen did in the minds of his contemporaries but things are moving that way.'

So wrote Peter Dobereiner after Ballesteros had shot a course record equalling 65 in the first round of the Dutch Open. A fortnight had gone by since the swashbuckling young Spaniard, with his dark eyes, flashing smile and absolute abandon on the golf course, had exploded into history at Royal Birkdale, and still the shock waves had not yet abated. Huge galleries had flocked to see him in Scandinavia, where he was struck by lightning, but finished third; in Switzerland, where he was runner-up; and they poured in colourful profusion across the links-like fairways of Kennemer, desperate to catch a glimpse of the boy who was being hailed as a golfing genius. He did not disappoint them. Recklessness cost him a 73 and the lead in the second round, but he responded by attacking the course with still greater fervour and, in the final round, left the entire field standing as he swept to an eight-stroke, record-equalling victory of 275, thirteen under par.

'That's the only way he knows how to play golf,' concluded Dobereiner admiringly, 'full steam ahead and damn the torpedoes.'

After that it was as if somebody had opened a floodgate which once released could never ever be shut again. Ballesteros, like a helpless rock star being hoisted above the heads of a screaming crowd, was seized by the publicity machine and carried along on an increasingly frantic vortex of media attention and public adoration. Sponsors beat a path to Barner's door, television stations formed mile-long queues and scores of teenage groupies, a phenomenon hitherto unheard of in European golf, followed him round the golf course and clamoured outside his hotel room.

'You cannot believe how women loved that guy,' says former European Tour player, Simon Hobday, enviously. 'The women just absolutely loved that bloke. There were six hundred, seven hundred groupies at every tournament. They were just after Ballesteros. All ages, too!'

Once, when a reporter asked a group of teenage girls at a tournament which pop star Ballesteros reminded them of, one of them replied, 'with all the youthful conviction at her command, "We have been here every day to see him this week. He's better looking than anyone in pop." '

'He had a following from 'seventy-six on,' recalls Doust. 'Gary Hallberg told me he was at a fraternity house in North Carolina – and Seve was the contemporary of all the university kids there – that when Seve nearly won the Open in 'seventy-six they went absolutely bonkers. So immediately he had a constituency that stretched around the world. Again because I think the game needed someone like that. And he had Trevino on his side. Trevino was always known as this great colourful Mex and now you were getting a great colourful Spaniard, who was not similar to Trevino in many ways but he was another Spaniard and that helped the mystique, I think . . . He was pretty sunny [by nature] and he was very funny and he was something unique. On the circuit here we hadn't had a magic figure since Jacklin. We had some very, very good players, like Neil Coles – wonderful golfer, wonderful striker of the ball – but no magic. And nobody was magic. And, I mean, for someone like Seve to come along, who was very good-looking and played the shots he played and was so good, I think he was worshipped, in a way, and loved.'

Ballesteros's impact on the whole of Europe, even at that early stage of his career, was that of a 'Continental Jacklin', as Ken Schofield, the executive director of the European Tour, has described him, for the spiralling myth which surrounded him effortlessly transcended political and geographical boundaries. 'Seve is big news all over Europe,' said Bernhard Langer in the autumn of 1976. The Spaniard and he are the same age. 'Even in Germany, where golf does not often get into the newspapers. And anything which makes the people interested in golf is good for me. What he has done is a tremendous inspiration to other Continental players.'

'If you got Seve competing for victory against an English player, or a Scottish or Irish player in Britain,' recalls golf writer Alan Booth, 'they were all rooting for Seve. And that, to me, is strange in a way. But I felt the same way. I was rooting for Seve even if it was against Sandy Lyle. It's a peculiar sort of attitude you get. You want Seve to win. Why? Because he's different. He's a one-off.

You can't compare him with any other player that there's ever been.'

'You were *fascinated* by Seve,' remembers Mark Wilson, now consultant to Schofield on the Tour. 'Every time you talked with Seve you became more and more fascinated. He went through that phase where he was desperate to learn English. I remember one time he came to me and he was very upset – he was very upset often – and he remonstrated with me quite fiercely, because he was asked at Birkdale, "How do you feel now?" and he said, "*Mucho Contento*," and the newspaper I was working for saw this as a great headline and they put it right across the back page. And Seve came looking for me and he was not happy. Because, he said, it highlighted and exaggerated his lack of English. It was at that stage he declared that he would learn and speak English perfectly. Then came that phase when he had a marvellous grasp of English, not as we understand it, but he was literally translating Spanish into English. He didn't have colloquial English at all. One day he shot 74 and he came in and we asked: "Seve, how could you shoot 74?" And there was this marvellous quote. He said: "Some days you wake up and you open the eyes and all is bright. Some days you wake and you open the eyes and all is dark. Today all was dark." The English would have said, some days you get out of the wrong side of the bed. But Seve had this marvellous way of turning Spanish into English. And so it went on, and then he became more than good.'

Ballesteros, who could hardly have been less affected by his runaway victory in the Dutch Open, whirled on through Europe like a hurricane, notching up a third place in the German Open, a fifth place in the Irish Open, a win in the Donald Swaelens Memorial Trophy in Belgium and a share of eighth place in the Benson and Hedges International. By the time he reached Paris for the Lancome Trophy he was, as Pat Ward-Thomas noted, 'riding a crest of rare confidence.' That is not to say that he had become conceited or full of himself. Indeed, Hobday echoes the sentiments of virtually every other person interviewed when he says that, 'he didn't become big-headed at all. He became more confident, yes, but he didn't become big-headed. You take a guy like Faldo, for example. Dear, oh dear, oh dear, oh dear. Faldo suddenly thought he was God's gift. Mind you, he was.'

'He was one of the most confident sportsmen I ever met when he was eighteen,' remembers Doust. 'But I didn't find it very offensive. I don't think anybody found it offensive . . . He was very aloof sometimes. He was a bit like the Kennedy family. You were either for him or against him, and if I wrote anything critical of him he thought I'd let him down. And that was the only problem we ever had, really, is that he expected me to be – not his mouthpiece, but his cheerleader.'

The extent of Ballesteros's self-belief at that age is simply illustrated by the fact that he composed his winner's speech on the eve of the final round of the Lancome Trophy when he shared the lead with no less a personage than Arnold Palmer.

Palmer, at forty-six, was no longer at his peak, but he was still a champion and still capable of drawing huge galleries. Thus, when the maestro and the prodigy who had elicited so much comparison with him teed off the following morning, a vast crowd of excited spectators surged after them. It was Palmer who drew first blood. Hitching up his trousers and smashing the ball powerfully down the fairway, he went out in 34, opening up a four-stroke advantage over the Spaniard. The writing, it appeared, was on the wall. But Ballesteros was not finished yet. Gathering himself for the fight, he began to attack the course with fearless iron play and flawless putting, in a way reminiscent of Palmer's own famous back nine charges, birdying five of the last eight holes for an inward half of 31 and victory.

Henry Cotton, reviewing the tournament, observed that he 'is now the top European golfer and not afraid of any player in the game. I heard some of the golf stars here this week talking about him – they can't avoid doing that because he is here to stay – but I do not agree that he is a seven-day wonder. There may be better strikers of the ball, more mechanical players, but he was the best golfer, even though he won by the minimum.'

Towards the end of the season two rather galling incidents occurred, though neither of them detracted in any way from the glory of Ballesteros's achievements in 1976 when he became, ultimately, the youngest player ever to win the Order of Merit, with earnings of £39,504, and the first Continental player to do so since Flory van Donck in 1953. He was also named Sportsman of the Year in Spain by *El Mundo deportivo de Barcelona*.

The first incident took place at Wentworth during the World Match Play, where Hale Irwin, who was playing Ballesteros and who was irritated by a rule which existed in Europe at that time but not in America allowing the tapping down of spike marks, accused the young Spaniard of trying to repair his pitch marks instead. It was all very unpleasant and resulted in Ballesteros losing both his temper and the match.

The second thing that happened also involved a rule and took place at the World Cup in Palm Springs, California. Ballesteros and Manuel Piñero were paired with Dave Stockton, the US PGA Champion, and Jerry Pate, winner of the 1976 US Open, on the second day of play. At the sixth hole Piñero's approach shot finished 3 feet short of the green and Ballesteros's about 6, so that the former's ball interfered with his partner's line. 'Manuel, can you move your ball?' asked Ballesteros. Piñero obligingly marked his ball, picked it up and dropped it into the palm of his black caddie Victor who, as he was going to clean Piñero's ball as soon as it was on the green, had a towel draped over his hand.

'That is not allowed,' shouted Pate, a Southerner, who was watching Piñero like a hawk.

In that instant both Ballesteros and Piñero realized that they were about to violate what is now Rule 21c (then 23), which states that 'a ball may be cleaned and lifted [off the putting surface] except when it has been lifted: Because it is interfering with or assisting play (Rule 22, formerly 23).' Piñero snatched his ball out of Victor's hand before the caddie had moved a muscle and before the two referees who were following the match knew what was happening. They played out the hole in silence. On the seventh tee Pate started saying that the Spaniards should be penalized two strokes.

'Who was the caddie?' demanded a referee.

Piñero claims that Pate then said something to the effect of 'The caddie's that black guy.' But he didn't react immediately, not having understood what Pate meant. When some Spanish friends who had overheard it translated it for him a few holes later, he was furious. 'When I left the eighteenth green, I was out of my mind with anger,' recalls Piñero. 'Seve was the same. I said to him, "If they penalize us two strokes, I'm going to hit Pate." ' He tried to sit down next to Pate when the players went to sign their scorecards, but Ballesteros took the chair away and sat in it himself. The Spaniards had managed to better their opponents by three strokes after Piñero had birdied the seventh hole while Ballesteros had eagled the ninth. The American cause had been weakened by Pate who had dropped three consecutive shots from the seventh. At length, the referees appeared and informed them that the Spaniards wouldn't be penalized in view of the fact that nobody had actually seen the caddie clean Piñero's ball. The Americans were outraged.

'That incident at the sixth hole affected my whole round,' cried Pate, forgetting that it was his score of 69 that had prevented Spain from taking control of the tournament. 'I played badly because of it.'

Ballesteros fixed him with a cold stare. 'You were not affected because you never played well anyway,' he said clearly, putting an end to any further discussion.

The following day Ballesteros and Piñero stormed to an emotional two-stroke victory over the United States with an aggregate score of 574, becoming the first Spaniards and only the second European team to win the World Cup.

Back in Britain, IMG had belatedly woken up to the realization that a star had been born. Roddy Carr, who is now chief executive of Amen Corner, one of Severiano's three companies, but who was then responsible for the recruiting of young players for IMG, remembers the young·Spaniard as being 'absolutely exceptional. Absolutely. I mean, he was what I'd consider a matador, the ultimate matador of golf . . . the way he attacked the game, the contempt [with respect] and the aggressiveness. No matter where it was, where it went to, what lie, what position he was in, it was just GO FOR IT. And it was wonderful.'

'Well, he'd be the ultimate guy you'd want to manage at that stage,' says John Simpson, Nick Faldo's manager and friend at IMG. 'One of the best, if not *the* best golfer for many, many years. Good-looking, modelled his clothes well, was good with people . . . He was confident, but a very, very nice guy. Very sympathetic. He always had a good heart. He would always see other people's point of view. Loved kids. He had a good feeling for other people, which I always thought was a very nice attribute to have . . . And everybody loved Seve. And he could play like hell, you know. So he'd be the ultimate golfer you'd want to have. And we could have done a helluva lot for him.'

It was for all of these reasons that Mark McCormack, head of IMG, was so annoyed at having been pipped at the post by Barner and so determined that Ballesteros should be lured away from him. Doust claims that 'the Spaniard became the central figure in McCormack's plan to dominate and control tournament golf on the Continent.' He cites as an example meetings held in October 1977 between McCormack and a dozen members of his team, the minutes of which were published in *The Sunday Times* and read: 'It seems that Ballesteros is unhappy with Barner, and now may be the time to approach him. The stronger we become in golf, the more Barner is able to do for Ballesteros, so it is important to have Ballesteros. It was felt that an investment in hiring the person closest to Ballesteros to work for us in Spain [e.g. Manuel Ballesteros or Jorge Ceballos, chief executive of the Spanish PGA] should be considered if this would guarantee us Severiano Ballesteros as a client. At present, Ceballos is an obstacle in our way. He certainly has a big influence on [Antonio] Garrido and we think he is trying hard to influence Ballesteros as well.'

However, all of these advances came to nought. Ballesteros, for the moment at least, was content to stay with Barner.

'I can say this,' comments Carr, 'that the strategy of IMG to get Seve would have probably been the most aggressive strategy of all time. At the end of the day, one of the great things about IMG is that they keep trying. They're probably at this stage trying . . . But the bottom line is that Seve was never going to be an IMG element, anyway. Never. It's just not him. He was always going to control his own destiny. But whether he would have stayed with IMG for one or two or three years, who can say. IMG would have been a helluva lot better than Ed Barner was. IMG are the best in the business, really, and at that stage, Ed Barner was nothing. Nothing. He had no real qualification in that particular area, in my opinion . . . I was never directly involved in the recruiting of Seve because I said from day one: "Forget it." Why? Because there was no chance. There was never going to be a chance, because that's the way he does things. He controls his own destiny.'

One thing Ballesteros couldn't control, couldn't even staunch the flow of, was his rising tide of popularity. 'When I became famous,' he told me, 'I feel like I lost a big part of myself. And this is the most difficult thing that can happen to anybody. I mean, I would say' – he paused, searching for words – 'it's not good to be famous. I think it's good to be recognized but not to be famous because it's like carrying a big stone on your shoulder all the time and it's difficult. Now I beat the pressure, but before I went through a very difficult time.'

Piñero nods compassionately. 'Seve was afraid of people when he was young – afraid of being with people – because he comes from a very small village. I don't think he actually liked publicity, and he had to live with it. Seve likes to be alone with a few friends. He's a very private person. Now he's more outgoing but before he was introvert. When he was eighteen or nineteen he had to have dinners with old people, dinners with presidents of companies and when he went to restaurants everybody knew him. So it was a very, very difficult life. But to explain that in Spain is impossible. I understand it. I *did* understand what he was going through, but you cannot explain it. I have a lot of friends and I have private conversations about it and some of them say, "Seve is not a friendly person." I say, "He can't be. You don't understand what he's going through. He can't be, because he's got so much pressure inside himself." To people on the outside, it will seem like he's always apart, but in a way, for his career, it is good that Seve wasn't a diplomat. Seve wouldn't be the same if he tried to change his attitude. It would affect his game. Because he needs to be hungry on the course. I think it's a psychological thing. For example, Seve has to be tight on the course – he needs to be nervous. He's like a car. He needs to be in overdrive.'

Ironically, the sensation Ballesteros was causing throughout the Continent went almost unnoticed in his own country. 'Seve has never had very good publicity in Spain,' explains Piñero, 'because in Spain we have a very peculiar way of seeing things. Fifteen years ago nobody knew what a golf professional was. Seve was the centre of attention in the golf world when he was eighteen, but in Spain he wasn't. He was the best player, but they didn't understand what that meant. And I always, in private and in public, excuse Seve for the early years. To me, it doesn't matter what he did. He was allowed to make a lot of mistakes because he was in a situation where very few people would have the character to take it. He was put in a situation where, when he was sixteen he was caddying for a hundred pesetas a day and when he was nineteen he wouldn't pour the tea for less than £10,000. *In two and a half years.* You cannot go from one extreme to the other in that time. It's impossible. You have to be very mature to understand what's going on. So, to me, in those years, all the mistakes Seve made I can accept.'

' 'Course he found [fame] difficult to deal with,' says Dave Musgrove abruptly. 'You can understand that, can't you? He had no background to it. That was obvious at the time. He didn't like it. He didn't like being mobbed for autographs. He didn't like having to go to receptions and presentations and all that crap.'

'Well, it's very difficult for somebody like him, at the age of nineteen, to become so responsible for everything,' says Chino Fernandez, Ballesteros's most steadfastly loyal friend. 'A person of his age having to sit with people maybe three times older than him, and even though they speak the same language, they don't *speak* the same language because of the difference between their ages and everything. So he have to mature very quick. And I think he avoid one step of his life because he became famous very young. He didn't live one part of his life. And it was very tough for somebody of his age. Sooner or later, it gets you.

'So now I think his attitude is one of self-defence. He wants to be by himself. That's why for people who never live the same way, it's difficult to understand. He didn't live from eighteen to twenty-five. He wasn't allowed to be young. He was under the focus of the world at that age.'

5

Fire and Ice

No man is a hero to his valet.

Mme Cornuel (1605–84)

Scientists, who have a label for everything, describe a person
or thing that precipitates a change while remaining unchanged
itself as a catalyst. Dave Musgrove was such a person. He
walked into Ballesteros's life in April 1976 – a thirty-two-
year-old Midlander with grizzled hair, beetling brows, steely
grey eyes and wit like a scimitar – and for four seasons was
the calm eye at the centre of the storm that is the Spaniard.
Musgrove is, and always was, unshakeably down to earth.
Ballesteros, at the age of eighteen, was dark, intense, explosive and overemotional. Doust described their relationship as
'a marriage of strong wills'. Ultimately, it ended in divorce.

Musgrove had begun his caddying career some twenty years
before, at Hollinwell, a Nottinghamshire golf course close to
his home in Kirkby-in-Ashfield, near Mansfield. He had continued to caddie throughout his teens and, when he became
a draughtsman for the National Coal Board, had habitually
taken his annual vacation during the Open Championship so
that he could try to find a bag. In 1972, by which time he
had left the Coal Board for the aerospace engine division of
Rolls-Royce, he was offered voluntary redundancy. He took
it. Once, years later, when he was asked why he had done it

– what the appeal was in caddying, he said it was the call of the open road. 'The chance of a big cheque and the freedom of the road. And if you've ever worked in an office you'll know the difference.'

By then Musgrove had already worked for several of the top players, including Roberto de Vicenzo, through whom he had come to know Manuel Ballesteros and Chino Fernandez. He was caddying for the latter in the PGA Championship at Royal St George's in 1975 when he first saw Ballesteros. 'I saw this lad practising away and the first thing I noticed was he had legs longer than his body and a great big pair of hands. He stood a long way from the ball to give himself plenty of room to swing. I looked at the golf bag [a Dunlop] and it said 'Ballesteros'. So I said to Fernandez, 'Is he any relation to Manuel?' 'Yeah,' he says, 'he's his brother.'

If Musgrove was impressed then, he soon became even more so, for the young Spaniard improved markedly during the course of the season. But it did not occur to him to try and caddie for him until almost twelve months later, when he arrived at the French Open at Le Touquet to discover that Fernandez had hurt his finger and withdrawn. It was not a catastrophe. The competition for bags then was not as stiff as it has become, and Musgrove simply settled down in front of the clubhouse to wait until a player without a caddie happened by. Before long, Manuel appeared.

'Need a caddie?' said Musgrove hopefully.

Manuel hesitated. 'Best thing you can do,' he said, 'is wait for my brother to come. He's playing good.'

So Musgrove waited. When Ballesteros came striding up the path, he remembered the Englishman and greeted him shyly.

'Do you want me to caddie for you?' asked Musgrove, coming straight to the point.

'You – work for me?' said Ballesteros, making sure he understood the question.

'Yeah.'

'OK.'

'So we set off,' says Musgrove, describing their first round together. 'He'd never seen the course before. He chipped up for a four on the first hole, birdied the second, birdied the third, hit a great drive on the fourth, a par five, and then hit a three-iron on the green and missed the putt for eagle. I thought: "This is all right for a nineteen-year-old." The next hole, a par three, he hits it middle of the green and missed it from about twelve feet. But he went off his head. Shouting and screaming. Anyway, he shot 66 and won the pro-am and didn't seem to think a lot of it. Didn't think it was a big deal, I don't s'pose. Very hot that week. Incredibly hot. He played all right, but every time he hit a bad shot or got into trouble his head would come off. I don't know where he finished – not bad [joint eighth with earnings of £569]. 'Course there was no money in those days. I tell you who won it. Vincent Tshabalala from Darkest Africa.'

After the French Open Musgrove started to work for the Spaniard regularly, only surrendering the bag to his friend Dick Draper at the Open at Birkdale because he didn't want to let Roberto de Vicenzo down. But by the time Ballesteros swept to his first European Tour victory in the Dutch Open, Musgrove was running low on funds. He informed his boss that he was returning to England to earn some money with which to subsidize his caddying.

'Aren't you going to go to Germany?' said Ballesteros, aghast.

'I said, "I've got to work," ' recalls Musgrove. ''Course he never would pay any more money, like.'

If Ballesteros can be said to have one major flaw in his character, it is an obsession with money. Tales of his meanness are legion. Given the circumstances of his childhood it is understandable if not excusable but it has, nonetheless, been the source of a great deal of heartache and controversy during his career, much of which could have been avoided had he been less mercenary. After all, how much money can one spend? Not surprisingly, it has been the men who have carried his bag who have complained longest and loudest (apart, that is, from the sponsors who pay him appearance money). Most caddies feel, quite reasonably, that they play a valuable part in the success of their player and that, when the said player becomes a very rich man through their combined efforts on the golf course, he should allow more than a few crumbs to fall from his table. Musgrove, for instance, says he was paid a 'minimum wage and 5 per cent. Well, minimum what he paid which happened to be better than normal. But it could never be described as good.'

Minimum wage on Tour these days is around £250 per week, but in 1976 it was less than £100. When Pete Coleman, now Bernhard Langer's caddie, worked for Ballesteros some years later he earned £120, plus 5 per cent, while Draper received £250 for his week's work at the Open in 1976.

'A lot of people ask me how much money I got off him for winning the Open in 1979,' says Musgrove. 'And I always say, I was there for ten days and the total amount of money that changed hands was, I had to lend him a fiver. Which he paid me back.'

'I've had my ups and downs with him on money,' comments Ian Wright, who caddied for Ballesteros in 1988 and 1989. 'I don't think generally he's a mean person, he's just careful . . . I felt, in the position he was in, he could have paid for a few more of the flights and things, particularly when the bad years came. You always felt . . . that he could have provided flights to the States, which is what other players do for their caddies. But he always paid a fair wage and a good percentage so one balances out the other, I suppose.'

In January 1977 Ballesteros experienced first-hand what it was like to be underpaid. He was drafted into the Spanish army, where he earned the princely sum of £2 a week as a private. In Spain, national service is compulsory. But where a conscripted serviceman has to serve up to twenty months, a volunteer, provided he has a primary school certificate, can choose his own posting. Ballesteros, of course, didn't have a certificate. He was too proud to sit for an Army examination either. 'I will not go through any examination whatsoever,' he told Jorge Ceballos, who later became his manager. 'Not even the US Qualifying School that the Americans want me to do. I have nothing to prove in golf and I do not regret not having as much culture as other people. I shall learn my own way through life.' However, it was some months before the authorities who wanted him to undergo written tests relented.

At Birkdale it was announced that he had been assigned to the staff of a Spanish general on a US base in Saragossa, but he ended up serving most of his time at a small nine-hole golf course outside Madrid, the Centro Deportivo Barberan; where he gave exhibitions and instructed Air Force officers in correct backswing technique.

'He only pretended to [go into the Army], didn't he?' Musgrove says sourly. 'Well, he didn't do a great deal, did he? It never stopped him playing. Just did a bit of time in the winters. He never did a great deal in the army. Basic training, that was about all. He never did as much as Elvis.'

Doust, who went to interview him for *The Sunday Times* the week before he was sworn into the Spanish Air Force, observed that since he had turned professional Ballesteros had grown enormously strong and was filling out almost daily . 'He is six feet tall and weighs twelve stone, eight pounds, a stone up on last year [in 1992 he weighed twelve stone, nine pounds]. He can carry eleven golf balls in one hand and the Air Force doctors found he could expand his massive chest from the normal 95 to 105 centimetres in one searing breath.' He was also struck by how natural and at ease Ballesteros seemed in his own environment, how little affected by the successes of the previous season. 'Spoilt, yes; confident and magisterial, yes. Subject to some of golf's blackest moods, Severiano Ballesteros remains a warm and friendly boy, generous of his time and amazingly untouched by fame or fan mail.'

By spring Ballesteros was ranked tenth in the world – Jack Nicklaus and Ben Crenshaw were No. 1 and 2 – and had been given extended 'leave' by the Spanish military to play in the US Masters and on the European circuit. Those players and journalists who had spent the early part of 1977 commenting wistfully on what a shame it was that Europe's best player was confined to barracks and would be unable to defend his position as leading money winner, were thrown back on their heels as Ballesteros suddenly laid down his rifle, combat jacket and boots, and embarked on a crusade far more important to him than defending a country not at war. In his first European Tour event, the Spanish Open at La Manga, he showed glimpses of his best form and finished joint third.

Ballesteros followed his fine Spanish Open performance with a rather poor thirty-fifth place finish in the Madrid Open, but recovered almost immediately and was placed fifth in the Italian Open. After that, there was no stopping him. He won the French Open at Le Touquet, was twentieth in the PGA Championship and then overcame Faldo at the first extra hole of a play-off for the Uniroyal International, despite being plagued by back trouble and receiving pain-killing injections all week. Then in July he was fifteenth at the Open Championship at Turnberry. 'He was going nicely and then he blew it towards the end of the third round,' recalls Musgrove. 'The last round he was thumping his driver on the floor and bent it, and he was trying to straighten it up again and it broke. So he had to drive off with a three-wood. He said: "These holes are playing long." I said: "This is where normal people play from." '

The next week Ballesteros overcame further back problems to finish three shots clear of the field at the Swiss Open. He swept all before him in Japan, where he won the Japanese Open and the Dunlop Phoenix, and in New Zealand, where he won the Otago Classic. Finally, in December, he teamed up with Antonio Garrido in the Philippines to bring glory to Spain for the second time in the World Cup. By the end of the season he was Europe's leading money winner once more, had gone fifteen straight tournaments without once three-putting and had a stroke average of 71.06. Only Byron Nelson, Ben Hogan and Sam Snead had triumphed so often in a single year, and no player had ever won in seven different countries in a season. In Europe he was a phenomenon, and his ability to compete at an international level was indisputable. All that remained now was for him to prove that he was a world-class golfer by contending with, and beating, the world's best players: namely, the Americans.

Sunday, 2 April 1978, Greater Greensboro Open, North Carolina. Severiano Ballesteros took three putts to get down on the final green of the tournament today, but it couldn't have mattered less. Victory was his by a shot. Long after he had signed his scorecard, having established an unassailable

81

lead, America's finest were still limping off the golf course, battered, bewildered and besieged. One by one they would gather their wits, dust themselves down, pause before the leaderboard to shake their heads in puzzlement, and then head for the locker room like broken men.

The cause of all this devastation was in the press centre, wreathed in smiles. 'I was lucky,' said Ballesteros feelingly. 'Everything went wrong for me but it all came right in the end. I don't know how I win tournaments. I came here and my game has no confidence. I was very worried that I miss cut. No-one likes to do that. The last two rounds I get confidence and I do my best, but I never think I win.'

The facts of the matter were these: that Ballesteros, exactly one week before his twenty-first birthday, had just become the first foreigner to win his first regular US Tour event – previously he had only played in the Masters, which is a major; the first non-member to win on the US Tour since Harold Henning at the 1966 Texas Open; the first player ever to win after only qualifying by one stroke; the first player to win his first regular Tour event since Ben Crenshaw (1973 Texas Open) and Marty Fleckman (1966 Cajun Classic); and the third youngest player to win a regular tournament, being a few months older than Raymond Floyd was when he won at St Petersburg in 1963 and Horton Smith had been when he won the 1928 Oklahoma City Open.

'Everything went wrong,' reiterated the young Spaniard, who was explaining in his halting English why he considered his achievement to be more incredible than all the dry statistics in the world could show. 'My plane left Madrid last Saturday at one p.m., but after three hours, in the middle of the Atlantic, the captain tell us that an engine give trouble and we turn back. I was very frightened. We land again in Madrid and, I tell you, if there had been a tournament in Europe I would have gone there. After six-hours wait we set out again in another plane and land in New York at La Guardia instead of Kennedy. There is a further four-hour delay before I connect to Greensboro, and I arrive Monday morning nearly twenty-four hours late and very tired.'

Subsequently, Ballesteros had recorded scores of 72 and

75 in the opening rounds to scrape through the qualifying and, after following them with a 69, had been five strokes off the pace going into the final day. He had all but been forgotten about. Even if he had not been, he would still have been considered by the average American golfer or golf writer as a rank outsider. Then, on a lightning-blue day, when temperatures went soaring into the high 80s and humidity sapped the resistance of the strongest, the raven-haired Spanish youth blazed a fiery trail to glory, going out in 31 and demolishing Fuzzy Zoeller and Jack Renner *en route*. Counting those in 1977, it was his sixth consecutive tournament victory, for he had won the Kenya Open at the beginning of the new season.

Of all the American players perhaps Ben Crenshaw, who had first played with Ballesteros at the Open in 1977, was most overwhelmed by his brilliance.

'Well, he played so instinctively and he played really to just slash and burn every golf course he could play,' says Crenshaw, himself one of the gentlest, kindest, most-gifted players the game has seen. 'He played with total abandon . . . To me, he's been the most exciting player that I've ever seen besides Palmer. I've always been an admirer of Seve's. He's an artist, he really is. To watch him try to figure out problems is fantastic, because when he's in a little bit of trouble he has great facial expressions. He really does wear his heart on his sleeve. He's got just an incredible imagination, and you can see what he's trying to do to the shot. All the time, he's working on something. I've seen him pull off some of the darndest shots I've ever seen . . . His instinct is incredible. And he looks so good. His hands go on the club and the way he sets up to the ball, he looks like he was born with a club. It's magical. But he's a fierce competitor, and I think he's very funny. I think he's got a great sense of humour. He gets down, like the rest of us, but he fights his way out of it. I'm really happy to see him play the way he's playing right now, because he's great for the game, *God, he's great*. I think he's marvellous, I really do. I always have.'

Two days after his victory at Greensboro, Ballesteros was offered his US Tour card. Ordinarily, he would have had to go through the rigours of the US Qualifying School just like any other player but, in an unprecedented move, Deane Beman, the PGA Tour commissioner, said that the Spaniard had proved his ability and would have sixty days to accept the offer. This met with mixed response. Many of the American Tour pros were outraged that Ballesteros should be made an exception of, and called for the decision to be rescinded. Frank Beard, a US Tour pro, reminded everyone that the whole purpose of the Players' School was to prove that a professional was a good enough player to compete, and pointed out that neither Graham Marsh [twenty-eight wins worldwide] nor Peter Oosterhuis [four times European money-list winner] had been given an exemption. 'So why Ballesteros?' he whined. Obviously, Ballesteros himself felt complimented but there were rumours that, because US Tour regulations stipulated that all members had to play a minimum of fifteen events on their own circuit and no more than three elsewhere, Ed Barner was trying to negotiate a deal with Beman whereby the card offer would remain open indefinitely, and would also allow the Spaniard to fulfil his commitments in Europe.

Nothing has quite such a bracing effect on Ballesteros as antagonism, and he responded to the American cold-shoulder by surging into the lead at the $112,500 Tournament of Champions, at La Costa, a fortnight later. Indeed, he played so aggressively, so passionately and so well, that after three rounds he had a four-stroke advantage. Then, incredibly, he lost.

Now if Ballesteros had been just another twenty-one-year-old golfer and had been subject to all the usual pressures and fears which govern the performances of young players, this loss would simply have been put down to inexperience and forgotten about five minutes hence. But he wasn't. He was absolutely unafraid. Yet in his final round, on a sunny, breezy day perfect for golf, he dropped two strokes at the relatively easy opening hole when he drove into a bunker, another stroke at the fifth where he was in the water, and another at the sixth where he failed to get up and down. Altogether, he had a miserable outward half and the tally at the end of it was 40. Gary Player, meanwhile, the Masters champion, who had been seven strokes behind at the start of the day, had gone out in 32. Unusually, the tournament was won and lost on the front nine, and the only clue to Ballesteros's collapse might lie with his playing partner, Lee Trevino. It seems the Mexican held an animated conversation (or monologue) with him the entire length of the first hole, while Ballesteros tacked his way from tee to green, but that for the remainder of the round a deathly hush hung over their little group. Since Ballesteros once said, 'The only time I talk on a golf course is to my caddie – and only then to complain,' one is left to conjecture that his concentration was upset by the chatter but that he left it too late to ask Trevino to keep quiet.

A week later he was in contention again. As Musgrove says, 'He don't give up, you see, he's very intense. He never gives up. But then it takes a lot out of him.' Ballesteros showed no outward signs of weakening at the Madrid Open when he shot an opening 66 to establish a three-stroke lead, but he did admit that after playing seven seventy-two-hole events in eight weeks he was feeling the strain, not only of golf but of the increasing number of interviews that the Spanish media, who had lately woken up to the concept of a golfer as a star, were demanding of him. But Nick Faldo, who partnered him, said, 'It was as if he had a 66 written on the board before he went out so easily did he do it.' Ballesteros just shrugged and remarked, 'A little lucky, I think.' He credited his fine round to a tip of Musgrove's. 'Dave is a very good caddie. I have confidence in him and if I go to America next year, he comes with me.'

A trio of three-putts on the back nine cost him the Madrid Open title, but he still finished third and followed his fifth place finish in the Spanish Open with a second in the French, which the South African Dale Hayes won by an astonishing eleven strokes. At last he reached Britain, where he overpowered Faldo and marched confidently to victory in the Martini International. There is a lovely story of how, on that day, all the Spanish restaurant staff in London, among whom the bold young Severiano had become a folk-hero, deserted their posts and drove up in convoy to the RAC Epsom to support him. Whether or not it is true, it conjures up delightful pictures of Ballesteros, like a Latin Pied Piper, leading a band of merry chefs and waiters, all in their white uniforms and hats and carrying their cooking utensils, along the fairways. Whatever – he entertained the galleries with a succession of magical shots, the most singular of which was a two-iron approach to the difficult eighth, a kidney-shaped green which falls away sharply on three sides, which he holed for an eagle two from 150 yards.

It was not long after this that he and Faldo, by now his chief rival in Europe, gave the following illuminating interview to Renton Laidlaw, in *Golf World*:

RL: Do you really think you can do justice to your [ability by] splitting yourself between two major world circuits?
SB: It will be tough for me. It means a demanding schedule but I have been offered my card and I have enough confidence in myself to feel I can cope successfully as long as my programme is carefully worked out. We'll just wait and see.
NF: I think you are going to find it extremely difficult to play well on both sides of the Atlantic. Will you be getting any special treatment over there to make it easier for you? There are so many rules – I mean, having to play fifteen tournaments to retain your card – that sort of thing.
SB: We are trying to arrange the whole thing with Mr Beman, the US commissioner, at the moment, and I think it will work out all right. I'm hopeful that I can get the type of deal which will enable me to become a transatlantic golfer without tiring myself out.
RL: What lessons have you learned in the past twelve months that have helped you become a better player, Seve?
SB: Before this season I played good some rounds, bad others. This year I play much more steadily. Before, I tried to attack the golf course with every shot. Now I attack when it is best to attack and I play safe if that is best. I'm not so impetuous. I think my way round better. I suppose you could put it all down to gaining in experience.
NF: What he means is that in the past year he has moved from being good to being bloody brilliant!
RL: How worrying is your back trouble?

SB: It's worrying enough for me to have seen several specialists, but I think it is OK if I do not overdo the practice . . . I can live with the problem. It's OK and, after all, I am not as bad as Lee Trevino who has to hang upside down every morning to get himself into shape. [Ironically, it was not two years hence when Ballesteros found himself having to dangle upside down from a Gravity Gym machine, a type of portable trapeze than can be fixed to any doorframe, at least three times daily in order to stretch the muscles in his back.]

RL: Any golfer as successful as you, Seve, is very much in demand. How do you cope with the pressure?

SB: You just have to. There is far more to professional golf than just playing in tournaments. There are regular meetings with the press, photographic sessions to fit in . . . I suppose I have to be choosy up to a point, but I try to please most people. I'll admit that it can be tiring at times but it's part of the price you pay for success.

NF: I agree with Seve. You certainly cannot afford to get fed up with all the extra demands. The hassle of interviews for the newspapers, radio and television is something we can all live with and all want to live with because it is a measure of success and being successful is a nice feeling.

RL: How much has Severiano helped you?

NF: We are good friends, as you know, off the course – although we thump each other in private. No, seriously, there is a lot of rivalry between us and it's great . . . [Seve] has a tremendous feel for the game . . . but what impresses me most about him is the way he works the ball. There is not a shot that he cannot hit . . . He's exciting to watch . . . All he ever sees is the pin and the hole. He is dedicated to winning, is super-confident and will win many more events in the next few years. Didn't Lee Trevino say recently that every fifteen years a player of Nicklaus's class is born and he believed Seve was the latest Nicklaus? I agree with that view. That's how highly I rate him.

[Years on, when asked about their friendship, Faldo said with a laugh, 'Well, it's the usual line: "We're friends and . . ." But we're very different. That's just the way it is. We all get on well and in the Ryder Cup we all knit together really well, but you're all playing competitors. You have to have some slight barrier up just because you're trying to be competitive with each other.' He felt that it was Ballesteros's putting and short game that made him such a good player at that age. 'He hit the ball all over the golf course, to be fair. And even when he was playing well and he hit it solid, they were still going right and left. He just managed with his short game, and he's one of these guys that takes every opportunity.']

RL: Is it true that you don't like America, Seve?

SL: Maybe. I'll whisper it – 'Yes', for various reasons . . . I cannot ever see myself full-time in America . . . One of the big problems I have faced in America is that you have far too much time to think. Sometimes you play in the morning at seven o'clock, are finished by noon, and are not playing again until two o'clock the next day.

RL: What's your one big burning ambition?

NF: Winning the Open Championship would be the greatest thing that could happen to me.

SB: I'd like to win the British Open. That's my ambition. Coming second to Johnny Miller in 1976 at Royal Birkdale is a bigger career highlight than some of my victories – that's how important I consider the Open.

The Open in 1978 was at St Andrews. Ballesteros was in peak form when it came around and more contented and at peace with himself than he had been in ages. 'Ballesteros never stops smiling,' Frank Keating remarked in the *Guardian*. Nor did he. And at press conferences he engaged in teasing skirmishes with his critics, saying, in heavily accented English, 'You cannot write all the time about me in the rough, because there's no rough here.' He was even happier after scoring 69 in the first round to share second place with Jack Newton, Raymond Floyd and Tom Weiskopf, one stroke behind the Japanese, Isao Aoki.

'In 1978,' says British professional Ken Brown, 'he was playing absolutely brilliant golf. I played the first two rounds with him and he played almost fearlessly – much more aggressively than he does now. I was singing his praises and Jerry Pate, who we were playing with, was trying to sort of say that he wasn't that good.'

Unfortunately, Ballesteros's boldness and derring-do robbed him of the chance to win his first Open Championship a year sooner than he did. In the second round he stood on the tee of the infamous Road Hole seventeenth and, like Arnold Palmer before him, curved a 325-yard drive far into the crowd in front of the Jigger Inn. All he had needed to do was to par the final two holes in order to gain a two-stroke advantage, and the assumption was that he had elected to go for maximum length rather than safety. But Brown says that it was the wall of undisciplined photographers in front of the tee, all clicking and whirring at the wrong moments, that put him off. His second shot from the tee was played with great ferocity – 'the stroke of an angry young man,' someone said – and travelled some 350 yards into the great unknown. From that position, he managed to reach the green with a four-iron and two-putted from 30 feet. He shared the lead with Ben Crenshaw and Aoki at the end of the round on 139, and was only four strokes off the pace going into the final day's play. But after his third round 76, a closing 73 left him tied for seventeenth place.

'He should have won,' says Musgrove firmly. 'He played a lot better at St Andrews [than he did at Lytham], but he hadn't learned to play the course. He should have walked away with it. It was like five in the afternoon and he was seven under par for the tournament, turned for home and the wind dropped and, by the time he got to the seventeenth, he'd realized what chances he'd missed. So he hit one out of bounds, the other side of the hotel – to the *right* of the hotel – and lost his rag. But he played incredibly . . .'

It is only when one looks at Ballesteros's record for a season such as 1978, when he finished at the top of the money list for the third consecutive time, that one can see why it is that people talk about him being in a slump when he goes for three tournaments without being in the top ten or for a month without a victory. Between leaving St Andrews and arriving at Walton Heath for the European Open, he finished first, first, joint fourth, joint second and first. His initial victory was the German Open which, by all rights, he shouldn't have been attending. In April he had been honoured with an invitation to play in the US PGA Championship at Oakmont, the first official exemption ever issued to a foreign player, but, having been mistakenly advised by Barner that the US PGA was not one of golf's major events, had graciously turned it down.

'That was just because, as a major – and it still is the situation but it was even more so then – it wasn't very important,' explains Joe Collet, one of his managers. 'It continues to be the least exciting. It's the one that he's usually prone to miss the cut in, and he had very good commerical possibilities in Europe at the time. It wasn't just the fact that he got an appearance fee, but I think it meant pushing an endorsement deal . . . with Braun [the tournament sponsor], which was a clothing company . . . They [the press] criticized the management [UMI] for doing something which, arguably, was detrimental to his career in the record books, but on the other hand it was financially rewarding and he was an important guy and he played in an event whose field was vastly improved by the fact that he was playing in it. I don't feel bad about it. I'd feel bad about it if it happened five years ago when he was at his peak, and he gave up a major to chase money which he didn't need. But at the time he was very young and the PGA wasn't a very big deal. It still isn't as important as the Masters or the Open Championship.'

While Collet is unquestionably right about the US PGA Championship's inferiority to the other three majors – and Ballesteros himself ranks the Open Championship first, the Masters second, the US Open third and the US PGA last – he is wrong about how little it probably mattered, given that Ballesteros was still young and not yet the force to be reckoned with that he later became. Ballesteros was at the top of his game when he reached Cologne for the German Open and if he had gone to Oakmont instead, who knows what he might have achieved. He had a four-stroke lead on 131 after two days' play and, in his final charge for victory, reduced the 594-yard ninth, one of the longest holes in golf, to a drive and a three-wood.

'Can you believe that?' said Gary Player, who was in the field, with a typically theatrical expression of awe. 'The Ballesteroses of this world will be shooting regularly in the fifties in years to come. Thank goodness I've got my titles won.'

The following week Ballesteros, told by Musgrove that he needed to shoot 32 on the back nine at Vasatorp to win the Scandinavian Open, proceeded to do exactly that to defeat Dale Hayes by a stroke. It was his eleventh victory in eight countries and on four continents in sixteen months. A fortnight later he won the Swiss Open.

Through that period of his life Ballesteros can only be described as a phenomenon. Tom Weiskopf said that he was the most charismatic player that he had seen since Arnold Palmer, and Jack Nicklaus and Robert de Vicenzo predicted that he would win the Masters several times. Everywhere he went he left a lasting impression.

'The first time I saw him was at the 1978 Madrid Open,' recalls Nick Price, the US PGA and Open Champion. 'He was hitting five-iron shots on the practice tee that day and they were probably going the same distance as my three-iron was. I just couldn't believe how strong he was. He just had so much strength and he swung the club with such ease and grace, and you couldn't figure out where all the power came from. I think the thing that was so outstanding in those days was the way he could get up and down from anywhere . . . He hit shots that most of us couldn't even dream of. He hit these little finesse wedge shots and little bump and run eight-irons and things. He just had wonderful hands and wonderful hand-eye co-ordination. I think what he did with his game [in later years] was to try not to hit the ball as far and he became a better all-round player. He may not have that kind of eye-opening game that people used to enjoy but golf's not about that, unfortunately. John Daly's in that league now, in that if he wants to have any longevity he's going to have to throttle back.'

'I feel very privileged to have seen him play in those years,' says Irishman David Feherty. 'There are a lot of parallels between him then and John Daly now, because it is a very expensive way to play the game, giving people what they want. You can't afford to give people what they want in this game. "Hit the driver, hit the driver," they'd all shout, and he'd get the driver and have a lash at it . . . He would actually give the crowd what they wanted . . . His game was extraordinary in that he hit the ball in the middle of the clubface a lot, even when he hit it a long way wide, and that's always, I feel, a sign of a player that's committed. You know, when he does start to swing well, he's going to be very, very good.'

'As a player, he was a breath of fresh air,' remembers Mark James. 'Gave it a dirty great hit and got it round with a magical short game and brilliant putting, much as he's done throughout his career. It was obvious he was incredibly talented. He could perform brilliantly in any department of the game and there's very few people who are capable of that.'

In Liz Kahn's biography *Tony Jacklin: the Price of Success*, Jacklin observed that, 'Ballesteros is a shot in the arm. He is just something else. He plays the game in the right spirit – smashes it long, ambles after it, looks for the hole, whack! and it all looks such fun. He gives you the feeling that he's actually enjoying it, and he is . . . He's won in America, which is great, and it will be interesting to see what he will do there in the future. At the moment, he's doing it all and enjoying it all, but when it gets too much, for whatever reason, that's when the problems start. He'll not be human if he doesn't go through some form of what I've been through.'

There was no doubt that Ballesteros did give the impression he was enjoying himself. And why shouldn't he have been? He had everything a young golfer could ever dream of. He had fame, he had wealth, he had an adoring following and he had a divine talent for the game. He should have been the sunniest, most contented man alive. The fact that he wasn't has a lot to do with the fact that nothing in this world is ever entirely what it seems. Take, for instance, the Hennessy Cup, a biennial match between Europe and the British Isles. Ballesteros played a shot there which has deservedly gone down in history. He came to the tenth hole of the Brabazon course at The Belfry, one up in his match against Faldo, and stood looking contemplative while the Englishman struck a mid-iron off the tee. Faldo was not being particularly cautious, nor was he playing safe. He was just doing what any rational golfer would do when faced with a 255-yard par four, with water down the right and the green tucked in the midst of a ring of trees, around a corner and across a pond. As a consequence, he was startled when the Spaniard plucked the cover from his driver. So were the crowd. They strained against the ropes to obtain a better view. With a minimum of fuss and bother, Ballesteros smashed the ball towards the distant flagstick. It soared out into the pale sky, carried a 50-foot tree some 250 yards from the tee, faded into a cross-wind and dropped onto the green, 10 feet from the pin, as easy as you please. There is a picture of Faldo walking open-mouthed from the tee. It was truly a marvellous golf shot and merits the comparison it had with Gene Sarazen's fairway wood for an albatross at Augusta.

The shame was that Ballesteros's performance on the golf course that week was slightly marred by two things, one of which was the comments of Angel Gallardo, the captain of the Continental side. 'Gallardo,' wrote Mitchell Platts in *Golf World*, 'the much respected Spaniard who had tugged at our sleeves four years earlier to go and witness a boy he regarded as a golfing genius, insisted [that]: "Seve thinks only of money. He does not think enough about the team." ' The young Spaniard . . . had stated that summer that he might not play. 'But Gaetan Mourgue d'Algue, much involved at that time in organizing the match, intervened. He offered to increase the appearance money from £2,500 to £4,000. Seve played but Gallardo was unamused by his compatriot's attitude that week.'

The second incident was the bombshell Ballesteros dropped after Europe lost to Britain 14½ to 17½, when he announced that he wouldn't be helping Spain to defend its World Cup title that year. He said it was ridiculous for a professional to be asked to play for a return of £1,000. When it was put to him that many players considered it their patriotic duty, he declared that Spain had never encouraged him and neither had the Spanish Golf

Federation. He said that he felt more loyalty to his fans in Britain.

Manuel Piñero, his first World Cup partner, who feels that 'one of the most important things for a professional in any sport is to play for your country, and if you refuse to play for your country I'm not happy with you', was livid and told him so. 'I have a great admiration, not only for Seve but for all the Spanish professionals, because of our background,' says Piñero, 'because of what we've come through. And because of that I will not accept anybody who tries to keep my opinions quiet. And I know sometimes that Seve will not a hundred per cent agree with what I say, but to me it doesn't matter. I think that's why I have quite a good relationship with Seve. When it comes to important decisions I think that Seve feels that he can come to me and say, "Manuel, how do you feel?" I will give always my honest word. But sometimes my honest word – and it did happen twice – is not to say "Yes" or to say "You are the best and you have the reasons". Sometimes my honest word has to be, "Seve, you're wrong and you have made a mistake." '

Musgrove had a very similar relationship with Ballesteros at that time, if rather more stormy, as was apparent at the European Open. On the eve of the tournament at Walton Heath, Musgrove was standing beside the practice green waiting, slightly impatiently, for Ballesteros to finish putting. He was anxious to get home. Only one of the headlights on his car was working and he was worried about driving after dark. Musgrove cast a glance at the Spaniard's bowed head and his rhythmic stroke. He was convinced that nothing would be gained by owning up to his predicament, and even thought that Ballesteros might deliberately extend his practice session out of spite. So when twilight drew its silvery cape across the course, Musgrove simply took the golf clubs, put them beside the Spaniard's street shoes in the clubhouse and left the course. The following morning he was standing in the car park, as usual, when his employer whisked in.

'Fetch the clubs,' ordered Ballesteros when he spotted his caddie.

'*I* haven't got them,' said Musgrove coldly. 'I left them with you last night.'

Ballesteros stared at him. 'You have got them,' he insisted. A rather fruitless row ensued, followed by a frantic search for the missing golf clubs. They were nowhere to be seen. Ballesteros, his face a picture of misery, was forced to borrow a set from the local pro and 'played badly, scored badly, played as best I could, but what can you do?'

The irony was that after six holes PGA European Tour tournament referee George O'Grady came out to tell them that the clubs had been found. A well-meaning official had seen them in the clubhouse the night before and had put them in an empty member's locker for safe-keeping. There was nothing Ballesteros could do. Under the Rules of Golf he had to complete his round with the borrowed set, which he did and scored 75.

'The funny thing was,' says Musgrove sardonically, 'he actually played better with the borrowed set.'

Earlier in the week there had been another clash between the two of them. Ballesteros's practice session had not gone well and, eventually, after a series of imperfect shots, he rammed his club back into the bag and stalked moodily off the range. Musgrove glared at his departing back and began to gather together balls, clubs, tees and towels. At last he heaved the bag onto his shoulder and swung round in time to see the courtesy car which had been waiting for Ballesteros start forward.

'HEY!' screamed Musgrove at the top of his lungs.

The driver stopped in confusion. Musgrove marched menacingly up to his window and swore at him. 'What d'you do that for?' he demanded.

The man shrank back into his seat, alarmed. 'He told me to,' he said pleadingly, jerking a thumb towards the passenger seat.

Musgrove threw the clubs into the car with some force and climbed in after them. 'Well, you're a right bastard,' he said to the back of the Spaniard's head. Ballesteros kept his eyes fixed on the road.

'So I got fired again,' says Musgrove drily, 'and re-employed the following morning at £1 extra a week.'

He turns his grey gaze on the horizon. 'People would never believe me what a bastard he was.'

Doust can. 'He was very, very, *very* tough on caddies. I mean, really cruel.'

Nick de Paul, who caddied for Ballesteros when he won the Open in 1984, agreed. 'Seve gives you hell every other hole out there, complaining about everything from golf to life in general. But you have to take the abuse – that way he's not battling on his own – which is all part of the business.'

In the book he co-wrote with Musgrove, John Hopkins says that, 'after several tumultuous years with Ballesteros [Musgrove] could no longer tolerate the abuse that was heaped upon him at, it seemed, almost every turn. Caddying for Seve at the Open at Lytham was hell, he was to say later. "Three weeks later he was still chewing me out. But there were also wonderful moments with Seve. He is so gifted it's not true." '

By the end of 1979 they had parted company. 'I'd had enough of him and he'd had enough of me,' admits Musgrove. In 1978, however, any rocky patch in their relationship was just another thing for Ballesteros to store away in his memory and, like an oyster with a grain of sand, use to spur him on to still greater achievements. He has a memory like an elephant when it comes to remembering snubs, and has a habit of bringing them up months or even years later without prior warning. In the middle of that season, for example, he was having a relaxed conversation with several journalists in the lounge of a Southport hotel when he suddenly brought up the subject of the Tournament of Champions, which he had lost by shooting 79 on the final day. 'They [the Americans] all come over to me, smile and say I have bad luck. They pat me on the shoulder. But they are happy and I see it. Why they not want me to win?' He gave a short laugh, the way he does when he is very hurt or bitter. 'Everybody said how sad it was. I led for so long, then I shot a bad last round. They say it was too much pressure for me. Not true. I lose because I was never meant to win.' Then he smiled.

'But let me tell you something else. In my *destino* there are many wins to come.'

6

Car-park Champion

I suppose I was lucky to pitch straight into the hole to win
that way. It might take me a million attempts to do it again.

Seve Ballesteros, Sun-Alliance Match Play Championship, 1978

They all kept trying to say he was lucky, but Jack Nicklaus
holed in one on the first day.

Dave Musgrove on Ballesteros's 1979 Open victory March 1992

It is not unreasonable to assume that most golfers who have
scaled the slippery ladder of success on the professional circuit
have arrived, through trial and error at a less costly time in
their lives, at the conclusion that if they have a less than one
in ten chance of making a birdie from a position where they
could just as easily make an eight, there is likely to be more
profit in playing safe.

Ballesteros is not among them. At a very early age he
developed the ability to stand on the tee of a perilous golf
hole and, where another player might find his view to the
green interrupted by an impenetrable forest of dark, forbidding pines, or even a greedy lake, replete with ducks, see
only the fairway stretching like a shining verdant carpet to
the foot of the distant flagstick. All hazards were invisible to
him. They did not exist. After a period this sleight of mind
became second nature and, when he reached the eighth hole

at Torrequebrada in the first round of the Spanish Open in April 1979, he had mentally obliterated every obstacle in view before fully realizing that, in the intervening months since he had successfully cut the corner off the dog-leg and made birdie in each of the four rounds of the Spanish Under 25's championship *en route* to victory the previous year, a steep mountain of wilderness, trees and boulders had sprung up and rendered that route impassable. He held a brief consultation with a two-dimensional sketch in Musgrove's yardage book. It confirmed to him that if he took the flight-path preferred by crows to the green, a distance of 310 yards, he would be shaving as much as 86 yards off the total length of the par four. Obviously, there was no choice. He measured two club lengths back from the markers to give himself the optimum target line and prepared to drive. Musgrove, who had tried vainly to dissuade him, was watching from the skyline, muttering under his breath.

Ballesteros launched himself into the ball with conviction. It soared out over the trees, vanished and the sound of disintegrating wood was heard. The Spaniard's face clouded with dismay. He set up over a provisional ball and smashed it in the same direction as the first. For an instant it hung provocatively above the horizon, tantalizingly near its destination, then gravity impelled it downwards and it ended among the rocks. Ballesteros was fuming. He refused point blank to hit another shot and went storming off up the slope in search of the last two. Naturally enough, given the depth of the scrub and the prevalence of bushes, any balls to be found were not his own. He had no option but to return to the tee, which he did with a countenance as black as thunder, and play a safe one-iron up the fairway.

'Next time you watch where ball go,' he said angrily to Musgrove as he put down a nine on his card. Eventual score: Torrequebrada 1, Ballesteros 0 (or 81 and a missed cut).

There is no doubt that Ballesteros is a compulsive gambler. Like all of his breed he occasionally suffers heavy losses – the Spanish Open is but one instance of this – but these are counteracted by windfalls, which happen often enough and are lucrative enough to make the risk-taking worthwhile. The English Classic, held at The Belfry in the last week of June, provides a fine example.

Until that tournament Ballesteros's season had been singularly uneventful by his own high standards, although he had finished ninth in the Madrid Open, seventh in the Martini International and tenth in the PGA Championship, and had been marred by his experiences at the French Open at Lyon, where something happened which was to cast a shadow over his young life for some considerable time. His good friend Salvador Balbuena died.

The fact of Balbuena's death was shocking in itself, for he was a gifted player of just twenty-nine who had a chance of making the next Ryder Cup team. But the circumstances of it were worse. At dinner on the eve of the tournament he suddenly said: 'I have a pain in my heart. I am going to die.' Piñero, Jose Maria Canizares and Antonio Garrido, who were with him, at first were astonished then thought he was joking. Moments later he fell dead of a heart attack on the street outside the restaurant. His stricken comrades withdrew instantaneously. The remaining Spaniards decided to compete and donate their prize money to the widow and her two children. Ballesteros, who was among them, was almost inconsolable with grief, breaking down several times in public; but for the sake of Marcia Balbuena he composed himself sufficiently each day to be able to play and hand in his card, and eventually finished third.

Nevertheless, he was out of form and out of humour for several weeks after the French Open, and inwardly miserable for much longer. In June he failed to qualify at the US Open in Toledo, Ohio. He walked off the course and, fighting back the tears, went straight into the locker room. There he sat, with his head in his hands, looking disconsolate and lonely. 'This year in the winter I practised harder than ever,' he mumbled, more to himself than to anyone else. 'I run every day. I train. But for what? Look what happens – nothing.'

It didn't help that his back was causing him a great deal of discomfort, and that the American specialists he had seen had made gloomy predictions about his future as a professional sportsman. To reporters, Ballesteros commented that he should make his fortune quickly lest his career didn't last as long as he might wish it to. On the subject of his indifferent form, he also said that 'the difference between a 65 and an 81 is this' – and held up his hand with his thumb and forefinger about half an inch apart.

But his spirits lifted with his return to Europe, and when he arrived at The Belfry for the English Classic after ten days of rigorous practice, he was lean, smiling and hungry for confrontation and speculation. The opportunity for both came sooner than he expected. During the first three rounds of the tournament he scored 73, 71, 71, and it gave him the edge over his opponents. This was somewhat blunted by the capriciousness of the wind and the unpredictability of his driver at the outset of the fourth day, and, upon reaching the eighth hole, he discovered that his pursuers were closing in on him and that Nick Faldo was only a stroke behind. Ballesteros was not pleased. He stood on the tee of the 460-yard par four and regarded the distant flagstick with grim resolution. It was high time he laid his cards on the table. A par at this hole was unacceptable; nothing less than a birdie would do. That the lake, strategically located on the left of the fairway, might enter the equation did not occur to him. He had erased it from his mind's eye. Musgrove recalls the situation well. 'It was cold and the course was in crap-arse condition because it's a crap-arse golf course. The anti-golf course. I mean, I can remember when they used to play the Ryder Cup on golf courses, but they gave that up.'

The Spaniard set up on the tee, took a long backswing and drove the ball powerfully away. Faldo, who had just putted out on the eighth green, saw it depart in an ugly arc towards the water. Its owner came striding after it, gesticulating to Musgrove. But Ballesteros's consternation turned rapidly to joy. Destiny had dealt him an ace. An upturned greenkeepers' boat had deflected his ball onto the bank, where it was now sitting pertly, a mere yard from the brink, as though a crash-course in swimming had never been one of its intentions. Ballesteros was thrilled to find it in play, and promptly struck an eight-iron to 12 feet and holed it for birdie. Poor Faldo, wandering down the ninth and expecting the Spaniard to have dropped a shot, could hardly believe his eyes when the leaderboard made clear that he had in fact gained a shot.

The scales of fortune tilted in his favour, Ballesteros swept to a six-stroke victory, overcoming Neil Coles and Simon Hobday with a final round 71 and an aggregate of 286. Faldo and Sandy Lyle shared third place. As Ballesteros observed, the season's first triumph could hardly have come at a more opportune moment with the Open Championship little more than a fortnight away.

'I needed it for my confidence,' he admitted.

Wednesday, 18 July 1979, Open Championship, St Annes-on-the-Sea, Lancs. A chill wind, melancholy and uneven, whistled through the moonlit stands of Royal Lytham and St Annes. Several hours had passed since the storm which had been its forerunner had abated; yet still it would not die down but caused leaves to swirl about the quiet brick houses and palely gleaming railway, white horses to leap from the inky ridges of the sea and the ghostly shapes of Open Championship tents to wrench hopelessly at their moorings. The night-watchman huddled deeper into his greatcoat, and continued his beat. Left, right, left, right, left, right. Past the pro shop and the practice green, past the press centre and the clubhouse, over the eighteenth fairway and up to the recorder's hut, where the winner would hand in his scorecard on Saturday afternoon. A distant clock chimed; a dog barked; a short shower of rain splashed down. Then night fled on silent wings before the dawn.

A watery sun was climbing unconvincingly into the sky when Ballesteros, his face ruddy with cold and excitement, crunched along the road to the practice range before teeing off in the first round of the Open. Musgrove toiled behind him. Once there, he selected a space, pulled on his glove and began to warm up, twisting and stretching in an effort to ease his aching back. The frozen crowd pressed closer to the barrier. Their breaths rose like cartoon bubbles into the air. After a while Ballesteros paused, flipped the ball bucket over with the end of his sand-wedge and stepped into the bunker. He hit a few shots. Musgrove, who was polishing the Spaniard's golf clubs, watched them land with something akin to pleasure. Earlier in the year he had remarked to Ballesteros that great bunker players, such as Player, Jacklin, Bob Charles and Peter Thomson, always won at Lytham, for there were 365 sand-traps on the course. And Ballesteros had replied, with no small amount of pride, 'I am the best bunker player.'

In practice rounds his performance had been encouraging, if erratic. Every morning Vicenzo had waited for him on the putting green and they had worked on their strokes together before playing the course. On the first day Manuel, who was also participating in the Open, had accompanied them, Vicente carrying his bag. Baldomero Jnr had come along, too, for the walk. Not two holes hence it became clear that Severiano was being offered conflicting advice by five determined characters – his three brothers, Musgrove and Vicenzo – albeit with the best of intentions. Finally, Vicenzo lost his patience. 'Look,' he said to Ballesteros, 'sometimes when you play you listen to too many voices.'

The young Spaniard could not dispute the truth of that. So he made a decision: he would learn only from the Argentinian, for Vicenzo had won the championship before and had played in five of the six Opens held at Royal Lytham. 'Roberto is the master and I am pupil . . .' he said later, 'and I'm using all the knowledge from his life . . . He really tell me many things on the golf course – where to play and how the ball will bounce. The most important thing he tell me is, "Seve, when you take the golf club back, play with your heart. Don't change your mind. Just pick up the club and hit the ball. Don't think about bunkers or out of bounds or pathways, just hit it." Is very good advice.'

Essentially, Vicenzo's lessons were these: 1. The foundations of a low score at Lytham must be laid on the front nine; 2. Patience is a virtue in major championships; 3. A draw is more helpful than a fade at Lytham because most of the trouble is on the right; 4. A long-hitter with the courage to bypass the conventional routes to the green might find 'loopholes' (as Musgrove calls them) in the rough, i.e. bald patches, which give a better angle of approach; 5. The transient nature of seaside climates means that all links holes have split personalities.

Ballesteros did not employ his apprenticeship to good effect immediately. In the opening round, playing with Ken Brown and Lee Trevino (who was so fearful of catching his death that he wore pyjamas under his clothes) in gales of more than twenty-five miles an hour, he shot a two over par score of 73, which left him in joint sixteenth place at the end of the day. The inclement weather was partially responsible: if Mark Twain had visited Britain for an Open Championship he never would have dreamt of saying, 'The coldest winter I ever spent was a summer in San Francisco.' Nevertheless, Bill Longmuir, a little-known player from Basildon in Essex, proceeded around the golf course as though it were a fine spring morning, making six birdies in the outward half to turn in 29. 'I could see a line to the hole,' he said. 'I couldn't miss a putt.' By the twelfth hole he was eight under par and practically lapping the field, and his sole objective was to score 59. 'I felt so good with the putter, I thought: "I'm going to shoot an unbelievable score here and nothing's going to stop me." ' A fraction less zeal on Lytham's cruel back nine and nothing might have. But after making bogeys at the fourteenth and fifteenth holes, Longmuir lost some of his momentum, and his 65-foot putt at the last lipped out for a 65, which equalled the course record and led by three strokes at the close of play.

Unused to being upstaged by foreign nonentities, the Americans were nonplussed. They came staggering off the golf course like bruised and disorientated survivors of an earthquake, and stared open-mouthed at the scoreboard. Tom Watson took one look and said: 'Six under par is beyond all reason.' He and Jack Nicklaus, the defending champion, had both recorded one over par scores of 72. The Golden Bear was more candid. 'I don't believe the score and I don't believe the player,' he said shortly to the press. 'It's a fictitious name you guys have stuck at the top of the leaderboard.' He was disgruntled that he had not managed to break par, despite making an ace with a five-iron at the 212-yard fifth. Sharing his displeasure were Gary Player and Tom Weiskopf, who had amassed respective scores of 77 and 79. Other US citizens had fared better. Hale Irwin, the reigning US Open Champion, was Longmuir's nearest challenger on three under par, while Jerry Pate was a stroke further back.

Thursday, 19 July 1979. After the first round Ballesteros switched drivers. He had not felt comfortable on the tee all year and had thus rotated six or seven of these woods on a weekly basis in the hope that one of them might prove superior to the rest. Wednesday's club was a relatively untried youngster. Its sojourn in the bag came to an abrupt end because it actively contributed to the Spaniard's 73 and caused him to think, with irrefutable logic: 'Well, I can't hit fairways with this one, so it can't be more difficult with my old one.' Fairways, unfortunately, showed themselves to be every bit as difficult to hit in the second round with the elder statesman driver as they had in the first with the child prodigy – indeed, as they had done since the beginning of the season – for the simple reason that it was the swinger of the club rather than the club itself who was at fault. No-one was more aware of this than Ballesteros. Some months earlier it had become a matter of such concern to him that he had sought help from John Jacobs. 'Because,' he said worriedly, 'I can only slice the ball.'

Jacobs was delighted to oblige. 'I can remember exactly what I said to him, and that was that he'd got the club too strong – which he still suffers from at times – and was too much underneath. In other words, his five-iron was sitting rather like a four-iron. That, in itself, tends to take the club back too straight, and the shoulders get too tilted and the club comes underneath the ball. I had to make the club weaker and get him to turn away from it.'

So Ballesteros was cured of slicing, but not of waywardness. No amount of practice or self-control could hold his vast swing in check. In the opening rounds at Royal Lytham he relied on the teachings of Vicenzo and his own courage to save him as he lashed mightily from the tees, forcing the galleries to break and run for cover, then attempted to retrieve his ball and to play it from a variety of unorthodox lies. His wildness was accentuated by the blustery conditions. At the tenth hole on the second day, Ballesteros hit a drive so far off line that Trevino felt compelled to point out the cause. He did so in Spanish, explaining that his erratic driving was due to the fact that he was not clearing his left hip adequately before following through. In fact, this was a violation of Rule 8-1 but nothing was done about it. Ballesteros was excessively grateful. His tee shot at the 542-yard eleventh flew miles over the fairway bunkers and set up a birdie chance, and further strokes were snatched back from par at the fourteenth, fifteenth (where he chipped in from 25 yards) and seventeenth holes. Then a driver and a superb five-iron, punched from the downhill slope of a grassy knoll to 4 feet at the eighteenth, earned him his eighth birdie of the round.

'One hesitates to say vintage stuff at the age of twenty-two,' said Peter Alliss, as Ballesteros acknowledged the acclaim of his fans with a grin and a wave, 'but, my word, vintage stuff indeed.'

Alliss later wrote that the true par of the last five holes on that day was considered to be 4,5,4,5,4; because of the prevailing westerly wind. Ballesteros's figures were 3,3,4,3,3. Before the close of play they had helped to lift him into second place on 138, two strokes behind the leader Irwin and one ahead of Longmuir. The American had played some of his best golf for a 68 – although his driving had been adversely affected by the multitudinous layers of clothing he wore to prevent hypothermia – and was astonished when he heard that the Spaniard had not only matched the course record with a 65, but had completed the back nine in 32 strokes. 'What did he do?' he queried. 'Cut across?'

Ballesteros was typically wry in his press conference afterwards, turning the most innocuous questions on their heads and using them to laugh at himself. Regaling reporters with stories of his adventures on the golf course, he confessed that his ball had finished in the rough so often that in the end Musgrove had said sardonically: 'Why don't you close your eyes and hit it? Maybe then you'll put the ball on the fairway.'

'I always play for the fairway, though,' said Ballesteros ingenuously, 'but I never go there.'

Asked whether he would like to see the fairways made wider, he responded, tongue in cheek: 'No, I would like to see the fairways more narrow, then everybody play from the rough. We should play one time the Open with no fairways. Then maybe I come close to winning.'

Friday, 20 July 1979. Rarely can two golfers have provided a sharper contrast of manner, appearance and style of play than Ballesteros and Irwin, paired together in the third round. Jekyll and Hyde had more in common. If this was not readily apparent, it soon became so. The second hole at Lytham is a beguiling par four of some 436 yards, with a railway running the length of it. It tests a man's mettle by encouraging him to flirt with the tracks and thus open up a better line to the green. Irwin, tall, upright and bespectacled, drove first, electing to place his ball safely in the centre of the fairway. His swing is high and classic, his forte is target golf. Straight driving and accurate iron play allow him to plot his way round the golf course like a chess master.

Then came Ballesteros, swarthy and handsome, his white smile flashing as he asked Musgrove his opinion then selected a one-iron. With youthful bravado and a touch of arrogance, he whipped the ball away to the right. A train clattered down the line; the gallery moaned; the ball disappeared out of view. The Spaniard looked faintly disbelieving. A provisional was played and he and Musgrove went to hunt for the original. They located it deep in the bushes. It was quite unplayable and, there being nowhere within two club lengths to drop, he was unable to continue with the provisional as he would have done if the ball had been lost or out of bounds, and had to walk back to the tee all alone, swinging his golf club self-consciously. He played his third shot onto the fairway, his fourth into a bunker, his fifth onto the green and sunk a tricky putt for a double-bogey (the only one he made during the championship). At the next hole, also a par four, he dropped a third shot. He stayed remarkably calm. On another day he had said that, 'You have to be very patient on this course because it's very easy to make bogeys and bogeys and never stop. Here you have to wait. When you attack the golf course, the golf course kills you. You have to wait and the birdies coming. When you attack, the bogeys coming. So it's better to wait, I think.' He continued to observe his own rules and was rewarded with birdies at the sixth and eighth holes.

The Golden Bear was up ahead and had made his move, holing a wedge shot at the third and birdying the seventh to turn in 34. But Lytham's finish is notoriously impregnable – only Ballesteros had managed to break through its defences – and it defeated him then as it had in the first two rounds, when he had gone out in 32 and 30 and come back in 40 and 39 respectively. This time he notched up three consecutive bogeys from the eleventh, for an inward half of 39 and a one over par aggregate of 214. Watson, the pre-tournament favourite, and Longmuir, who had had a 77, were two strokes further behind.

Out on the golf course it had begun to pour. Spectators huddled together beneath umbrellas. Ballesteros pulled on his rainsuit and Irwin rubbed unhappily at his glasses. Until then the American had been in control, his methodical accountant-like approach to the game paying dividends. But icy gusts of wind and rain affected his concentration, and he dropped shots at the tenth and eleventh before coming to grief at the penultimate hole where his tee shot missed the fairway, his three-wood recovery plugged in a bunker and he took four more to get down for a double-bogey six. Ballesteros had problems of his own. As Irwin had distanced himself on the leaderboard, he had grown increasingly agitated, finally throwing caution to the wind and playing with a passionate fury that was beautiful to behold. It did, however, cost him dropped shots at the fourteenth, fifteenth and seventeenth holes, but at the end of the day he was in contention with Ben Crenshaw and Robert Byman on 215.

Rodger Davis later recalled him commenting, prior to the start of the tournament, that because the rough was so thick that even if you missed the fairway with a one-iron you could only chop out sideways with an eight- or nine-iron, nothing could be lost by taking a driver, since at least then you would be nearer to the green and would be able to hit a mid-iron close to it or even onto it. 'Which I actually believe was the right way to play it,' says Davis. 'I think he was totally right in every respect there.'

Brown is sceptical. 'He had no idea where the ball was going, whatever anybody says,' he insists. 'Off the tee, it could have gone forty yards in one direction or forty yards in the other, but it wasn't going to go straight. He was putting particularly well but his tee shots were as crooked as they could be. People say he knew where it was going but I saw him hit too many tee shots where, if he knew where it was going, he wouldn't have hit it there. It's strange because the one that you'd have thought he'd win [the 1978 Open], he didn't, and the one that you didn't think he'd win, he did.'

So Ballesteros and Irwin, as diametrically opposed as an Arabian sheikh and a county librarian, came to the eighteenth hole still separated by two strokes – the same number that had divided Tony Jacklin from Bob Charles in the final round of the 1969 Open before the Englishman had hit the perfect tee shot, far beyond all danger, and settled the contest. Nicklaus had not been so fortunate. Six years earlier he had arrived at the last with victory within his grasp, but had failed to hear the applause after Charles and Phil Rodgers made birdies at the sixteenth and, assuming he needed a four to win and a five to tie, had pulled carelessly into a fairway bunker and missed the play-off by a stroke. Player, too, had brought drama to the final hole, playing his third shot left-handed with a putter from against the clubhouse wall in 1974 to win the championship for the third time. But in the event the fifty-fourth hole did not prove as important for Ballesteros and Irwin in the grand scheme of things as it first threatened to when the American hit his 'worst drive of the championship' into the rough; for both he and the Spaniard then overflew the green and had to get up and down for par and matching scores of 75. The gallery could not have cared less. The only thing that mattered to them was that their hero had lived to fight another day, and they communicated this with such tumultuous clapping and cheering that Ballesteros, obviously pleased, took off his rain-jacket and waved it gratefully above his head.

In his post-round interview he was quietly confident. 'I

was not much lucky today,' he said. 'Maybe I save the lucky for tomorrow. If I start well on the first four holes, I think I have a chance to win.'

Saturday, 21 July 1979. The windows of the men's locker room at Royal Lytham provide an unparalleled vantage point from which to observe Open Championship drama, positioned as they are behind the eighteenth green, and during the course of the tournament one can occasionally see professional golfers or caddies gazing from them with rapt faces. Now, however, no-one was there. Everyone who could be outside was, braving the drizzle in order to pay tribute to the Spaniard marching so triumphantly up the final fairway. All except Bill Longmuir, that is. He sat alone in the deserted locker room, thinking wistfully about what might have been. Of what could have happened if he had managed to recapture that state of grace which had made his record 65 so easy and so natural in the first round. Of how different his life might have been if he had made par instead of 82 in the last. Of how wonderful it would be to be Open Champion with £15,000 to his name, instead of twenty-ninth with £665.

A roar shattered the silence. Reluctantly, he stood up, climbed onto the bench and looked out of the window. He could see Ballesteros, expression rapturous and putter raised to the gallery, striding down the eighteenth. 'My God,' thought Longmuir, sitting down again and running his fingers through his hair. 'What a situation to be in. *I* could be winning the Open.'

He cast his mind back to the first time he had met Ballesteros, at a pro-am at Boyce Hill Golf Club. 'He was very Latin, didn't speak much English.' Longmuir didn't consider him remotely special. 'When he finished second in the Open in 'seventy-six, I remember my old boss at Thorpe Hall asking me what I thought of him and I'll never forget saying – it's one of the worst things, I s'pose, you can say about a player: "I don't think he'll last. He's got too ambitious a game." I felt that he was a bit of a flash in the pan, so to speak. I thought his brother Manuel was a better player, I really did. And I think he did at that time. I remember him being interviewed, saying, "My brother's a far better player than me. You've got to watch Manuel." And Manuel was a steadier player – a good-looking, solid swinger of the club.

'But going into 'seventy-nine, Seve was probably my favourite player. He's an eye-catching player for another player to watch. With Seve it was his balance and his ability to hit any type of shot . . . He was such a complete player, you know. He was not only a long hitter, he had a beautiful touch around the green, he was a fabulous putter and had a very good head on his shoulders, too. He was a very mature player . . . And you could see his confidence was growing month by month as he played. There was just no looking back for him, really. Coming into 'seventy-nine I would have put my house on him winning a major tournament.'

Had he indeed gambled the roof over his head on the Spaniard's success, Longmuir might have had something more to show for his trials and tribulations at Royal Lytham than a bruised heart and a comparatively empty pocket. As it was, he simply gathered his belongings, walked to the car park and began the solitary journey back into obscurity. Just another moth whose wings had been burnt on the bright flame of Ballesteros's desire.

No gulf in professional sport is wider than that between a good player and a major champion. Talent alone is not enough to bridge it, nor is desire, stamina, physical strength or mental resilience. 'Hitting the ball,' says Player, 'is just one piece of the puzzle. Nicklaus had the complete puzzle filled in, and I think I had it filled in pretty well otherwise I couldn't have won nine major championships.'

So far as Jacklin is concerned, the first time that Ballesteros showed that he might have that delicate balance of fire, humility, audacity, patience, intrinsic wisdom and absolute simplicity inherent in all major champions, was when he fought so long and so brilliantly at Royal Birkdale in 1976. 'He showed he could handle the pressure, and when you've done it once you can always build on it.' Jacklin watched and took note, knowing that 'there are a lot of people with a lot of ability but some of them haven't got the right sort of intelligence – common sense – to make it happen for themselves. To recognize that golf isn't just about hitting the ball and having a pretty swing. It's about much, much more than that – adjusting to different environments and circumstances, feeling comfortable wherever you go, never letting anything get in the way of your determination to succeed . . .'

'It is,' says Nicklaus, 'about knowing when to be patient, when to be aggressive, when to be cautious, when to put all of those things into the game – which is all basically management of oneself.'

Ballesteros had spent a restless night dwelling on every one of the above and on his golf swing in particular. He was worried about his driving. It still wasn't right, and he feared that any technical weaknesses in it were being exacerbated by his back problems. Thus far, the latter had been relieved by treatment. Every morning since the Open had started, Ballesteros had woken up, partaken of his favourite breakfast of scrambled eggs, toast and milk (he rarely drinks tea or coffee), and driven down to the local physiotherapist for a swim and a massage. On Saturday he decided against it. He didn't want the time of the appointment on his mind.

At midday he left the house he had been sharing with Baldomero Jnr, Jorge Ceballos, and Ed Barner and Joe Collet and their two wives, and went down to the golf course to begin his preparation. It was a bleak, stormy day. Clouds scurried across a sullen grey sky, while the northwester which drove them turned the back nine into an ordeal. Ballesteros pulled on a navy blue sweater and strode briskly through the milling crowds to the range. The other contenders, Rodger Davis among them, glanced up involuntarily when he appeared. 'He always had this aura about him,' recalls the Australian. 'The way he walked was a very confident walk. The way he talked was always very confident – nothing negative came out of him. And in some ways . . . he was a little bit intimidating to other players, because he just gave off that aura that he was going to win. And you had to try and stop that somehow in your mind . . . He just always looked naturally positive, naturally confident, naturally, "Yes, I'm here to win it." And he had the putter to do it. I think, if you could say Seve had a weakness in his bag it would have been his driver. Nearly every great player has had a weakness and I'd say Seve's was his driver.'

At ten past one Ballesteros went to cross from the practice green to the first tee. Vicenzo, his friend and mentor, stopped him. '*Tienes las manos. Ahora juega con tu corazon,*' he said fervently to the young Spaniard. 'You have the hands, now play with your heart.'

Royal Lytham is unusual among the Open courses in that it begins with a par three. Ballesteros, youthful and dashing beside Irwin, teed off first, striking a seven-iron to 15 feet. The American's shot was more tentative and only just limped onto the putting surface, from where he two-putted for par. With scarcely a pause, Ballesteros stepped up his own ball and stroked it swiftly across the green for a birdie. It was like a knife in Irwin's heart. One hole played and half his lead gone. His expression was an exact mirror of Johnny Miller's at the same stage in the final round of the 1976 Open, after his young rival had made one of his vintage pars. But on the next hole his face grew long. Ballesteros had no intention of repeating his experiences of Friday, so he played a safe two-iron down the fairway and made a conventional four. Irwin selected a three-wood, pushed it out to the right, left his second shot miles short of the green, hit his third to the back edge and three-putted. A six was marked down on his card and he surrendered the lead for good.

'We will forget about Irwin,' remarked Ballesteros to Musgrove after parring the third. 'Other players are coming into the game.'

Davis was the first to challenge the Spaniard's one-stroke advantage, taking a share of the lead when Ballesteros bogeyed the fourth, then birdying the next to seize control of the tournament. Elsewhere in the field Ben Crenshaw, Nicklaus, Mark James and Isao Aoki vied for position on the upper reaches of the leaderboard. The Japanese toppled soonest. He had birdied the third, fifth and sixth holes to turn in 33 but, like James, was unequal to Lytham's gruelling finish. Crenshaw, aware of the struggle to come, concentrated on gathering birdies, whipping the ball cleanly into the air with his smooth and stylish swing, and gaining strokes at the sixth, seventh, and ninth holes to move into second place. Ballesteros, meanwhile, had dropped another shot at the sixth. On the seventh tee he remembered Vicenzo's words and drew courage from them. 'It's the one with the biggest heart who will win,' he confided to Musgrove. And made birdie. When he reached the turn he was one under par and joint leader once more, while Irwin was two over.

All of this time Ballesteros, though he lashed fearlessly off the tees, uncaring of retribution, was holding himself in check, remembering not to press – to wait. Afterwards he said: 'The only real time I attack is on the thirteenth. I was watching the scoreboard to see how is my position . . . and I told my caddie that maybe we can hit the green.'

He came to the 339-yard dog-leg par four – the beginning of Lytham's brutal closing stretch – after making two crucial putts, one to save bogey at the tenth and one for par at the twelfth, and the adrenalin was still rushing through his body. Standing on the tee, his face taut with concentration, he looked strong and unyielding. 'He will not be afraid if he gets the chance,' Musgrove had said. The conventional way to play the thirteenth is to take a long-iron off the tee and hit a wedge into the green. But Vicenzo had told Ballesteros always to hit driver and chance falling foul of the fairway bunkers. Curiously enough, the Spaniard had resisted the temptation all week. Now, with a gale at his back and his name at the top of the leaderboard with Crenshaw's, he gave in to it. 'We'll go for it today,' he told Musgrove.

'You could say thirteen was a bit of a birdie hole,' remembers Davis, who by then had blown himself out of the championship with a double-bogey at the fourteenth and bogey at the fifteenth, 'but, you know, the wind was so strong there was really no birdie hole out there.'

Ballesteros set up over the ball and stared at the flagstick. To have even a prayer of making the green he had to carry the ball 300 yards over a trap. It was not easy, but then again it was not impossible. Summoning all his reserves of power and skill, he smashed his drive from the tee and, like the ballplayer Carlton Fisk, tried 'to will the ball to stay up there and never come down'. It almost worked. A degree less wind, a milli-second longer on the clubhead and the ball would have carried the extra yard it needed to clear the bunker. Instead, it flew an incredible 298 yards, caught the top of a mound and toppled into the sand. By the end of the Open he had been in fifteen bunkers and had got up and down from fourteen of them. 'The sand-wedge was the key to my win,' he said later, 'certainly not my driver.' Now, however, with 68 yards to the pin, he took a wedge, hitting it down hard on the ball to force it over the high wall of the trap.

'I hit it just about perfect,' recalls Ballesteros, 'but the spin pulled it off the green to the right.'

That's when *destino* laid a hand on the young Spaniard's shoulder. He had a 10-foot putt for birdie and it never for one second looked like missing the hole. It positively flew in. And if ever victory shone in the eyes of a player it did so now, as Ballesteros, black hair flying, putter thrust forward like a sword, charged across the green like a matador, punching the air with his fist. 'All week,' Davis says, 'Seve had been just flowing along, flowing along . . . And if you looked at his face there, he was the winner . . . When that happened, all of a sudden everything just lit up and nothing was going to beat him.'

Ballesteros seemed to sense the end was near. His stride quickened and became more jaunty; his face was dark with intensity and a fierce joy. The unruly gallery surged after him, trampling the barren landscape and buffeting his forgotten partner in their frenzy to see him play. Irwin was too drained and demoralized to put up a struggle. His entire round had been a chapter of disaster, and he watched the Spaniard's three-putt at the fourteenth and magical 35-yard chip for par at the fifteenth with the jaundiced eye of the veteran theatre critic. Even Ballesteros's next feat, his most spectacular yet, failed to elicit a response. He simply walked to the green with the air of a man who had been called upon to witness more improbabilities in one day than most men could reasonably be expected to in a lifetime, and leaned dispiritedly on his putter.

Few shots have cast as long a shadow over a champion's

career as Severiano Ballesteros's into the car park beside the sixteenth fairway in the final round of the Open. It was viewed, especially by the Americans, as symbolic of his entire performance that week – wild and outrageously lucky (he hit eight fairways in the first three rounds and one in the last) – and it earned him the nickname, 'The Car-Park Champion'. Even Irwin, who finished with a 78, said afterwards, 'I can't understand how anyone can drive as badly as that and still win an Open Championship.' Actually, that particular tee shot was premeditated. Ballesteros *intended* it to finish where it did – some 24 yards from the fairway and 64 yards from the green. 'I drove to the right because the wind was helping from the left,' he insists, 'which meant an approach from the fairway – with the wind behind – would be very difficult and an approach from the right rough, almost into the breeze, much easier. I knew the rough out there was not bad because the spectators had trampled it down, and that if I hit a big drive I could get close to the green and make a birdie. I also realized that if my ball finished among the cars I would get a free drop.'

As he marched hurriedly from the tee, the crowd stampeding past him, he felt a flicker of alarm. What if he had miscalculated? What if he had over-compensated for the wind? A moment later his fears were allayed; his brothers Vicente and Baldomero shouted urgently to him: 'Don't worry, you are two strokes in front.' Crenshaw had just double-bogeyed the seventeenth. 'When I realized that, I told myself just to make par,' says Ballesteros, who, under special tournament rules was allowed to drop clear of the car he found his ball underneath, without penalty. He paced off the distance to the green himself, selected a target about 15 feet away from the flag which was slightly softer than everywhere else and hit a perfect sand-wedge to that precise spot. Then he holed the putt for birdie to lead the Open by three strokes with two holes to play.

The rest, as they say, is history. After parring the seventeenth from a bunker, Ballesteros played a conservative three-wood from the tee at the last, deliberately aiming away from the fairway to avoid the treacherous bunkers. It hooked out over the rough and disappeared from view.

'What's over there?' he asked Musgrove anxiously.

'I don't know,' came the droll reply. 'That's the one place we haven't been this week.'

But the ball had found a perfectly playable lie and the Spaniard hit an easy five-iron to the front of the green. With that, any sense of decorum that the crowd might have had was lost and, like a river bursting its banks, they poured down the stands and over the fairways, engulfing Ballesteros in a tide of warmth and adoration, just like they had with Jacklin ten years before him, and carrying Irwin and the two caddies helplessly along with them. When the American had fought his way free he was waving a white handkerchief in surrender – to the people as well as to the Open Champion.

'You're different people, but you always know what a guy feels when he's winning his first major,' says Jacklin. 'You never forget, because you're so incredibly nervous and keyed up. You never forget the way you feel in those moments. I can recall it now and it's twenty-three years ago. You just feel so unbelievably full and nervous and aware and, *God!* – your senses are so sharp. You're just flying by the seat of your trousers, basically learning the whole thing. You've got to have a lot of courage to see it through.'

Few men have as much of that precious resource as the young Spaniard who broke through the gallery that summer's evening, arms held high in a victory salute, and a smile of unalloyed happiness on his face.

'So much was made of Seve's wildness that week,' says Crenshaw, who finished joint-runner up with Nicklaus. 'You know, he hit some errant shots and everyone will agree, but the only thing that counts is your name on that big board and the score. He shot the lowest score. I don't think there's any question that Seve wasn't hitting the ball anywhere like he'd like to, but it takes a champion to overcome that and to learn to get out of places like that and make a score under Open Championship conditions. That's what's important. And that's an impressive victory.'

'I won by three shots,' says Ballesteros summarily. 'I won because I played better than anyone else, not because I was luckier than everybody else. I've watched the video many times and I don't see any luck there at all. Luck is when you hit a tree and bounce out onto the fairway.'

Fortune did not make him the youngest winner of the Open this century, *destino* did.

Musgrove's only concern was that Ballesteros made a four at the last to be the only player under par with a total of 70 and an aggregate of 283. At the edge of the eighteenth green the Spaniard had told him proudly: 'I can take four putts from here and still win.'

'No, you can't,' retorted Musgrove, 'because I've got a bet on with one of the caddies that the winning score will be under par.'

Ballesteros holed out for a par. As he did so, there was a scuffle in the gallery, then first Baldomero Jnr and then Vicente raced across the green and embraced him. They clung to each other, weeping, until officials led Severiano away to sign his card. Manuel, who was in the clubhouse, watching it on television, was no less emotional: 'I could not bear to be near the green itself. I felt the pressure of that last hole a hundred times more than if I had been playing myself.'

'Was great emotion,' confessed Ballesteros with an unashamed grin in his press conference afterwards. 'Will be very difficult to forget that time. Very, very difficult. My brothers just cuddle me, and it was very emotional, especially for the oldest one. He tell me after the third round, "I can't watch you putt because my heart was bang, bang, bang," and he was very, very happy.'

When the prize-giving ceremony was over, there was a small cocktail party held for the Open Champion in the R&A caravan. Afterwards, Ballesteros was walking across the putting green carrying some champagne he had been given, when he spotted Michael Williams, the *Daily Telegraph* golf correspondent. Much to Williams' astonishment, he immediately went over and handed it to him. 'Take this,' said Ballesteros with a smile, 'and have a drink with all the other writers for all the nice things they've said about me.'

Later, he went back to the house where he had been staying to celebrate, accompanied by Mark Wilson. 'It wasn't a wild party but there were certain people enjoying themselves,'

Wilson recalls. 'I'm guessing there were no more than twenty people in the house . . . *He* certainly did not join in the celebrations. Everybody else could celebrate, but not Seve. He was going to be playing golf the next week and that was it. I don't know of Seve ever breaking the strict training rules. I've never heard of Seve going wild, I've never heard of him having a bender, I've never heard of him having a night out. Which is amazing because they all go off the rails occasionally. But he suddenly went into a corner on his own and he was talking. He just wanted to talk, he didn't want to drink. As you know, he doesn't. And I remember I said, "How much is this going to change your life?" And he said: "It won't." He was a young man, and I laughed. He knew what I meant, but I laughed. Because it changes everybody's life. And almost every player, like a Pools' winner, says: "It's not going to change my life". And you know damn well it will. And he suddenly looked at me – he was very serious – and he said, "If you think I change, you come to me and you stand in front of me and you say: 'Where is Seve Ballesteros?' *'Where is Seve Ballesteros?'* And I will know what you mean." '

7

The Green Road to Glory

A man conscious of enthusiasm for worthy aims is sustained
under petty hostilities by the memory of great workers who
had to fight their way not without wounds, and who hover
in his mind as patron saints, invisibly helping.

George Eliot, *Middlemarch*

In the spring of 1977 Ballesteros made his first trip to
Augusta, Georgia. He had not long emerged from the Spanish
Air Force and, with his military haircut and tanned good looks,
resembled no-one so much as a young Elvis, leaning eagerly
out of the window of the Cadillac, impatient for a glimpse,
however fleeting, of the sacred turf of Augusta National Golf
Club. As far back as he could remember he had imagined this
moment. A decade ago, at least, he had sat at the feet of
Ramon Sota, a small intense boy with a pensive, wistful face,
and listened enraptured as his uncle, who had played Augusta
half a dozen times between 1964 and 1972, finishing sixth on
his second visit, talked of the golf course that was home to the
US Masters Championship: of wide fairways lined with rare
and beautiful trees; of hidden perils which visual splendour
belied; of greens so swift, so undulating and so mysterious
that a man might play them all his life and never master
them; of great champions who won there and broken men

who fell; and of memories, achingly sweet or bitter as gall, that remained indelibly etched on every golfer's mind for the rest of his natural life.

The driver of the Cadillac slowed and turned down Magnolia Lane. Ballesteros sucked in his breath sharply. Vistas of sky, clouds and emerald foliage flashed across the windscreen as they swept along the cool, fragrant tunnel and up to the stately white clubhouse. For a moment Ballesteros sat unmoving, entranced by the magnificence of it all. Then he was out of the car and running swiftly to see the golf course. It was a warm day. A faint-blue haze had settled on top of the towering pines and below it golfers moved about lazily, like ants in slow motion. The fairways dropped away from the clubhouse in a series of low curves, as closely shorn and perfect as astro-turf, artistically striped and dotted with snowy bunkers. Spectators flowed in a river of living colour across the jewel-green grass, a slender ribbon of creek shone through the trees and everywhere there were flowers: jasmine, azalea and dogwood. Ballesteros gazed with childlike wonder at the loveliness of the scene. He had a strong feeling of déjà-vu. There was something familiar about it all, something that reminded him of Pedreña. 'Seve,' he said to himself, 'one day you will win this tournament.'

But 1977 was not to be Ballesteros's year. Even if Augusta had not been one of those golf courses where experience means everything, he would still have been disadvantaged from the start. His stint of national service meant that he was suffering from lack of competitive practice and, as a consequence, while lashing furiously at balls on the range before the tournament even began, he strained a muscle in his back. This did not put him in the best humour. He had already formed the notion that the hierarchy at Augusta were conspiring against him, something which had become clear to him when he saw he had been paired with Jack Nicklaus in the opening round, and the least negative sign served to enhance this impression. He was convinced that he was being tested, deliberately put under pressure.

Nicklaus, of course, was blind to this resentment. It would never have occurred to him that the Spaniard might regard their partnership as anything other than an honour of the highest order, and he read nothing into his silence, contemplating his golf swing in an abstract manner and reviewing it favourably on another day. 'I saw this sort of long, flowing golf swing that I liked very much. I saw a fella that had trouble controlling the ball at times yet didn't worry about it because he was very long, which was much the way I played when I was young. I liked that. I liked his aggressive enthusiasm for the golf game and I felt like he would become a very, very good player.'

Ballesteros's initial scores at Augusta reflected his state of mind. He shot 74, 75 in the first two rounds and came within a whisker of missing the cut. At the weekend he acquitted himself rather better, finishing thirty-third behind Tom Watson with a score of 291, three over par. Joe Collet, a brilliant young lawyer who had joined UMI in January and whom he had only just met and was sharing a house with, strolled companionably around the fairways with him every day, finding him quiet and serious off the golf course. 'He was really not very talkative because my Spanish wasn't very good and his English wasn't very good, and I didn't know a whole lot about golf and he wasn't interested in a whole lot of other things, but we became friends because I was somebody there that he could talk to.' Together they went to the cinema and out to dinner most evenings. On Ballesteros's birthday (which falls during the Masters every year just like Faldo's, interestingly enough, falls during the Open), Collet and Ed Barner baked him a cake. 'We invited some of his Spanish friends over and had a little party, which he wasn't too thrilled about. Never has been thrilled about having his birthday that week. He was very gracious and appreciative, but . . . OK, that's fine, let's eat the cake. Now that's over, let's watch TV.'

Later in the year, when relating his experiences at the Masters to Dave Musgrove, Ballesteros revealed that he had been forced to play the final round of the tournament with old balls because he didn't have any new ones.

'Well, he wouldn't go and buy any, would he?' says Musgrove sardonically. 'Years afterwards I reminded him of that. He says: "*How you know this?*" I said, "You bloody told me!" '

The following season Ballesteros finished joint eighteenth at Augusta and in 1979 he was twelfth. His love affair with the golf course, untainted by his uneasy relationship with Masters officialdom, had developed into an obsession. What Vicenzo had prophesied – 'Seve won't win the Masters once, he will win it many times' – Ballesteros fervently believed. He was certain that, with the right preparation, the green jacket could be his in 1980. Accordingly, he devised a new winter practice regime. Instead of merely hitting thousands of balls into oblivion each day he began to work on his draw, the essential shot for Augusta. That done, he would walk down to the beach at Pedreña as the sun was going down and, for the first time since he was a boy, plant a makeshift flagstick above the watermark and practise his putting: at low tide the sand had the same glassy quickness as the greens at the Masters. Lastly, before going to bed, he would stand before a full-length mirror in the stables and study his takeaway. Something Tony Jacklin said to him shortly after his victory at Lytham had stuck in his mind. He and the Englishman were friends and often played golf together. Once, when they were driving to St George's Hill to get their clubs repaired by Barry Willet (who is now Mizuno's clubmaker on Tour), Jacklin said to him, 'You know, you're never really going to be as good as you want to be until you learn that you can't hit the ball flat out all the time. For what it's worth, I'm telling you, you've got to learn to control the ball and you've got to learn to control yourself. It's no use taking your anger out on the ball, because you can't win every tournament hitting it into car parks all the time, like you did at Lytham. You will *not* last. Nobody's nerve can stand that. You've got to learn to go at eighty-five per cent and put it on the fairway all the time.'

Ballesteros set his jaw stubbornly. 'But I am not like that,' he said proudly. 'I have to go for everything.'

'Seve,' said Jacklin with quiet emphasis, 'you won't be there to go for everything if you don't learn not to put yourself under such extreme pressure.'

Looking in the glass at his reflected golf swing, Ballesteros had to admit that Jacklin had been right. Not long after they had spoken he had realized that, if he wanted to achieve the level of consistency necessary for victory in the Masters, or indeed in any other major championship, he was going to have to shorten his backswing and learn to take the club back more in one piece, and thus had embarked upon the necessary changes.

On 3 March 1980, having dedicated his entire winter to restructuring his swing (taking more than 18 inches off the top of it) and rehearsing for Augusta, Ballesteros flew to America for a trio of warm-up events. In the first one, the Inverrary Classic at Fort Lauderdale, he finished fifteenth to Johnny Miller. The second was the Doral Eastern Open, held over a 7,065-yard course nicknamed the 'Blue Monster'. Ballesteros, who was touring pro at Doral at the time, soon fell foul of the beast. It failed to recognize a friend and, aided and abetted by high winds and eight large lakes, caused him to shoot 74, 73 and miss the cut. Still, he continued undaunted to Sawgrass for the Tournament Players Championship. On the opening day of the tournament he went out in 37 in perfect conditions, and then, illogically, came back in 32 in the wind. The next day a thunderstorm suspended play for an hour and he had five bogeys and five birdies for a 73. He regained his composure, recorded two 69s and finished third with Tom Watson behind Lee Trevino and Ben Crenshaw. That week he had stayed in a hotel in Jacksonville and had devoted all his spare hours to practising his putting on the beach. 'It's very good because the roll is true and it's quick,' he explained. Eight days later, more than a week before the season's first major began, Ballesteros was at Augusta National preparing for his fourth US Masters.

Tuesday, 8 April 1980, Augusta, Georgia. There has long been a tendency among the higher beings whose domain Augusta National is, to consider the home of the Masters as the very axis upon which the rest of the world turns. They have scant regard for the conventional rules of modern society, believing them to have no application whatsoever to themselves, and instead create laws of their own which the combined might of the Vatican and the White House could not have repealed.

In 1980 one of their more notorious policies was their racial one: until 1983 no white man carried a bag at Augusta and it was 1977 before a black man (Lee Elder) played. As a result, Ballesteros came alone and simply enlisted the services of his regular Masters caddie, Marion Herrington. Herrington duly made preparations to go out and measure the golf course. Ballesteros stopped him. Herrington, like Musgrove and most of his other caddies, only worked in yards. To this day, Ballesteros finds it impossible to think in anything but metres. 'I will do all by myself,' he declared, and set off armed with pencil and pad to carefully pace out the distances from the fairways to the greens, from the bunkers to trees and from other landmarks, such as mounds, to possible pin placements. Then he padded for several hours around the putting surfaces, in a hunched attitude rather like the Golden Bear perusing his line to the hole, studying every undulation, slope and borrow.

When he had finished he stood behind each one, as he had seen Nicklaus do, and looked back up the fairway – playing the hole in reverse in his mind – so that he could see where his approach shot should come from, for the secret of Augusta's treachery lies in the allure of her spacious fairways. 'Augusta,' says Crenshaw, 'is the most tempting golf course I think I've ever seen. It *goads* you into trying different shots because there's so much to gain. If you're right on your game and you live dangerously for a day and you can just skirt the trouble here and there, you can come off with a brilliant score. But if you're not, that's when it's really punishing . . . I think people tend to overlook how you must be good with your irons that week if you expect to win, because if you can't position your approaches you play defensively all week. It's very difficult to keep the ball below the hole, but that's the idea. You're rewarded when you do. Every time.'

In practice Ballesteros played with Trevino and Graham Marsh, who observed that the Spaniard was putting exceptionally well. Michael Williams walked with them to the second green.

'How long have you been here?' he asked Ballesteros.

'A year,' replied Ballesteros cryptically. In spirit he felt he had. Afterwards, he remarked to the press that he felt more in control of his golf swing than he ever had in his life before.

The Masters began on one of those crisp, sparkling blue days reminiscent of the best seaside holidays. A fresh wind gusted through the pines, searching for, but not finding, sandwich wrappers and drinks cartons, and toying instead with the psyches of hapless competitors. Ballesteros teed off at midday with Craig Stadler, the aptly named Walrus. In contrast to his playing partner, he was in a buoyant mood, further improved by birdies at the second, third, sixth and eighth holes, and was not discouraged when he dropped a shot at the fourth, where he had missed the green with a one-iron. The back nine, too, asked no questions he couldn't answer. He gathered birdies at the eleventh, thirteenth and seventeenth holes and was unlucky not to card two more: at the fourteenth he pitched to 10 feet but missed the putt, and at the next dropped a shot as light as a butterfly 4 feet from the pin and saw it lip out.

'This is the best I have played at Augusta,' he said delightedly when he came off the course. His score of 66, six under par, gave him a share of the lead at the close of play with Australian David Graham.

Friday was a gloriously hot and still day. Ballesteros, who was off early, went out in level par. This tends to suggest that he recorded a commendable string of threes, fours and fives, but appearances, as we know, are often deceptive. In reality, he was up to his old tricks again. Whether for the benefit of Larry Nelson, his playing partner and old Ryder Cup rival, or for the sheer pleasure of kicking over the traces, he thrashed at his drives with such force that he was almost carried after them. Thereafter, he would pursue the ball into forests and flowerbeds, tearing the heads off azaleas in his efforts to salvage pars. But on the inward half his philosophy of 'an eagle or a seven' began to pay off. He made threes at the tenth and eleventh and birdied the thirteenth and fifteenth with two wonderful long iron shots into the green.

At the sixteenth he called for his eight-iron. Herrington shook his head. 'It's a seven-iron,' he said with certitude to the Spaniard. Ballesteros hesitated but took the club anyway, and hit his tee shot 80 feet past the pin. Herrington was aghast. 'I'm so sorry, I'm so sorry,' he kept repeating.

'Don't worry,' said Ballesteros magnanimously. 'It was not your fault. It was mine for listening to you.' At least, that's what he usually says to his caddies.

He teed up on the par four seventeenth, seething with suppressed anger. All his aggression was channelled into his next shot, which snap-hooked off the tee at an angle so extreme that it flew through the top of a pine tree, bounced on to the adjacent seventh fairway, rolled between two bunkers and came to rest some 10 feet away from the flagstick on the seventh green.

'Where did that other ball come from?' queried Graham when he reached the green to find a strange ball on his line to the hole. 'No one's playing mulligans, I trust? Oh, it's Seve's ball, is it? Well, good enough, that explains it.'

Ballesteros emerged from the trees, looking slightly embarrassed. 'Nice drive,' commented Graham with some sarcasm. 'Would you like to play through?'

'I am a good driver, yes?' snapped Ballesteros, his temper flaring. 'This is the first time I hit the seventh green today. I missed it the other time.'

'I'd trade balls,' said Graham drily. 'Yours is closer to the hole.'

Ballesteros marked his ball and, as soon as the green was clear, took a free drop nearby. He was now faced with a shot of extraordinary difficulty. Before him, and completely obscuring his view of the green which lay 150 yards away, was a vast scoreboard, a large mound and several pine trees. While marshals scurried about shepherding the astonished flock who suddenly found themselves in his way, Ballesteros considered his options.

'Are you going to make a birdie?' shouted a Southern wag.

'Yes,' said Ballesteros positively. He selected a seven-iron, settled over his ball and swung through it with one of those exquisite swings of his which are all feel and no hit. A roar went up from the green. Ballesteros was off and running, the gallery surging after him. He found his ball 15 feet from the pin and rolled it in for birdie. Nelson was rendered speechless. What was there to say? Ballesteros finished with a par for a 69 and a halfway total of 135, three strokes ahead of Rex Caldwell and Graham.

The latter, who had been proceeding with less caution than he perhaps ought to have, had fallen horribly from grace at the twelfth, the same hole where Tom Weiskopf chalked up a 13 the previous day after putting five balls in the creek, and had squandered his chance to equal or better the Spaniard's lead.

In any golf tournament, regardless of whether or not it calls itself a major, it is impossible to predict with confidence the eventual outcome when only two rounds have been played. The Masters is no exception. Ballesteros might well have had a three-shot margin when he teed off on Saturday, but three shots is a reserve parachute barely worth its weight around Amen Corner. Six would be more reasonable. Nevertheless, there were now two distinct camps of anticipatory opinion at Augusta: those who thought Ballesteros was a great golfer who was playing well enough to retain his advantage and win, and those who thought he'd be lucky to. The second brigade were already clapping their hands together in glee and saying, 'I told you so,' rather tiresomely when Ballesteros reached the sixth hole. Certainly his start had been erratic. He had gone bogey, birdie, bogey, par, before his drive at the par four fifth had ended in a stand of pines. Fortunately, his ball was lying in the very place where a tree had recently been uprooted. Unfortunately, he had no clear line to the green. This realization came together with a new and sobering thought: a bogey or even a double bogey was inescapable. Indeed a six would reduce his lead to one.

Afterwards he said that it was a lesson from his childhood that had helped him at such times. 'If the water is rough in Santander Bay, you must fight harder in the boat and not give up, not worry about sinking. That's what I learned from my father. Others worry about sinking and they are finished.'

He counselled himself to remain calm at all costs, selected a sand-wedge and lofted the ball high over the trees and back on to the fairway. When he walked off the green he was thankful he had done no worse than bogey.

In light of the ensuing drama, there can be little doubt that the par five eighth played a crucial role in turning the tide of the tournament, even in those early stages of it. Up until that point Graham, who was partnering Ballesteros, had been slowly gaining ground on the Spaniard and, psychologically at least, felt he was virtually in the driving seat. That was his first mistake – and his last. Ballesteros, having driven powerfully up the fairway, consulted his yardage book and decided to go for the green, some 245 yards away. A three-iron was chosen for the task. He set up over the ball and sent it soaring into the blue. It came to a stop 6 feet from the pin. Before Graham's incredulous eyes, Ballesteros stroked the putt in for eagle.

The Australian was visibly shaken. He immediately took six and, despite the fact that he was in third place with Jack Newton, Andy North and J.C. Snead at the end of the day, never really threatened again. Ballesteros turned in 35, one under par, and came home in a relatively steady 33, for a score of 68 and a total of 203. His nearest challenger was the robust American Ed Fiori, a distant seven strokes away.

For a young man poised on the brink of history, Ballesteros was inordinately composed and unexcited. He knew that victory on the morrow would make him the youngest winner of the Masters ever – Nicklaus was eighty days older than the Spaniard's twenty-three years and four days when he marched to glory at Augusta in 1963 – and that he would become, along with the Golden Bear, Francis Ouimet and Bobby Jones, one of an élite group of players who had won two or more major championships by the age of twenty-three. As such, he responded to the attention he received with grace and goodwill, but slipped quietly away as soon as he was able. He had invited a handful of his Spanish friends and an American woman journalist over to his house for dinner. When they arrived they found him in an ebullient mood, determined to be the perfect host. He supervised the buffet meal and was, by turns, during the course of the evening, amusing, entertaining and an articulate conversationalist. Later, needing the cool comfort of solitude, he left his guests and watched, without really seeing, *Saturday Night Fever* in another room. By ten he was in bed. For a while he was restless and lay with his headphones on, staring wide-eyed into the night; but the gentle tones of his Barcelona psychologist filled him with confidence and allayed his fears, so that when sleep finally drew him into its dark embrace, there wasn't a shadow of self-doubt in his mind. He believed he was the best and, he told himself, when day broke he would prove it.

In the morning a woolly blanket of clouds hung in loose folds about the tops of the tall pines of Augusta National, enveloping the golf course in a congenial, motherly warmth. Ballesteros was off at twelve minutes to two. At a quarter before the hour, he walked from the putting green to the tee with Jack Newton. Outwardly, he was the epitome of tranquillity, but inside the butterflies were flapping around like eagles. 'Everybody gets nervous,' he admits. 'I think any time you don't have any nerves out on the course it's because you are not interested in the game.' He was relieved when he had hit his opening drive on the fairway and even more so when he had pitched up to 6 feet for birdie. At the third he was closer still, holing from 5 feet to steal another shot from par, and on the fifth he sank a big, swinging putt right across the green. When he reached the tenth hole, he was three under par for the day and leading by an incredible ten shots. Victory, it seemed, was a foregone conclusion: in the clubhouse Ballesteros's green jacket had been selected and laid out ready for its new owner and congratulatory speeches were in preparation. People began to yawn from an overdose of champagne and allowed their gazes to drift from the television screens to which they had been glued for three and a half days. In all likelihood, the inward nine would be a procession.

Then, for the first time since the tournament had begun, Ballesteros faltered; he three-putted the tenth. Newton saw his chance and grabbed it, making a four there and a birdie at the eleventh to close the gap between them to eight strokes. Ballesteros was unperturbed. Provided he didn't lose another shot to par, no harm was done; besides which, for the bold player there were still plenty of birdie opportunities to come. He stood on the twelfth tee calmly reflecting on this, and considering his next move. Ahead of him lay one of the toughest par three's in the world. The slick green is bordered by Rae's Creek, the graveyard of a million hopes, and guarded by one cavernous bunker and two smaller sandtraps. A wall of trees stands behind them, and herein lies the danger, for they trap and deflect the wind, causing it to swirl unpredictably above the putting surface. Contemplating them now, Ballesteros decided to aim to the left with a six-iron and let the breeze bring the ball in to the pin. Then he did something utterly out of character; he changed his mind at the top of his backswing and tried to hit the ball straight at the pin. It sailed right, hung suspended for an irritating age in the air, then plopped unceremoniously into the water. Ballesteros was shaken. He swore viciously and slammed his club into the ground. After a moment, he stalked to the water's edge to drop another ball, peering into its murky depths with a black scowl. One chip and two putts later and he had notched up a double-bogey. Newton, meanwhile, had birdied to reduce the Spaniard's lead to five.

On the thirteenth Ballesteros teed up and launched himself into his drive. It drew pleasingly round the corner of the dog-leg. The green was now just 180 yards away, tucked against Rae's Creek. 'Three-iron,' he ordered. Herrington was sure it was a four, but didn't like to say so. He watched Ballesteros line up over the shot with some concern. Then . . . calamity! The Spaniard hit the ball fat, striking the ground inches behind it. It climbed weakly into the air, dropped short on the grassy verge of the green, paused, then tumbled into the creek with a splash. The gallery gasped. Spreading rings of ripples chastised him silently, while ten thousand pairs of eyes swivelled and pinned on him in horror. What had he done!! What would he do! Would he *lose*?! Ballesteros felt the cold fingers of fear clutch at his heart. Sweat pricked his skin. He started towards the green with the heavy-limbed languor of a nightmare. The drone of the disturbed crowd grew louder and louder as he walked. They hummed like killer bees. He bent to lift his ball from the tepid water, feeling persecuted, and dropped it over his shoulder. The referee was not satisfied and told him to drop it again. Rage bubbled up inside Ballesteros and threatened to overflow. 'This man is trying to put me off,' he thought, and stared icily at the referee.

'Are you sure, *Sir*?' he asked menacingly.

Then, hurtling through his subconscious came a flash of memory, vivid and arresting. With picturebook clarity, he could recall the spring of 1978. He had been striding down this very fairway in the final round of the Masters when Gary Player, whom he was paired with, suddenly turned to him and said: 'These people don't think I can win.' Ballesteros had stared at him in surprise, then turned to look at the gallery. There was little doubt that that conclusion had indeed crossed the minds of several of them. They had begun to chatter among themselves and drift away disinterestedly, the way they do when it becomes obvious that the match they are following is out of the running. Ballesteros, who had started the day seven strokes behind the leader, Hubert Green, was heading for a 74 and playing that way, but Player had done better. He had reached the turn in 34 and had since picked up two birdies. Nevertheless, the inalterable fact was that he was still a distant three shots adrift of Green entering Amen Corner, one of the most treacherous stretches of holes in golf. The crowd regarded the little man in black with pity. 'What prayer does he have?' was their collective thought.

Player felt them write his chances off as keenly as if it were a lash across his shoulders. He responded to it with a sudden flash of rage. 'These people don't think I can win,' he said resentfully to Ballesteros. 'You watch, I'll show them.'

There followed one of the greatest back-nine performances in the history of major championships. Player scored 30 on the inward half at Augusta and rimmed the hole with putts three times. 'Had they dropped, I would have shot 27,' Player says. He grins. 'I would never have been invited back.' An incredible seven birdies in the final ten holes allowed him to overcome Green, Watson and Rod Funseth by a stroke and win the green jacket.

'I'll never forget,' says Player, 'and I want you to put this in Seve's book, because it's a good thing to spread a little love around the world because so many people spread bloody nasty things, but I'll never forget as long as I live the way he hugged me when I won the Masters. He came up to me on the eighteenth green in front of two hundred million viewers and he hugged me. Which is fantastic. And he was very complimentary because he said I taught him to win the Masters.'

Few things have had as much influence on the course of Ballesteros's destiny as Player's words that day on the thirteenth fairway. Now, as he dropped his ball for the second time, he remembered them, and also the note he had found in his locker just before teeing off. '*Buena Suerte*,' Player had written. 'Good luck, I'm pulling for you.' Ballesteros took a deep breath, selected a sand-iron and chipped onto the green. But despite his best efforts he could do no better than bogey, while Newton holed out for a four. Ahead of them Gibby Gilbert made a three at the fourteenth to move to within four strokes of the Spaniard.

Ballesteros was still smouldering when he drove off the next tee. 'So stupid,' he said to himself. 'What are you doing? Now you must try very hard or you lost the tournament.' A spectator's voice forced its way into the maelstrom of his thoughts, loud and jangling. 'Come on, Jack!' it shrieked. Ballesteros went white with fury. He threw the man a murderous glance. Adrenalin, thick and heady, coursed through his veins. 'These people don't think I can win,' he thought rebelliously. 'I'll show them.' He took out a six-iron and hit a magnificent shot out of the rough and onto the green. It ran to 25 feet and he two-putted for par. Later Newton said he believed that approach to have been critical to the Spaniard's success. 'Seve had to get it on the green, but also to the right place on that big rolling green. From anywhere else he could have three-putted.'

By now Ballesteros had marshalled his thoughts and was ready for the final challenge. 'Slow backswing, very important' he said to himself as he addressed the ball on the fifteenth. Then he powered a drive down the fairway and hit a four-iron over the water to 20 feet. When he reached the green, he glanced at the scoreboard. Gilbert had birdied the sixteenth and was only two strokes behind. Ballesteros leaned with some trepidation on his putter while he waited for the Australian to putt out. But the green was far quicker than either man had judged, and Newton ran his ball 10 feet past the hole. Ballesteros watched and learned. His own putt was lagged to 4 feet and he tapped it in for birdie.

Only the sixteenth now stood between Ballesteros and the US Masters title. The seventeenth and eighteenth were certain pars, but the sixteenth is a daunting par three of 170 yards with water running from tee to green. Ballesteros, however, was done with heroics. He took a six-iron for safety and two-putted for par.

'It's finished,' he said to Herrington. 'The tournament is ours.'

Monday, 14 April 1980, London: *Daily Telegraph* – 'On the day Severiano Ballesteros clinched the US Masters golf title, Spain's national radio began a news bulletin with a Spanish swimming record. No mention was made of the Spaniard who became the youngest winner of the Masters with a thirteen under par total of 275.'

Thursday, 17 April 1980, La Costa, California. The days following Ballesteros's victory at Augusta were so frantic and filled with activity that in no time at all they had merged into a confusing reel of places, colours and strange ingratiating faces, like half-remembered scenes from the windows of an express train. First, there had been the prize giving and a lengthy and demanding press conference, at which he had been more or less asked to quantify the exact proportions of luck and good judgement used in his triumph. Newton, who had finished runner-up to Ballesteros with Gilbert, took issue with the blind insistence of American reporters that fortune was the overriding element in the Spaniard's successes at Augusta and Lytham. 'It takes a lot of guts to win a major championship,' he said shortly, 'and Seve has won two of them. Here is a superstar and it's about time everybody realized it.'

That evening there was an honorary dinner at the golf club, where, Ballesteros complained, he was given a steak scarcely bigger than a peseta. Then, of course, there were the inevitable celebrations, attended by the usual raucous crowd. It was 5 a.m. when he finally went to bed and he was up again by eight to catch a plane to Atlanta. At eleven o'clock he was collected from the airport and whisked away to a photo session. For an interminable period of time he was called upon to look suave and pleased with life while flash bulbs exploded in his face. After that, he was rushed to a television studio for the Mike Douglas chat show, put on a flight to Los Angeles where he was meeting Ed Barner for dinner and, at length, shown a televised re-run of his Masters win. No sooner had he caught his breath than he was back on an aeroplane and winging his way to the Tournament of Champions at La Costa, California.

Upon reaching the golf course, he collected his credentials from the players' registration desk. The official dispensing them beamed. 'Your mother called from Spain,' she informed him.

'My mother?' said Ballesteros in puzzlement. 'She spoke English?'

'A little.'

The slow light of comprehension dawned across his face. 'Not my mother,' he told her with the sly grin of a man not unused to getting calls from women purporting to be near relatives. He was still smiling when he left the clubhouse in search of his caddie.

'Well done, Seve,' said Trevino as the Spaniard passed him, clapping him on the back. 'Remember me telling you to go to Augusta a week early?'

Ballesteros had not forgotten. 'How do I win the US Open?' he asked hopefully.

'Get them to cut down the rough,' Trevino laughed.

Eventually, after disentangling himself from two persistent salesmen who were determined that he should endorse their shirts, Ballesteros went out to play a practice round, alone but for his caddie and a dozen spectators. Coming off the third green he was stopped by a television crew. They only wanted to ask the same questions he had heard a hundred times before ('How was his back? Why didn't he want to play in America?'), but he was patient and tactful and gave them as much time as they needed. That night he wandered down to the clubhouse restaurant – which had made a special concession to him not wearing a jacket – and had supper with Dudley Doust and Michael Williams. He said three things of note during the meal: a. The Swiss Open was one of his favourite tournaments because he loved to go to the local disco; b. Sandy Lyle would one day win the Masters; c. Appearance money was essential to the European Tour.

When the tournament was over and Ballesteros had finished eighteenth behind Tom Watson, he flew to Spain for the Madrid Open. There he was greeted as a conquistador by his comrades but went almost unnoticed by the nation at large. Piñero had spent the night after the Masters on the telephone to every newspaper in the country in an effort to establish whether in fact Ballesteros had won, but to no avail. 'Severiano who?' they had echoed blankly. But, from those people who did know him and who did understand how momentous his victory was, Ballesteros received a deluge of congratulatory telegrams and phone calls. King Juan Carlos and Adolfo Suarez of Spain both wrote letters, Bob Hope requested a round of golf with him and Muhammad Ali rang to tell him he was the greatest.

On the surface, all of this left him unaffected. His family had come down from the north to welcome him home, accompanied by a coachload of excited villagers driven by Ramon Sota, and he was drawn willingly back into the warm and familiar cocoon of friends and relatives – simple, generous-hearted people with simple values – experiencing a strong sense of relief as he did so, rather like a cat that has been too long in the cold snuggling into a sheepskin rug on the hearth. Thereafter, his evenings passed in a dusky-hued whirl of pavement cafés, red wine and laughter.

On the surface, he enjoyed life to the full. How could he not? *Destino* had been good to him so far. At twenty-three years of age he was handsome, wealthy, popular and hugely gifted, the winner of sixteen official Tour events and two major championships and the subject of international, if not national, acclaim. But inwardly he was beginning, by infinitesimal degrees, to alter beyond all recognition. The

135

incessant demands of the public and of sponsors, and the constant pressure on him to perform, made him increasingly moody and withdrawn. Away from the golf course, during those sultry Madrid evenings, he was able, for a few hours, to forget who he was and what he stood for; but when the harsh light of morning returned it always brought the tournament, and along with that came the probing glances and intruding questions of strangers intent on invading his private world.

On the first practice day of the Madrid Open, Ballesteros went hunting for Dave Musgrove. Musgrove, however, was caddying for Michael King and refused to change bags. He had not heard a word from the Spaniard over the winter and didn't see why he should. There was a small confrontation of wills. Musgrove and Ballesteros adopted mutually aggressive postures on the practice range, and glared stubbornly at one another for some minutes. Ballesteros's brown eyes were the first to drop. He knew he was in the wrong – not that he would ever have dreamt of admitting it. 'I didn't tell him to go,' he said defensively to journalists. 'Last season he got very excited towards the end and he talked too much on the course. That was not good.' Baldomero, his brother, was then prevailed upon to caddie for him.

In the second round Ballesteros shot a career-best 63. It was the triumphant result of a personal ambition to make everyone he felt had insulted him eat their words: Musgrove, for instance, had been palpably rude and quite scathing when rejecting his offer of employment; the Spanish media had failed to recognize the enormity of his achievement at Augusta, although a national press conference was now scheduled; and the Americans continued to doubt his ability to win major championships without divine intervention. Pursued by these imaginary demons, Ballesteros played like a man possessed. He strode along the fairways, eyes fixed on his target, muttering to himself over and over again: 'I can win every tournament in the world, I can win every tournament in the world.' The spectators stared at him curiously but shrank back when he glowered at them, and once or twice when Baldomero made an incautious remark he had his head snapped off.

'You have a 30, six under par,' he had p
innocently to his young brother at the turn. But Balle.
mood had been further blackened by an 8-foot putt misse(
the ninth, and he only said irritably: 'It should have been a
29.'

Then on the back nine Baldomero told him that the
King of Spain was in the gallery. Ballesteros didn't glance
up – didn't hear him even, so absorbed was he in the task
that he had set himself.

In the third round the young Spaniard scored a 70
to Piñero's 69, gaining a four-stroke advantage, and the
upper hand psychologically going into the final day. Piñero,
however, is long on courage and fortitude, and had closed
the gap to a shot by the time they reached the sixteenth
hole. There, Ballesteros showed his mastery. He extracted
a seven-iron from a desperate lie among the pines, putting it
6 feet away from the pin for birdie while Piñero, who is not
blessed with magic powers, had to chip out onto the fairway
for bogey. Ballesteros eventually won by three shots with a
score of 69 and an aggregate of 270, eighteen under par. It
was his first major triumph in his native land.

The subsequent festivities were entered into with gusto
by the gathered clan, but were cut short by the collapse of
Baldomero on a street corner in Madrid. 'Baldomero is a very
nervous person,' explained Ballesteros, 'and he is not used to
carrying a golf bag that weighs twenty kilos up and down hills
for four days. Eight kilometres a day for a man thirty-three
years old made him very tired. His nerves, plus the pressure,
plus all the eating and alcohol and smoke . . . Baldomero just
. . . stops breathing.' For an instant Ballesteros was paralysed
with fright at the sight of his older brother lying motionless
on the pavement, but soon recovered himself and was about
to give him mouth to mouth resuscitation when he revived.
Baldomero was taken to the hospital for examination, kept in
overnight for observation and released the following morning.

Two days later Ballesteros was already in rehearsal for the
Spanish Open, his fourth consecutive tournament after the
Masters. Contrary to all expectations he showed no outward
signs of fatigue but, rather, was bursting with vitality and good

137

...... at El Escorpion had been guaranteed by ...., sponsors of the event; who, having paid .... at Torrequebrada the previous year, where .... missed the cut, now found themselves writing ......00 in appearance money, £2,000 if he qualified ...... days and an additional £2,000 if he won the ...... ze.

B...... secured the first and second parts of the bargain early enough, scoring 68, 72 in the opening rounds, but his temper and Eddie Polland, the former Ryder Cup player, cost him the third. 'In contrast with Ballesteros, who could frequently be seen beating his club on the ground in frustration,' wrote Michael Williams in the *Telegraph*, 'it was refreshing to find Polland accepting any minor unintentional shots without a tantrum and, instead, a rueful smile.' Polland won by five shots from the Spaniard and Mark James.

In retrospect, Ballesteros's achievements in the early part of 1980 are nothing less than extraordinary. Beginning with the Tournament Players Championship in March, he finished third, first, eighteenth, first, second, first – this last being the Martini International where he beat Brian Barnes. Throughout that period he maintained an air of youthful defiance and invincibility, the only indication that he might be succumbing to the inevitable strain of contending every week being the PGA Championship at Royal St George's, where he was suffering from a chest infection, and informed the media morosely: 'Winning is very difficult in any company.' He then proved it by finishing thirty-second.

Five days before the US Open Championship was due to start at Baltusrol, Ballesteros flew to New York to begin his preparations.

Friday, 13 June 1980, Baltusrol Golf Club, Springfield, New Jersey. The existence of newspapers is proof that no two people can ever tell a story in exactly the same way. It can't be done. Human nature doesn't allow it. One can hardly be surprised, therefore, at the number of variations on a theme one hears of the following events – particularly when some of the storytellers are given to sensationalism and others are hoping to absolve themselves of blame. Suffice to say that they began, in Ballesteros's version, at least, when he experienced a premonition on the flight from Madrid to New York. One minute he was reading magazines and looking distractedly out the window, and the next he was overcome by a sensation of impending doom.

'Seve,' he said to himself, 'you should not be going to the US Open. Something bad is going to happen.'

Things began to go wrong almost immediately. Upon registering for the tournament Ballesteros was given a players' badge and a caddies' badge, the latter being for his brother Baldomero. He then discovered that Baldomero was not allowed beyond the locker room, let alone into the dining room, and an acrimonious discussion with a USGA official ensued. But in vain. The official could not be swayed. Ballesteros stamped off crossly to find his golf clubs, encountering Hale Irwin *en route*; who, though there had been little love lost between them in the past, invited him out for a practice game. Ballesteros accepted, played well and had a thoroughly enjoyable time, finishing 2, 4, 4 – all birdies. Irwin remarked to journalists that the young Spaniard was, 'driving respectably and swinging the club both smoothly and slowly.'

When he came off the golf course he had recovered his humour and was smiling. It was but a fleeting phase. Soon he was in conflict with Barner, who was insistent that he should attend a cocktail party half an hour's drive away in New York City, because UMI was negotiating a new contract for him with Rolex. Ballesteros refused point blank to go anywhere. Why should he? He had a major championship to play the next day. Barner used a variety of pleas, ploys and entreaties to try to persuade him, but in the end Ballesteros had his own way: he stayed in his hotel room. As it turned out, it wouldn't have made a blind bit of difference if he had gone to the cocktail party or even if he had made a comprehensive tour of the nightlife of Manhattan afterwards. The following day he recorded a dismal 75, five over par, and drew perilously near to missing the cut.

It is at this point that the stories of the people involved in this incident (and indeed those who weren't but might just as well have been) start to diverge. Ballesteros has an excellent memory, there's no question about that. According to Joe Collet, who was taking care of the Spaniard that week, 'He has such a good memory that sometimes he thinks he's the only one that remembers it in the way that it was. But he does have the same frailty that a lot of us have, that [his] perception of reality is not always what everybody else's perception is . . . He has his impression of what happened [at the US Open] and I have mine.'

Collet's impression is this. Because Ballesteros wasn't yet fluent in English, he had always made it his job at the beginning of every tournament to search out the draw, take it to the Spaniard and check that he knew his tee-off times. The US Open was no different. On Wednesday evening he had taken a starting sheet from his briefcase and said to Ballesteros: 'Do you know what time you are playing on Thursday and Friday?' After Ballesteros had reeled off the times confidently, Collet had not given the matter another thought. But on Friday morning when he was walking through the hotel lobby, on his way to get a courtesy car, he caught sight of Ballesteros wandering aimlessly out of the dining room.

'Seve!' cried Collet in amazement. 'You're off in a few minutes! What are you doing here?'

Ballesteros was taken aback. 'Oh, no,' he said, 'I don't go off for another hour.'

'You go off right now,' Collet said in a chilling tone.

The colour drained like a sponge from Ballesteros's face. In an instant he was in a courtesy car and speeding dangerously through the traffic to the golf course. He was out of the door before the car stopped and running to fetch his shoes and clubs, but by the time he reached the first tee, seven minutes too late, his playing partners had hit their second shots. USGA official John Laupheimer had no choice but to disqualify him under the Rules of Golf for the breach of Rule 37-5.

Dudley Doust's interpretation of events is totally different to Collet's and yet they were the only two people allowed into Ballesteros's hotel room after he had returned from the course. He claims that it was Collet who failed to remind Ballesteros of his starting times, and that when Ballesteros and his brother had set off that morning at 9.25, for what they thought was a 10.45 tee-time, they had done so in a relaxed fashion, laughing and joking all the way to the course and taking no notice whatsoever of the queues of rush-hour traffic. It was only when they had pulled up at the club and a British journalist came rushing over to tell Ballesteros that he was due on the tee, that they had realized anything was amiss.

Another story is that Baldomero was supposed to have checked the starting time and told Ballesteros, and that there had been some breakdown in communication between the two brothers. But Collet says he has talked to Baldomero about it and that Baldomero just answered tersely: 'I know how to read. But Seve had it set in his mind that it was another time and, because he seemed to know, I didn't question him.' No matter. The end result of all these scenarios is the same. When Ballesteros heard he was to be disqualified he flew into a terrible rage and pleaded for a reduced sentence. However, the rules of the game are specific. Ballesteros had to swallow his medicine and, not liking it one little bit, went snarling to the clubhouse to empty his locker and left the golf course at speed.

'Of course, it was big news,' continues Collet. ' "Europe's Order of Merit leader makes idiot mistake." And there were reporters hanging about the hotel trying to get pictures and interviews and, of course, he just wanted to hide. He was so embarrassed, it was terrible. And a good friend of ours [read: a good friend of Seve's], Susan Minkley – she takes the statistical count out on Tour; she's a California girl – she was very fond of Seve and she just felt terrible about it. She had a Cadillac and she offered to help get us to the airport because it was a big hassle getting a taxi. And I'll never forget, I had the room next to Seve's, and I was looking out the window and all the reporters were hanging around the car park. So I said, "Baldomero, you go down to the lobby like you're expecting Seve to follow. Susan, get your car and sneak round the back. Then we'll go down and

141

drive off and avoid all the confrontation." It almost worked. Everybody went to the lobby when they saw Baldomero, and Seve and I bolted down the stairs. But just as we were jumping in the car, a couple of them got wise, and came around and took pictures. And Seve smiled and waved and closed the door and we drove off. But it took him quite a while to admit that maybe it was his fault about the tee-time, and I kind of got blamed . . . And it wasn't true. In fact, if it wasn't for me, he would never have got there at all.'

That was not the opinion of a sizeable number of officials and members of the press, who felt that the whole affair might have been stage-managed by UMI. 'More than one world-class American . . . felt very strongly that . . . Ballesteros had demeaned the US Open in particular and golfers in general with his disgraceful performance at Baltusrol,' wrote Ben Wright in *Golf World* (September 1980). 'The players in question feel that the gulf between American and European golf . . . has been immeasurably widened by the talented Spaniard's inexplicable conduct, and it is difficult to disagree with them, although I had to point out to them that Ballesteros's two "handlers", who should have ensured his presence on Baltusrol's first tee at the appointed hour, are American.'

Wright goes on to speculate whether anyone may have been responsible for Ballesteros missing his starting time so that he would save face after a first round 75 had left him twelve shots adrift of eventual winner Jack Nicklaus and Tom Weiskopf, and these include a high ranking official of the USGA . . . He told me: "It is hard to understand Ballesteros's behaviour, particularly since he was also accompanied by his brother. It was obviously very hurtful to us that the British Open and US Masters Champion should behave in such an unprofessional manner. No-one in a privileged position in American golf will be anxious to bend over backwards to help Ballesteros in the foreseeable future, at least until he has wiped the slate clean." '

A week after the US Open Ballesteros was offered £5,000 to play in the Greater Manchester Open, but turned it down. His brother Manuel said in a statement: 'Seve is still upset by what happened in America but that has nothing to do with him turning down the offer.'

Those were gloomy times for Ballesteros. Whether at home in Pedreña or out on Tour, all served to remind him of the trauma of Baltusrol. His days were haunted by it; his sleep was disturbed by it. He had nightmares where he was blindfolded and facing a firing squad but woke up an instant before he was shot, and others where he was late to the first tee while playing in the World Cup with Piñero, and disqualified. 'Many times I see people, at night,' he said to Doust. 'Not in dream, no, no. I tell you, *people*. I wake up and see somebody leaning over my bed – maybe a man, maybe a woman – but when I open up the light, nothing. It has gone away.'

In press conferences he was even more self-deprecating than usual, constantly alluding to his pet themes of missed tee-times and luck, but it was not until the Dutch Open at Hilversum that he actually confronted the spectre of the US Open head-on.

'It was my fault,' he admitted. 'I was stupid. But I felt like a dog which has been kicked.'

Then he pulled himself together, assumed a Laughing Cavalier aspect and swept to a four-stroke victory, much to the delight of the huge galleries that had turned out specially to see him. It was one of few bright sparks in what was a comparatively dull second half of the season. The editor of *Golf World* commented: 'All of [Ballesteros's] wins were in the early part of 1980 and I am left wondering if there is any significance in this. For the rest of the year he was disappointing and his attitude and approach to the game that gives him his living left something to be desired . . . The smiling face is not instantly there now – a few wrinkles have appeared – and he showed at the World Cup that he wants nothing to do with any golfing activity which does not guarantee him money on the table before he starts. As Peter Alliss says of him, "I hope he does not get too tough and that he takes time to smell a few flowers on the way." '

But Trevino, asked what he thought was the matter with his young friend, jumped to his defence. 'The kid is going through the first slump of his life,' he said abruptly. 'People keep asking him what's wrong and it's bugging him. He can't go into a restaurant and enjoy dinner anymore. I really feel sorry for him because he really is a tremendous player and a good guy. He asked me how I handled my bad times and I told him: "Seve, there will be days you can't do anything right. You have to stay with it and work your way out of it." '

Halcyon days: Severiano (*left*) and friend as boy caddies in Pedreña.
© *Joe Patterson/Yours in Sport*.

Conquistador: police struggle to hold back the tide as Lytham crowds rush to acclaim the new Open champion. © *Allsport/Steve Powell*.

ABOVE: Friends and foes: Nick Faldo spent the early part of his career 'hoping there was going to be some competitive rivalry' between himself and the Spaniard but 'Seve was too good.' Photographed here for a *Golf World* interview in 1978. © *Phil Sheldon*.

LEFT: Less than a year after winning the 1979 Open, Ballesteros becomes, at twenty-three years and four days, the youngest Masters champion in history. © *Phil Sheldon*.

Severiano, his face a picture of happiness, relaxes on the family boat with the man who was to prove his greatest friend, mentor and influence – his father Baldomero.
© *Chris Smith*.

Magician: Ballesteros conjures up a breath-taking chip shot into the hole to win the 1983 Masters. © *Phil Sheldon*.

After holing the winning putt at St Andrews in 1984, Ballesteros explodes into a joyous celebration of his second Open triumph, punching the air repeatedly and turning a full 180 degrees as he salutes the galleries. It was a moment he later described as 'the pinnacle' of his career. © *Phil Sheldon*.

Young, gifted and supremely confident, Ballesteros, his precious golf clubs on his shoulder, poses in front of the Pedreña farmhouse where he was born. © *Chris Smith*.

Brothers in arms: Ballesteros raises Tony Jacklin's hand in a victory salute after helping him lead the European team to a historic triumph in the 1987 Ryder Cup at Muirfield Village.
© *Phil Sheldon*.

Matador: Ballesteros, his cape whipped back by wind and rain, turns warily to face the opposition. © *Chris Smith*.

8

Pride and Prejudice

And Winston Churchill always said, adversity is what makes you a man.

Gary Player, Palm Springs, March 1992

In order to understand the events, and far-reaching effects, of 1981, it is first necessary to know that they had their roots in the evil of appearance money. One should also realize that appearance money did not always have the notoriety it does now, and that in 1971, when John Jacobs was handed the responsibility of trying to make a non-viable golf circuit into a marketable enterprise, he considered player inducements to be an essential ingredient in the tournament division's long-term success. Before the appointment of Jacobs the British Tour, such as it was, had been run by the Professional Golfers' Association with the aid of a handful of freelance financial advisers. As a result, it had made little progress. An average season consisted of seven or eight events with a total prize fund of £250,000, and individual purses of less than a tenth of that, in which the winner and four or five other players made money, eight or ten broke even and 150 were out of pocket.

To Jacobs, a former Tour player, it was unacceptable that this situation should be allowed to continue. He set about contacting the existing Tour patrons and explained to them that in future a minimum prize fund would be imposed. As a consequence, several key sponsors withdrew their support. It quickly became obvious that if the British Tour was to survive, two things needed to happen: a. It had to expand into Europe; b. Europe's top players had to be encouraged to support their own circuit rather than that of the US. With this in mind Jacobs created a rule which stated that any player who had won a major championship had the right to negotiate for appearance money. This idea was not as revolutionary as it sounds. It had been an open secret since the days of Henry Cotton, and possibly long before, that certain professionals received incentives to play. In 1971, however, Tony Jacklin was alone among the Europeans in meriting them. After he had won the US and British Opens, he was paid in the region of £2,000 for events on this side of the Atlantic and £10,000 for those in Japan. IMG, his representatives, made the most of their good fortune, Jacobs watched the Tour flourish and everybody was happy. Until Ballesteros came along.

It is possible to assume that UMI had asked, or had been offered, appearance money for Ballesteros from the time he finished second to Miller at Birkdale, although officially he was not entitled to it until after he had won the money list at the end of that year. Certainly Musgrove has a clear recollection of the Spaniard saying to him in September 1976, during the Sun-Alliance Match Play Championship at Kings Norton, that he had been paid to show up. 'They're giving me money to play,' the Spaniard had remarked. By 1979, even before he had won the Open, Ballesteros was able to command fees of more than $5,000 per tournament; in 1980 he was paid £7,000, with additional bonuses for winning; and in 1981 Ed Barner decided – inflation being what it was – that his client could ask for £11,000, plus first-class airfares, expenses and a bonus for winning.

That was the straw that broke the camel's back. Early in the previous season several sponsors had expressed outrage at the figures they were being expected to pay Ballesteros and, as is their way when they feel they are being held to ransom by a player, had run crying to Ken Schofield, the executive director of the new European Tournament Players' Division

(ETPD). The first stirrings of dissent were felt at Tour head-quarters. A ban on appearance money was discussed. Word reached Ed Barner. In March, when the British press met for the launch of a major deal between Ballesteros and Slazenger (worth £250,000 over five years), he took the opportunity to inform them that unless sponsors paid the going rate, his client would not be playing in their tournaments.

He might just as well have tossed a match at a keg of dynamite. The resulting explosion was heard right around the golfing world and was the beginning of what Schofield bitterly describes as, 'that very, very public and very lamentable year.'

It's strange how full of irony life really is. One moment a rule is being created to allow Jacklin to reap the maximum benefit of his two major victories through appearance fees, and the next there is talk of that very same rule being abolished immediately because Seve Ballesteros is making too much money from it. According to Jacobs it was discussed anyway. Of course, these incidents took place almost ten years apart, during which time the PGA and the Tour had gone their separate ways, Jacobs had resigned, the total prize fund for the season had risen from £0.7 million in 1975 to a projected £1.8 million in the 1981 season (as compared to the £22 million of 1992), and the appearance-money rule had been adapted so that the winner of the preceding season's British Order of Merit was also entitled to receive it.

Joe Collet says that clandestine meetings between Schofield and those sponsors who wanted to cut the throat of the appearance-money monster had been held then, but that due to lack of support from other patrons their campaign had proved ineffectual and had ultimately resulted in surrender on the part of the Tour. 'Then it all got out of hand again and, I don't know who was to blame, but the fees got bigger and bigger, and more and more tournaments realized they couldn't even get a field unless they paid Tom, Dick and Harry. And there were probably more people who weren't at the top of the Order of Merit, who were asking for plane tickets and hotels and things, and so the sponsors went back to Ken again. The details have escaped me, but what I do remember was there came a point in time when Seve was going to be singled out as an example.'

That point was in the autumn of 1980. The ETPD committee had rendezvoused at Wentworth to review the appearance-money situation. Once before when they had met, Jacobs had tried to convince them that the reason the rule had been instigated in the first place – to attempt to compensate top European players for earnings which they could otherwise make in prize money alone in the US – was still justifiable. Ballesteros, for instance, was the winner of two major championships and three money lists. Under the present system he was entitled to, and could make, far more than any other European player from appearance money. How could he now be expected to play on his own continent for peanuts when he could make ten times as much in Japan or America? 'I'm very sorry,' Jacobs had declared to the room at large, 'but I think you're wrong. You're dealing with a very proud Spaniard and you're saying that he shouldn't have appearance money, but you're still allowing Lee Trevino and Tom Weiskopf [and every other US golfer] to have it. Why?' This time there was nobody to argue Ballesteros's corner. The committee, led by chairman Neil Coles, ruled that with effect from the first tournament of the new season no ETPD member could request appearance money, although he would be allowed 'expenses' of up to $10,000. Perversely, American players who commanded fees of up to $40,000 for appearing in Europe were free to continue to do so. And as if this policy was not farcical enough, there was also a loophole in the rule which meant that although a player or his manager couldn't actually *ask* for appearance money, there was nothing to stop a sponsor offering it to him.

But farcical or not, the rule was imposed. Before the 1981 season had begun, the die was cast, and the wheels of misfortune had begun to grind inexorably along the path towards destruction.

Wednesday, 22 April 1981, Madrid. Lightning, like the devil's pitchfork, split the dark sky above Puerto de Hierro, sending the small group of players who had ventured out to practise scrambling hastily for cover. Since dawn the rain had fallen with relentless efficiency. Play had been suspended when the golf course was reduced to a relief map of rivers and ravines and, with more rain forecast, the prospects for a four-round tournament were bleak. Inside the clubhouse the atmosphere was no less charged or stormy. Brandy glasses clinked and cigarette smoke swirled thickly as the Madrid Open committee pondered a singular conundrum: the disappearance of Severiano Ballesteros. They had before them a letter of explanation. At least, if it didn't exactly *explain* why he had gone absent without leave, it did inform them of his whereabouts. Regretfully, Ballesteros would not be defending his Madrid Open title at Puerto de Hierro that week as he was under obligation to compete in a conflicting event on the Japanese Tour. Would the committee be so kind as to grant him a release?

A stunned silence greeted this announcement. It was followed immediately by a cacophony of Spanish cries and appeals to a higher power, as members of the committee gave free rein to a wide spectrum of emotions. They were enraged; they were embarrassed; they were embittered. Ballesteros was Spain's finest player, not to mention the title holder of the Madrid Open and a major draw card in terms of ticket sales, and all posters, programmes and other promotional material had been prepared with this in mind. What on earth was to be done? And what of the manner in which the release had been requested? That, too, should be taken into consideration: 1. Ballesteros had flown to Japan on the Monday of the Madrid Open; 2. The letter had allegedly been delivered on Tuesday; 3. Under the rules of the ETPD, any member who wishes to play in a tournament which clashes with an ETPD event must obtain a release from the ETPD.

The Madrid Open committee debated these issues at length in two separate meetings and it was late in the day before they decided – although strictly speaking the request should never have been addressed to them in the first place – that the Spaniard should be given a release.

'So what happens now?' asked Peter Dobereiner the next morning. 'Possibly a fine. Possibly a refusal to pay the fine.

Possibly a resignation from the ETPD. Possibly no Ballesteros in the Ryder Cup team. At all events the most promising career in world golf will come under serious threat and that is the greatest of pities because the new rule forbidding the asking of appearance money, which Ballesteros sees as an act of personal victimization, is no more than the expression of a pious hope. There are many ways in which a top golfer can be persuaded to include a tournament in his programme and players take advantage of them, as is their due.'

People like to say that bad things happen in threes. They don't really. They happen in twos or fours or even twenties. It all depends on when you start counting them and when you stop. If you began in June 1980, for example, you would say that the black dogs were barking when Ballesteros missed his tee-off time at the US Open. But if New Year's Day in 1981 was your starting point, then you would probably include the two minor car crashes Ballesteros was involved in. They were both his fault, and caused the wreckage of two different vehicles.

'My driving is like my golf,' he said mockingly when questioned about them. 'I am never on the fairway.'

The next thing that occurred was the European Ferries' press conference in London on 11 February, where Ballesteros signed a five-year contract as touring professional at La Manga in Spain. He informed the gathered media that he would be competing in only six or seven tournaments in Europe that season, most of which would be in Britain. Instead, he intended to play around seven events on the US Tour and at least five on the lucrative Japanese Tour. 'They want to see me in Japan,' he explained. 'They play for double our prize money and they are also offering me as much as $30,000 or $40,000 a tournament.' He made no bones about the fact that the decision to spurn the European Tour was a means of retaliation against the new rule. 'Sponsors don't have to pay me appearance money, but also I don't have to play in their tournaments,' he observed, knowing full well that he would continue to be offered money in suitcases. 'I think it should be left to the sponsors to decide who they want and how much they want them. If they want all the publicity then they must pay for the good players.'

But when Ballesteros arrived at Augusta in April to defend his US Masters title, after a lacklustre performance in the Greater Greensboro Open, he was considerably less blithe. Four days earlier London Weekend Television had released a documentary in which he was seen to say that, 'Appearance money will never disappear,' and to state categorically that he owed the game nothing. 'Do you not know how much I give to golf? I start when I was nine and since then I live until I am now twenty-three. That all the way for golf. You think that is not enough? I think that is enough.' According to Doust, he had also received a hostile letter from the executive director of the Tour. 'One thing you should know straight from me,' Schofield allegedly wrote, 'is that no one player can, from this day forward, expect to clear $250,000 in appearance fees before teeing off on the European Tour.'

These troubles were clearly weighing on Ballesteros's mind. He was sullen and taciturn during his interviews, and would give little away save that he had undertaken to play in Japan during the week of the Madrid Open. His game, too, was not what it should have been. After parring the first six holes in the opening round of the tournament, he proceeded to drop seven strokes in eight holes through Amen Corner and finally returned a card of 78. His outburst in the winter – 'Every day, business and rain, business and rain. I have no time to think, I have no time to relax, to concentrate on practising my game. I tell you, I have *never* been so poorly prepared for a season. I will play no good at the Masters' – appeared to have been a prediction. The following day he scored a four over par 76 and crashed out of the tournament after missing the cut by six shots.

On 6 May, having played truant for a fortnight in Japan, Ballesteros returned to Europe for the French Open at St Germain. He refused to take on the mantle of the prodigal son, insisting instead that he was the 'white sheep of a prodigal family'. If the tournament committee fined him he would not pay it, whether it was five pounds or five thousand. 'I have many other places to play apart from Europe. Maybe I will

151

play the Japanese Tour.' There was no doubt that he believed the Tour to be making a scapegoat of him and felt that the creation of the appearance-money rule had been inspired by the jealousy of lesser players. It plainly cut him to the quick that the ETPD failed to appreciate what he had done for European golf. At the same time, he regretted the chain of events that had brought him into conflict with the Tour. 'It is very sad. I feel sorry for the people who want to see me play in Britain and I hope they understand my position.'

In the first round of the tournament he shot 72. Afterwards he was in a melancholy mood and commented sorrowfully that it sometimes rained and one had to put up an umbrella. 'At the moment in my life it is raining very hard.'

He soon found out that it never rains but it pours. In the second round a heavy downpour flooded the course and play was suspended. John Paramor, the tournament director, at once set out across the course on his buggy, sounding intermittent blasts on his Klaxon to alert players that they should stop, as he is directed to do under the rules of tournament golf. But the Klaxon's voice is adversely affected by damp weather. Brian Barnes played on for forty minutes after failing to hear its thin cry, dropping three strokes to par in the process, before being told to stop when he was 20 yards short of the eighteenth green. He then learnt that Ballesteros's group had been given special instructions to suspend play while Barnes was on the fifteenth hole. 'Is there one rule for Seve and another for Barnes?' he demanded furiously, and went to take the matter up with Paramor. As far as he was concerned, he should be allowed to start again from the fifteenth where he would have stopped had he heard the Klaxon. He continued to press his case while his playing partners continued their round, at which point his argument became academic because he was disqualified for failing to resume play.

Ballesteros's own round included nine birdies, but he was thoroughly depressed by the misadventures which had prevented him from gaining more. At the par-four seventeenth, where he was left with 110 yards to the pin, he had taken a wedge and flown the green by as much again, ending up in the bushes. But his score of 67 had put him in the hunt for the tournament, and closing rounds of 68 and 69 earned him a share of third place behind the eventual winner, Sandy Lyle.

When the tournament ended, Ballesteros returned to Santander with a heavy heart. He had a week to wait, and possibly longer, before he would know the inevitable consequences of his now irrevocable decision to resign from the European Tour.

14 May 1981, London. The *Guardian*: 'Severiano Ballesteros is no longer a European Tour player. His name has been removed from the Ryder Cup points list and from the official money list.'

Throughout the years, the blame for the events of 1981 and their repercussions has always been laid squarely at the door of UMI. But as I understand it, the whole affair really began and ended with Ballesteros. He wasn't coerced into doing something he didn't want to do. He did it of his own free will. As Roddy Carr says, 'Seve has never been one to take advice. He'll do exactly what he wants to do, anyway.' Early on in his career Ballesteros had told Collet and Barner that they should be more aggressive when asking for appearance money on his behalf. He felt he was as good as any American player and should be paid accordingly. His managers agreed. IMG were not slow in adopting similarly forceful tactics, and in no time at all the sponsors were weeping on Schofield's shoulder and the Tour had introduced the new rule. There were now two options available to Ballesteros. He could defy his own nature and give in gracefully to authority; content himself with playing for nothing but the love of the game each week while US golfers committed daylight robbery before his very eyes; and count his blessings when he was given the occasional cheque under the table. Or he could rebel. Characteristically, he took the line of most resistance.

'He was adamant that he should get appearance money,' recalls Collet. 'We told him that there were going to be sanctions imposed if he continued to be paid, and that the only way round that was to withdraw his membership and then as a non-member he could charge what he wanted and get paid.

And since he felt that it was more important to continue to be able to be appreciated and be compensated based on his merits than it was to be a member of a second-rate tour – which it was at the time – he agreed with our strategy to withdraw his membership. And we did that on the promise he had with John Jacobs that it wouldn't affect his Ryder Cup standings.'

With Ballesteros's permission, Collet sent a telex to Schofield. 'On the basis of which way you decide on the ruling,' he wrote, 'I'm provisionally withdrawing Seve's membership from the Tour.' 'That was my language. And Seve backed me up on it and Ed thought it was quite daring but to go for it. I thought I'd just teach them a little lesson.' But when this action came to light it was widely interpreted as 'a childishly transparent stratagem to intimidate the tournament committee'. The theory behind it was simple. If Ballesteros had already resigned from the Tour, he could not have broken any rules by playing in the Far East during the Madrid and Italian Opens, and should not therefore be subjected to disciplinary action. The ball was in the court of the ETPD. All they had to do was accept this piece of logic as unassailable, put any notions of fining him or suspending him out of their heads, and Ballesteros would withdraw his resignation.

'I wouldn't have the guts to do that today,' says Collet with a laugh. 'But I'm proud of myself that I did it then. I think it was a good move and had to be done. It made a statement. It said: "Look, until everyone is treated the same, Seve has the right to do what he wants. We're not blackmailing him or anything. It's voluntary." '

The ETPD accepted Ballesteros's resignation with effect from the date it was received, which meant that because he wasn't a member when he went to Japan – where he was understood to have been paid £60,000 appearance money – he would not be punished. Officially, he was now restricted to playing in his own national open and a maximum of two other European events as a non-member. In reality, he could accept invitations to play every event on the calendar. And he could rejoin the ETPD if he wished to by signing the standard players' declaration agreeing to abide by the rules. From that moment on he would be eligible to win points for Ryder Cup selection.

If only life was so simple.

With Ballesteros safely in Spain for a month of enforced rest, the battle between UMI and the ETPD began in earnest. 'My only contact [with Seve] at that time, rightly or wrongly, was through Ed Barner,' says Schofield. 'He was prepared to take out virtual injunctions against me talking to his client . . . My recollection is that there was very little in the way of letters between us. Most of it was a public shouting match at various press conferences and meetings. I can certainly vividly remember leaving one meeting at the Inter Continental Hotel on an impasse to go back to Wentworth, and being told that Ed's been on the phone nice as nine-pins, as if nothing had happened. Yet an hour earlier we were going to have all the lawyers in the world dealing with us. So that was the nature of the debate at that time.'

In June Ballesteros arrived in New York for the Westchester Classic, the richest event on the US Tour. He declined to comment on rumours that he had resolved his differences with the ETPD, prolonging the suspense with a mischievous grin, and set off to play the 6,600-yard course. The first hole is a par three of some 200 yards. Ballesteros missed the green right and dropped a stroke, holed an 18-foot putt for birdie at the next and parred the third. On the fourth he was addressing his putt when a sudden gust of wind moved his ball. He summoned a referee but to no avail. If the ball moves once you have addressed it – that is, taken your stance and grounded the club – you are deemed under the Rules of Golf to have caused it to do so, regardless of how obvious it might be that you did nothing of the kind. Ballesteros had to suffer in silence and, being human, allowed despondency to get the better of him and three-putted for a six. He was now looking for birdie opportunities and the seventh hole, a dog-leg par four of 333 yards, seemed to present itself as such. The conventional way to play the hole is to drive straight down the fairway and pitch at right angles onto the narrow green. Ballesteros elected to take a short cut through the woodlands. His drive caught a branch and fell short of the green, leaving him with no shot.

He plucked one, nevertheless, from his imagination, but hit it too strongly so it flew the green and collided with another tree. A bogey was made there and another from a greenside bunker on eight. Then at the ninth a pulled tee shot cost him an easy birdie. He turned in 44 and recorded an eventual total of 77, six over par. Needless to say, he wasn't smiling when he left the recorder's hut.

The next day, his chances of making the cut with a flawless performance were lost quite early in the round. He started on the tenth and by the time he had finished the thirteenth, where he drove wildly from the tee and lost the ball, had already dropped five strokes to par. He completed nine holes in 40, which rendered the remainder of the round a mere formality.

Off the golf course events had taken a new and rather bizarre twist. The ETPD had released a statement announcing the impending return of Ballesteros to the bosom of the European Tour, and claiming that the appearance-money dispute had been resolved. They were still saying the same thing a week later when Ballesteros teed up in the US Open at Merion. Barner, on the other hand, was insisting in 'increasingly extreme language' that it was more bitterly contested than ever. He called a press conference and informed the media with brutal frankness that the ETPD announcement was premature. Nothing whatsoever could be gleaned from Ballesteros. He was secretly afraid that anyone he spoke to would remind him of his missed tee-off time at Baltusrol, so he avoided conversation altogether. His normally sunny demeanour had vanished, to be replaced by a surly, non-committal façade, and he went about his business on the golf course with singular unenjoyment, like a prisoner in a workcamp who feels himself persecuted by his gaolers. This had no effect on his ability to manufacture miracles but it did alter his response to them. On the fourth hole in the first round he visited three bunkers in an attempt to reach the green. When he came to play his fourth shot from the unfamiliar environment of the fairway, he found his ball had been cut and was smiling at him. He pitched up to the putting surface and there succeeded in holing a 50-foot putt across a steep slope for par. Thunderous applause greeted this effort. For once, Ballesteros made no acknowledgement, but simply walked away as though weighed down by a burden too oppressive to bear.

The following Wednesday, having scored 73, 69, 72, 75 to finish forty-first at Merion, he issued a statement in which he said that he had decided not to accept membership of any tour organization for the rest of the year. He regretted that this would exclude him from the Ryder Cup, but could see no other choice. 'Having been the object of apparently intentional efforts to portray me as disloyal and mercenary,' he wrote, 'and then further being discriminated against in specific ETPD regulations, and finally to be excluded from the ETPD Order of Merit while other non-members are included, I can only say that it has hurt my feelings very much. Where I once felt at home, recent actions by some have made me feel very uncomfortable.'

In July Ballesteros made one of his rare appearances in Europe at the Scandinavian Enterprise Open, for a fee of almost $25,000 (the same amount he had been paid to play in the French Open). Whether for this, or for some other reason, he appeared to have had a change of heart. For one glorious week he was his old smiling, wryly self-deprecating self again. He marched the fairways as if he owned them, thrilling the galleries with his boldness and vigour.

'He had great imagination and flair and he had zest and ambition,' recalls Zimbabwean Mark McNulty. 'He didn't just want to be a great golfer. He wanted, I think, to be Severiano Ballesteros, the great golfer.'

'He was very intense,' says David Feherty. 'I don't think he was intentionally aloof, but he had that incredible burning ambition, that single-mindedness. A guy like Faldo is the same, although he's chosen to do it a different way. He's done it in a more clinical fashion. Ballesteros just followed his instinct. You know, there's the hole, let me get the ball into it in as few as possible.'

On the seventeenth hole in the third round the Spaniard drove deep into a forest off the tee. Most golfers would have seen only one avenue of exit: a short chip onto the fairway.

Ballesteros, thankfully, is not one of them. Having prowled about in the undergrowth for some minutes searching for options, he at last spotted a tiny fragment of sky through the surrounding foliage – a conceivable escape route only if you are one of those people who believe that trees are 90 per cent air. Ballesteros is, and his seven-iron flew cleanly through the gap and landed 10 feet from the pin for a birdie. Further manifestations of genius allowed him to record closing rounds of 68 and 66, for an eleven under par total of 273, to win his first tournament since the Dutch Open the previous summer.

The manner of his victory prompted Louis T. Stanley to observe a few months later that, 'The young Spaniard has demonstrated how a cavalier style of play, a boldness of method, can dominate opponents and courses alike. He has immense talent but unfortunately a Latin temperament that quickly becomes depressed. In many ways he is his own greatest enemy . . . Ballesteros must not put himself on a pedestal with an appearance-money price-tag on it. Quite naturally he wants to make as much money as he can from his skills but it is a mistake to use muscle in bargaining . . . Rather than risk the label of being called greedy, the Spaniard would be better advised to listen to mature advice. He will make plenty of money out of golf in good time. In the end public opinion and private friendships are more valuable than an inflated cheque. He has a considerable following and it would be sad if they were disillusioned.'

There is no telling why Ballesteros's fellow professionals first turned against him. It may, as he claimed, have been sparked by envy of his achievements and of the worth sponsors placed on him, or it may just have been a gradual erosion of the respect he had earned. It began when he broke with the time-honoured tradition of returning to defend a title, was fuelled by press reports of his avarice and then his resignation from the Tour fanned the flames. At any rate, his relationships with other players, even those who had once been close friends, started to deteriorate.

'Well, Seve in those years was going his own way,' explains Piñero. 'He thought he was right and he was doing things for himself, and a lot of people on the European

Tour, we thought he wasn't one hundred per cent right. But from what I can remember, the European Tour felt he tried to put them in a situation where it was: You or me? Seve or the European Tour? In 1981 he was a fantastic player. He had won the Masters the year before. But he forced them to choose. And I think that a lot of players felt that no matter how big you are, the European Tour has to be bigger. We all accepted that he was brilliant. That's why there was such a great discussion, otherwise there wouldn't have been . . . But one of the problems with Seve a lot of the time, is he thinks he is right all the time. And he is a person. He's right *on* the course. When you're winning a tournament and you shoot 66, you're right to get the number one prize. But when you make your opinions about the game you are a human being, and you don't win your rights by winning tournaments. I know if you win a major people will listen to you a bit more than if you're not winning anything, but then you have a responsibility to make decisions and to listen to people. The bigger you are, *I* think, the more careful you have to be with your decisions. The bigger you are, the more you have to listen to people. To me, Seve thinks he is a hundred per cent right too many times. And Seve is a human being, same as myself. Sometimes he doesn't look like a human being on the course, playing, but off the course he is a human being. He makes mistakes like anybody else.'

Only gentle Chino Fernandez spoke out in Ballesteros's defence, angry at what he felt was a 'hypocritical' attitude on the part of many of the players. 'When he was on top everybody wanted to play with him. Even on the putting green, they wanted to be nearby. When the appearance money came out in public, most of the same people that wanted to be beside him started talking against him . . . I talked to some of those players and told them that I thought they were unfair. Because every week there were a bunch of players that wanted to play a practice round with him. And then suddenly he was by himself. I don't think it was anything to do with appearance money, the way people reacted. I mean, those players didn't realize that because he was playing we had sponsorship and more spectators coming to the gate.

They didn't realize that. They could only be jealous because he was getting appearance money. I told them: "Well, next time it could be you. Or somebody else." And I said: "Who's guaranteeing that the sponsor's going to put the money that they want to pay Seve in the prize money?" They *want* Seve to play. And it's been proved that twenty-five per cent more people come through the gate when he's playing.'

Outcast by officialdom and fairweather friends, Ballesteros whiled away the long, lonely days in Pedreña, practising for hours and hours by himself, the way he had when he was a little boy. 'I felt everybody was against me,' he said later, 'and I became scared of people. I felt like I was in a restaurant alone and people whom I didn't know were talking about me.' At intervals he emerged from this term of solitary confinement to play in one of the few tournaments on his sparse schedule. He finished thirty-ninth in the Open Championship at Royal St George's, won by Bill Rogers, and was the only European to make the cut in the US PGA Championship at Atlanta Athletic Club.

But by now it was becoming increasingly obvious that, one way or the other, the great appearance-money debate had to be resolved. How it actually was is another of those wonderful mirage-like stories – the 1981 Ryder Cup saga is the most infamous (as we shall see) – which looks all very realistic and convincing when contemplated from a distance, but has a tendency to fall to pieces under close surveillance. Ostensibly, Ballesteros was fast using up his exemptions in America, was tired of flying back and forth to Japan, and had finally accepted that the European Tour would not be bending the rules on his account. On 11 August he formally reinstated himself into the ETPD. This was taken to mean that he had settled his differences with the tournament committee over appearance money. Barner then sent out a bland statement to the effect that, 'The accomplishments of ETPD members in this year's Open Championship indicate that the day is not far off when ETPD events may not need the extra drawing power of American professionals. This could signal the end of guarantees and a dramatic rise in the prize money on the European Tour.' Ballesteros was then welcomed back into the fold with open arms and all was seen to be well.

Soon after this ceasefire Schofield came across the Spaniard in the transit lounge at Heathrow airport, where he was awaiting a connecting flight to Liverpool for the European Open. They exchanged careful greetings, then stood for a moment or two in awkward silence. 'I just want to play golf,' Ballesteros suddenly burst out.

'I just want you to play golf,' said Schofield reassuringly. And they made a pact then and there that they would not be revisiting the 'desolation' of that year with anyone – which they haven't. But they did endure an initially unpleasant period where the same journals that had reported that Ballesteros had been 'stripped of his membership' and had 'his hand slapped because he was asking for appearance money' after his resignation, insisted that he had been 'forced to admit that he wasn't bigger than the game and, tail between his legs, had re-entered the ETPD.' But then it all died down and these days hardly anyone ever mentions it.

As to who was responsible for the whole unfortunate business, no-one can ever say. Collet admits that at that age he thought he was 'a pretty tough, savvy manager. I probably just thought it was a pretty clever thing to do. It may not have been in the best taste, but it turned out all right on the commercial side. The regrettable part, really, was the fact that we had no control over, and we had no reason to believe it would be a problem, the Ryder Cup situation.'

Jacobs thinks that the blame should be apportioned equally between all three parties involved, and that one individual should not have to stand trial for the misdeeds of several. 'Who was at fault? The Tour was at fault, in the first place. It was premature to do what they did because Seve was Masters champion at the time and it meant he couldn't cash in completely here in Europe when the prize money was still not comparable at all with that of America. Secondly, Seve's advisers were not very helpful. But Seve himself is very strong-minded and very wilful, as you know. I mean, the strength of his whole game is the strength of his character. He's a *very* strong character and he was very, very upset.'

'I don't think Seve ever took the view: "I'm the greatest in the world and they can all go to hell",' says Jacklin. 'I don't think that for a minute. But I do think he was a pawn in a game for a while. He was – "mismanaged" is the wrong word maybe – but I don't think his manager did him any favours, certainly, PR-wise, and it was Seve who was carrying the can for it . . .

'I think he was badly represented, that's what I think,' continues Jacklin. 'I went through that with IMG. When you're young, as I was and Seve was, you need the guidance of somebody who's older and wiser to tell you how to behave, and what you must do and what you mustn't do. And all you were to those managers – Ed Barner for Seve and Mark McCormack for me – was a money-making machine, and they never looked upon you as anything other than someone who was going to make it for them. Send you off to play these tournaments after the British Open . . . When I won I went to Westchester and I said, "You know, I'm not interested in playing here." Understandably, I was exhausted. He said: "£250,000 first prize [which was the biggest first prize in golf then] and you can't get interested!" I said, "I'm not a machine, Mark." And your involvement with them is such that you can't get out, or at least you can't get out without a lot of hassle. And you're playing golf and you don't want hassle, so you let it go . . . They just use you as money-making objects.'

'I regret 1981, of course I do,' says Schofield feelingly. 'I mean, I was so close to what was happening and the general mood of the situation, in terms of the Ryder Cup, that I think it doesn't do any good to look back. If you were going to try and look for something good that came out of it, the only positive thing could be that it left such a deep impression on everybody, not least Severiano, who, for a time in his life felt he might never play Ryder Cup golf again . . . the pain and discomfort of 1981 may have given him an extra dimension to say to himself, "I will now show the world how committed I am. If anybody ever doubted it, they must have been very mistaken." So in a perverse way, it may have done some good.'

What wasn't so good, from Schofield's point of view, was the speed at which the spectre of appearance money returned to haunt him. All things considered, Ballesteros never really stopped getting it. With the exception of the Open Championship and events on the US Tour, he was paid every time he teed up in 1981. And then gradually it became generally understood that if you had won a major championship or had finished in the top three on the Order of Merit, you were entitled to appearance money. A decade on, it had spread like a virus and become a massive problem again, with players like Ballesteros, Nick Faldo and Ian Woosnam earning well in excess of £60,000 before they had struck a golf ball each week. So Schonfield climbed up on his high horse and read the riot act about the principles – or lack of them – involved in appearance money, and the whole thing started up all over again. Only this time Ballesteros wasn't held up as an example.

I don't think there's anything the matter with it,' argues Collet. 'It's business . . . The guys that gripe about it are the guys that don't have enough charisma to be able to command it. You should talk to Lionel Provost who runs PromoGolf in France. This whole thing of appearance money created stars, and stars created spectacles and now France is a major golfing power in Europe. If they hadn't brought over stars and paid them fees, where would golf in France be? They still have no French golfers that are worth two cents. And who does that affect? That affects the Chris Moodys of this world who benefit from having bigger purses and more tournaments to play in. I think there's a very sound argument to be made in favour of it.'

In 1992, after a two-year investigation into appearance money by the tournament players' committee, with the co-operation of every sponsor, golf association and federation, the European Tour finally came up with a set of guidelines on how a golfer may be officially encouraged to consider your tournament in his playing schedule. 'Most people are adult anough to know that business is business,' says Schonfield frankly. 'If Nick Faldo has signed a contract with the General Accident Assurance Corporation immediately after they've secured sponsorship of the European Open and, yes, part and parcel of that is that he will play in three of their tournaments, I don't think anybody regards that as appearance money. *I* certainly don't. The players don't.

The sponsors don't. Mr Barner's position was different. His was: "Here is a gun. You send me a cheque for $25,000 and my man will play. No cheque, he will not play". You know, that was it.'

The interesting part about 1981 is that, according to Collet, the battle only ended when the European Tour 'basically just gave up and said anybody could get appearance money. Ever since then, there's been no problem. Until 1991, when they started saying, "Boys, now that the Tour's grown a lot, wouldn't it be better in an ideal world if we didn't have this? And most of the golfers said, "Well, if we can be sure that nobody's cheating and everybody's being treated the same, fine." So then the PGA devised this bonus pool thing . . . and they also invented this Champion's Challenge format, where they coincidentally pay rather high fees for this other event which is the same week as the PGA Championship, but only the top guys are invited, and then they play the PGA Championship because it's such a *great* event. But they've tried to meet 'em halfway and I respect their creativity with what they're trying to do. I'm not going to say it's hypocrisy and double standards. I'm going to say, I think the Tour understands that this is a fiction of our times and it goes on. It's like, everybody smokes pot, so what are you going to do? Keep arresting people? Or, short of making it legal, you just place a little fine on it so that you can show that socially it's unacceptable behaviour *but* we're not going to persecute people. That's kind of what they've done with appearance money. They've said: "We realize there's no way we can stop it; we've gone through this battle with Seve. Let's just all call it something else and agree that they do something else and, as long as those two conditions exist, we'll just turn our backs to it." For my business, it's business as usual. Nothing has changed. We won a major battle for European golfers to be on equal footing with American golfers coming over here, back when Seve did that, and everybody should applaud him for taking that stance.'

At the end of that controversial season, Louis T. Stanley wrote an epitaph for the Spaniard in the *Pelham Golf*

Yearbook: 'The tragedy of 1981 has been the virtual eclipse of Severiano Ballesteros. The endless, tiresome hassle over appearance money left him isolated and a stranger to the European Tour. His visits to America were disastrous and best forgotten. Scandinavia produced a ray of hope, but one swallow does not compensate for the losses. The decision not to agree to his demands is right. In no way can the Spaniard justify special treatment. The hard and expensive lesson he has learnt from the sorry business is that the game can do without him. By now nobody comments on his absence. He belongs to yesterday and nothing is duller than old news.'

9

No Easy Ryder

The curiously comical aspect of everyday events conceals from us the very real suffering caused by our passions.

Barnave, *Scarlet and Black*, Stendhal

The Ryder Cup affair began innocently enough – like all of these things do – with a phone call and a promise. At that time Ballesteros was still considered the *bête noire* of professional golf, was still in the United States and was still giving the ETPD a run for their money (so to speak); but he was fast wearying of the struggle. He missed the amiable eccentricity of British and Continental Tour events and the easygoing camaraderie of Europe's players, he missed Spain and Spanish food and speaking Spanish, and he missed his home and family. And so it was that a month or six weeks before the Benson and Hedges International at Fulford in York, the last event with points counting towards Ryder Cup selection, he was sitting in his hotel room, pondering the chances of a peaceable reconciliation with the hierarchy at Wentworth – and the subsequent resolution of the apparently irreconcilable differences between them, when the telephone rang.

'Yes,' snapped Ballesteros abruptly, for he has a passionate dislike of the instrument.

'Hallo? Hallo, good evening, sorry to trouble you . . .

Would it be possible to speak to Seve Balles . . . ? Oh, Seve, it's John Jacobs here.'

The conversation that ensued was one of notable ambiguity – notable because how else could it have retained its news value or capacity to wound or provoke anger for more than a decade? In essence, Jacobs, who was to captain the 1981 Ryder Cup team, was trying to persuade Ballesteros to return to Europe and attempt to play his way into the Ryder Cup, which he could do quite easily by improving his Order of Merit standing, since the top ten players on the money list would automatically be awarded places. The final two members of the team were to be elected in a meeting at Fulford, venue of the Benson and Hedges International, by the Ryder Cup committee – in this case, Jacobs, Neil Coles, and Bernhard Langer, the season's leading money winner. 'If you don't qualify automatically,' Jacobs allegedly told the Spaniard (*Golf World*, September 1991), 'I can't promise you a hundred per cent that you will be in, but I promise you that you will have my vote.'

'Which I believed meant I would be in,' says Ballesteros, 'because he was the captain and the captain is the one who chooses the players. If I was the captain, even though I might have consulted with Bernhard Langer and Neil Coles, the other people on the committee, ultimately it would be my decision. Anyway, those were the words Jacobs used.'

Jacobs, however, insists that what he actually said was: 'Seve, I can't guarantee you'll be in the team. I'm one of three. If you will come and play in the Irish Open and the B&H, that strengthens my position very much more.'

'But that's not easy to explain to someone that doesn't speak English very well,' says Jacobs, 'and who probably didn't understand the actual voting situation. He said: "Oh, I'm playing very badly." And he was very down and he was cross and he was anti. And he didn't come and play, and therefore I had no leg to stand on. But Seve's reported as having said that I said that I could definitely get him on the team. And I couldn't.'

Now in 1981 the Ryder Cup was a subject already very

near to Ballesteros's heart. No sooner was Jacobs off the line when he had repeated the exchange, verbatim, to Joe Collet and Ed Barner and, partly for the reasons previously listed, i.e. that the European Tour 'basically just gave up and said anybody could get appearance money,' etc, and partly because he believed Jacobs to have virtually pledged him a place on the team, he was reinstated as an ETPD member before many moons had passed and was looking forward with some pleasure to the matches at Walton Heath on 18 September. There was only one snag. Because the negotiations between UMI and the Tour had taken several weeks to conclude, they had effectively put an end to any hopes that Ballesteros might have had of trying to earn his way back into the Ryder Cup team. As a result, he (or his management company) decided that it was hardly worth him entering the few European Tour events remaining that did officially count towards Ryder Cup selection – not even the Benson and Hedges, which aroused an enormous amount of displeasure and almost certainly had a bearing on the final outcome of the situation – when he was bound to be one of the wild card choices of the committee anyway.

Well, the day of the meeting at Fulford rolled round and Ballesteros was conspicuous by his absence. Jacobs, rather unhappily, set off in the afternoon to interview the existing team members on whether or not they thought the Spaniard should play at Walton Heath. Of the ten of them, excluding Langer, but including Nick Faldo, Bernard Gallacher, Des Smyth, Jose Maria Canizares, Eamonn Darcy, Sandy Lyle, Sam Torrance, Howard Clark and Manuel Piñero, only Gallacher felt that Ballesteros merited a Ryder Cup place. 'You're the captain,' he told Jacobs, 'but if I were captain I would want Seve in the team.' 'Everybody else said no,' recalls Jacobs. 'The Spanish boys, for instance, like Piñero, who are his friends, all thought that Seve was behaving very badly by arguing and not coming to play and so on. So when this meeting started, with the three of us, I said: "Well, what do you think about Seve?" And both [Neil and Bernhard] said: "NO!" I said: "Well, that's the end of that then." *I* wanted him in but . . .'

But Jacobs didn't say so – at least, not in so many words. He seems to have taken it for granted that Coles and Langer were aware that that's what he would have liked to say, had the circumstances been altered, and then accepted his position as hopeless without bothering to try to assert himself, which he had every right to do as captain.

'But everybody *knew* I wanted Seve,' insists Jacobs. 'Because I went and argued his case at the Tour headquarters in May and they were there then. Neil Coles knew, but Neil was adamant that he shouldn't be in. Neil would substantiate that he and Bernhard Langer said no.' He clicks his tongue in exasperation. 'When people say, "*John Jacobs* voted against Seve . . ." *I* was a committee of three. Now in 1979 Seve was on that committee. *He* was the leader of the Order of Merit. And we sat down at the Irish Open at Royal Dublin, Seve, Neil Coles and myself, to choose the next two [wild card players]. And on that occasion Neil Coles said, "John, you're the captain, tell us who you want". I didn't get that in 1981, because if I had I would have said Seve straight away. But then Neil knew I would have said that.'

To Ballesteros, the news that he had been cast cruelly aside by the Ryder Cup committee was a bolt from the blue – utterly unforeseen, unheralded and unexpected. It struck him forcibly, like a body-blow. He felt fury, he felt pain and sheer bewilderment, but, more than anything, he felt the deep sting of betrayal. 'Manuel Piñero and Jose Maria Canizares had both said I should not be on the team,' he later recalled. 'That was a pity. I was very disappointed at that because I always felt that I helped them and that they were good friends. I don't know if it was jealousy or whatever but it was the one time they could help me and the one time they could hurt me, and they chose the second option.'

'I do remember John Jacobs asking me how I felt,' says Piñero defensively, 'but in the end it wasn't our decision. It was the decision of three persons. And today, because of what happened to the Ryder Cup and because of what happened with Seve's career, those three persons are still trying to find an excuse for what happened. But if we hadn't won the Ryder Cup in 'eighty-five, and if Seve wasn't as good as he's been, nobody would have any discussion at all. Nobody. You have to make the decision that seems right at the time [because you haven't got the benefit of hindsight]. I don't remember very well, but I think I said to John, "Seve's good enough to be on the team, but he's not doing the right thing to be on the team." But if you put me in the same situation again, I'd probably do the same thing. I did what I did and I stand by it. I will not try to excuse myself.'

Piñero's role in the drama, however, along with that of every other team member, ended when he gave his opinion to his captain. Thereafter, the responsibility for what was, ultimately, a masterpiece of tragicomedy, became the sole property of Messrs Jacobs, Coles and Langer. They started their meeting by establishing, collectively or individually, that Ballesteros was not going to be in the Ryder Cup team, and then turned their attention to selecting the players who were. There were three contenders: Mark James and Tony Jacklin, who occupied the eleventh and twelfth positions on the Order of Merit, and Peter Oosterhuis, who played the US Tour more or less full time, but who had never lost a Ryder Cup singles match, and had also just won the Canadian Open. 'We all agreed on Peter Oosterhuis,' says Jacobs, taking up the story. 'No question. He was the obvious next one. And, of course, it would have been Peter Oosterhuis and Seve. That's who it *should* have been. *Not* Tony Jacklin. Tony was at the end of his career. Tony couldn't knock a putt in to save his life . . . [although] he was still a very good player . . . But it always hurt me that Tony should be that upset because we chose someone who was ahead of him in the averages. Tony and Vivienne [Jacklin] were tremendously supportive of me in 1979. But I had to dismiss all these things in lending my voice, and the three of us were absolutely at one about Peter Oosterhuis. And we had a lot of discussion about Tony or Mark James, and in the end the three of us came down to Mark James. But I stupidly said, "Well, we didn't pick Tony because we think he was probably too old." As opposed to me saying, "Well, I don't think he's playing as well as he used to and his career's coming to an end." '

Jacobs was correct about Jacklin's reaction. He was upset.

Very, very upset. But the battalion of emotions that marched through the fevered mists of his brain when he found out that he wasn't on the team were mere cadets when compared to the detachment of crack troops that went on the warpath when he found who he had been replaced by. In theory, the Spaniard's Ryder Cup place had been given away to Oosterhuis, while Jacklin's had been handed to James. In practice, it made not an iota of difference. The facts, whether you dress them up as sheep in wolves' clothing or wolves in sheep's clothing, are always the facts. Ballesteros, one of the greatest players ever to strike a golf ball; and Jacklin, who was still a good golfer by anyone's definition, even at the ripe old age of *thirty-seven*, and who had played well enough at that stage in the season to hoist himself into twelfth place on the money list, had been passed over in favour of one of the players who had wantonly disrupted the 1979 Ryder Cup.

'The thing that surprised me,' says Ballesteros, 'although I have great respect for him and we are now good friends, was that Mark James was picked and I wasn't. In 1979 Mark James was fined for bad behaviour during the Ryder Cup. It was a joke that they went for Mark James instead of me in 1981.'

Now let us turn the clock back a few years so that you can fully appreciate the punchline.

The Ryder Cup owes its existence and its name to Samuel Ryder, an English seed-merchant who had been advised to take up golf for the good of his health (physical, that is). After a time he came to prize the professional game above all else and because of this did two exceptionally generous things: a. He engaged Abe Mitchell, one of the finest post-war British players, as his personal teacher, so that Mitchell would not be burdened with the duties of a club professional and would be able to devote his energies wholly to practice and to tournaments; b. He donated a trophy to the PGA in 1926 for use in an international match, the purpose of which would be to foster goodwill between the golfers of the USA and those of Great Britain and Ireland. The former was a noble gesture and worth a good deal to Mitchell and to golf generally, but it is the latter for which Ryder will always be remembered. He invented a tournament which might, ultimately, come to symbolize an entire game.

The early Ryder Cup matches were doubtless entertaining and full of incident, but by 1977 they had become so predictable and dull they were in danger of extinction. Only three times since their inception had the British carried home the trophy: every time the Americans teed up they won. This had its thrills initially but these quickly wore off, and the day came when Tom Weiskopf, having earned himself a place on the team, elected to go elk hunting rather than participate in the matches. Jack Nicklaus then wrote to Lord Derby, the president of the British PGA, saying he feared for the future of the Ryder Cup unless something was done to revive interest in it. Knowing that, at twenty, Ballesteros was the best golfer in Europe, he suggested that Continental players be included in the British and Irish team.

Thus, when the 1979 Ryder Cup team went to the Greenbrier at White Sulphur Springs in West Virginia, two of its members were Spanish. That was the match that five men and a dog went to see, for it was held in the Deep South and Lee Elder, the first black Ryder Cup player, was on the American side. It was also the week where Sam Snead, who had once been pro at the Greenbrier but who had fallen out with the club, sneaked onto the premises to see Ballesteros, whom he had long looked forward to meeting. And it was the week where the Spaniard sacked his caddie, a local boy, after only one day. Jacobs, who was captain that year, considered Ballesteros and Antonio Garrido to be the most outstanding of Europe's twelve players, and sent them out first in the fourballs on the opening day. That was all well and to the good, but they came up against Lanny Wadkins and Larry Nelson. Wadkins is a formidable opponent under any circumstances, but Nelson was in the peak of form and playing electrifying golf. When the pair of them reached the turn, they had a betterball score of 28, which led inexorably to a win of two and one. 'Garrido and I played against Larry Nelson and Lanny Wadkins three times and they beat us three times,' says Ballesteros admiringly. 'They played brilliantly.

Nobody could have beaten them. They were unbelievable.

'We played against Fuzzy Zoeller and Hubert Green in the first day foursomes and there was a bit of an incident on the sixteenth green, where we won the match. Antonio conceded a putt to Hubert and he threw the ball back to him with his putter. I guess Hubert was upset because he was losing. Whatever, he started to say something in English and Antonio got upset, and it was a very difficult situation there. I remember I had to stand in between them. They both got very cross and I nearly had to act as referee. At that moment I could see that the Ryder Cup was important. Even though we didn't play for money, we played for pride.'

Pride or no, when the fat lady sang it was the American anthem that played: the US team had strolled to yet another victory, with a score of sixteen to ten and two matches halved. At least, that is what the record books say. What they don't say is that behind the scenes the Europeans had been handicapped by the tomfoolery of Mark James and Ken Brown.

'They behaved unbelievably stupidly,' says Jacobs, still capable of experiencing incredulity at what occurred after all these years, 'and I'm blowed if I know why. Right from the word go, when they appeared at the airport dressed as though they were going on a camping holiday . . . they just set out to be as disruptive as possible. It welded the other ten together. The other ten performed wonderfully. You must appreciate, we were going into the singles one point behind and I hadn't had the services of those two, and Seve and Garrido had only won one point . . . What did they do? Well, the opening ceremony is a flag-raising thing and it's televised, and on that occasion we were all to meet in the room that had been set aside for any team discussions. Those two guys didn't show up . . . Finally they did show . . . but they wouldn't stand to attention and just chatted away. At the dinner the night before the Ryder Cup started, when people were taking pictures, they covered their faces. Wouldn't have their pictures taken with the team. I mean, incredible things . . . James pulled a muscle on the first morning playing with Ken Brown, so I had to play Brown in the afternoon with Des Smyth. And, of course, he hit a couple of bad shots early on and then just didn't talk to anybody. Just hit it and walked up the fairway. And I had to apologize to Des Smyth in front of the whole team.'

Ballesteros, who Jacobs describes as 'a superb member of the team', was so horrified at how demoralized the other ten players became that he immediately went, cap in hand, to Angel Gallardo, his captain at the Hennessy Cup in 1978, and apologized profusely for his own behaviour then, which had also been less than exemplary.

The truly amazing thing about the Ryder Cup saga, though, is that, if you met those two delinquents now, you would refuse to believe that the complete episode was not a figment of the over-active imagination of the media and one or two officials. I mean, Brown is as quiet as a mouse, with nice manners and a sweet smile, and James has a wonderfully dry sense of humour, and is one of the most popular and admired players on the circuit. Both of them have played in several Ryder Cups since 1979 and have been models of decorum and contributed greatly to the overall success of the matches. The contrast is so striking, in fact, that when I interviewed Jacklin I put it to him that they might have been unfairly criticized.

He looked at me as if I had suddenly grown horns. A spasm of pure white rage crossed his face. He made an almost visible effort to control himself, then burst out vehemently: '*Unfairly criticized!* I would have sent them home. If I had been the captain, I would have sent them home. They didn't turn up for meetings, treated everything as a joke, didn't stand to attention for the Queen when the flag was raised; Mark James ordered six hamburgers – there was only him there! – and just signed the bill and left it. I mean, pranks that my children would have never ever played. Beyond belief, as I say. It wasn't just childishness, it was sheer effort to disrupt everything. They folded their arms when the flag was going up and the anthem was being played . . . and just general behaviour that was totally unacceptable. I remember my wife then, Vivienne, and Lesley Gallacher, taking them outside during dinner one night, and just saying, "What do you think you're playing at?" They were just like . . . like yobs. And I would have sent them home. But the effect that their behaviour had on the team was devastating, because there was no team unity there at all. It

174

was ten [good] guys and those two. And we were putting a front on. But you can't play and win matches like that. And so what I could never understand was why Jacobs condoned it. But what we tried to do, and what I did – I said, "The guy [Jacobs] deserves another chance. He had those two in the team." And then he goes and picks one of them again! Now I don't understand that kind of mentality. If somebody treats me badly and lets me down, I'm not saying they don't deserve a second chance, but I'd certainly find a different way to give them a chance. I wouldn't give them the chance to screw up again.'

Brown had no excuses when I questioned him about it. 'In those days it was less of a team effort,' he says simply. 'We were a team but there wasn't really team spirit, which is what Jacko and Seve brought in in 'eighty-three. It was just a catalogue of minor incidents that would have ended if the captain had stood up and said: "Come on, lads, this is a team effort." But that wasn't Jacobs' way. But I'm not blaming the captain at all. If we'd been doing things properly [in other words, if they had not had plastic shoes, poor quality bags and bargain-basement team uniforms], we wouldn't have been doing these things at all. Did I regret it afterwards? Well, I'd have loved someone to say something at the time. At the actual time of the event I didn't really think we had done a terrible amount wrong, but when you add it all up . . .'

However, this sorry chronicle does explain why Ballesteros and Jacklin were so outraged by the actions of the Ryder Cup committee in 1981. To begin with, an attempt *was* made to salve the feelings of the Englishman, by inviting him to Walton Heath in an official capacity, but there was nothing but an embarrassed silence on the part of those people who had, willingly or unknowingly, conspired to ensure that the Spaniard was left out of the team. 'I told them to stick it in their ear,' said Jacklin candidly some while later. 'I was so disgusted with the way that it was dealt with. And I didn't want anything else to do with the Ryder Cup . . . And if I was mad Seve was twice as mad, because he was that much younger than I was and his Spanish blood was boiling, as you can well imagine.'

Indeed it was. The week after the decision was made, Ballesteros told the press that he did not deserve to be in the team and that it did not bother him one way or the other. That is typical of him. The more hurt or angry he is about something the more he will try to turn it around and either use it against himself or pretend it couldn't matter less. He usually accompanies this with a brave and extra-bright smile, which is so transparently not a happy one that every heart in the room goes out to him. But years on, when he was asked by Robert Green of *Golf World* whether he thought he would have been selected if he had played in the Benson and Hedges International, Ballesteros replied, 'We are talking about revenge here. It's like Nick Faldo not playing the German Open . . . and the captain saying: "If he doesn't play the German Open I'm not going to choose him." It's like revenge – it's a personal feeling between two [people] against the team and against European golf. That's not the way to do it. If I were the captain I would pick the best players as wild cards, even if I didn't like them personally, because that is the best way for the team and for European golf. It's a tremendous mistake to let personal feelings interfere with that decision.'

In thinking this he was not alone. A number of journalists, supported by the public and a proportion of the players, took Jacobs and his cohorts 'to court' on these and other charges, and returned a verdict of guilty. Bill Longmuir considered Ballesteros's omission from the team to be 'the most ridiculous decision that has ever been made'. He unconsciously echoed Jacklin, who had called it 'the single most ridiculous thing that's ever happened in the Ryder Cup.' '[Seve] had not really played enough golf in Europe to establish himself in the numbers situation,' says Longmuir. 'He was having a war with the European Tour . . . and he was playing a fair amount in America. But he was in no man's land, really. He was an unhappy man, there was no question about that. But the bottom line, in my mind, was that at that time he was still our best player. He was our greatest strength. Somebody voted against him, I don't know who it was, but it was the wrong decision. Seve is such a force to be reckoned with that you cannot afford to leave him out of the Ryder Cup team. I know, he's done the wrong things at times and said the wrong things but, you know, he's a golf pro, he's not a politician.'

'I think most people were of the opinion that if Seve had wanted to play in the Ryder Cup, all he had to do was tee up in the last tournament and win something like £1,000,' says James. 'And since he's obviously capable of that, most of us wondered why he didn't do that. And also, he treated the Tour with such contempt that year that I don't think anyone had any sympathy for him, and I think he would not have enhanced the team spirit at all. I think he was very unpopular with most players around that time. He was milking the Tour and players simply didn't like it. The prize money wasn't high enough then to be able to stand huge appearance money fees. I wasn't very pleased. I would have liked the situation to change. But I think the feedback from players in general that year was that they weren't keen on Seve . . . If he wanted to play in the Ryder Cup, he could have just played the last event and he would have got in. So he wasn't keen on playing in it.'

'All he had to do was play one more tournament and he would have been in the team anyway,' agrees Langer. 'And he decided not to do that. Just to prove the point. He [also] went to Japan, and gave his card back. He didn't want to be a member of the Tour. And [he did] all sorts of things which weren't very good for the image of the Tour. And then in return he expected the committee to vote him on the team. We probably should have done on his playing ability, but we felt he wouldn't have been a good man for the team. It's a team effort and when you have people going their own way, totally opposed to what [rules and regulations] they should abide by, and then you get those people in the team, it's difficult. It might not be fair to the others.'

'Seve felt that he had been betrayed,' recalls Collet. 'Putting aside the fact that he had played from a rather strong position and withdrawn his membership – that's all fair in love and war – but overtures were made, you know, "Come back, everything will be all right and it won't affect the Ryder Cup." And then you do that and it's reneged on . . . To this day, Seve does not know what happened. And we never will. Because John Jacobs, Bernhard Langer and Neil Coles all tell a story which absolves them completely of any blame. So one of them is not remembering what happened correctly, put it that way.'

Ballesteros continues: 'Two years later, at the 1983 match in Florida, Bernhard Langer approached me during the opening ceremony [Langer denies this] and said: "Seve, I want to explain about the situation in 1981. I want to make sure that you understand that I wasn't the one who voted against you. Neil Coles and John Jacobs did." I said: "Thank you, Bernhard, nice to hear that from you. I appreciate it." Nearly two more years later, Jacobs called me in to the office at the PGA European Tour and we had a chat. Ken Schofield, the executive director of the Tour, was there. Jacobs said that he had read an article in which I said I didn't understand why Jacobs had voted against me. Jacobs said: "No, that's not what happened. I asked Neil, and Neil said no, and I asked Bernhard, and Bernhard said no, and so I was in the position that I didn't have any other way to go. So we all went for no." '

One morning in April 1983, nearly eighteen months after the deplorable and rather fantastic sequence of events that culminated in the repudiation of two of Europe's best players by the Ryder Cup committee, Jacklin was practising his putting stroke only minutes before going out to play a tournament, when Schofield walked up to him and calmly asked him to captain the 1983 Ryder Cup team.

Jacklin was dumbfounded. His immediate response was: 'How the hell can they invite me to do this when what's gone on's gone on?' But since he didn't hold Schofield responsible for what had happened, he agreed to at least consider the proposal. 'I was angry, angry as hell. But I kept saying, "If I do it, I want to do it my way." I said, "I want Concorde; I want an unlimited amount of clothing; I want our guys to feel equal to the Americans when they stand on the tee." And every demand I made, they accepted. It came to the point where they had accepted all that, so I was that far down the road, and then I sort of said to myself: "Now hang on. Are you going to keep a vendetta going with this thing for ever?" And it was clear that the Ryder Cup was going to survive much longer than me or anybody else. So I decided at that point to let bygones be bygones and to do it.'

But the biggest hurdle was never going to be persuading Jacklin to captain the Ryder Cup team. It was going to be winning over Ballesteros, who, at that time in his life, could scarcely have been more disinclined to participate in the matches or less well disposed towards anybody who may, even by association, have been guilty of complicity or duplicity in the 1981 affair. This is where Schofield was smart. He knew that Jacklin would be the ace in his pack. He realized that in Ballesteros's present frame of mind the only man who could hope to win him over was the player who had suffered the same fate he had and at the same hands. 'Well, if I couldn't do it, nobody could,' agrees Jacklin. 'Lord Derby, who was president at the time, didn't want to talk to him. So I went to talk to him at the Prince of Wales Hotel in Southport. He listened and listened and listened and he started arguing. I said, "There's no point arguing with me because I *know* . . . But at the same time, Seve, you've had a bloody tough stretch. You've been on the carpet for appearance money and this, that and the other, and I'm not sure your image is everything it should be in this country. You're a great player and you've got my total sympathy. I know what you're going through. You're Spanish, you're trying to play somewhere else, you're trying to do your best everywhere, you want everybody to love you and it's getting mixed up. But trust me when I tell you, if you do this and let bygones be bygones and we can make this work, you will have an unbelievable following in this country because they'll adopt you as their own."'

But the wounds were still too raw for Ballesteros to forgive and forget as easily as Jacklin might have wanted him to. All the hurt and anger he had been suppressing for so long came rushing out in a tide of invective as he told the Englishman, in a few choice phrases, exactly what he thought of those who had spurned him. When he ran out of steam he didn't exactly say yes, but he didn't say no either. 'I thought he was going to do it,' admits Jacklin. 'I was able to say to him, "We're going to go by Concorde, we're going to have the best golf bags, we're going to have the best cashmere blazers, we're going to have whatever *you* want. We'll do the thing together. You can be my sounding board on the golf course. Together we can make it happen." And, of course, he came round. And that was the beginning.'

In the second week of October 1983 the European team flew by Concorde to Florida – unlike their luckless British counterparts of 1951 who, it was recorded, 'travelled cabin class in the *Queen Mary* instead of first class when they crossed the Atlantic for the Ryder Cup match. The savings were approximately £1,250.' When they arrived at PGA National in Palm Beach Gardens, they found that the Americans, while less complacent than they had been in the past, were confident that victory was a foregone conclusion.

'The heat,' explained Nicklaus, the US captain, listing off the reasons why his team were unlikely to be beaten. 'The Europeans won't be accustomed to it. There's the Bermuda grass. They won't know too much about that. Then there's the fact that we win most of the time . . . If you *feel* you should win then more often than not you do.'

How prophetic his words almost were, but not in the way he intended them to be: after the first day's play Europe led the United States by 4½ points to 3½. One of those points – earned in the afternoon fourballs against Raymond Floyd and Curtis Strange – had been contributed by Ballesteros and Paul Way, who, to the amazement of all, the European captain had paired together.

'[Paul Way] needed help,' says Jacklin frankly. 'I know how I felt when I played my first Ryder Cup in 1967. You're as nervous as hell. You need the comfort of somebody looking after you. That's why. I mean, there's another view; you say, "He's a cocky little bugger, he'll get by." But that never works. The stress and the tension are so difficult to cope with.'

Ballesteros accepted the pairing without a murmur, and it wasn't until lunchtime on the second day of play that Jacklin realized anything was amiss. Angel Gallardo approached him wearing a nervous frown. 'You should talk to Seve,' he told the Englishman.

'Why?' said Jacklin, alarmed.

'Well, he's not happy.'

Jacklin needed no further bidding, and at once went looking for the Spaniard. He found him in the far corner of the locker room, brooding.

'Everything all right?' said Jacklin briskly. 'Any problems?'

Ballesteros made no reply; he was wrestling with his conscience. He stood up abruptly. It was a sweltering day and the air was sticky and oppressive. His pink shirt clung to him wetly. He peeled it off and, flinging it down on the bench, blurted out: 'This *boy*! This Paul Way! I can't believe it. I'm holding his hand all the time. Every shot, I'm trying to play my shot, I'm trying to play his shot. I feel like his father.'

'Seve,' said Jacklin quietly, 'you are his father in here.' He touched his temple. 'That's why you're playing with him. Is that a problem?'

Ballesteros held a mental debate. He came to a decision. 'For me,' he said proudly, 'it's no problem.'

'And they [Ballesteros and Way] went out there in the afternoon and won again,' says Jacklin. 'And ironically, Paul Way won his singles match and Seve only got a half – which, because Seve is so hard on himself, he blamed himself for. "If *I'd* won my match we would have done this, that and the other . . . !" But, I mean, his contribution has not just been what he's personally achieved during the matches. It's the rub off that other people have had because of his presence, as well.'

'He's always been the absolute inspiration to the team,' says Ken Brown, 'and Tony got him a hundred per cent on his side. In 1983, a couple of matches he almost won single-handed.'

'I thought he was God at the time and I thought: "We cannot lose," ' recalls Way. 'We only lost one game so I was nearly right . . . I found it easy playing with him because he encouraged me and wherever I put him, specially in the foursomes, he would make up for it. So it eased the pressure, really . . . I always remember he over-helped me. He was going, "Do this, do that." And I just didn't really listen to him after a while. I just did what I wanted. But he was very helpful.'

It was in the singles matches at PGA National that Ballesteros hit one of the greatest golf shots in the history of the game. His opponent was Fuzzy Zoeller, the 1979 Masters champion and a strong, exceptionally talented player. The Spaniard had fallen behind at the second but had recovered with four consecutive birdies, whereupon the American promptly won four holes in a row. They were all square when they came to the last hole, a magnificent 578-yard par five, with sand all down the left and water down the right. There, Ballesteros hit what he later described as 'one of the worst drives of my life.' It buried itself almost invisibly in the deep, tangled and all but unplayable Bermuda grass rough on a bank above the face of a bunker. He slashed at it with all his might with a wedge, but only succeeded in moving it 20 yards forward into another bunker, where it finished on an upslope, just underneath the lip. It was the stuff of nightmares. What could he do but play out sideways with a sand-wedge?

Zoeller, meanwhile, was having problems of his own. After driving into the rough, he had played out sideways and now faced a two-iron shot to the green. He turned to watch the Spaniard, who was pacing up and down like a tiger, his face dark with fury and determination. There was a three-wood in his hand. He was going to try for the green. Zoeller stared at him in amazement. He watched as Ballesteros climbed into the bunker, aimed 50 yards left of the flagstick, wriggled his feet deep in the sand and then lashed at the ball with every ounce of strength in his body. It shot out of the bunker like a rocket, flew an incredible 245 yards and finished on the fringe of the green, from where he got up and down for a half.

'That was one of the best shots of my life,' said Ballesteros afterwards, while an incredulous Nicklaus described it as 'one of the greatest shots I have ever seen.'

'I think that was one of the greatest shots that was ever struck,' says Ben Crenshaw sincerely. 'I mean, it was unbelievable. And only Seve has the audacity to try something like that, and he did it. It was just unbelievable.'

But Ballesteros' joy was blighted by Europe's loss by a single point (11–12) to the United States. 'I think we were very unlucky,' he says. 'There was a lot of frustration because we thought we played well enough to tie at least. It was like losing in a play-off – it was very sad. Nearly the whole team cried on the eighteenth when we lost.'

Incredibly enough, there is an epilogue to the saga of 1981. Jacobs claims that ten years later, at the end of season PGA European Tour dinner which, as he says was 'a great *tour de force* for Seve,' Ballesteros walked up to him and said: 'I'm told I was wrong.' 'And we made our friendship up again,' he explains. 'And he said, "But why did Bernhard tell me you have voted against me"? And I said, "Don't fall out with Bernhard because Bernhard is a super guy as well. I'm very fond of Bernhard". But I'm quite sure that Bernhard would have wanted to make his peace with Seve at the 'eighty-three Ryder Cup. *Of course* he would. And I don't want to disrupt that. But I promise you what I've told you is true. And what makes me so cross is that people would think that I voted against him. I was the *only* person who was arguing for him – not only because I *wanted* him in my team in 1981, but fancy playing the Ryder Cup at Walton Heath without Seve Ballesteros! He was even better then than he is now.'

The odd thing is that in Collet's account of the conversation between Jacobs, Ballesteros and Gallacher (who appears to have been acting as a kind of intermediary between them) at the Tour dinner, there is no happy ending. 'Bernard Gallacher,' explains Collet, 'was talking to Seve, trying to get him to see his side of the John Jacobs story. I already talked to him and said: "Don't bother him. He doesn't want to hear about it." But Bernard did it anyway, and Seve told him the same thing I did and then he got frustrated about the whole thing. It's better forgotten now. Leave it. Seve will always admire John Jacobs for his contributions to golf; he's always going to be a friend of Bernhard Langer's, because they've been rivals but they've been contemporaries . . . and Neil Coles you can take either way. Neil Coles is Neil Coles and nothing's going to change.'

'Well, Coles has always liked committees,' says Jacklin, who believes that while Jacobs was responsible for keeping him out of the team, Coles was one of the reasons the Spaniard didn't play, 'which is why the Tour wanted the selection thing

183

through a committee so no one man could be blamed. That's why I changed it. Because I said, "I'm quite happy to have three choices and stand by my convictions." You can't have a *committee* picking three players. That's nonsense. Anyway, we proved it to be nonsense and everybody involved in that operation as it happened in 1981 should be ashamed of themselves as long as they breathe.'

10

Amen Corner

It's a work of art. It's like playing a Salvador Dali landscape. I
expected a clock to fall out of the trees and hit me in the face.

David Feherty, Augusta National, April 1992

If you were someone who knew nothing and cared even
less about men who hit golf balls with sticks and you drove
unseeing past the interminable T-shirt and memorabilia stands
that line the streets of Augusta in the second week of April,
you could quite easily be through the town and out the other
side without ever realizing that you had only been minutes
from a show as finely choreographed as any on Broadway.
No billboards disfigure the landscape with pictures of golfers
in primary colours. No white-coated marshal shows the way.
And there is nothing to suggest, in the grim façade of Burger
Kings, malls and drab hotels lit by neon signs with missing
letters, that behind them lies a golf course as lovely as the
Garden of Eden, where spring is eternal and the flowers are
always in bloom.

Nowhere does life imitate art more closely than at Augusta
National.

Ever since 1930, when Clifford Roberts, a New York
investment broker, persuaded Bobby Jones to partner him in
the creation of 'a retreat of such nature and such excellence that
men of some means and devoted to the game of golf might find

the club an extra luxury where they might visit and play with kindred spirits from other parts of the nation,' it has thrived on élitism, perfectionism, the observance of tradition and the careful maintenance of an illusion which, though beautiful, is an illusion nonetheless. At Augusta, one is invited to suspend disbelief. To consider the world – at least during Masters week – a place free from poverty, discord, suffering and sordid commercialism. To marvel at the glorious (artificial if nature has made them anything but) azaleas, rhododendrons and dogwood, the divine blue of Rae's Creek (dye added), and the harmonious effect of a colour-coding system so regulated that a man carrying a white polystyrene cup would not be allowed onto the premises until he had either disposed of it or exchanged it for one in the appropriate shade of sunshine yellow or bottle green. To wonder at the bravery of the golfers who, like latter-day Daniels, tread a wary path through the lions' den that is Augusta. And to be uplifted, as the tournament nears its dramatic conclusion, by the triumph of human spirit.

To keep reality in abeyance for a short time is no hardship; Augusta is an escapist's paradise. The arcane rules of the club make it still easier. For example, advertising of any kind, whether inside or outside the grounds, is expressly forbidden, as is the mention of any tournament barring the four majors and the British and US Amateur championships. All references to money are considered obscene. Tickets for the main event cannot be begged, borrowed or stolen, and the privileged few who already hold them have had them handed down like family heirlooms. But while some of the measures taken to preserve the sanctity of Augusta National have, over the years, seemed unnecessarily draconian, they have nevertheless combined to ensure that the Masters is not only the most unique event in the world but also the most aesthetically pleasing. The golf course itself is gorgeous. There is no sensation to compare with that of lying in the shade of a whispering pine beside the twelfth on a warm spring day, drinking pink lemonade, breathing in jasmine and watching the greatest golfers who ever lived pit their wits against an opponent as ravishing as Augusta.

'This place has no present tense,' said Thomas Boswell in *Strokes of Genius*. 'Cathedrals have a similar quality, and the mansions of state. But they don't command three hundred and sixty-five acres, nor do they often create such ambience. This is life, buffed and burnished.'

When Bobby Jones first visited Augusta, he was struck by the sensation that the land before him, then a nursery, 'had been lying here for years just waiting for someone to lay a golf course upon it. Indeed, it looked as though it were already a golf course, and I am sure that standing today where I stood on this first visit, on the terrace overlooking the practice putting green, one sees the property exactly as I did then. Year by year I myself have sat in the same chair on the same little balcony, upstairs, looking through the wisteria down at the same scene, while the same coloured waiter comes out and says, "You like the same as last year, sah? Beefeater on the rocks?" Everything, indeed, is the same and it is only by looking at the scoreboard that you can tell which year it is – a Palmer year or a Nicklaus year . . .'

Or even a Ballesteros year.

I tell you all this in an attempt to explain why it was that the Spaniard fell so deeply in love with Augusta that he named one of his companies Amen Corner, after that wicked stretch of holes from ten through thirteen; and to help you understand why his performances at the Masters through the years, and the public's perception and reception of them, have been inextricably linked to subtle changes in his own personality and to the ebb and flow of his career. Collet describes his regard for the golf course as 'almost a reverence'. Ballesteros admits that it's true. 'I love this course,' he says fervently. 'It is like Pedreña where I learned to play as a child. I feel I am at home here. That is why I àm happy. I treat it with respect, like an older person. Sometimes I take a few advantages, but always there is respect.'

His affection for Augusta blossomed with his victory in 1980, fluctuated slightly when he missed the cut in 1981 and grew strong again when he finished third in 1982, one shot behind Craig Stadler who beat Dan Pohl in a play-off. On that occasion he was let down by his putting. The greens had been replanted with bent grass – the pace of which was so excessive that he felt it added a stroke per round to the difficulty of the course. Tom Watson observed that the putting surfaces were the fastest he had seen since Oakmont in 1962 – which Sam Snead had likened to trying to putt down a marble staircase – and Billy Casper took half a dozen putts on the second hole.

In 1983 the greens were quicker still. In practice Peter Jacobsen, trying to re-enact Casper's six-putt, started the ball rolling about 18 inches above the hole and watched it rim the cup, gather momentum on a slope as smooth as glass and eventually come to a reluctant halt 15 feet past. Later, a notice appeared in the clubhouse to the effect that the cut on the greens was one-eighth of an inch, on the tees, one-quarter of an inch, and on the fairways, seven-sixteenths of an inch.

Ballesteros was advantaged by the fact that, when he arrived at Augusta – well in advance of the tournament – his putting was what American Mike Nicolette described as 'phenomenal', and he was in fine fettle generally. In the preceding weeks he had played in the Doral Open, where he had missed the cut, not being match-fit, in the Honda and Bay Hill Classics and in the Tournament Players' Championship, and had done reasonably but not exceptionally. However, he was enjoying his golf again and, the hurts and recriminations of 1981 long behind him, was relaxed, approachable and looking forward to the new season. More importantly, he was happy with his golf game. On practice days he strode jubilantly along the spacious fairways as if the worries of the world had suddenly leapt from his shoulders, with great crowds of people pouring after him. Bold approach shots were experimented with, daring chip shots holed and velvet putting surfaces scrutinized endlessly.

Watson, who said that his own game was like a light which could be switched on at any time, explained that it was the speed of the greens that made the golf course so difficult. 'The key to playing well here is to have a great touch. I think you've got to be able to control your touch. If you cannot control your touch then you're going to have a big problem at Augusta.'

'The greens are brilliantly designed,' agreed Ben Crenshaw.

'The fifth and the fourteenth greens are really supposed to resemble St Andrews' greens and they do. They're very similar. I've always thought, too, that if you have a golf course that's entirely filled with trouble, then you're not allowed to think – you don't have room to think. But at Augusta you widen the scope and you actually have room to think because the danger's not imminent. Imminent danger is where you can see it directly before you in some form, but deferred danger is what you feel is lurking out there somewhere . . . I think it's a higher art form that way.'

Ballesteros was more succinct. 'Every time you make a mental mistake you pay for it.'

He made his first mistake at the first hole on the first day of play, when his opening drive hit a tree. It rebounded onto a sloping lie near a fairway bunker, from where he proceeded to play his recovery shot into a greenside bunker and take bogey. All the signs pointed to an indifferent start. But Ballesteros merely laughed in the face of adversity and went on to make six birdies – one of them at the 535-yard eighth, where he was the only man in the field to reach the green in two. Had his tee shot at the sixteenth not spun away so sharply that it caused him to three-putt from long-range, he would have completed round one in 67 strokes. As it was, he finished a shot behind the leaders Raymond Floyd, Jack Renner and Gil Morgan on four under par; along with J.C. Snead, Charles Coody, Jim Hallett and Arnold Palmer – whose day it really was. Fifty-three years old and in contention for the Masters! All Augusta resounded with the cheers of his Army. Walking off the course the Spaniard, who had plenty of his own supporters, was cornered by an American sportswriter, who asked him bluntly if he was playing better than he had when he won the Masters in 1980 and was 'all over the place.'

Even a man with a hide as thick as that must have quailed beneath the look Ballesteros gave him and it was followed by a curt: 'Why you only want to see bad shots? Why you not want to see my good ones? I hit only two bad shots that day and I was ten shots ahead with nine to play. I cannot be all that bad.'

On Friday the heavens opened and the Great Flood descended. Streets became rivers, pretty blue streams evolved into muddy torrents and the press room flooded to a depth of 3 inches. The powers that be, while ruing the potential cost of such a disaster and wishing that they could just touch a button and have a new backdrop of blue sky and fluffy white clouds wheeled in, congratulated themselves that they had built a dam in Rae's Creek and had thus prevented the eleventh, twelfth and thirteenth holes from being washed away. But for the first time in ten years play was abandoned.

Saturday was Ballesteros's birthday. He celebrated it with his beloved father, who had accompanied him to the Masters for the first time, and with a small circle of close friends, whose tickets he had provided; including Dr Campuzano, his first sponsor, Jorge Ceballos, his new manager, and a Miami airport official whom he had befriended some years earlier when the man had helped him with some lost luggage. He was twenty-six, a year younger than Nicklaus had been when he won his sixth major, and within reach of his second victory at Augusta.

The Golden Bear's hopes of a fifth green blazer had been raised, too. But shortly before the second round his back muscles went into spasm and he had to withdraw. Hardly had this been announced when dozens of scribes had rushed to the champion's locker room and hung about in the doorway, trying vainly to catch a glimpse of the prostrate Bear. After a time it was decided that it would not only be more profitable but also more professional to despatch a single spokesman to the great man's bedside with a tape recorder. This done, it transpired that Player, in his role as ministering angel, had prescribed a Bute pill (usually given to horses) but it had failed to provide relief. 'Doctors have told me that I can change my swing, stop golf or put up with the pain,' commented Nicklaus. 'I don't like those options so I'll just carry on.'

Ballesteros, after repeated excursions to orthopaedic specialists, physiotherapists and acupuncturists, had adopted the same philosophy. After his victory at Lytham in 1979 he told journalists: 'I have a troubled back since 1977 when I played the Masters. It was just after I came out of military service and I had been practising at Augusta the day before the tournament. I felt very uncomfortable with my back, and through the year is coming worse. For the next year I don't really have pain, is just uncomfortable. I feel like my shoulders are heavy, like I'm carrying a weight, and it was very difficult for me at Lytham because, maybe you see before I hit the ball, I swing three or four times because I feel stiff. The cold is bad for me. However, is no pain, but everybody ask me about my back. All the time you ask and I say, "It's good, it's good," but still people say, "Seve, how is your back? Seve, how is your back?" Then it work in my mind and that put me very much off.'

The state of his health was not a matter of pressing concern to Ballesteros prior to the second round. Far more trying was the weather: heavy showers during the night had left the course saturated and the going slow and, despite the best efforts of thirty-five greenkeepers and their squeegees, morning drizzle compounded the problem. Shortly before noon play commenced from two tees. Ballesteros put his patience hat on and went boldly into the gloom, seizing the opportunity to mount an offensive while Augusta's defences were lowered. Darkness fell before his mission was completed, but he was still a stroke behind Morgan, who had two holes remaining, on six under par, standing on the eighteenth tee. Keith Fergus was the clubhouse leader with a score of 139, while Jodie Mudd and Nick Faldo were a stroke further back. Ballesteros's final hole was completed before breakfast on Sunday. The sun sailed briefly across the sky as he putted for a 70, but soon vanished and the third round was delayed while rain fell and put paid to the proposed thirty-six holes.

Player waxed lyrical about Ballesteros's talent and his victory in 1980, observing with obvious pleasure that the Spaniard had been 'very complimentary because he said I taught him to win the Masters.' He beamed. 'Wasn't that something? That's a very nice compliment from a wonderful golfer like that. I have so much respect for the man and the golfer because I understand what he feels like. He also came from a poor home and he *had* to survive. It's all very well to sit on the side and criticize. People are always going to criticize people who do well. The highest tree gathers the most wind. And the highest tree must have the strongest limbs and branches to take that. He's a trier; he's a battler. You know, both of our careers are very similar, and we've been very similar in our attitudes towards the game – to try your best, to give everything you've got. And when you've finished a round, if it's 78, you gave it 78 of your best. I've shot 80 but it's been 80 of my *best*.'

In the third round, Ballesteros's finest efforts were foiled by his inability to convert the few chances he had on the unpredictable greens. An indiscriminate mixture of rain and shine had left them neither wet nor dry but somewhere in between, and each time he made a charge for the top of the leaderboard his progress was arrested and made a mockery of by his blade. Nevertheless, he came off the course with a one over par 73 and his confidence still intact. His aggregate of 211 had left him in second place, one stroke behind Raymond Floyd and Craig Stadler, the defending champion, and one ahead of Watson, Mudd and Fergus at the end of the day's play. Before repairing calmly to the practice green to work on his stroke he told the media that, though he had played well, 'my putting is not what it should be.' He was reticent about his chances of victory. 'This course is not easy,' he said firmly. 'I'm just trying to stay cool. Winning any one of the Big Four is great, but I'm still young. I don't have to be in a hurry.'

Lee Trevino used to say that a lot of American players would like to hear him admit that Ballesteros was wild off the tee and – as a consequence, I suppose – lucky. 'You'll never hear the great players say he's lucky,' he remarked in Dudley Doust's book in 1981. 'They'll say he's great, though. How great? Every generation or so there emerges a golfer who is a little bit better than anybody else. I believe Ballesteros is one of them. It won't be long before he's the greatest international player of all time. I'd say even more successful than Gary Player who, right now, is the finest international player who ever held a golf club. And Roberto de Vicenzo was [also] fantastic. But Seve, before he retires, should be better than them all. On a golf course he's got everything – I mean *everything*: touch, power, know-how, courage and charisma. By the time he finishes, in about twenty years, he may not be equal to Jack Nicklaus – nobody will ever be equal to Jack Nicklaus – but he'll be more than equal to the rest of us – myself, Watson, Byron Nelson and even Ben Hogan. Seve Ballesteros, through the 1980s, will be the successor to Jack Nicklaus.'

That Trevino was absolutely and indubitably right has long since been proven; not even the most parochial American would dare to contradict him now. But in 1983 they could and did, making constant allusions to the Spaniard's 'parking-lot shot' and to his marvellous recoveries, as if he were being unfairly favoured by a sort of golfing genie. This grated unbearably on Ballesteros's nerves. He regarded it as a gross insult to his ability and took it to refer particularly to his erratic tee shots.

'Oh, you know I am a very wild driver,' he told sportswriters sarcastically. 'This is the only course in the world that is wide enough for me. Every fairway is two hundred yards wide, so I can use my driver.'

Gullible, they wrote it down, they drank it in. They perpetuated the myth.

They could hardly have been more wrong.

'Of all the courses in the world,' explains David Graham, 'Augusta National places the most emphasis on strategy and is the best example of what a major is all about. Every shot here offers an option. That's the key. You've always got a safe side of the fairway or the green to aim at, where you know you can find your ball sitting on short grass. But from those safe spots you are not, by any means, guaranteed a par . . . Caution here is an invitation to make bogeys.'

'You need to play every club in your bag,' says Ballesteros. 'You have to be long, you have to be straight, you have to play shots right to left and left to right – especially the irons, you need to be a good player round the greens, you have to putt very well and you have to think. Because Augusta is the kind of golf course that has been designed to make you think.'

'It's very much a tactician's course,' concurs Crenshaw. 'And it's a little bit of a dichotomy, I suppose, because people say, "Well, it's so wide open . . ." Well, it is. But it's a place where you have to pick your spots in order to gain the best angles. So you're always trying to hit a certain spot. There's not too many courses that resemble St Andrews, but Augusta's meant to have that sort of style or philosophy of thinking behind the building of the holes. Jones always talked about it being a "psychologically punishing" golf course. There's something terribly debilitating about having sixty yards to drive in and you drive and you're in the wrong position and then you have a tough angle to try to get the second shot in . . . A hole like number 13 – everybody is trying to go down the left side, close to the creek. But if you hook the ball into the creek then you say, "[Why did I do that when] I've got a *hundred* yards to the right of the creek to play with?" That's what Jones means by "psychologically punishing" play. And that can be as punishing as any rough on either side of the golf course. I'm not saying it's a fair punishment but it's a punishment you can live with a lot easier. There's no thinking involved when you get up to a hole and there's trouble on both sides. There's no thought process. You hit the ball and you try to stay out of trouble. But if you have trouble on one side and you have another side that's open wide and then you get a different angle to the green, now you're really stimulating thought inside a player. It's like outdoor chess. And that's when it gets interesting.'

Five days after they struck their first shot in earnest, Ballesteros and Watson stepped out onto the tee in the final round of the US Masters. Before them, as vivid and panoramic as an expressionist painting, stretched the crisp fairways of Augusta, hemmed with towering pines and airbrushed two shades of green. The world's No. 1 player and the Young Pretender rehearsed their swings before the pleased gallery with graceful, economic movements. When they were announced by the starter, they powered their drives down the fairway and walked briskly from the tee, each preoccupied with his own thoughts. After the first round Ballesteros had told the press that he thought an eight under par total would win the tournament. 'I'd be happy to take it now and go home,' he had said with a laugh. He still felt the same way now. But his confidence was running high, and when he reached his ball he took out an eight-iron, struck it smoothly to 6 feet and was away with a birdie.

It was a perfect day for golf. The sun beamed down from a cobalt sky, and the gentlest of breezes ruffled the leaves and pulled at the hats of the gay crowd as they crossed from green to the tee. The second hole at Augusta is a 555-yard par five named Pink Dogwood, which makes it sound like a walk in the park. Actually, it's anything but. Ballesteros appealed to its better nature with a fine drive, a majestic four-wood to 12 feet and a single-putt for eagle.

'Hell,' grumbled Tom Kite, who later emerged from the pack to finish joint runner-up with Crenshaw for the tournament, 'I can't even stop a wedge that close to the hole on that green.'

But the Spaniard had only just begun. He narrowly missed a birdie putt at the third and he did make one at the 205-yard fourth, hitting a towering two-iron shot to within a few inches of the flag, and establishing a three-shot lead that no player seemed capable of challenging. Watson was literally punch-drunk with incredulity. 'I felt like a fighter getting knocked down twice in the first round,' he said. 'I was in a daze . . . I still thought I could win, though. A lot of things can happen. Byron Nelson made up six shots in eleven holes at Augusta. It *can* happen. Specially on the back nine.' But the nearest Watson came to presenting a threat was when he drew within two shots of the lead after eagling the eighth. Thereafter, he seemed to go into a decline. A three-putt at the ninth was followed by more of the same at the tenth and eleventh, while Ballesteros reasserted himself with a birdie at the ninth to turn in 31.

'I always knew that he had great touch, great feel,' said Watson admiringly. 'That's his strength, his ability to manoeuvre the ball with a club, especially with the shorter clubs. His weakness has obviously been a tendency to get wild and hit the ball sideways. I'm familiar with that because I do the same thing. But when he's on, he's certainly a very exciting person to watch and also to play with. He impresses me with the type of shots he can play. He works the ball left to right and right to left, which is essential for a great player to succeed and have a great career.'

It wasn't a poor drive but an over-ambitious approach shot that caused him to take bogey on the tenth, and a wayward iron off the twelfth tee cost him another. Undaunted, he smashed a huge drive into the forest on the notorious thirteenth. All the imagination in the world was of no earthly use to him there; he could do no more than chip out onto the fairway. But he did have the courage to fire his three-iron approach straight at the pin, though it was positioned on the edge of the green at Rae's Creek, and very nearly made a birdie.

The rest of the field, in varying states of awe, astonishment and dejection, had been left to eat dust.

'We just couldn't keep up,' admitted Crenshaw; while Kite exclaimed: 'It's like he is driving a Ferrari and the rest of us are in Chevrolets.'

The spectators at Augusta are among the most disciplined in the world. They do not stampede, catcall or drop litter, and they regard the slim ropes which line the fairways as sacred and inviolable boundaries. It would be more than their lives were worth to think otherwise. Now, moving with that half walk, half scurry of children who have been forbidden to run in a school corridor, those of them who had not already done so joined the flood of people rushing towards the Ballesteros/Watson match, leaving the downcast and scowling Walrus and others like him to wallow in their own misery, and were vociferous in their support of the proud young Spaniard.

Throughout the round Ballesteros had worn an intent and unsmiling expression. It never altered even as he came to the final hole leading by four shots, and it remained unchanged when he flew the green with his approach shot – drawing a gasp of alarm from the scattering crowd, and then began the long march up the hill towards the clubhouse and victory. His ball had overflown the putting surface by at least a clublength. It lay on an awkward downhill lie among the gallery. Ballesteros surveyed it impassively, hands on hips. His father watched anxiously from the crowd. Then he chipped and the startled gallery saw the ball bound forward a few paces and die on the bank of the green. But Ballesteros neither swore, looked heavenward for advice nor cried 'Why me?' in an anguished tone, all of which would have been perfectly natural and even appropriate under the circumstances. He simply stepped up to his ball and, with the confidence and delicacy of touch that is God-given, chipped the ball into the hole. Then, finally, as the gallery burst into thunderous applause, a smile broke like sunshine across the young Spaniard's face.

If a man strives his whole life to achieve perfection, and if he measures that perfection by the attainment of his profession's highest honour, then the hour of his victory should be his alone to cherish, and should be sweet and untainted – not marred by the petty jealousies of others. For Ballesteros, that hour was over in moments. Watson had preceded him into the interview room and had remarked sourly that, if Ballesteros's chip shot at the eighteenth hadn't hit the flagstick and dropped into the hole, it would have run off the green.

'Sure,' snapped Ballesteros, when this was repeated to him. 'And I suppose then I take ten putts and don't even finish in the top ten.'

He was too filled with joy to allow himself to grow angry over something so trivial, but the implication – that he had been lucky rather than the best player in the field – was not lost on him, and he put it to the back of his mind to be reflected on on another day.

'Would you say you are a better golfer than you were when you won in 1980?' queried a reporter.

'No,' said Ballesteros, 'just more experienced.'

Another asked whether he was planning to quit Europe for the US Tour.

The Spaniard shook his head. 'I love to be an international golfer. I love to play in Japan and Europe and the US.' He grinned. 'Anyway, I love to travel because I meet different girls.'

'Is it an ambition of yours to win the US Open?'

'Yes,' replied Ballesteros, tongue in cheek, 'but I don't think I will. I'm not *straight* enough for those courses.' His face was deadpan and the implication went over the heads of both the American journalist laboriously taking down his answer and his compatriots. 'One day,' he added, eyes twinkling mischievously, 'I will come over and play the US Tour full time and see how good I am.'

21 April 1983, Madrid. Ballesteros, the 'lucky' champion, was in a car park once again – this time facing a 200-yard shot of nightmarish difficulty to the green. He assessed the risks and weighed up his chances. They were less than even. Undeterred, he smashed the ball away. It climbed high into the blue yonder and disappeared behind the stands. The crowd, ten thousand strong, erupted. Ballesteros allowed a pleased smile to lift the corners of his mouth, rapped his club smartly against his shoe, and threaded his way back through the smiling spectators into the Bernabeu football stadium, home to Real Madrid, where he was demonstrating trick shots.

The Masters champion had arrived home from America to find himself a national celebrity, feted by ministers and kings. To begin with, he had tried to hide away in Pedreña but, having been forced into the limelight by the impending Madrid Open, where he was defending champion, he had resigned himself wearily to the attentions of public and press. The football stadium exhibition had simply been a platform for an announcement, by the Mayor of Madrid, Tierno Galpan, that two public courses were to be built in the city as a tribute to the young Spaniard.

'This is exactly what we need to give everybody a chance to play golf,' a pleased Ballesteros said afterwards. 'It will make the game popular. I've waited for years for this to happen . . . I am flattered that they want to name the first one after me. The Mayor sent me a cable congratulating me on winning again at Augusta and so did the King of Spain. The newspapers and TV gave very big coverage to the Masters, compared with almost nothing when I won the first time. Now they know about golf as well as football in Spain.'

The curious thing was that, although two of his most cherished dreams – winning the Masters and helping to make golf in Spain accessible to the masses – had come true in the same month, Ballesteros seemed listless and dejected.

Indeed, his mood was unchanged even after he had finished third in the tournament behind Sandy Lyle.

The reaction of the press to his Masters' win was equally downbeat – more critical than congratulatory. *Golf World* said that 'It was undoubtedly an important victory for the Spaniard. Since winning his first green jacket in 1980, only nine months after capturing the Open at Royal Lytham, he has won several tournaments around the world but has somehow failed to live up to everyone's expectations . . .' And Mitchell Platts, profiling Ballesteros, commented that, in the years since his first win in the Dutch Open in 1976, the Spaniard's career had seemed 'punctuated by troubles. Seve has smiled. Seve has sulked. He has been labelled an enigma. Certainly there are times when it is difficult to trace a reason for his sudden changes of [mood] . . . Many of his problems have been attributed to a fanatical desire to succeed coupled with a reputation for being somewhat avaricious . . . In his defence there is another side of Seve. [The] tales of meanness have some foundation but there are times when he shows a generosity . . . which few could emulate. In Madrid three years ago he was eating in a small tavern when he recognized several relatively unknown British golfers dining at a corner table. He immediately sent over a couple of bottles of wine. Then, while competing on the Puerto de Hierro course, he was disturbed . . . at the top of his backswing . . . by a couple of small boys eager to . . . get a glimpse of Spain's newest sporting hero. Such an intrusion into Seve's work routine would usually darken the skies; on this occasion he quietly and kindly gave the two youngsters a friendly [lesson] in etiquette.'

Platts added: 'Nobody doubts that he does his job on the course but he has sought the sanctuary of the locker room more than any other player in Europe.'

On this note, the new season began. When he arrived at Royal St George's in May for the PGA Championship, he had already lost one play-off in Italy to Langer and had narrowly missed out on another at the French Open. At a comparative point in 1982 he had won four tournaments in a row (counting the 1981 Spanish Open and the World

Match Play Championship), and was, as Michael Williams said, 'almost in the Walter Hagen position of being able to ask: "Who is going to be second?" ' Nothing had changed in the intervening year. After a minor setback in the second round – when he lost his temper and broke his driver – he compiled closing rounds of 67 and 71 to edge out Brown and Lyle at Sandwich, the first golf course he had ever played in Britain and one he had once described as 'Hell'.

Two other things of interest happened before Ballesteros crossed the Atlantic for the Westchester Classic: 1. After finishing thirteenth in the Silk Cut Masters and winning £1,500, he was disqualified and given last place and £200 because a spectator had spotted a discrepancy in his published first round scores; 2. He played nine holes of La Manga's South Course on his knees, accompanied by Manuel, Juan Mellado, the club pro, and Mike Bamber, the chairman of Brighton Football Club. Said Bamber: 'It was an amazing performance. He only did it for a bit of fun but he played brilliantly. He went on his knees for every shot, even for two in bunkers, and only stood up to putt. He told me that that was the way he perfected his swing when he was learning to play golf. I've never seen anything like it in my life.'

On Friday, 17 June, following the first round of the US Open, Johnny Miller declared that there were only two types of tournament golfer: Severiano Ballesteros and the rest.

Ballesteros, who had prompted this compliment by shooting 69 to share the lead with John Mahaffey, accepted it graciously enough but at the same time hinted that there was a deliberate campaign by the media to put him under pressure. It wasn't that he was feeling depressed or ill-tempered – quite the reverse; after winning the Westchester Classic, by hitting two shots of near genius on the final hole for an eagle, he was positively bursting with high spirits. But he wanted to let them know that he hadn't forgotten past slights, nor the aspersions they had cast on his ability over the years.

How, a questioner wanted to know, had he managed to cope so well with Oakmont's gruelling layout when the vast majority of the field had been crippled by it?

'Well,' said Ballesteros, poker-faced, 'I hit the driver three times and I expect to leave the fairway two times, but I get lucky and I hit it two times. I think I was very lucky today. I'm only twenty-six and I think I play the US Open ten or fifteen times more. Maybe one day I will get lucky and win. That's the only way I can win this tournament – get lucky.'

The American press were bemused. They looked to each other for help. Finally, one said: 'How do the British journalists describe the way you play?'

'In the United States, I'm lucky. In Europe, I'm good,' came the swift response.

Fernandez believes that the reason Ballesteros makes the comments he does about luck is 'to make himself even stronger, to make himself work even harder. Because he knew inside himself that he could win majors. I mean, you can be lucky once, twice, three times, but not always. People who play golf know that you're not lucky every day. If you get good results it's because something else is in it.'

The following day violent storms disrupted play and Ballesteros did well to shoot 74. Nevertheless, he was only three strokes off the lead and considerably more relaxed and at ease than he had been at the same stage in the 1982 US Open, when he had scored 81, 79 to miss the cut. On that occasion, too, there had been rain delays and general mayhem as a result. By midnight on Thursday the tee-times had still not been posted, so Collet resolved to get up early the next morning to find them out. When he did, it was to discover that Ballesteros was off in less than an hour.

'So here I was,' recalls Collet, 'a year after the US Open incident and he's going to miss his tee-time again. So we frantically got a car, and this time I went with him, and the car went along the edge of the road, honking, and we got there like fifteen minutes before. He was really upset about it. He said: "*How could this be?*" I said, "Well, we asked the right questions, talked to the right people, and they were just so disorganized they couldn't give us the answers, so what are we supposed to do?"'

No such disasters befell Ballesteros in 1983, and when thunderstorms brought the tournament to a halt in the final round he was lying third on the leaderboard behind Nelson and Watson with five holes still to play. Statistics show that on that day he went out in 38, while his two main rivals scored 33 and 31 respectively; that when he bogeyed the tenth and twelfth he was overtaken by Calvin Peete and Gil Morgan; and that when the curtain closed on the final drama Nelson was the winner and Peete and Ballesteros shared fourth place. What they don't explain is why the Spaniard finished fourth. They don't reveal that the Ballesteros that played Oakmont that week was of a species that had not previously been thought to exist. He was cautious, conservative and concerned only with making pars. He was a metronome. He told the media, 'You have to play here like a robot, by hitting one-irons straight down the fairway.' And he did exactly that. In short, he played in a way that Faldo has since perfected.

The 1983 US Open appears to be the first time in Ballesteros's career that there is any mention of him playing 72 holes in that restrained manner, so obviously alien to his nature. Subsequently, he has done it on numerous occasions and almost always to the detriment of his game. But he has remained convinced that he played the course the way it should have been played and that he should have won. In 1991 he told Guy Hodgson of the *Independent*: 'I had a chance of winning going into the last round. But I think someone realized Severiano might be the champion, so they moved the tees back as far as they could. I'm not the most accurate driver. It made a big difference to me. I got 74 but if the tees had been further forward, as they had been for the rest of the tournament, I would have done much better. The US Open is always tees and greens, very tight. There is very little opportunity to manufacture shots. You have to play like a robot, straight, straight, very mechanical. The [price] for [not] being accurate off the tee is too great. I've never been a robot. I'm famous for being in trouble. Then you can make shots, show your ability a bit more.'

There is a hint of paranoia in this statement, just as there was in a comment he made to the tall Fijian, Vijay Singh, about his performance at the 1983 Open at Birkdale. He had complained then that the punishing rough greatly reduced the chances of the flair players and made it 'a mechanical game'. He then proceeded to pussy-foot around the golf course for three rounds, only remembering midway through the final day that boldness not wariness had made him a champion and finishing sixth.

'Lost ball at the second hole,' the Spaniard told Singh. 'Two thousand people watching! We shouted fore but we never found it.'

The second half of the year passed without mishap. At the Irish Open, which he won, it was announced that the ball he had used in the Masters, a Titleist with 384 dimples on it, had been outlawed by the United States Golf Association (USGA). The approved ball had only 320.

'It's no problem for me,' said Ballesteros cheerfully when told. 'Why don't we all play with stones.'

In September he dropped a lawsuit he had brought against the RJ Reynolds Tobacco Company in the United States for using his likeness without permission to advertise their cigarettes, and drew nearer to winning the Order of Merit again. 'Sure, I want to win the money list,' he said at the Swiss Open in Crans-sur-Sierre. 'But I only want it, Nick Faldo *needs* it. He must be a little bit afraid of me to come here this week. I've won it three times already so now I want to be the number one in the world. Last year I was third behind Craig Stadler and Ray Floyd, but this year I win nearly $400,000 world-wide. In eight years I win two million dollars. That is not so bad, I think.'

Compare Ballesteros's record with that of Arnold Palmer, whom he was to beat so spectacularly in the World Match Play in October. When Palmer was twenty-six he had just struggled through his first year on the US Tour, he had won less than $8,000 and had finished thirty-second on the money list. Ballesteros, on the other hand, had won three majors and more than thirty championships world-wide and had earned more than twice as much money in 1983 alone as Palmer had in seven years. When the season drew to a close he was runner-up to Faldo on the European Order of Merit and was almost universally acknowledged as the No. 2 player in the world. Only Watson was ahead of him.

11

Hallowed Ground

I want to be the best again, of course. But right now I must be honest, and by looking at the results and the way I feel, I cannot lie to myself. I never lie to myself.

Severiano Ballesteros, Pedreña, June 1984

The eyes that peered out through the foliage were dark gold, liquid and expressive. They vanished as their owner dropped to his knees and, crunching about among the fallen pine cones and twigs, tried to gain a clearer perspective of the distant flagstick, then reappeared with their black brows drawn together in a fierce frown of concentration as Ballesteros realized that he would have to play the shot blind. The fifteenth green at Puerto de Hierro lay some 195 yards away, round a corner and screened by a small forest. On it, American Tom Sieckmann, his playing partner in the opening round of the Madrid Open, was practising his putting stroke and, upon glancing up and seeing only the backs of the enormous crowd thronging about in the distant rough, wondering rather impatiently what had become of Ballesteros.

Ballesteros was deliberating his options. 'I had two chances,' he remembered later (most people would have said those were slim and none). 'I could hit a low hook or I could hit a high fade.' Having decided to pursue the latter course, he selected a five-iron, opened up the face, aimed 50 yards left of target and smashed the ball into the air. It flew away in a curve as geometrically precise as the line-drawing of an architect, cleared the trees by inches, pitched 10 feet from the pin and trickled to a halt 20 feet away. Siekmann looked skywards as if he expected manna to follow.

'Where on earth did that come from?' he said.

He repeated the question when the Spaniard came striding down the fairway, and Ballesteros explained that he had hit his approach shot over the trees on the left. Siekmann gaped. He stepped out of the way with new respect and shook his head disbelievingly as Ballesteros holed his putt for birdie.

That Ballesteros was inspired by this single spark of brilliance in what had otherwise been an unexceptional day, became obvious over the remaining holes. His pitch to 9 inches at the last ensured a birdie and a score of 71 – one of the few sub-par rounds he had recorded all year. He followed it with a level par 72 to make only his fourth cut in seven events, and his eventual second place was a fighting one for he was struggling with a hook. Nevertheless, he had not yet grown desperate over the state of his game. 'It is a little slump,' he said, 'but I am always like this,' and his hands described giant peaks and troughs.

It was now the end of April and Ballesteros was in Spain for one of his infrequent appearances at a European Tour event. After almost six years of abortive attempts on the part of US Tour commissioner Deane Beman to persuade him to switch his allegiance from Europe to the United States, Ballesteros had finally crossed the Atlantic and, since the beginning of the 1984 season when he had become a member of the US Tour, thereby committing himself to fifteen events, had been based in America. The reason for this was not simply that a middle ground had been found between what Ballesteros wanted and what US Tour regulations stipulated. Indeed, no compromise had been reached at all. It was because the Tournament Policy Board had, just like the poor ETPD committee before it in the case of the appearance money dispute, been forced to see it Ballesteros's way. In 1978, when Beman had taken the unprecedented step of offering him his Tour card, the Spaniard had asked whether or not he would still be free to play in Europe as often as he wanted to. He was informed that although he would only be given three releases a year to play in overseas events, he could, as a foreigner, play wherever and whenever he wanted to on his home country circuit. Ballesteros replied, quite reasonably, that Spain did not have a circuit and that the European Tour should be regarded as such. Beman wouldn't hear of it. He didn't see why the rules should be rewritten for a twenty-one-year-old who hadn't yet won a major. But as time went on and Ballesteros marched victorious from one Open and two Masters, he became considerably less hard line in his views. At length, he had given in altogether and the Spaniard had won the right to treat Europe as his home circuit and had joined the US Tour.

Like the hopeful voyagers before him, who, in good faith, set forth to discover the New World, Ballesteros quickly grasped that all would not be plain sailing. In 1983 he had collected more than $200,000 on the US Tour in a limited number of appearances, in addition to the £113,864 he had made in official earnings in Europe. By the end of June 1984, he had played in twelve events, had had only two top ten finishes – a third place in the Tournament Players' Championship and another in the Tournament of Champions – and was thirty-sixth on the money list. He had also failed to qualify for the final two rounds at Augusta after unwittingly taking two practice swings in a hazard on the thirteenth hole and incurring a two-stroke penalty.

'When I decide to play in the US this year I knew there was a big risk involved,' admitted Ballesteros. 'I won two out of eight tournaments I entered last year so this time people expect me to win six out of fifteen. But that's not possible. The standard is too good. Over there any one of fifty players is a possible winner, but here you're looking at maybe sixteen. Nothing has gone right for me. If I miss the green I always seem to finish up with a double-bogey. When I'm going well, something always seems to happen and I lose a lot of confidence. There was a lot of publicity about me missing the cut in the Masters, but that really summed up my problems. I dropped shots because I grounded my club in a hazard which I didn't know was there and it cost me my place in the last two rounds. The cut was so close that I would have been only five shots behind the leader, and I would have still been in with a chance of winning.'

His last tournament before returning to Europe was the US Open at Winged Foot – 'the toughest golf course I have ever played and the toughest of the championships to win.' By then the appeal of the Great American Dream had plainly worn thin. He was fed up with hot dogs and mediocrity, and filled with a deep and insatiable longing for *paella* and the sweet hills of home. On practice days it seemed that his wish might be granted sooner rather than later. Winged Foot had been set up with traditional USGA severity; Ballesteros's erratic driving and indifferent putting did not augur well for his chances. But when the tournament commenced, he put away his driver, took out his one-iron and, in the oppressive, ninety-degree-in-the-shade temperatures of New York that summer, exhibited a combination of magic and fire that thrilled the American crowds and earned him an opening 69. It turned out to be a flash in the pan. Having teed up in the second round a mere stroke behind the leaders Hale Irwin and Jim Thorpe, he came crashing down with a 73, and was eleven shots adrift of Irwin going into the final day. At that point he announced, to the consternation of all, that he was abandoning his full-time commitment to the US Tour. His next tournament would be the Lawrence Batley in England, three weeks hence, and in the interim he would be recovering in Pedreña. Of the remaining US events, only the Buick Open and the PGA Championship had been pencilled into his schedule. He had no plans, for the time being, at least, to play the obligatory fifteenth tournament.

So Ballesteros returned to his beloved Pedreña. Surrounded by the friends and family who adored him, he began, as he had a thousand times before, to heal the wounds which had been inflicted on his pride and self-confidence by callous reporters, envious players or by his own capricious golf game. This he did by lying on the beach, playing tennis and *pelota*, meeting old friends and devouring liberal helpings of his mother's cooking. Vitamin tablets, too, were swallowed in large doses, for a blood test had revealed that a mineral deficiency may have been responsible for his tiredness and lack of vigour. Twice a day Ballesteros worked on his golf game, under the watchful eye of Manuel.

'Away from the course, everything is great,' he assured Peter Higgs of the *Mail on Sunday*, when Higgs arrived in Pedreña a fortnight before the Open Championship to interview him. 'But I am not happy with my game.' Adopting the principle of all great players by following a negative thought with a positive one, he went on to explain that, although he had not been playing well when he went to Sun City in South Africa for the Million Dollar Challenge he had won the tournament by five strokes. 'That's the way in golf sometimes. I feel great, I expect to do well and nothing happens. Other times . . . I'm unhappy about my swing and I win the tournament.'

His victory in Bophuthatswana gave him considerable satisfaction because he had lost a nine-hole play-off there to Miller two years earlier in particularly galling circumstances. On the first extra hole Ballesteros had hit his tee shot to 6 inches. The American was 6 feet away but sank the putt with aplomb, and they went up 16, 17 and 18 three times before Ballesteros missed a 4-foot putt for bogey to hand the title to Miller.

'He couldn't come to the party afterwards,' recalls Brent Turley, who had accompanied the young Spaniard on behalf of UMI. 'Manuel tried to get him to do it but he was back in his room, crying. It was a very emotional experience for him. It was just something he could not accept. Now that is something that would be interpreted by many as being a human failing – which we all have. But it's also the guts of why he has been so successful.'

Back in Pedreña, Ballesteros omitted to mention to Higgs that, on his return journey from Johannesburg to Spain, he had decided at the last possible second to take the night plane from Madrid to Santander instead of the one he was booked on the following morning. When he arrived home, he learned that the second flight had crashed in a runway accident and not a solitary passenger survived.

Destino had come to his rescue once more.

'You know, maybe why I don't feel too good is because

1983 was a tough year,' mused Ballesteros. 'It was a great year, the best. But I was under a lot of pressure and now I'm suffering a little reaction. That's why, maybe, I'm a little jumpy and nervous and my concentration has not been good.

'St Andrews could be the place where it will come right. If I didn't think I could win, I would stay at home . . . I have to be honest and say that my confidence and attitude aren't at their best. But I will be tough there, that's for sure.'

Wednesday, 11 July 1984. When Ballesteros had first set out for a practice round on the eve of the Open Championship at St Andrews, a genial sun had been shining, which had lent lustre to great rolling greens and an ochre hue to the mounds and hollows. Seagulls had wheeled carelessly above the cornflower-blue bay and pilgrims had clattered joyfully through the streets of a 'city given over soul and body to a tyrannizing game' – pausing only to gaze wistfully at the shops, restaurants and museums which paid homage to that game – before spilling out onto the sacred links of St Andrews.

Now, however, it was early evening. The sun was sliding down below the gothic spires and medieval roof-tops of the famous grey town, and a mysterious half-light prevailed. At that hour of day, the Old Course was no longer a thing of beauty. Indeed, a dispassionate observer, standing in the shadow of the Royal and Ancient clubhouse and looking out across the flat, mousy links, would soon see her for what she really was: a sullen, ugly, frowzy old woman, riddled with ambiguities; as craterous and barren as the moon. Small wonder that when Sam Snead first came to St Andrews in 1946, she struck him as being 'an abandoned sort of place . . . so raggedy and beat up I was surprised to see what looked like fairway among the weeds. Down home we wouldn't plant cow beets on land like that.'

Fuzzy Zoeller, the US Open Champion, was equally unimpressed in 1984. 'A guy could get lost out there,' he said. 'I stood on the second tee and started hunting for some sign of the course.'

The sages nodded wisely. They had heard it all before. Each and every one of them had experienced the same sense

209

of disappointment when they had first laid eyes on the Old Course, the conviction that whoever built it – whether God or man – had played a cruel joke upon golfers world-wide. The slow dawning of respect had come later, along with the thrill of discovering each of her many faces, and then the blossoming of a love-affair that would last a lifetime.

'St Andrews is the course where you look down the register of champions and every one of them is a brilliant champion,' enthuses Ben Crenshaw, a convert. 'All through the ages it's probably been the most loved and most hated golf course. Most of them have learned to love it. There's a lot of learning to be done. There's a lifetime of learning on that golf course. For a mind like Bobby Jones' – and I think he's close to being the most cerebral player that ever lived – it fascinated him. He hated it at first. Didn't like it because he couldn't understand it . . . Later on he became more tolerant of it, and the more he learned about it the more he loved it, because it was a puzzle. Later on, he said it was by far his favourite golf course.'

Ballesteros had already been through the entire emotional spectrum with links courses in general (beginning with his passionate loathing for Royal St George's in 1975), and had lately reached the stage where the intensity of his feeling for the home of golf could almost be described as worship. These and other thoughts were flitting through his mind as he rounded the turn at St Andrews, flanked by his loyal friends, Chino Fernandez and the Brazilian Jaime Gonzalez. There was a rare smile on his face. Rare, because he had not often had cause to smile in 1984. Not only because he had been homesick and preoccupied with the state of his game, but also because he felt alienated by the Spanish golfers who had once encouraged him and protected him. For that, of course, he had no-one to blame but himself. He had offended the nationalistic pride of many of them by demanding a large fee before he would con-sider participating in the 1978 Hennessy Cup, then refusing to play in the World Cup a few months later; by resigning from the Tour in 1981 over the appearance money issue and then causing a rumpus when he found he hadn't been chosen for the Ryder Cup; and by deserting Europe for the fatal charms of the dollar.

Piñero had been quoted as saying that it was 'very difficult now to understand Seve at times . . . I don't think he changed himself, I think the people changed him. In the early days he was allowed to be himself. He had his close friends, the ones on whom you can always rely; but after he wins the big tournaments then everyone claims to be a friend of Seve and wants to be a friend of Seve. They are the hangers-on. So I don't think the ways of Seve today are necessarily of his own doing. They have been shaped for him. I think Seve is introverted. Everyone gets to him and he cannot handle it. He doesn't like to be mobbed by people all the time. What he needs now, more than anything else, is a close friend and not the hangers-on. I spoke with Seve and I said that it was important for him to realize that away from his job he is still an ordinary person and that he must try to be his own person. I think Seve is a nice guy, but he has his problems. He has lost his way. What he needs now is more understanding.'

No two players were more willing to provide Ballesteros with all the understanding he needed than Fernandez and Gonzalez. He had gone to them both during the Lawrence Batley tournament at The Belfry, one week before the Open, and begged them to help him. 'Well, he had played already for nearly six months and he didn't break 70 one round from January to July [in an ordinary Tour event],' recalls Fernandez. 'He asked me if we could play a practice round together. I said yes and one day we went to the practice range and I spotted what I thought was wrong. He was reverse-pivotting.' Ballesteros had started to work on the fault almost immediately but, upon arrival in St Andrews, was still not entirely convinced he had resolved it. Thus, he had come out onto the links with Chino and Jaime for one last attempt to search for the key that would turn his game around.

When twilight crept in purple robes across the quiet golf course, the three friends knew they had found it.

'They told me I was turning too much instead of just transferring my weight,' says Ballesteros. 'They both told me the same thing so I did something about it. And it worked especially well for me.'

Thursday, 12 July 1984. By the time Ballesteros teed off in the first round of the Open Championship, the white horses which had lain still for most of the morning were rearing energetically in the sparkling Bay of Firth. Such is the luck of the draw in this tournament. Some players encounter nothing but blue skies and sunshine during the opening rounds, others have to cope with rain and gale-force winds. But today the weather was as perfect as could be expected at St Andrews and it contributed greatly to Ballesteros's manifestly good humour. Several things were responsible for this sudden change of heart. One was the presence of his mother, now sixty-four, who had never been to the Open before but who had come determined to see her son win; another was the overnight improvement of his golf swing and the subsequent lift of his confidence and spirits; and the third was the arrival of Carmen Botin, his girlfriend of two years, with whom he was staying at a nearby farmhouse.

The Ballesteros who strode so jauntily along the front nine of the Old Course bore little resemblance to the glum Spaniard of recent months. So cheerful was he, in fact, that it seemed at any moment as if he might break into a whistle. 'It was as if he was at home at St Andrews,' recalled Nick de Paul, his American caddie, later. 'He hardly put a foot wrong. If the others had realized just how totally in charge he was, I think they would have been very jittery.'

Round the Loop flew Ballesteros and then along the holes called Bobby Jones, High, Heathery, Hole o' Cross, Long, Cartgate and Corner of the Dyke, adhering all the while to his strategy of avoiding the Old Course's treacherous fairway bunkers. But just as it began to look as though he would hardly be able to help scoring 68 or better, he reached the seventeenth – the Road Hole. There he tried to cut his drive, hit a poor fade instead and was compelled to take a four-iron from relatively thick grass. It ascended into the blue with all the enthusiasm of a snooker ball and fell back into the rough. Next, he attempted a wedge shot to the green but it, too, died and rolled in front of the bunker. He was now 'looking at a six'. Quelling his nerves, he putted bravely round the rim of

212

the bunker. The ball ran down to about 8 feet and he holed the putt for a 'bogey that felt like a birdie'.

'Today was one of the best rounds of the year for me,' said Ballesteros after his round, beaming down at the world's press from the lofty height of the interview platform. 'Two more rounds like that and I will definitely be in contention on Sunday.'

At the close of play he was lying third on the leaderboard on 69, three under par, along with Faldo, Tom Kite and Gonzalez. Ian Baker-Finch, the twenty-three-year-old Queenslander, was a stroke ahead of them, while the leaders, Greg Norman, Peter Jacobsen and Bill Longmuir – the same Longmuir who had conjured up a near-miraculous 65 to lead the Open at Royal Lytham in 1979 by one stroke – were on five under par.

Joe Collet has always maintained that Ballesteros is not a superstitious man but only has a keen sense of traditionalism. Nevertheless, there are dozens of examples to support the theory that he is. He refuses to carry No. 3 balls, for example, never studies a putt from the left-hand side in case he misses it and, since his first victory at Royal Lytham, has always worn navy blue and white on the final day. He did the same throughout 1983 after winning the Masters in a pale blue sweater, white shirt and dark trousers, always putting them on for the last round of a tournament. During his champion's press conference at the Lancome Trophy, he indicated his clothes and said proudly, 'Already five times champions this year.' But the final proof is provided by Longmuir, whom he approached just prior to the Open in 1985, offering to give him lessons to help him with his game. 'If I see your name on the leaderboard, I'll know I'm going to win the golf tournament,' said Ballesteros cheerfully.

'Yeah,' thought Longmuir wryly, 'but what about me?'

Longmuir has never led the Open since, but to this day, if he runs into Ballesteros in the weeks preceding it, the Spaniard will say, 'How are you playing? Are you hitting it all right? Have you qualified?'

It is, as Longmuir says, quite funny really.

Friday, 13 July 1984. On the second day of play Ballesteros was no less exuberant. 'If I was worried a little about my game,' he said later, 'I thought of my friend Fuzzy Zoeller. All year he had not done much but then he went to the US Open and won it. In this game you can never be sure.'

But now the Old Course – subtly at first, for she had been robbed of some of her powers by the benign conditions – exerted her influence on the tournament. She was aided in this by the wind, which began by gusting teasingly but gradually grew more malevolent; by the sun, which had hardened the browning fairways and greens to a state of rare unpredictability; and by the two most notorious holes on the course, the fourteenth and seventeenth. 'There's no other golf course in the world that changes so much with every little puff of wind,' says Crenshaw. 'There's an intricate set of problems on every hole. You're thinking about contours, little humps and hollows. They all add up to what you can and can't do on a certain day. Things that you shouldn't do, things that you ought to do, things that you ought to have done.'

Ballesteros did everything he ought to do, and did it magnificently, for sixteen holes. Then he came to the seventeenth – where he met his nemesis.

Peter Thomson, winner of four Open Championships, one of them at St Andrews, once remarked that, 'as a planner and builder of golf holes world-wide,' he had no hesitation in allowing that if one dared build a par four such as the Road Hole today, one 'would be sued for incompetence.' Mark James said he wasn't sure who had designed it, but that he'd heard he had escaped, while Crenshaw suggested that the reason the 461-yard seventeenth was the greatest par four in the world was because it was a par five. But Ballesteros, who had been two shots clear of the field after thirty-four holes in 1978 when it put paid to his chances, simply described it as 'the hardest hole I've ever played. The pin placings are so difficult. Maybe one day they decide not to put the hole on the green!'

Now, as he stood on the penultimate tee and surveyed the most infamous and dreaded hole in golf, with its black railway sheds, its side-angled view of the monstrosity that is

214

the Old Course Hotel, its scruffy grass and mottled heather, he resolved to improve upon his bogey of the previous day. But it was not to be. The wind was swirling nastily above the heads of the gallery, and it seized his six-iron approach and pulled it into the cavernous Road Hole bunker. Ballesteros needed two shots to get out and all of his skill to hit the second to 4 feet and hole it for a five. He was not alone. Of the 312 golfers who pitted their wits against the Road Hole in the opening rounds, 223 made bogey or worse.

That evening the young Spaniard who had, at the age of twenty-one, cheekily told a questioner that the way to play the seventeenth at St Andrews was to hit a 'good drive, good second shot and one putt', laughed and promised: 'Tomorrow I will par the Road Hole.' On Saturday, after his third consecutive bogey, he amended his vow. 'If I don't par it Sunday, I will come back and play it Monday until I par it.' In victory, the first thing that crossed his mind was: 'I keep my promise. I won't have to come back tomorrow.'

At the end of the day Ballesteros was three strokes adrift of the leader, Baker-Finch, on 137, seven under par. Nick Faldo and Lee Trevino shared second place with him, while Bill Longmuir was on 138. Tom Watson, who had played in the worst of the weather, Fred Couples and Lanny Wadkins were on 139.

Saturday, 14 July 1984. Soon after noon on the third day of play, when the air was mild and a brisk wind followed the field out to the Eden Estuary, Tom Watson, winner of five Open Championships, found himself the grateful beneficiary of a slice of good fortune. His approach shot to the first green, having pitched millimetres short of the Swilcan Burn, bounded safely onto the green – thereby saving him a bogey or worse.

'Luck plays a great part in the game no matter where you play,' said Watson, freckled and smiling, 'but in links golf you have to depend on the bounce.'

In 1984 Watson, the No. 1 player in the world (prior to the Open Championship), was depending upon the luck of the bounce to help him make history by equalling Harry Vardon's record of six Open titles. On Saturday it seemed he would not be disappointed. He had seven birdies and one bogey in a round of 66, and at the end of the day was sharing the lead with the indomitable Baker-Finch on 205, eleven under par. Ballesteros, who had had fourteen pars, three birdies and a bogey, was two strokes behind with Bernhard Langer, while Wadkins, Trevino and Hugh Baiocchi were on 212.

Of Ballesteros, Watson said: 'Seve's a very determined player but I think superstition gets in his way. I believe sometimes he feels the golfing gods are against him and other times I think he feels that the golfing gods are with him. And I think sometimes that can be a hindrance.'

Afterwards, Jorge Ceballos, the Spaniard's manager, said that he had felt all along that it would come down to Ballesteros and Watson. '[Seve] told me he would claw his way through anything to win because he wanted it so badly. It did not matter about his golf and how he had been playing up till then. His form had nothing to do with it. He was going to get this one because he wanted it much more than anybody else.'

Sunday, 15 July 1984. On the morning of the final round, when the loveliest water-colour blue washed over the sky above St Andrews and the air was filled with the mingled aroma of salt, crushed grass and heather, Chino Fernandez drove slowly out of town. He had failed to qualify and felt duty-bound, therefore, to take his family back to London. 'I left a message for Seve, but he never wants to read anything before he goes out. He doesn't like it. Maybe it's superstitious, but it's in case something he doesn't like upsets him before he goes out.'

Nothing happened to disturb Ballesteros's equilibrium at all. Indeed, his composure, as he walked down the steps to the first tee, greeted Langer perfunctorily and turned to gaze out over the Old Course, was remarkable. So was his appearance, for he was strikingly tall, broad-shouldered and handsome, his face a deep rust-colour above his white polo-shirt, his hair like a raven's wing. There was not an eye in the gallery that wasn't pinned on him. He set up over his ball, glanced at the ribbon

216

of green and gold fairway which ran between the bright banks of spectators, and smashed his drive smoothly away.

The previous afternoon, following his round, Ballesteros had been interviewed about his antagonists, and had commented that Watson was a great player and 'he's playing his best now and is confident and I think he is the man to beat.' Later he was to say that his initial objective had been to ensure that his arch-rival was denied the Open trophy. 'That was my first job. To try and beat Langer and then to concentrate on the others.' He set about this task with a singular determination, hitting his approach shot to 10 feet and keeping his nerve when Langer almost holed his from the fairway, knowing that golf is about how and not how many. But fury flitted like a dark angel across his face as his birdie putt stayed wilfully above ground while Langer went to ten under par. 'Pete Coleman was caddying for Bernhard,' recalls Nick de Paul, 'and Pete had caddied for Seve for a time, so he was thinking it was one-up to them. I thought: "Things are going to be tight this afternoon." And I know Seve was thinking the same.'

Behind them Baker-Finch, who had proceeded blithely round the Old Course for three days with barely a scratch, had his first real experience of the darker side of her nature when he hit his approach shot into the Swilcan Burn. Watson moved swiftly and mercilessly to take advantage of his slip. But three putts at the second and fourth holes negated the advance he had made at the third, and when Ballesteros made his first birdie of the day at the fifth, holing from 13 feet while Langer struggled to a bogey six, the American and he were tied at ten under par.

At the sixth hole there was an incident which may have been more significant in the grand scheme of things if Ballesteros had been anything less than completely in control. He pulled his drive, scowled and muttered, 'It's in the bunker.' Someone in the gallery cackled. Ballesteros spun round, eyes flashing. 'You think that's funny?' he asked. There was complete silence. Only the fresh blustery wind and the dull roar of the sea could be heard. Eventually, the Spaniard moved off and, when he found that his ball wasn't in a bunker at all, made par while Watson took three putts at the fifth and Baker-Finch took six at the sixth. Two holes later a five-iron to 6 feet gave him the outright lead of the Open for the first time since he had walked off the final green at Royal Lytham in 1979.

Now the weather began to change and grey clouds stole over the top of the flapping marquees. Ballesteros, tense, confident and excited marched resolutely through the gloom, hitting shot after immaculate shot. At the short eleventh, however, having just three-putted from 70 feet at the tenth, he misclubbed and his eight-iron tee shot rolled off the putting surface and came ominously close to the edge of the evil Strath Bunker. He took out his putter and tried to stroke the ball up the steep bank onto the green. It crawled reluctantly to the top of the hill and hung there. 'One more roll and it would have gone right to the pin,' says Ballesteros. As it was he made bogey while Watson birdied and resumed control of the tournament.

Thus did it continue – the delicate shifting of the balance of power – for by now, though separated by a fairway, they might have been the only two men in the field. The huge crowds, high as kites on the melodramatics, whirled dizzyingly about them in a kaleidoscope of colours, their faces looming spectre-like through the dust. At the twelfth hole Watson was over-ambitious and saw his drive vanish into the bushes in no-man's-land. But he birdied the next just as the Spaniard did the same at the fourteenth, and they were tied once again at eleven under par. On the fifteenth tee Ballesteros reached into his golf bag and, calmly and deliberately, pulled on the navy sweater he had worn to win at Lytham. His face was absolutely rigid with determination. When a putt which, had it dropped, would have given him a one shot cushion going into the Road Hole stopped on the lip of the cup on the sixteenth, he simply squared his shoulders, set his jaw and marched on with his head held high, the gallery pouring after him. 'All the way round I felt good and clear and calm,' he recalled later. 'I held my game together through the excitement, particularly over the closing holes, and that is the key to my winning. I stood up to the pressure.'

But now he heard the siren call of the Road Hole, who had lured so many men to their doom. He himself had suffered three of his five bogeys at her hands. Nevertheless, he believed the line he had taken all week to be the right one, so he drove out to the left. The ball homed unerringly in on the area of rough where it had finished on the previous two occasions. This time he had a good lie. He also had 200 yards to the pin and an area of green no bigger than a postage stamp to work with. He chose a six-iron. Normally, he hits a six-iron no more than 165 yards, but knowing the adrenalin was pumping and knowing too that he might get a flyer out of the rough, he was confident it was the right club. Into the overcast sky it arched, then down onto the dangerous green. It was a stroke of genius. And no-one but a champion could have played that shot, under that pressure, on that hole *and* almost make birdie from it.

Years on, Ballesteros is still amazed by his own audacity. 'The more I look at that shot,' he says laughing, 'the more impressed I get myself. Because if you look at that shot, to put the ball where I did on the green, I guess, was very lucky.'

'You are a lucky player.'

'Yes,' replies Ballesteros, accepting it as a statement of fact. 'Always have been.'

'As we came off the seventeenth green Seve said, "There's going to be a play-off," ' recalls de Paul. 'I said, "If we birdie the last there won't be any need for a play-off." I think it got him thinking positive.'

When Ballesteros had hit his drive to the last hole, he turned and looked back at the seventeenth. There was Watson, solid and seemingly invincible, in prime position on the fairway. 'Well,' thought Ballesteros to himself, 'Watson is Watson. He is going to make a par and he can make a birdie at any time.' And he struck his pitch shot carefully to 15 feet to attempt to finish with a birdie.

Watson had rather less confidence in his ability to bring the Road Hole to its knees than Ballesteros gave him credit for. He was uncertain about the club he should take. First, he thought it might be a three-iron and then he thought it was a two. At last, he selected the latter. Even before it had bounded off the back of the grass and onto the dreaded road, he thought that destiny was closing the door on history. And when he saw his ball pressed up against the wall, watched his chip race past the flagstick and stood by helplessly as his par putt failed to fall, he knew it was.

In the vast amphitheatre of the eighteenth green, Ballesteros played his final stroke – 'the happiest of my life.' Then, as the ball vanished into the hole and the crowd erupted, he exploded into a frenzy of ecstasy and triumph, punching the air over and over as he turned to salute the people who loved him.

More than 200 miles away Fernandez, driving through England, was listening to the drama unfold like a brilliant radio play on his car stereo – which he wouldn't have done if he had been in Spain, for at the precise moment of Ballesteros's victory the Spanish broadcasting networks had switched over to a horse-race. 'When I heard that he won and in his speech he thank his friends, it was fantastic,' says Fernandez. 'The only thing is, he still has to pay me whatever he owes me. He said, "Well, fifty per cent of this is for Vicente and Jaime who helped me." I still have to get my twenty-five per cent!' He bursts out laughing. 'No, but it was very nice . . . I was very happy and I called him and thanked him for what he said. I told him, "I would have been very disappointed if you hadn't said anything." But he's not that kind of person.'

'I can't tell you just what it means to me to win at St Andrews,' said Ballesteros, wreathed in smiles. 'It has made my year without a doubt. When I won at Royal Lytham in 1979, I win with the heart. But this time I won because I prepared myself so well. I had good preparation of the mind, good determination and good thinking on the course. It meant so much to me to do it at St Andrews and have the Spanish flag flying at the home of golf for a year. My first Open win was very special but this proves that it was not a lucky fluke.

'Maybe it will make people think a little more of me.'

Years on, sportscaster Tony Adamson went to Ballesteros to ask him to autograph a poster of his triumph at St Andrews – that famous image of the Spaniard with his fist clenched and his face dark with emotion.

'That was some moment, that,' said Adamson, who had

220

been right beside the final green and had been almost moved to tears by the wonder of it all.

'Yes,' agreed Ballesteros. 'The pinnacle.'

12

The Dry Season

Action is transitory, – a step, a blow
The motion of a muscle, this way or that –
'Tis done, and in the after-vacancy
We wonder at ourselves like men betrayed:
Suffering is permanent, obscure and dark,
And shares the nature of infinity.

William Wordsworth, *The Borderers*

John Brodie, an intelligent, good-humoured Californian who
was once a Quarterback for the San Francisco 49ers and who
is now a successful Senior PGA Tour player, likes to tell a
story about a golf enthusiast friend of his who went up to
Dave Marr and said to him: 'David, who's the best player
in the world? The players know, don't they?'

'Well,' replied Marr, 'I suggest that you go out onto the
practice tee and look around and whoever most of the guys
are looking at is probably pretty good.'

The man followed his advice and walked down to the range.
When he arrived there he saw a group of about eleven players,
including Norman, Strange, Woosnam and Faldo, all standing
about watching Ballesteros hit balls. He went straight back to
find Marr. 'Oh,' he said, 'I see what you mean.'

By 1985, when Ballesteros flew into Georgia for the Masters, he was the No. 1 player in the world, both officially (in

so far as the rankings that existed at that time could be called official) and by consensus of Tour professionals across the globe, and had been accepted as such well before he became Open Champion for the second time, though his victories in 1984 had been spread thinly. After winning the Million Dollar Challenge, struggling unsatisfactorily through the spring and early summer events and triumphing at St Andrews, he had not won again until the World Match Play in autumn, but he had been variably placed third, second, eleventh, second and fourth in the remaining European events.

His principal rival during the season had been Bernhard Langer, the dedicated, athletically built German. Both men came from very similar backgrounds: Ballesteros was the son of a farmer, Langer a bricklayer; the former started playing the Tour at the age of seventeen, the latter at eighteen; both were caddies; both never had handicaps; both came from undeveloped golfing nations; and both were gifted and extremely hard-working. A strong element of competitiveness existed between them, possibly because they were so alike, but for the most part it was healthy and conducive to fine golf. In 1984, however, it was accentuated when Ballesteros beat the German into joint second place at St Andrews, lost to him in the Irish Open, beat him 2 and 1 at the World Match Play and then finished fifth to him on the Order of Merit, and at the Match Play it bubbled over into open hostility.

'Seve never speaks to me so why should I be nice to him,' Langer told journalists on the eve of the final at Wentworth, thereby adding insult to injury, for he had already been quoted as saying that the Spaniard was 'intimidating' on the golf course, which implied that he thought he was guilty of gamesmanship.

Ballesteros was angry and hurt. He retaliated by declaring that he 'would prefer to play Greg [Norman], he's more friendly,' and the next day held a heated and very public exchange with Langer in the press centre as to the exact meaning of his comments.

'I don't know how it started,' says Langer now, of the discord between them at that stage of their careers. 'We're very different. We never were very close friends. I think we

respected each other but we were big rivals for many years
. . . I said he was intimidating, but I didn't really know
what intimidating meant so I used the word in a different
meaning and it all came out rather badly. The press made
it even bigger. Seve's not easy to play with. He doesn't talk
and he never says good shot – or very seldom. He practises
putting when you're over the ball and you can see him out
of the corner of your eye. He's over there, fiddling about.
And he must know these things, and I don't think it's right.
That's what I meant. He intimidates other players. I used
"intimidating" – what the right word might be I still don't
know – but what I meant was he's very difficult to play with,
specially in match-play. He read it in the papers or was just
told by the press. He was kind of shocked. He didn't think
we had a problem and he was very surprised. And we didn't
really have a big problem. The only thing I was saying was
that he's not easy to play with.'

A few days later they sat down together and talked over
two things: Langer's comments to the press and the role
he had played in the Ryder Cup controversy of 1981. 'We
cleared the air,' remembers Langer. In ensuing interviews
they made appropriately complimentary speeches about each
other. Langer listened while Ballesteros assured reporters that
he bore the German no malice, and then the Spaniard stood at
the back of the press centre while Langer explained he had
believed the word intimidating to be an innocuous one and
had really intended it as a compliment to Ballesteros's powers
of concentration.

Henceforth, an uneasy truce had existed between them,
which was still in operation when Ballesteros came to Augusta
in April 1985, brimming over with happiness and contentment. He had started the year well, by successfully defending
his Million Dollar Challenge title and by winning the rain-
shortened USF&G Classic in New Orleans by two strokes
from Mahaffey, but then had missed the cut at the Tournament Players' Championship (TPC) after shooting 76, 74.
This set-back did not dampen his spirits. He took a week's
holiday at Doral in Florida, during which time he did not hit
a single ball but just swam, lay on the beach and fished, and

then reappeared at the Masters on his birthday looking tanned and refreshed. Failing to qualify at Sawgrass did not seem to concern him in the slightest. 'Last year I finished equal third in the TPC, came to Augusta and missed the cut,' he said, smiling round at the worried faces of the British journalists. 'Perhaps my play this time in the TPC will be a better omen for the Masters.'

To begin with, it seemed it would. In the opening round Ballesteros scrambled round the golf course and was fortunate to escape with a 72, but by the second day the work he had put in over the winter was beginning to pay off and he was playing with a fluid and beautiful rhythm. He scored 71 in that round and 71 in the next and, like the shadow of a black hawk, loomed large over the tournament when the final day dawned. Langer, whom fate had decreed should be drawn with the Spaniard, was not the only one afraid of him.

'I'd lost to him in the World Match Play three times,' recalls Langer, 'once in the final, once in the semi-final and once in the second round, and in 1984 he won the British Open and I finished two behind. So it became more and more difficult for me because it seemed like the more we played head to head, the more I lost, even though there were several tournaments where I beat him. So at first I wasn't too excited about the pairing. But I said, "I'm not going to watch him today, I'm just going to play my own game. Whatever he does, it will not bother me." I told myself that the night before. I said, "If he practises putting on the green, I will tell him to go away. If he does anything else, I will tell him what bothers me and I will not be upset if he doesn't say anything." So I had a really clear picture of what I was going to do the next day. And I didn't have any problems.'

On a grey, humid day in the south Ballesteros, dark-eyed and intense, teed off in the fourth round of the Masters, his brother Manuel at his side. Langer, golden-haired and fresh-faced but no less determined, came after them with his even, unhurried stride. Ballesteros drew first blood. His bunker shot at the second hole almost went in for eagle, while Langer, from virtually the same place, took three to get down for a bogey six and was two behind the Spaniard before they had reached the third hole. But gradually it became obvious that Ballesteros had lost his touch on the greens. Putt after putt evaded the hole and denied him birdies, while Langer converted his chances with a three at the third and a two at the sixth. Ahead of them, Strange burnt a fiery trail to the turn. Teeing up on the tenth hole, he was four under par for the day and four ahead of Ballesteros, Langer and Gary Hallberg.

It was at that point that Langer glanced at the leaderboard for the first time. Realizing how much ground he had lost, he resolved simply to try his best, regardless, and to attempt to play the perfidious back nine in four under par. Ballesteros, meanwhile, had grown frustrated and his agitation was reflected in the colour of his language (he rarely swears) and in his grimaces and heavy sighs. He looked on bleakly while Langer made successive birdies at the twelfth and thirteenth holes. Strange's flight to glory had already ended in tears. A three-putt on the tenth and a disastrous encounter with Rae's Creek at the thirteenth had brought him crashing down to earth. Ballesteros fought on gamely, making par after par after par but no birdies. It was not good enough. His last chance was a critical and brilliantly executed chip shot on the sixteenth, which would have brought him to within a stroke of the German with two holes to play had he holed it. But it narrowly avoided the cup, and the Spaniard threw himself to the ground in despair for he knew that he had now left the way clear for Langer.

Walking off the seventeenth green Ballesteros put his arm around Langer's shoulders. 'It's all yours,' he said. 'Well done. You've played some great shots.'

Looking back at that tournament now, through the brightly lit tunnel of time, it is possible to see it as the start of a dry season in Ballesteros's career – of a period when major championships seemed beyond his reach, when he lost his spontaneous smile and swashbuckling, devil-may-care attitude, and when he became increasingly discontented and preoccupied with holding his great swing in check. At the time, however, it was not noted as being particularly significant. Yes, Ballesteros had finished joint runner-up with Strange and Floyd on 284, two strokes behind his arch-enemy Langer, and yes, it had meant a lot to him to win so it was obviously very painful for him to lose. But it didn't really matter, did it? Wasn't it still an achievement to be second?

And so it was that when Ballesteros teed up in the PGA Championship at Wentworth in the last week of May (for a fee of £30,000), he gave every appearance of having bounced back from his experience at Augusta without any after-effects at all; indeed, he probably did, for it was only in the light of the events of the next two years that the 1985 Masters was of any consequence at all. Six weeks had elapsed since he left Augusta. In the interim, he had participated in a £250,000 Skins game in Australia, along with Nicklaus, Watson, Faldo, Lyle, Langer and Norman, where he had earned £25,000 for winning only one hole; had flown to Boston to visit his girl-friend, Carmen, who was at college there; had finished equal fifth in the Italian Open; and had acquired a racing bike. This last had become his new obsession. In the fortnight preceding the tournament, he claimed to have ridden twenty miles daily along the mountainous routes surrounding Santander, wearing five sweaters and two pairs of trousers to help him pedal away the pounds. He had also been using a hand-strengthening device given to him by Gary Player.

'All the top players have strong legs,' insisted Ballesteros. 'Look at Jack Nicklaus and Tom Watson. It's foolish to say you don't have to be fit to play golf. I want to be a better golfer and the stronger you are, the more confident you are.'

He proved it by finishing joint fourth behind Paul Way.

In June Ballesteros returned to America for the US Open at Oakland Hills. In horrendous, blustery conditions he returned opening scores of 71, 72, and was six strokes behind the leader, T.C. Chen, after two days of play. Then, when all eyes were on him after a third round 69, that strange, cautious aspect of his personality revealed itself and smothered his usual boldness and flair. He became obsessed with taking irons off the tee. He plotted his way carefully round the front nine of the brutal USGA layout like a man playing chess for his life, and it was not until he reached the turn and found that he had nothing to show for his attempts at self-preservation but a 37, that he lowered his guard and came home in 34. By then, of course, it was too late. Andy North had seized control of the tournament and Ballesteros was not even in the running.

Even Trevino expressed astonishment at the Spaniard's handling of the closing rounds. 'Seve has unbelievable potential,' he said, 'and there is not a shot in golf that he can't hit, but he hasn't quite got down to managing his game yet.' But the unnatural conservatism which had gripped Ballesteros's game in several major championships rarely did so in ordinary Tour events. When Trevino encountered the Spaniard in the Irish Open, he noted with awe that, 'I looked into his eyes and I could see the killer instinct coming out.'

The victim on that particular occasion was not the Mexican but the new Masters champion. Langer scored an incredible last round 63 at Royal Dublin to catch Ballesteros, who had had a 66, and force a play-off. But at the second extra hole, where they both had identical putts of 12 yards, the Spaniard sank his for a birdie three and victory. The following week Ballesteros won again. On the first day of the French Open at St Germain, he played golf of such flawless and exquisite quality that he scored 62, nine under par. It was the lowest round of his career on the European Tour. Twice before he had scored 61 – once in a pro-am in Madrid and once in a tournament in Japan – but rarely had he played a round more solid or more perfect. He hit every single fairway off the tee and was putting for birdies or eagles on every one of eighteen holes, going out in 33 and coming back in 29. By the fourth round he had a seven stroke lead and a 69 ensured him victory by two shots over Sandy Lyle. His prize money of £13,751 amounted to less than a third of what he had been paid in appearance fees.

None of these things served to comfort him when he recorded a 75 in the rain-lashed first round of the Open at Royal St George's. His momentum was interrupted when there was a lengthy delay in obtaining a ruling for him on the fourth hole, and he never seemed to recover it. He scored 74, 70, 73 in the remaining rounds and finished equal thirty-eighth on 292, ten strokes behind the Open Champion, Sandy Lyle.

Lyle's victory was important for several reasons. In the first place, it meant he was the first British golfer in sixteen years to win the Open. In the second, it drove home the point that the balance of power in world golf had shifted away from the United States to such an extent that three of the last six winners of the Masters and three of the last seven Open Champions had been Europeans. By the end of 1985 the Europeans had done the impossible and won the Ryder Cup, and the top three names on the world rankings were Ballesteros, Langer and Lyle.

There can be little doubt that the Spaniard was almost single-handedly responsible for the meteoric rise of European golf then and for the glorious heights it has reached now. It was Ballesteros who first went to America, Ballesteros who became the first European to triumph there since Jacklin, Ballesteros who convinced the Europeans that the Americans were not invincible and Ballesteros who gave them the courage to believe in themselves. As Ken Brown says, 'After he won Greensboro we knew that if he could win in America, we could, because we knew how we compared with him and that we could beat him on any given day.'

'Seeing Sandy and Nick win the Open Championship and watching Bernhard win the Masters, I gave a little credit to myself,' Ballesteros was to say years on. 'I think I was the one who proved we had this ability to win majors. I think I helped give confidence to the European players.'

So the Europeans crossed the Atlantic one by one and by 1986 Brown, Faldo, Lyle and Langer were all playing there regularly and all except Brown had won one or more tournaments there. Ballesteros, for his part, had encountered the same resentment of foreign participation from American Tour players that Jacklin did in the Seventies. 'You're only a nice guy here if you don't win,' he said at Augusta in 1980. 'They smile when I lose. But they don't say anything if I am winning. Except, maybe, that I am lucky. That's OK with me.'

And when Langer won the Masters, Ballesteros told him, 'I am happy that it was one of us Europeans that won and not one of them' – meaning the Americans.

Watson remembers Ballesteros being very unpopular with many US Tour players in those years and thinks it had 'a lot to do with his focus when he's on the golf course, his desire to win. I think that manifested itself in some players' eyes as being cold or distant.'

Jacklin sees it more as jealousy. 'By 1985 he was right in his prime as a player. His abilities were recognized around the world. I mean, even the Americans, who are reluctant to admit that anybody's ever better than an American, couldn't help but believe that here was somebody that was special. He was *the* man of his time, as Hogan was, as Palmer was, as Nicklaus was, in a given era that they dominated. And there was no question that Ballesteros dominated.'

'I've *never* understood why,' says Ben Crenshaw of the insular prejudices of certain American pros. 'I was always for the foreign players. I wanted them to come. Some were thinking that, "Well, he's coming over here and he's taking up my spot." I like to know where I stand, what you can learn from them. It's all a learning process. I don't know. I've always felt we should welcome them. But our Tour can sometimes be construed as taking care of its own.'

'The guys on [the US] Tour call it cherry-picking,' explains Jay Townsend, an American who plays on the European Tour. 'They don't want Bernhard and Seve and Jose and Sandy and Nick to go over there and play when they want, make a bunch of money, like they do, and go home. They look at how these guys are coming over and taking from them, they don't see that they're going over to Europe and taking out. I think a lot of it's jealousy. It used to be that the Americans were the undisputed best players . . . and now, in the last ten years, the [foreign] golfers have become stronger, and the Americans don't like it. They don't want anybody coming over on their Tour. It's their own deal.'

In 1985 Ballesteros saw less of the American players than he ought to have done for the simple reason that he spent most of his time in Europe, despite being a member of the US Tour. He finished joint seventh behind Langer in the European Open and then strolled comfortably to victory in the Sanyo Open, the week after the Ryder Cup. Throughout this period he was having problems at home, for his father was extremely ill. In a rare week when he was well enough to travel, Ballesteros brought him over to the World Match Play in Britain. Vicente came too and caddied for his brother, and Ballesteros beat Langer for the second time in the final. When he returned home, he won the Spanish Open, prompting the Secretary of State for Sport, Roman Cuyas, to offer 75 million pesetas (£326,000) for golf course construction after Ballesteros had gone on television to plead for more spending on municipal courses. The government's offer meant that six basic nine-hole courses could be laid out.

On Friday, 1 November, while Ballesteros was at the Portuguese Open, the following announcement appeared in the *Daily Telegraph*: 'Severiano Ballesteros's membership of the US PGA Tour has been revoked by the Policy Board meeting in New York. He will not be allowed to play in Tour co-sponsored tournaments in the US next year because he has played only nine Tour events this year instead of the minimum fifteen. He remains eligible for the Masters, which he has won twice, for the US Open and the PGA Championship. Ballesteros can also play in the USF&G Classic in New Orleans in March as defending champion.'

To say that Ballesteros was shocked would be an understatement. Outraged is more accurate. Afraid of saying something he might regret, he refused to discuss the matter with anyone other than Ceballos, Schofield and Beman. His only comment then was: 'If the decision stands, it will be a terrible mistake. It's anti-social.' Later he insisted, 'the first thing I knew about a possible ban was when Mr Beman wrote to me [in] August. I just thought I'd lose my membership, but still be able to play under the old sponsor's invitation rules.'

'Seve has set himself on a course of confrontation with us,' retorted Beman. 'Now we have gone back to the old rules after his failure to comply with the new ones.'

The irony of the situation was this: not two years previously Beman, in his desperation to bring the charismatic genius of Ballesteros to the American public, had created 'special privileges' for European players, allowing them to treat the whole of Europe as their home circuit. Now, he was not only punishing Ballesteros, he was also rescinding the privileges of every other European player in the top 125 on the US money list. Non-US Tour members would in future be allowed to play no more than six tournaments a year.

The influential American magazine *Sports Illustrated* dealt harshly with Beman, saying: 'The PGA Tour has told the best golfer in the world to get lost and we agree with Ballesteros who says "it was a thoughtless decision that can only harm international golf." '

Ceballos, who was almost as shaken as Ballesteros, pointed out that Ballesteros had fulfilled his fifteen tournament commitment in 1984 but had felt that there was too much pressure on him and that it had led to a disappointing season. He also said that Ballesteros had already received twenty-six invitations to play in America in 1986. 'What are those sponsors going to think?' he asked.

'Ballesteros upset Beman because he stood up for what he thought was right,' says John Brodie. 'And if you ever begrudge a man for doing that then you're wrong. I think you should listen to a man who thinks he's right even if he is in fact wrong; and I think there's a lot of discussion about whether or not he was wrong there, [in view of] the fact that it was so vehemently stated that, "This will be the way you do it", when the rules out here change *so often* and they sometimes change for very peculiar reasons. I just think that if we took under our wing what was the best interest for golf and that became one of our priorities over here, that they would do the same in Europe and you'd have no problem. And, to me, the Europeans have a much better outlook on life as it applies to golf than do the Americans.'

'When they started, you know, going at it,' recalls Collet, 'it was more like Seve criticizing Deane personally about the rules they had for the way the Tour worked, that they selfishly favoured the Americans, that they were a little archaic and should be renewed. In fact, we wrote him a letter which suggested three alternatives: that they either reduced the number of tournaments one had to play in to retain one's membership, increased the number of exemptions that a player could have without being a member, or counted a couple of tournaments as those you could play on merit. And they said: "None of those are possible." And a couple of years went by and lo and behold the TPC is now one that you can play if you qualify, period. So, too little, too late.'

But while the question of whether or not Ballesteros deserved to be banned from the US Tour was being hotly debated by the golfing press, a far crueller tragedy was being played out behind the scenes. Baldomero Ballesteros, Severiano's father and his best friend, was dying. His four sons rallied round him but in March 1986 he passed away. Severiano, who had been closest to him, was devastated. It was the most traumatic event of his young life and the scars it left remain unhealed to this day.

'It was very hard on him,' says Fernandez sympathetically, 'because just when his father started to live the life Seve wanted him to live, he was gone.'

It is Collet's belief that that, more than anything else, was the reason why Ballesteros failed to play in the required number of events.

'It's kind of an emotional subject,' says Collet. 'I don't think you'll get much out of Seve . . . His father was dying of terminal cancer. He had had one lung removed. Seve interrupted his schedule to be with him and to help make arrangements at the hospital, and he didn't convalesce well, developed pneumonia in the remaining lung and expired. And it really shook him. He was very close to his father. And the fact that they were getting him checked up during the year – they went to Houston, I think, for the operation – made it very difficult for Seve to fulfil his commitments . . . He's very proud and it's not easy for him to pick up the phone to anybody, whether it's to his wife or to me . . . He just doesn't. A phone is some kind of an aggravation that's there. He only calls when he absolutely has to or when he's bored and there's nothing else. If he wants something, he calls, if he doesn't, he hopes you don't call him. And so what he should have done was call Deane Beman, and say: "Listen, Deane, I don't know if you know this but my father's terminally ill. I know I've made some commitments to the Tour, but he's the most important thing in my life and I really need to be with him. It's so upsetting for me, my mind isn't on the game, and I just can't play all those weeks. I hope you understand."

'He probably didn't fully appreciate that it would be an issue and then by saying nothing he created an issue,' explains Collet. 'It's very difficult for him to talk about his father. But, having sat back as a witness, I think that's what happened. I think had he called [Deane], that it would have been OK, because Norman had a similar problem one year . . . and they gave him a rain check. But that was because they were businesslike enough to address the problem pro-actively, whereas that's not Seve's nature. He's more reticent about doing things that a lot of people would do and he reaps the harvest. Because it's an emotional issue, he would sound to himself like he was making excuses if he talked about his father.

'So he just avoided the whole discussion and it looks like he was irresponsible.'

The fifteenth hole at Augusta National has a reputation for changing lives and influencing destinies. It was to this par five that Gene Sarazen came in the last round of the 1935 Masters, trailing Craig Wood by three strokes, and hit one of the greatest shots ever played – an albatross two – going on to win the green jacket and the play-off, and put the championship, then only in its second year, on the front pages. Fifty-one years later Sarazen, still wearing plus-fours and still sitting on his favourite balcony overlooking the golf course, was retelling the story for the umpteenth time. 'My caddie tried to talk me into hitting a three-wood. But I took out my turf-rider [four-wood] instead. The moment I hit it, I felt something in my bones. Walter Hagen was playing with me and Jones was on the green. Twenty-one people were behind the green. The sun was going down. I wasn't sure it had gone in the hole until I saw all twenty-one people jumping up and down.'

At virtually the same stage in 1986 Ballesteros was striding unknowingly, like a goose across a grave, along the fairway of a hole that would have a more shattering effect on his career than any other single event. He seemed tense and, as one newspaperman put it, 'too anxious to prove the ridiculousness of his situation, even if it was of his own doing.' Already the US Tour ban had cost him dearly. He had lost his job as touring professional for Doral Country Club and, apart from the USF&G Classic where he had missed the cut, and the Florida Cup Classic on the TPA mini-tour where he had finished twenty-second, had been denied competitive practice of any kind for the Masters. As a result, he was disinclined to talk to either journalists or officials. 'Whatever happens now, this will be a bad year for me,' he had predicted after the death of his father. When he did speak it was to inform the media in no uncertain terms that when the tournament was over he would be the champion.

'I will win this,' he declared. 'It will be mine by the time I get to the sixteenth on the last day.'

On Sunday, 13 April 1986 Severiano Ballesteros came to the fifteenth hole of Augusta National in the final round of the Masters, leading by two strokes. All around him tidal waves of applause swelled and crashed, as the great gallery swung between the brilliant young Spaniard and the extraordinary spectacle of Nicklaus, aged forty-six, rising like a phoenix from the ashes of an ailing career. The day was a fathomless, indigo blue. Sunlight and shadow flickered across Ballesteros's damp shirt and warmed his skin as he set over the ball on the 500-yard par five and prepared to drive. He knew as soon as he had struck it that it was a good shot. It boomed off the clubface into the clear sky and finished far down the fairway. Vicente, who was caddying for him, clapped him excitedly on the back. He scented victory. Two holes previously, when Ballesteros had hit a huge drive round the corner at the thirteenth hole, followed it with an approach shot to 6 feet and holed the putt for his second eagle of the day, the brothers had shaken hands, as if in premature congratulation.

'I thought when I eagled the thirteenth I was the champion,' Ballesteros said afterwards.

Elsewhere on the course, that extreme pressure which only comes into play on the closing holes of a major championship, and which crushes the very life-blood from the uninitiated, was beginning to take its toll. Norman, the overnight leader, whom

Ballesteros had caught by the turn, succumbed to it with a double-bogey at the tenth and missed his putt to tie at the eighteenth. The Golden Bear's charge had been launched at the ninth. Playing with the fearless determination of a man who has nothing left to lose and everything in the world to gain, he made three successive birdies, and was only halted when he failed to get up and down on the twelfth. By the time he reached the sixteenth green, he was on seven under par and two strokes adrift of Ballesteros, having birdied the thirteenth and eagled the fifteenth. A birdie putt of one yard would elevate him to eight under par.

Ballesteros and Watson were on the hole behind him, quietly waiting for the tumult to die down. The latter was on the green, facing a 20-foot putt for eagle which would take him to seven under par. Reluctant to play until there was silence, he stood there motionless as the minutes ticked by. When he finally did putt, he missed. Ballesteros, meanwhile, was standing patiently on the fairway visualizing his approach shot and birdie putt. He had 210 yards to the flag. With a four-iron in his hand, Ballesteros lined up his shot. A sudden hush, unnatural after the clamour which had preceded it, had settled over the cool green fairway. A breeze lifted his hair.

One last glance at the pin . . . an intake of breath . . . a ragged, short, uneven, uncommitted golf swing . . . a gasp . . . a splash . . . a spreading ring of terrible ripples . . . calamity!

Nicklaus heard the roar as he walked to the penultimate tee. 'It wasn't the sound of a cheer but it was the sound of a cheer,' he recalled later. Ballesteros, cold with shock, holed out for a six; then three-putted the seventeenth. It was over.

'For a while we all felt that Seve, under the severest pressure, would always pull off the magical shot,' says John Jacobs. 'I think something of that left him when he dumped it in the water at Augusta. But I think he just stood waiting and waiting behind Nicklaus eagling and birdying and holing putts, and everybody screaming and yelling. And obviously he took too much club. He was still leading by one or two at that stage, and he packed up on it – you could see he did. And I've talked to him since. He overclubbed because "the only way I could lose the Masters was if I put it in the water short." But he knew it was too much club and he stopped on it. And then, of course, Nicklaus birdied the seventeenth. And Seve had to stand there and watch this.'

'You know, everybody says, "Well, Seve hit that shot in the water," ' says Crenshaw vehemently. 'Anybody, *anybody* can miss a shot like that. But it was so painful for him. And everybody said he was completely downcast for two years. Maybe he was. Who knows?'

'That shot, to me, looked like a fella who had not played a lot of golf that year, had not prepared,' recalls Nicklaus. 'And whether that was his fault or somebody else's fault, I don't know. But when he hit his second shot, he quit on the ball. It was not a good swing for him. It was a very defensive hope-the-ball-goes-on-the-green shot. It was not, "I'm going to hit the ball and knock it on the green." It was not that kind of a swing. It was the kind of swing that I find myself making quite often early in the year, when I haven't been playing much golf. And I just sort of related to that. And that was obviously the shot that cost him the tournament, and it probably cost him a couple of years mentally.'

'I don't want to take anything away from Jack,' says Ballesteros, who eventually finished fourth after Nicklaus came home in 30 to win his sixth Masters. 'He played fantastic golf. But I think for me not to win was almost a miracle under all the circumstances. Eight out of ten times I would have won. It was *destino*. It took a long time before I was confident with my four-iron again. You know, this is mental game. It really works on your mind. I lost my confidence, no question.'

How deep were the wounds or how lasting the scars, did not become obvious at once. The full extent of the damage to Ballesteros's psyche was only revealed gradually, over four or five years, until now it seems that of all the things that have shaped his character and governed his fate, none have had the impact on him that the 1986 Masters and the death of his father did – for the two are inextricably linked. But that April Ballesteros appeared to recover before the last putt was holed at Augusta. The very next week he was leading the Suze Open at Cannes-Mougins, jogging four miles daily with Vicente in preparation for the US Open in June and telling the press: 'I was the only one in contention from start to finish at Augusta but no-one even mentioned me on Monday morning. That hurt me. But I accept the challenge. I like it when the going is tough and I'll be going all out to win the Open.'

The changes in him were subtle ones. They were noticeable in the 73 he scored in the last round to lose the Suze Open; in the slip he made to surrender the Madrid Open to Howard Clark after leading by two strokes going into the final nine; in the bogeys he made in the fourth round of the Italian Open to finish equal fourth; in the 74 he shot in the opening round of the Spanish Open to finish equal third.

He took two weeks off then and when he came back there was a harder, more resolute glint in his eye. A putting tip on the eve of the Dunhill Masters from his friend Jaime Gonzalez made an overnight improvement in his touch on the greens. He took only twenty-eight putts in the first round and was a stroke off the lead. For the first time since leaving Augusta, he began to smile. In the closing rounds he played glorious attacking golf that was a joy to witness and overcame his playing partner Robert Lee by two strokes with a score of 275, thirteen under par. Afterwards, Nick de Paul described him as a new man. 'You've no idea how much he wanted that Dunhill Masters victory,' he said. 'I have seldom seen Seve so nervous over the closing holes as he was then. All those narrow defeats this season were preying on his mind. He was desperate to win again.'

Once Ballestcros had destroyed the mental barrier in front of him, he couldn't stop winning. To appreciate the sheer magnitude of his talent and the extent of his domination of European golf in the Eighties, one need look no further than his playing record. In the decade between 1976 and 1986 he won more than fifty-two tournaments, was runner-up twenty times, third eighteen times, in the top ten thirty-nine times and missed only four cuts in Europe (an incredible feat). In 1986 he followed his Dunhill Masters victory with successive wins in the Irish Open, the Monte Carlo Open and the French Open, finished joint sixth in the Open before winning the Dutch

Open (by a landslide margin of eight strokes), finishing tied first in the Lancome Trophy – following an unprecedented situation in which he and Langer called a referee after four holes of a play-off, having had to stop because night was falling, and asked if they could call it a draw and split the first and second prizes of £33,313 and £21,505 – equal tenth in the German Open and equal fourth in the European Open. By mid-July he had already been paid an estimated £230,000 in appearance money (approximately £25,000 per event). When he won in Holland he achieved one of his greatest ambitions, to become the first player on the European Tour to amass more than £1 million in tournament earnings. By the end of the season he was the No. 1 player on the Order of Merit for the fourth time, with £259,275, and his stroke average was 68.95. His playing statistics at the time of the Open were as follows: Driving distance – 277 yards; Driving accuracy – 56 per cent; Greens in regulation – 72 per cent; Sand saves – 75 per cent; Putting average – 29.25.

Two things put these statistics into perspective: a. On the Tuesday after the Open he sponsored a junior caddies' competition at Pedreña, the first event he ever won; b. During the same week he attended a ceremony to rename one of Pedreña's main thoroughfares *Calle Severiano Ballesteros*.

And so the season drew to a close and its hero returned to Spain in a blaze of glory. Its only blight had been the Masters. How much it was preying on Ballesteros's mind was shown at the World Match Play when, asked whether he would like to beat Nicklaus after what had happened at Augusta, he replied: 'There is nothing to avenge. Jack Nicklaus is a great champion. I will take revenge from the golf course, especially from the fifteenth.'

And so it was that, in the final round of the Masters in 1987, Ballesteros exacted retribution from the fifteenth hole and clawed his way back into contention with a birdie. Ahead of him, twenty-eight-year-old, Augusta-born Larry Mize, little known to anyone outside of his home town, had hit his approach shot to 4 feet at the eighteenth and made three for an aggregate of 285. Desperate to catch him, Ballesteros struck boldly from the tee at the seventeenth. He was rewarded with a

5-foot putt, which he holed for birdie. Norman followed him in from 35 feet. There were shades of 1986 at the eighteenth when the Spaniard bunkered his approach shot, but with marvellous composure he managed to get up and down and he, Norman and Mize were tied for the Masters.

It was early evening when the three men teed off on the tenth, the first hole of a sudden-death play-off, and the tall pines cast long shadows across the jade fairway. Spectators were packed solidly from tee to green. Mize hit the longest drive, but each of them hit the putting surface in regulation strokes, and Ballesteros's ball finished 20 feet away. 'I felt I hit my second shot perfectly,' he said afterwards. 'Had the ball bounced one more yard, it would have run round to the hole instead of rolling straight on to finish off the green. With Norman and Mize both having birdie chances, I gave it a little extra, running it three and a half feet past. The sun was directly into my eyes on the return . . . I don't think I did anything wrong but I must have aimed left.'

And missed.

'That was a harrowing moment for anyone that feels for a player,' says Schofield, who went back to the clubhouse with the distraught Spaniard, 'and I felt very bad for him at that particular moment. He was in tears. I said to him, "Hey, come on, Gary Player would take the view that he hasn't lost the Masters. No-one's beaten you over seventy-two holes." And he went the next week and won in Cannes – such is the strength of the man – and by the time he got there that's the phrase he was using to the journalists. So perhaps I'd been of some good. And I think you have to give someone something to cling to. No-one had beaten him over seventy-two holes. He lost in extra time. Small consolation, you might say, but at least it was something.'

But during that long, tortuous walk along the tenth hole, away from the gay crowds and the duel for the Masters Championship, Ballesteros was inconsolable. Head bowed and shoulders slumped, he wept for everything he had ever loved and lost – especially for his father, whom he had promised before he died that he would win the Masters at Augusta.

For that one moment in time, there was no sadder, more lonely man in all the world than Severiano Ballesteros.

13

A Measure of Greatness

I have found my heart again.

Rudyard Kipling, *Kim*

Ballesteros, in a mood of wistful contemplation, once remarked to Doust: 'Bad luck sticks in my mind more than good
luck. Sometimes I remember bad things that have happened
to me.'

Nothing was imprinted on his mind with such nightmarish
detail as the Masters he felt he had let slip. He could remember as if it were yesterday flinging himself to the ground in an
agony of despair on the sixteenth hole in 1985, when the chip
which might have won him the tournament failed to go in the
hole; he could not forget the winking pond on the fifteenth in
1986, nor the jarring feeling in his hands as the ball left the
clubhead, nor the deathly hush, nor the snaking ripples, nor
the blood turning to ice in his veins; and he still shuddered
at the memory of that interminable walk back from the first
play-off hole while Mize and Norman battled for the prize
that should have been his.

Four years had gone by since Ballesteros had last won
a major. During that time he had lost or been beaten in
(depending on your viewpoint) three Masters, two US Opens
and two US PGA Championships, and every one of them
haunted him and gnawed at his psyche.

'It is wrong to settle major championships by sudden-death,' he had said vehemently after the 1987 Masters, having relived the ordeal of the tenth hole a million times over. 'I didn't want to say anything at the Masters because it might have seemed like sour grapes but they must go back to the eighteen hole play-offs. Even five holes, as in the British Open, is fairer. I don't want to take anything away from Larry Mize who chipped in to win at the second hole, but I think it is more likely that the real champion will win in an eighteen hole play-off. It's very disappointing to miss out for three years in a row. I feel I could have had four or five green jackets instead of two. But I was much more disappointed [in 1986] after being two ahead with four to play and going in the lake. I feel as much the Masters Champion as Larry Mize because I tied after seventy-two holes.'

No-one was convinced – least of all Ballesteros. Later he admitted: 'I lost faith in my putting when I missed that short one in the play-off. I started missing a lot of short putts after that; especially the crucial ones.'

Gradually, as the seasons passed and the majors, golf's only real measure of greatness and the criterion by which Ballesteros measures himself, continued to elude him, that aura of invincibility which had surrounded him became eroded. He lost the Palmeresque audacity he had always had, the conviction that if it could be imagined it could be birdied or eagled, and along with it went some of the intrepidity which had been a feature of his game. He lost his nerve on the greens and his ability to win through will-power alone, regardless of form or good fortune. He lost, in short, like so many great players before him, that youthful belief in his own immortality.

Human nature being what it is, it wasn't long before people began to voice – albeit in whispers – the unthinkable. Could it be that Ballesteros's genius, so dependent on inspiration, had left him? Could the pressure-cooker atmosphere of the last nine holes of the majors be causing him to collapse? 'Nobody,' insists Robert Green, 'actually called it choking, but some people were wondering . . .' Or could it be possible that the most gifted player of the modern era was washed up?

'Perish the thought that we have seen the best of Ballesteros,' said Michael Williams, 'but as time [goes by] . . . one does begin to speculate.' Michael McDonnell agreed. 'The question used to be *when* would Ballesteros win another big title. But as he has not done it since 1984, some critics now want to know whether he will ever win again.'

The reasons offered for Ballesteros's decline were many and various. Some suggested it was because the course of true love had not run smoothly for him and Carmen Botin; they had been talking of marriage for four years and nothing had happened. Others said that it might be due to his pre-occupation with money, or even his ailing back, while there were those who were certain it was because he had tempered his golf swing to such an extent that he had taken the fire out of his game. 'What's happened to Seve is rather like what happened to Arnold Palmer,' Jacobs told Doust. 'They were both wild hitters and fantastic putters, but once they learned to play, which in Seve's case came [around 1985 or 1986], their putting left them.' His brothers, of course, were another problem. He had never won a major with any of them caddying for him. Fingers were pointed at the handshake between him and Vicente on the thirteenth hole of the 1986 Masters shortly before disaster struck, and at the voluble and animated conversations the normally taciturn Ballesteros had with every one of his siblings on the golf course. Then there was the matter of the row he had had with Vicente when he was sharing the lead in the final round of the 1987 US PGA Championship. Moments later, at the 533-yard par five third, a hole he had birdied for three consecutive rounds, he drove into the right rough, chipped out sideways, returned to the rough with his approach shot, went into a bunker, then into the water, and finally sank a 10-foot putt for a triple-bogey eight. He finished with a 78, an aggregate of 292 and a share of tenth place. 'I thought I had a chance,' Ballesteros, who had finished third in the US Open at Olympic earlier in the season after scoring 68, 75, 68, 71, said miserably. 'But nothing happened. That's really what has been happening all year. It's my *destino* this year.'

Whatever the cause of Ballesteros's inner conflict on the

golf course, there was no escaping the fact that it had a radical effect on him outwardly. His face, always an accurate barometer of his moods, now mirrored his emotions exactly and the feelings it reflected were not happy ones. Gone was the impudent grin and the ready wit; he became distant, surly and increasingly morose. 'I can remember doing an interview with him,' says Jacobs, 'and saying, "Seve, smile like you used to smile," because he was always scowling and looking miserable.'

'Every week everyone wants me to do 61,' protested Ballesteros at the Lancome Trophy in 1987. 'There is too much pressure on and off the golf course. Everyone wants just one minute from me and it turns out to be two weeks. If I am not careful I can get burned out and I do not want that. I want to keep playing for years.' But at the US PGA Championship he confessed: 'People tell me I have to be more relaxed, that I put too much pressure on myself. I'm trying to convince myself that I'm a happy man.'

No other player in golf has the power to move an audience, whether it be a gallery at a tournament or the public at large, the way Ballesteros does. No-one has his ability to make them suffer with him, pull for him, laugh with him or even weep for him, because no-one fights as bravely or as well. On 13 March 1988, almost eleven months after his victory in the Suze Open at Cannes Mougins, his last win anywhere in the world, he put the smile back on his face and sunshine into the lives of the emotional crowd who saw him, when he took the Mallorcan Open at Santa Ponsa by six strokes from Jose Maria Olazábal. A single swallow does not make a summer, but at least it is a start – one step taken along the slippery slope to recovery.

But by April Ballesteros had stumbled once again. He had failed to qualify at the TPC, and had been left to rue the chances he had missed when he scored 73, 72, 70, 73 at Augusta to finish seven strokes behind the winner, Sandy Lyle. Worst of all, he had shot 76, 78 in the Cannes Open, to miss his first cut since the Silk Cut Masters in 1983 where he had been disqualified for signing a wrongly marked card. He had not actually scored too many since the Sanyo Open in 1982. 'Everything was bad,' he said sadly. 'I gave everything last week in the Masters and I gave everything I had left here as well. Nothing went right.'

Precisely one month later, with no prior warning whatsoever, Ballesteros exploded gloriously into the limelight, when he beat Greg Norman, Ken Brown and David Frost with a birdie at the first extra hole of a four-way play-off for the Buick Classic. It was his first victory in America for three years.

Wednesday, 13 July 1988, Open Championship, Royal Lytham. Nothing in professional sport is as cruel, as tormenting, as hard a taskmaster as the ghost of past achievements. Ballesteros, who on Monday had played his first round of golf at Lytham since winning the Open in 1979, knew it well and intended to use it to his advantage. Before coming to the tournament he had spent long hours looking at videos of his triumph in the hope that the magic of those incredible years would revisit him. 'I think watching all those putts drop can encourage me to do well,' he said earnestly. 'I made a lot of putts on the last day. I think my putting is still as good. The only difference is that the ball doesn't go in the hole and I don't know why.'

On that first day, in the biting cross-winds of Lytham, he had played with Lyle for the price of a sandwich. 'I lost,' admitted Ballesteros with a grin, 'but it didn't matter because Sandy had to buy his own lunch. I didn't pay.' The Spaniard and the huge, gentle Scot had been firm friends since 1985 when Lyle had won the Open. Much to Lyle's surprise, Ballesteros had sent him a congratulatory telegram. 'It was a nice gesture. That was how it all started, really. I can't remember it word for word but it was like, "Congratulations, you deserve it." The gist of the rest of it was: "A word of advice. You can't please everybody. Just do your own thing." I've always tried to take that bit of advice. It's impossible, really, to please everybody. So you've just got to do what suits you and get on with it . . . It's too easy to say, "Yes, I'll do that for you," and before you know it you've spent an hour at the golf course and you haven't hit a golf ball yet.

246

'I would say,' observes Lyle, describing Ballesteros, 'he's slightly on the shy side, although he's all right with his own little clique of Spanish friends . . . I don't treat him any differently to how I treat my sisters or my father. I just talk to him and don't give him any bullshit, and if he's out of order I tell him. And if he thinks I'm out of order on certain things, he'll tell me. That's the way it is. If you try to be somebody you're not to him, then he'll see through you quite quickly . . . I've never been to his house but he's been to my house a few times. He's just part of the family, in a way. He watches videos, plays with the kids. He's down to earth, really. I think if you're a friend of Seve's, you're a friend for ever. It's just a matter of breaking that barrier.'

At Lytham, Lyle watched Ballesteros with slight incredulity as he retraced his steps over the last five holes of his victory. At the par four sixteenth, scene of the infamous car-park birdie, the Spaniard took a three-iron off the tee, a sand-wedge off the fairway and three-putted for bogey – the golfing gods having a fine sense of irony. 'The way I won was a miracle,' he said. 'I had no game plan then. I just teed up and hit it. I haven't lost that old aggression but now I try to tackle the courses the way they are meant to be played. Sometimes experience is an advantage, but it can also be a disadvantage. Until I won the Open, I just used to enjoy the game and do the best I could. Winning changed my life, but I feel fortunate to be where I am.'

Between Sunday and Wednesday, the final practice day, Ballesteros roamed the grey links in inclement weather and reminisced nostalgically about 1979. This was the hollow from where he had made eagle, that was the green where he made his matador charge and here was the 'parking-lot' from where he'd made history. Trotting beside the Spaniard as he strode the fairways, was his new caddie, Ian Wright, laboriously scribbling in his yardage book. At the Madrid Open in April, a week after he had missed the cut in Cannes, Ballesteros had approached the forty-year-old Yorkshireman and, on Chino Fernandez's recommendation, asked whether he would caddie for him. Wright, of course, was overwhelmed. Previously he had only worked for journeymen players like David Jones,

Brian Marchbank and Carl Mason, and his eyes lit up as he imagined basking in the reflected glory of a golfer as great as Ballesteros. He lost no time in agreeing. Terms were fixed and it was duly arranged that he should start at the PGA Championship at Wentworth in May. When the big day arrived, Wright went down to the golf club, heaved the Spaniard's bag upon his shoulder and waited at the tee. Ballesteros arrived for his practice round, drove off and marched rapidly down the first fairway. Two hours and ten minutes later, he holed his last putt on the eighteenth. 'I think,' says Wright, 'he was testing me.'

One can't help but wonder why it is that Ballesteros decided to find a regular caddie barely a month before a major. Previously he had felt so strongly about his brothers working for him that even when he was fined £50 for employing a fellow professional (Vicente) to carry his bag, the old rule regarding caddies having been amended, he refused to comply. 'It is a stupid rule,' he announced. 'I will definitely carry on using Vicente . . . Maybe the PGA needs the money. It's no problem for me. Fines are tax-deductible.' The matter was something of an embarrassment because Ballesteros was on the committee, but an escape clause was found and from then on it was only fellow members of the European Tour who were not permitted to caddie. But now it seemed that his brothers were too busy with their families to waste their time toiling round golf courses. 'Vicente has a wife and daughter and his job as a golf professional at La Manga,' Ballesteros said firmly. 'He needs to spend more time there.'

Whether it was chemistry, coincidence or simply that a change is as good as a holiday, Wright's presence had an immediate and positive effect on Ballesteros which might ultimately have precipitated his overdue return to form. At the time of their meeting the Spaniard was fourth on the World Rankings behind Norman, Lyle and Langer after a year with only one victory and one lost play-off (for the Westchester Classic). He had, however, had three seconds, six thirds and five other top ten finishes the previous season and had won more money per tournament in his restricted appearances than anyone else on the US Tour. At Wentworth, with a different caddie by his side, he seemed overcome with optimism for the future. Standing on the first tee in the opening round, he smiled spontaneously and said to Wright: 'This is the beginning of a new era.'

And so it proved. At the PGA Championship, a week when he was more amiable than he had been in months, Ballesteros finished joint runner-up with Mark James to Ian Woosnam, in the French Open he was equal fourteenth and in Monte Carlo he was third. A fortnight later when he left Pedreña, he was bound, with hope in his heart and a spring in his step, for the 117th Open Championship at Royal Lytham – the place where it all began.

Thursday, 14 July 1988. The greatest players who have ever lived have long been defined by their ability to raise their games to the big occasion. Thus, Jacklin, whose form was little better than indifferent when he came to Lytham in 1969, was able to reach inside himself and find courage enough to win the Open trophy; and Nicklaus, roused to fury by a newspaper article which declared him 'done, washed up and finished', was able to play the hardest back nine in golf in six under par and become the oldest winner of the Masters. Ballesteros, for his part, had been down on his luck and dispirited with his golf game before both of his Open wins, but by concentrating his entire being on his goal each time, he had achieved it, and his triumphs were triumphs of the human spirit.

Now he sought to do the same thing again.

A malevolent sky hung low over the red brick houses as Ballesteros made his way to the tee for the first round of the Open. His expression was absorbed but peculiarly eager. Earlier in the week he had described to Wright in minute detail his strategy for the tournament and now he intended to carry it out to the letter. A smooth swing, a careful putt and he was away with a birdie two. He marched to the next tee, head held high. A second birdie followed, then another. A tense excitement began to take hold of him and it transmitted itself to the crowd. Their numbers swelled. Clinging to their candy-striped umbrellas, they struggled after their hero, blasted by the ferocious gale. Ballesteros was just hitting his stride. He swung boldly from the tee, and almost every drive found its target. His iron play was peerless, his short game magical and his putting inspired. For a few moments, after gaining strokes at the sixth and seventh holes, he even found himself thinking in terms of a 29. But he missed from 4 feet for a three at the eighth and turned in 30.

By now Ballesteros was in full flight. Adrenalin surged through his veins, and the roars of the crowd intensified its already heady effect. At the fourteenth hole he came unstuck. A slight hook off the tee was followed by a wicked pull over the heads of the gallery and deep into a thicket. It had unplayable written all over it before it left the clubface. 'Instead of playing safe I got greedy,' admitted Ballesteros afterwards. 'I tried to reach the green with a two-iron, but it was a bad shot.' He dropped 50 yards away from the hole under penalty, played his 'best shot of the day', a blind seven-iron to 15 feet, and holed the putt for a bogey five. He marched on undaunted, leaning into the wild wind. His eventual score of 67, despite another unplayable lie, lifted him head and shoulders above the rest of the field. Only two other players had managed to break 70, Brad Faxon and Wayne Grady, both of whom were on 69.

'This is my best start in a major since the 1980 Masters,' said a delighted Ballesteros. 'Last year at Muirfield I had to wait twenty-eight holes before I got my first birdie. This time it took just one.'

Friday, 15 July 1988. The week before Ballesteros came to Lytham he had spent a good deal of time out on his boat fishing. He caught fifty-two sea bass on one day, one on each of the next two days and then fourteen on the last. 'When I'm out there on the water [with my friends and my girlfriend] I can switch off, forget everything,' he said. The therapeutic benefits of these activities were undeniable. Ballesteros was relaxed and approachable and looked to be enjoying himself again as he went about his business on and off the golf course.

On the second day the sun came out and touched the

links with its fierce yellow glare. A keen wind blew, testing the ingenuity of the competitors, and on the third hole Ballesteros found a bunker, dropped a shot and surrendered the lead. 'I got a ticking off because the one thing we'd planned especially was to keep the ball out of the sand,' recalls Wright, who rarely turned a hair during these admonitions which increased in volume and intensity as the months went on. But the Spaniard recovered almost immediately and, with birdies at the sixth and seventh holes, resumed control of the tournament. The fourteenth broke through his defences once again. He pulled his tee shot, hooked his second and failed to reach the green. His eventual score of 71 left him a stroke behind Zimbabwean Nick Price on 138, four under par. Stadler and Faldo were their closest challengers on 140, while Andy Bean was a stroke further back.

'The course is very difficult,' explained Ballesteros. 'Right now, I would settle for a couple of 71s over the last two rounds. I think four under par will be good enough to win.'

Saturday, 16 July 1988. On Saturday rain, opaque and unceasing, slanted across the links and pounded at the marquees with the thunderous roar of a waterfall. The ninth, tenth and eleventh greens quickly became flooded and at 12.20 p.m. play was abandoned. When fairways became lakes and gullies raging torrents, the R&A decided, for the first time in Open history, to extend the championship until Monday.

Sunday, 17 July 1988. On Sunday the atmosphere was strangely subdued. Ballesteros went out with Craig Stadler and Nick Price, swinging easily and concentrating hard. He and the Zimbabwean had known each other for years. When Ballesteros was playing regularly in America – as a non-member he was now restricted to just five Tour-sponsored events and approved non-tour events such as the Masters and World Series per season – they often met socially and went out for meals.

'Seve; I s'pose, doesn't really talk a whole lot on the golf course,' says Price. 'I play with a lot of guys who are a little more – not jovial – a little more talkative. But that didn't worry me because I just knuckled down and tried to do my own thing. But he was very, very courteous . . . Seve and I have always had a great friendship. He respects me for the person I am and I respect him for the person he is. I know that there are times when he just doesn't want to be spoken to, and you must give him his room then. And I do that. I respect that. You know, I don't go up to him and try to talk to him when he's having a bad time. No man's an island in that he can be consistent all the time. I think some people are just a little unfair and a little hard in judging him as a character. I think he's actually clammed up a little over the last few years because of that. I think a lot of people misunderstand him. But I understand him. I know Seve and I admire him because of the way he plays the game and the person that he is.

'But Seve,' adds Price, 'is a difficult person to get close to. He doesn't open himself up to too many people. I don't think he trusts a lot of people. Everyone wants to be a friend of his, and I think some people really try to get close to Seve. Not me. I like him to be a friend, that's all. But, generally speaking, Seve's a very down-to-earth person. I don't think he had many airs and graces off the golf course. I think on the golf course it's different. It's business. I'm sure there are a lot of business people around the world who have good friends and go out to dinner, but when they're in the office they're hard people. And unfortunately sometimes that's the way you have to be in golf.'

In the third round all three men seemed immersed in their own games, although the Walrus, who had suffered cruelly at the hands of Royal Lytham, was plainly wishing he could be anywhere else in the kingdom. Ballesteros sailed along serenely until the 490-yard par five sixth, at which point he had a run in with a small tree. 'I'm sure my driver hit something and kicked left into the bushes,' said Ballesteros. 'But you know me, I'm usually all over the place so maybe it was a normal position.' He was left with no shot. Inventing one, he reversed a sand-wedge and tried to strike the ball with the back of the clubface. It moved 6 inches. He persevered. This time it flew 60 yards. 'One for practice, one to come out,' joked Ballesteros, who then hit an eight-iron 195 yards to 30 feet and two-putted. He had only two birdies on that long grey day – one at the seventh and another from the rough at the thirteenth – but stayed calm and good-humoured until the end. At the close of play Price was leading by two strokes, on 206, over Ballesteros and Faldo.

In the interview room, the Spaniard was quietly confident. 'It will be tough in the final round and the winner will be the man who can best take the pressure. I have coped with it before, I don't see why I can't do it again. But you never know . . .'

Monday, 18 July 1988. On the night of Ballesteros's return to Lytham, when images of his last victory came rushing sweet and vivid into his mind, he went up to his bedroom in the rented house where he stayed, sat down on the bed and started to think. 'I was back at Lytham. I was a winner here. I am a better player now than I was then – better swing and more experienced,' he recalls. 'I convinced myself I could win.'

When he stepped onto the first tee in the final round of the Open, that conviction was still with him, and his navy blue sweater and white shirt were the same he had worn to victory in 1979 and 1984. He nodded pleasantly to Price and Faldo, and they drove and set off down the fairway. The first objective of every man in the field was to win as many strokes back from par as they could before the turn, for it is only by laying the foundations of a good score on the front nine that a player has a prayer of surviving Lytham's gruelling inward half.

The Spaniard, tense and excited, pounced first, birdying the sixth, and he and Faldo moved a stroke nearer Price on the leaderboard. A ripple of pleasure went through the crowd. They crossed to the next tee.

Then came a crucial development. On the seventh hole Ballesteros hit a beautiful second shot that pitched onto the front edge of the green, narrowly missed going into the hole and ran out to 15 feet. Price used the contours of the putting surface to bring his own in to 6 feet, but Faldo, whose approach was every bit as excellent as those of his playing partners, found his path to the flag blocked by a large mound and proceeded to three-putt. 'I hit two great shots,' he remembers. 'I just couldn't putt the bloody thing because of that hump. But the way Seve was playing, he was like a bull in a china shop. He was unbelievable. He was [also] very relaxed. I think that's one of the secrets in majors. You've got to be able to relax and, obviously, have all the strong stuff going on inside your stomach.' Ballesteros, with infinite poise, stepped up to the ball and holed his putt for an eagle, sending deafening cheers reverberating round the golf course. Price then followed him in. From that moment they were out on their own, distant figures on the big yellow leaderboards. The race had begun in earnest.

'It became almost a match-play situation then,' says Price, 'although I tried to just stick to the game plan that had got me there and I'm sure he did too. But he has a wonderful ability, like all great players, to elevate his game one notch.'

Ballesteros, racing to catch Price, lashed away from the tees with a fluid and powerful swing. One after the other his drives found the fairway and his iron shots flew boldly for the heart of each green. Birdies were made at the eighth, tenth and at the eleventh, where for the first time, the Spaniard took the lead. The atmosphere surrounding the leading match was electric. There were shades of Lytham in 1979 – in the fresh wind, in the frenzied gallery, in the grin Ballesteros flashed after making a particularly audacious recovery, in the aggression of his driving – when he lashed at his drives both his feet almost left the ground – and in the wizardry of his short game. But the Ballesteros who won then had been little more than a boy, with a raw and elemental vitality about him. By 1988 that fierce, almost primitive quality of his genius had been tempered and polished, and what was left was a mature and self-assured man and a golfer at the peak of his game.

Later, Price was to say that he thought that Ballesteros 'still had a lot of the [old] memories of Lytham fresh in his mind. I think the British Open in 1979 was so important to him that he felt he was unbeatable on that course. And I think he still feels to this day that he's unbeatable on that golf course. And he might be. Who knows?'

'I was surprised how good my nerves were,' commented the Spaniard afterwards. 'I didn't expect to be so relaxed and calm, the most under control I have ever been in that sort of situation in a major.'

'I don't know [whether you actually] "know" you are going to win,' says Faldo, trying to describe the sensation of being in contention for a major. 'It's there for you to grab, that's almost the feeling. Knowing that you're doing everything right. It's just knowing you can cope with situations, I think that's the nice thing. You know, things might be going wrong at different times but you think, it's OK, everything's all right, I'm coping.'

That, precisely, was Ballesteros's reaction to a dropped shot at the twelfth, which brought him level with Price once again on ten under par. At the following hole, when the Zimbabwean almost holed his second shot, Ballesteros sank an 18-foot putt for a matching three. In this manner they continued, thrust and counter-thrust, lunge and parry.

'I think the best way to describe the way I was that week is that I was so adaptable,' says Price – 'to the conditions, to the shots that I had to play. I just accepted it when I had a bad shot and if I got a bad break I accepted it and went on to the next hole. When you're not playing well, adversity works against you. Whereas, when you're playing well, sometimes adversity makes you think, oh well, don't worry, I'm going to have another three or four birdie putts in the next five holes.'

The sixteenth hole, appropriately, was the turning point. Both men took one-irons off the tee, Price hitting his 232 yards, Ballesteros 227 to the right edge of the fairway. The Spaniard deliberated over his 135-yard approach. 'It's a nine-iron,' said Wright. 'Hit it nice and easy and you won't be far away.'

'He hit a perfect nine-iron,' recalls the Zimbabwean, who struck a sand-wedge to 17 feet and two-putted. 'I mean, absolutely perfect. It wasn't a full one, it was just a nice, smooth nine-iron and he hit it up there to about three inches. I looked at it in the replay about three weeks later and

I don't know how it didn't go in, because it actually came into the pin on the left and finished behind the hole on the right. So it must have lipped the cup or something. It didn't put the trophy in his hands right then and there. He knew it, too. There was still two tough holes to go. But it sure helped his cause.'

To the seventeenth they went, Ballesteros now leading by a shot. But Price still hung on doggedly, erasing the memories of how he had let slip the Open in 1982, defying the men who had called him a choker. Even when his tee shot finished on a bare lie of caked mud, he didn't give up. He simply dropped clear without penalty, hit a brilliant one-iron into the green and two-putted to equal the Spaniard's par.

On the right-hand side of the eighteenth fairway at Royal Lytham, some 260 yards from the tee, is a pot bunker craftily designed to trap the errant tee shot. Ballesteros, whose honour it was, drove first, launching the ball into the grey sky. Price, shivering slightly in the chill air, followed its flight. It plummeted to earth and didn't bounce. 'I think he's hit it in that little pot bunker,' the Zimbabwean whispered to his caddie.

Ballesteros turned quickly to Wright with something akin to fear in his eyes. 'Is it past the bunker?' he demanded urgently.

'I think it is,' said Wright uncertainly.

'I knew then, when I stood on the tee, that if I hit a good tee shot I was going to have a very good chance to win,' recalls Price, 'because I thought the best he'd be able to do was make five out of there. And I hit absolutely the best tee shot I'd hit all day, about 290 yards [down the fairway] and into a perfect position.'

The Spaniard began the long, nerve-wracking walk to his ball. All around him the towering stands of spectators were rejoicing at the return of the conquering hero, the roar rising to a crescendo.

'Are you *sure* it's past the bunker?' Ballesteros kept saying over and over again.

'Yes,' replied Wright, his heart in his mouth. 'I'm sure.'

'When I got up there I was a little disappointed his ball had carried the bunker,' admits Price. 'Also he had a

Grave of Hopes: Ballesteros stands stunned on the fifteenth at Augusta in 1986 as a spreading ring of ripples signals the end of his bid for victory.
© *Lawrence Levy/Yours in Sport*.

ABOVE: Fate twists the knife in the Spaniard's heart once again as he three-putts the first extra hole of a play-off at Augusta in 1987. Larry Mize, the eventual winner, looks on. © *Lawrence Levy/Yours in Sport*.

INSET ABOVE: The Grail: after four years
in the wilderness, the Spaniard reaps the
ultimate reward for his efforts, the Open
trophy at Royal Lytham in 1988.
© *Allsport/Dave Cannon.*

LEFT: Severiano, seen here with Baldomero
Jnr, experienced mixed fortunes when his
brothers caddied for him and never succeeded
in winning a major with any of them.
© *Allsport/Simon Bruty.*

ABOVE: The Ballesteros mansion in Pedreña – a mere iron shot from the eighth tee. © *Phil Sheldon*.

OPPOSITE BOTTOM: 'Why me?' Ballesteros discusses the finer points of the rules book with referee Mike Stewart at the 1990 Desert Classic. © *Phil Sheldon*.

BELOW: Course of confrontation: Ballesteros and Paul Azinger cross swords at the 1991 Ryder Cup at Kiawah Island. © *Allsport/Dave Cannon.*

LEFT: Comrades: Jose Maria Olazábal hoists himself high on the shoulders of his compatriot in the 1992 Ryder Cup. Together, they have made one of the greatest partnerships in the history of team competition. © *Allsport/Dave Cannon.*

BELOW: David Leadbetter, guru to the world's best players, restricts the Spaniard's lower body movement on the practice ground in Jamaica. © *Allsport/Dave Cannon.*

ABOVE: Perfect couple: Ballesteros and Carmen at the Ryder Cup dinner at Kiawah Island. © *Lawrence Levy/Yours in Sport*.

RIGHT: Severiano with son, Baldomero Javier. 'It is my hope for him to be a professional golfer so I can make sure he doesn't make the same mistakes I did.' © *Lawrence Levy/Yours in Sport*.

Ballesteros's Open hopes fade with one more visit to the rough at Royal Birkdale in 1991. © *Allsport/Dan Smith.*

pretty decent lie so he could get it on the green. I knew that I'd have to make three. He pulled his second shot. He hit a pretty good second shot but it went over the back edge. But I just never ever thought he'd make five . . . And I just tried a little too hard on that six-iron, I tried to get it too close to the hole. Instead of just playing it . . . But, I mean, I was so fired up. I had visions of hitting that six-iron like this' – and he holds the palms of his hands about 4 feet apart.

In such circumstances are majors won and lost. Price hit his second shot 35 feet short of the pin, while the Spaniard's ball ended some 50 feet away in an awkward lie in the left rough. Silence, like a blanket, descended over the amphitheatre of the eighteenth green. The only sounds were the muffled crunch of Ballesteros's spikes through the grass and the low murmur of his voice as he conferred with Wright and considered his shot. Then he played a feathery, delicate, magical chip, which popped up, skipped onto the green, then rolled and rolled and rolled until it came to a stop a bare 3 inches from the pin. It was over. Price tried gamely to hole his putt, rushed it too far past and missed the return, and so finished second with a score of 69. Ballesteros tapped in his own for a 65 – which equalled the lowest final round in 117 Opens and included an eagle and six birdies – an aggregate of 273, eleven under par, and a two-stroke victory over Price. Faldo was third on five under par, and Fred Couples and Gary Koch were the best of the also-ran Americans on three under par.

'I had begun to think I was finished,' said an emotional Ballesteros in the interview room afterwards. 'My confidence was down after I hit the ball into the water to lose the Masters in 1986. I was worried. But I decided all I could do was try and try and wait for my chance and momentum to come back. It was my turn to win this week . . . A round like that comes only every twenty-five or fifty years. It is the greatest round of my life . . . so far.'

1988 was, arguably, Ballesteros's finest season. After the Open he won the Scandinavian Enterprise Open, the German Open and the Lancome Trophy in Europe, and the Taiheiyo

Masters in Japan. He was the No. 1 player on the World Rankings, the No. 1 player on the European Order of Merit for the fifth time with earnings of £451,559, the European Golfer of the Year and was named Spain's Sportsman of the Year by Spanish sportswriters.

Officially and unofficially, his achievements were unparalleled – even the Americans acknowledged it.

'As we approach the 1990s golf has home-grown heroes like Curtis Strange,' wrote Jerry Tarde in *Golf Digest*. 'We have international celebrities like Greg Norman. We have semi-retired kings like Jack Nicklaus and kings who play like they're semi-retired like Tom Watson. What we didn't have before July 18, 1988, the day he won at Lytham, was a living, breathing, practising superstar.

'Now we have one. Severiano Ballesteros, the best golfer in the world.

'Long may he reign.'

14

To the Courtroom

I badly want to win the tournament . . . but the money is not important. If I win, will I not eat the same breakfast on Monday morning?

Severiano Ballesteros, European Open, 1984

The best golfer in the world was stretched out on the sofa in the front room of his rented house at Lytham, wearing jeans, a sweater and a smile of pure happiness. He was thinking of Pedreña, his home, where fireworks had lit up the sky a few hours earlier as villagers celebrated his third Open Championship victory.

'They've had those fireworks for four years waiting for me to win a big one again,' said Ballesteros with a grin. 'They were so old we weren't sure they would work.'

He was calm, contented and affable enough, but he also seemed curiously subdued. His answers to the questions of the journalists who surrounded him were quiet and from the heart. The key to his triumph, he told them, had been his putting. Vicente had suggested he move his hands closer together on the grip; he had tried it and it had worked wonders. 'It's difficult to go out and play with confidence when you know your putting isn't good. It means you put pressure on your chipping because you know that you cannot hole the six- footers. There's no pleasure in that golf. OK, it

259

was called a slump, but even with poor putting I was always there . . . It is not possible to dominate any more all the time. I don't think it is possible for me to equal Jack Nicklaus's record of twenty titles. I don't want to take anything away from Jack, but the gap between players is much closer than it was then.'

At length, the interview drew to a close. The reporters closed their notebooks and gathered their belongings. They were just getting to their feet when the most extraordinary thing happened. For no reason at all, other than the fact he seemed desperate to get it off his chest, Ballesteros suddenly sat up and revealed to his astonished audience that, after years of anguish, he had finally bought out his contract with Ed Barner. 'It was almost an afterthought,' one of the journalists recalled later. 'We were all ready to leave when he started talking about it. The whole thing was rather strange.'

They settled down again to listen to his story.

In order to make sense of what happened next, one not only has to understand the circumstances that led to the break-up of Ballesteros's relationship with Barner but also something of the personality of the latter and what motivated him. Edward Lee Barner was born in Arizona on 10 May 1940. The son of a motor mechanic, he graduated with a degree in Communications and Public Relations and, after spending two and a half years working as a Mormon missionary in West Berlin, set his sights on a career in television production. By the time he was twenty-five he was a tour manager for a firm of Hollywood showbusiness agents, but in 1967, disillusioned with the entertainment industry, he left with the idea of moving into sports management. A year later he and Billy Casper formed Uni-Managers International.

That Barner had a unique gift for management was obvious from the outset. Joe Collet, who joined UMI in January 1977 as internal counsel shortly after leaving law school, remembers him as being one of the most talented men he had ever met for understanding what management meant, creating ideas and solving problems. 'He had a charming personality. He knew everybody he needed to know and if he didn't, he found out how to make them friends. Unfortunately, that didn't always last long term, but he had this tremendous boldness and charming way of getting to decision-makers and celebrities. Even Princess Grace of Monaco considered him to be a dear friend and they used to write letters . . .

'But like a lot of people who have a tremendous amount of talent, they have an equally negative side if you get on the wrong side of them. And Ed, I think, had a bit of a complex that people were not always straight with him at times and that used to really grate on him. One of the problems that he had with clients is that he felt they would be willing to do little side deals and not include him, whereas he was offering total management services. It was like a marriage. You had to have complete trust in the partner. And as long as he found them big impressive deals . . . they were happy to pay the going rate. But when the deals were a little bit smaller . . . then they thought: "Why should I be paying a manager a fortune?" It was a philosophical difference. So what happened in practice is that a lot of them would find little cheap deals on their own and not tell him and then that element of trust became eroded. He'd tell them what he thought sometimes, which maybe diplomatically speaking wasn't the shrewdest thing to do but it was very human of him to say: "I'm upset, I'm hurt, I don't like it." But he'd do it in such a way, with such finesse, that they would be really shocked. How could this amazing, personable person be so downright blunt and critical of their behaviour, which they didn't think was so bad? And a lot of clients had their feelings hurt and pouted.'

'He was a genius in some ways,' observes Miller, whose own parting from Barner in 1978 was acrimonious and resulted in a lawsuit. 'He was very, very talented at marketing and managing. If there was a weakness in him it was that he was a little bit too possessive . . . In other words, he would get you into things and then ask you if you wanted to do it and, of course, if you said no, he had already told them you were going to be there. That works OK when you're young and you need guidance and pushing along and directing, but when people get to the point where Seve was and where I was and where Billy Casper was . . . you don't want to be pushed, you just want to be helped. And Ed couldn't back off. That was his weakness and that's why he got into trouble with his clients.'

Ballesteros had signed his first contract with UMI on 17 October 1975, on the day that he and Manuel had gone so warily to Barner's hotel room after Orville Moody's dire prophesies. It was a five-year agreement and stipulated that the Spaniard had to pay the company 25 per cent of everything he earned, including winnings, appearance fees and endorsements. In return, they would provide him with a complete management service. Collet, who is a talented linguist and who now speaks Spanish, Portuguese, French, elementary German and a little Japanese, as well as being able to understand Italian and Swedish, was assigned as his account executive and was responsible for doing everything from arranging his schedule to negotiating geographically fragmented contracts. UMI had already conducted several endorsement deals for the young Spaniard, one of which had been a $5,000 per annum fee to play Mizuno clubs in Japan, acquired only weeks after Ballesteros had signed with the company. Barner had also discussed a new ball contract with Richard Brown of Dunlop Sports Company, Ltd, in 1976, the day before the Open. Brown claimed that: 'The day after it he made totally new demands.' But Barner was adamant that no agreement was made. But for the next three seasons the Spaniard did not play in the Dunlop Masters, and Doust maintains that it was Brown and Dunlop who led the sponsors' rebellion against appearance money in 1981. UMI, and principally Collet, negotiated more than two dozen contracts for Ballesteros in that first five-year period, including endorsements for everything from tomato juice to table-top games. Among the most lucrative were his Mizuno Sporting Goods contract, worth around $50,000 per annum, and his Slazenger contract which, beginning in 1981, was to pay him in the region of £250,000 over five years. His income at that time was estimated at approximately $1 million a season.

In 1981 Ballesteros's initial contract with UMI expired. When the renewal agreement came to be drawn up, there was a serious conflict of opinion between Ballesteros and Barner over what the former thought he should pay and the latter felt he should be paid. Finally, they compromised on 20 per cent on specific deals and no percentage on winnings.

'Neither side was happy with it,' remembers Collet. 'We just lived with it and tolerated it and let it run its course.'

'I think . . . the kind of things that bothered [Seve] are the ones that bothered other clients,' says Brentnall Turley, who worked for UMI for four years as general counsel and also as a director. 'Basically, there was not the veracity there on a lot of occasions . . . And that was one of the things that concerned Seve . . . Ed would get something done and do it very creatively and very effectively, but not be able to rein his temper and really obliterate all the good things that he had done. And if that's your manager, then other people say, "Well, your manager is really a reflection of you." And so you don't really want to be painted with that brush . . . I thought that if you could take all the really good things that Ed was capable of doing – and he was very talented – and be able to keep the other things from knocking them out of the saddle and killing them, it would be great. But unfortunately that never happened.'

'It's too convenient to make Ed out to be the bad guy,' responds Collet with some irritation. 'Ed was a perfectionist and he was extremely good at doing what he did, but he was furious when somebody did not live up to his standards of integrity, which in turn caused him to react – not violently, but to be very obviously upset. And when somebody that you've only had pleasant words with and who has been a great moral support to you, like a psychologist almost, for two or three years, suddenly turns around and just chews you up one side and down the other, it just leaves you completely demoralized. And people couldn't live with themselves and that's why they left the company. They couldn't face up to the fact that they had done something wrong . . . Some of the things that [Johnny Miller] did upset me as much as they did Ed. That relationship was already on the wane when I joined UMI. Of course, Brent Turley was Johnny's account executive as I was Seve's, and it worked to his advantage to have Johnny leave and then he could start representing him, and he made a nice living off working for him.'

'Ed has called me everything that he possibly could,' says Turley frankly, 'and basically he's said that I'm a very dishonest person and this and that and whatever, which is really a reflection of what has been said about him . . . Basically, I left UMI in 1976 and went and opened up my own law practice. Johnny came to me a couple of years later and said: "I want to leave UMI, would you be interested?" I said: "Yes, I would be." But Ed's position is that every client that left him was because of me. I didn't actively do anything. When Seve left UMI, [he] came to me because [he] knew that I'd lived through the Johnny Miller extrication.'

In March 1983, on the day that Ballesteros's second contract expired, Collet resigned. He had known for two years that Ballesteros wasn't happy with UMI and wasn't going to renew his contract. 'I tried to salvage it and Ed, occasionally, would try to compromise. But it was just better that they parted at that point in time because they didn't see eye to eye . . . I just was kind of getting burned out at that point. Seve was what made my job interesting for me.'

The problem was that the Spaniard couldn't just walk away from UMI without a backward glance. In the seven years he had been with the company, it had 'obtained scores of endorsement contracts for him which paid him several millions of dollars in revenue.' These deals were all covered by a clause in the initial contract he had signed which stated that, if a client left UMI, the company would continue to receive its commission in perpetuity, for as long as the client had a relationship with the manufacturer or sponsor concerned.

Ballesteros, who by then had put his affairs into the hands of Turley, a Los Angeles attorney named Jerry Phillips and Ceballos, objected to this clause and a bitter dispute arose as to how much Barner and UMI were entitled to receive from the proceeds of ongoing contracts they had negotiated on the Spaniard's behalf.

'[Seve] felt, on the advice of Brent Turley and other people, that he could beat that [clause] in court,' explains Collet, 'and

264

that the court would probably rule that a reasonable commission period at the end of the separation was fair but not for ever and ever. And it was that point that provoked an arbitration. Otherwise what could have happened is that UMI would be considered to have invoiced the deals that it had administered and sent him his share and retained its, and he would have been [able] to find other companies and do other deals and not pay UMI anything. But instead Seve chose to try and cut it off *right now* and Ed chose to try and keep it for ever and ever, neither one of which was quite right.'

In 1984 UMI initiated arbitration against Ballesteros and Spangolf Enterprises, the corporation under which he conducts some of his US business. The following year a hearing was held before an arbitrator, who issued an award favourable to Ballesteros, and more or less determined that all commissions as per the letter of the contract should be added up to a point some two years beyond the date on which the agreement between him and Barner and UMI ended. According to Collet, UMI then tried to retain money on the contracts that it had serviced 'because Seve wasn't being fair with them on other things. And so they had to have an accounting to determine how much would be offset from what one had against what the other owed him.

'We've had our ups and downs, too,' admits Collet, recalling his relationship with Barner during those long and tortuous days. 'I've had some rows with him. There was a period of time when it was better that we just didn't talk to one another because he'd keep asking questions that I didn't want to answer. He knew how to make you say what you knew . . . He was very clever at doing it. Some people he'd win over and they'd feel like they needed to get it off their chest so they'd tell him. And other people he'd make them feel like they were dishonest if they didn't . . . so they had to tell him. But in either event, it worked to his advantage and against them.'

Following the arbitrator's decision, Barner filed an action in federal court to 'vacate' the award and, when it was dismissed, threatened to appeal. Settlement negotiations ensued, the dispute was resolved and on 19 December 1986, while arbitration proceedings were still pending, both parties signed a written agreement entitled 'Settlement Agreement and Mutual Release'. Legal records show that 'the funds that Barner and UMI retained, even without considering the offsetting effect of the funds Ballesteros retained, amounted to substantially less than $1 million.'

*

Thus do we come to the incident at Royal Lytham in 1988, following the Spaniard's victory at the Open. It should be borne in mind that, while all of these legal battles and recriminatory rows were going on, Ballesteros was trying to play golf, come to terms with his father's death, overcome the devastating psychological effects of losing several major championships in the circumstances that he lost them and wage a Trans-Atlantic war with Beman.

As a close friend of his said at the time (quoted by Tarde in *Golf Digest*:) 'Anyone who knows Seve will realize he could never push this ferocious dispute out of his mind. All his professional life he has been inspired to great deeds by his craving to stick it to someone. Go through his record and you can match his triumphs to his mood. Here's when he stuck it to the European Tour because they wouldn't permit him to ask for appearance money. Here's when he stuck it to the American pros for calling him lucky. Here's when he stuck it to Deane Beman for not changing the qualification rules. But how could he stick it to Ed Barner when the process of sticking would only serve to enrich Barner even further. If he won a major, he would be slipping a six-figure cheque into the pocket of the man he wanted to rid himself of. You see his dilemma.'

Nevertheless, when Ballesteros did win at Lytham he was so filled with joy and relief at having cast off the double burden of his slump and the legal difficulties under which he had laboured for so long, that he momentarily dropped his guard. He forgot that the settlement agreement between himself, Barner and UMI had contained a clause which provided that '[t]he existence and content of this Agreement are confidential and shall not be disclosed by any party to anyone or to any entity, except to a government taxing authority', and therefore spoke sincerely to the journalists who surrounded

266

him about how much he had suffered in recent years. It was widely reported and in no time at all Ballesteros found himself back in the courtroom. Barner and UMI filed an action against him for alleged slander and trade libel, and for breach of the confidentiality provision in the settlement agreement.

In July 1989, Barner and UMI alleged that, at Ballesteros's Open Championship press conference, he had complained generally to reporters about the quality of the representation he had received over the years from Barner, citing as an example that in 1979 he had wanted to play in the US PGA, but that Barner had told him to play in another event (the German Open) where he could earn £5,000 in appearance money. This, Ballesteros said, had led him to believe that 'things were not quite right' with respect to his relationship with his manager. However, Barner insisted that he had, on the contrary, repeatedly urged Ballesteros to play in major tournaments but that the Spaniard had preferred to go where the appearance money was.

Ballesteros then told journalists that he had been forced to pay 'big money' to terminate his relationship with his manager. Asked whether that sum was more than $1 million, he replied, 'BIG MONEY', implying that it was in excess of $1 million. He apparently added that Barner did not deserve so much money for the services he had provided, and alleged that he had personally gone to see Barner to discuss the settlement, saying: 'I asked how much money he wanted. And I paid. I then said: "Be happy but I do not want to see you again."'

It was Barner's assertion that the above meeting had never taken place, and that Ballesteros did not pay Barner anywhere close to $1 million. He maintained that since Ballesteros's statements were widely republished in everything from the *Sun* and *Golf Digest* to the *Bangkok Post*, both Barner and UMI had suffered specific damages, in that they had 'lost certain business opportunities in connection with the marketing of leisure facility developers, sports equipment, professional organizations and sports personalities. The amount of these damages would be proved at trial but was believed to be over $100,000.

Ballesteros essentially denied every allegation that Barner

and UMI made. But he did admit that the personal meeting he claimed to have had with Barner and indeed their alleged conversation had never taken place. He also acknowledged that he had paid Barner less than $1 million.

'Seve was kind of feeling happy and he said too much and departed a bit from the fact situation,' says Collet ruefully. He remembers that day at Lytham with mixed feelings. 'And the way that they wrote it up, it sounded very bad for Ed. And he got mad and slapped him with another lawsuit – ostensibly as a violation of the settlement agreement. That went on for a period. It ended up settling the arbitration and settling the other thing. I don't remember the figures of either one.'

'Was it more than £1 million?'

'Less.'

'More than $1 million?'

'Somewhere in that area. It was a disagreement over percentages and philosophy and it had to go to arbitration to be resolved, and there were some conditions to that arbitration about not dragging the linen out in front of everybody, and one side, a few years later, felt that that hadn't been respected and so it cropped up again. And then that was settled (25 April 1990) and now everything's peaceful. That's where we'd like to leave it.'

When Collet had resigned from UMI in the spring of 1983, Ballesteros had asked him if he would consider moving to Spain and handling his business. Why he did so is a complete mystery to anyone familiar with his nightmare experiences with UMI and Barner. 'I told him I couldn't,' recalls Collet. 'Legally and morally, I couldn't.' A noncompete clause in the contract he had signed upon joining UMI prohibited him from taking any of the company's clients and starting a management organization of his own. But in November 1986, when that stipulation was no longer legally binding, chance brought the two men together again. 'We were always good friends, you see,' explains Collet. 'When he came to California, he'd call and say hello. We'd go out to dinner. And after three years of this, one day I said: "What's going on? How are things going?" "Well, not so good." And I said: "Well, maybe I'd be interested in doing something." And he said: "We never closed that door." '

In the years between leaving UMI and rehiring Collet, Ballesteros had put his affairs in the hands of his friend Ceballos, a Spaniard who had been important to UMI in maintaining a relationship with Seve during his years with the company. Previously an executive of the Spanish airline, Iberia, and also a former executive director of the Spanish PGA until he could no longer tolerate the accusations of favouritism in the case of Ballesteros, Ceballos had become director of the Spaniard's company, Fairway SA, in 1981. Fairway had been formed while Ballesteros was still under contract to UMI, to develop and manage his Spanish business, which at that time included Seve Tours – an Iberia promotion to bring tourists to Spain on golf holidays, and a soft drink line. It was, however, completely autonomous and independent of UMI. The Ballesteros brothers were the sole shareholders: Severiano owned 85 per cent of the shares, while Baldomero, Vicente and Manuel had 5 per cent each.

Today there are three main companies: Fairway, Amen Corner and Trajectory. Fairway is Ballesteros's personal management company. Headed by Collet, who has managed the Spaniard since 1986, it negotiates all his endorsement contracts and administers everything from fan mail to instruction videos. In 1981, as well as his equipment contracts, Ballesteros was paid to wear Rolex watches, drive a Range Rover (in partial exchange for giving three Leyland exhibitions a year), lend his name to Seve Tours and hold five golf clinics per season at $15,000 a time. Five years later, when Collet moved to Spain, there were twenty days a year when Ballesteros was obliged to be available for clinics, outings, photographic sessions, video taping sessions, press conferences, etc. Now, apart from his obligations at an actual golf tournament, he spends just one and a half days a season on extraneous activities and makes four times the amount of money. His principal endorsement contracts are: Sunderland Rainwear; Dunlop Slazenger International, Ltd; Sumitomo Rubber Company, Ltd, Japan; Hugo Boss; Rolex; the *Evening Standard*; *Golf World*; and American Express.

'Endorsements today are probably of secondary importance to another whole area for these guys, which just opened up in the last five years, and that's golf course design,' explains Collet. 'Endorsements don't pay that much . . . The company's objective is to get as much time and exposure as they can, and the manager's objective is to get as much money for as little time . . . You don't need a shoe endorsement that pays you £25,000 a year if you have to do a day's worth of [video] taping every year, or half a day's worth of photography, or you have to sign autographs at a stand at the British Open . . . I see Greg [Norman] in the media. He likes people, he's more gregarious [than Seve], but I see him doing [a lot of running around and a lot of Showbiz stuff]. One thing is that he likes to do it and he does a good job, but another thing is that his management (IMG), in order to generate the fantastic sums that they publish – I don't believe that they're accurate – in order to justify the credibility they're trying to project, have got to give a lot of time to the companies . . . Have you seen *Golf Illustrated Weekly*? They have a picture of Nick Faldo in there, like a side of beef. You know, how much the visor's worth and how much the shoes are worth. And it's all complete rubbish . . . In fact, if you look at the endorsements that Nick Faldo has or some of the other guys have, a lot of them are the ones that we didn't want. So I think we got our first pick. All those figures you see in magazines about what the guys earn is complete rubbish. I know, because that's my business . . . What IMG does, is they talk to you in terms of numbers . . . And what they're usually quoting you is the total value of the contract when you sum all the years together, including projections of win bonuses and royalties that could come in, and lead you to believe that's what they get in a single year in pounds when it's what they get over the length of the entire contract in dollars and it counts everything. So that's how the figures get distorted and they're four or five times what they are in actuality. If Nick Faldo got the sums of money that are attributed to him in *Golf Illustrated*, he'd own half the companies that he's working for. People love to believe those things. They say, "This is fantastic! It's so glamorous!" . . . I disagree with the philosophy of using the

270

media to print false figures which will generate more income by persuading sponsors that that is what other sponsors pay. I think it's in bad taste, really.'

Amen Corner began as a joint venture between Fairway and Roddy Carr's company, Camcorp. Carr had continued to play pro golf himself until 16 December 1979, at which point he missed a 4-foot putt in a tournament and quit the game. Thereafter, he had spent three years looking after women's golf in America for IMG, two years running IMG's office in Hong Kong and three years helping to set up Nicklaus's golf design operation in Europe. In 1986 he approached Ballesteros with the concept of taking over the rights to the Spanish Open and helping to promote golf and raise the level of the tournament in Spain. Ballesteros agreed immediately. They doubled the prize money from £80,000 to £150,000 and sold it three years later to Peugeot. In 1993 the prize fund for the tournament was £600,000.

In 1987 the Open de Baleares contract came up and it was decided to form a company that specifically and exclusively promoted European Tour events in Spain. Ballesteros became the new president of Amen Corner, as the company was named, and Carr took a share of it and became its chief executive along with Baldomero, the group chief executive of all the companies. At present, Amen Corner promotes three European Tour events: the Spanish Open, the Open de Baleares Open (or Mallorcan Open) and the Turespana Masters. The aim of the company is to make those three tournaments the best on the continent, and also to establish a Ballesteros memorial event, which will be played on one of his own golf courses and will, theoretically, live on for ever.

'The most impressive thing about [Seve] is he's highly intelligent,' says Carr, who has the greatest admiration and respect for Ballesteros. 'He understands the fundamentals of business. He would help me maybe twice a year when I need it, and he is always there at the right time with the right person to do the job in exactly the right way . . . He will achieve more in an hour than I would in two months.'

'He's very capable of sustaining a certain rhythm without a lot of interaction,' agrees Collet. 'We programme him and he says, "I want to do this, that and the other thing", and then we'll work out the details and then say, "OK, here it is." He does it and then we come back and give him another dose. We sort of do it in three-week dips.'

This, of course, is when Ballesteros is in Spain, which, for a time was rarely, because his actual residence was in Monaco, where he 'moved' in 1987. Needless to say, the Spaniard insisted that he wasn't a tax exile. '[T]hat's not the reason why [I moved here],' he told *Hello*. After all, I have in Spain all my organizers and my golf course firm, as well as three other businesses that I pay my taxes on. The low tax rates in Monaco are obviously very pleasant but the reasons I moved here are to maintain anonymity, which is provided here, and the weather, which means I can constantly train.'

Collet adds two more reasons: 1. Proximity to an international airport; 2. Intensive police surveillance and low crime rate. As he says, the Ballesteroses' two sons are 'invaluable' and at risk from kidnappers.

Ballesteros's third company is Trajectory, which essentially designs golf courses in Spain. His first three projects were done in co-operation with Dave Thomas, co-designer of The Belfry, after which he decided that if he formed his own company he would be able to 'express' himself better. He has since completed four courses in Japan, one in France (Pont Royal Country Club de Provence), one in England (with Thomas) and three in Spain, while more than six are under construction and another half dozen are awaiting permits for construction or something of the kind. All of them are very natural and reflect the influences of courses like Augusta National. 'I insist on incorporating the existing landscape,' he has said. 'When people visit a Ballesteros course they should have the feeling that they are in a naturally designed field.'

More and more of his time away from the golf course is taken up with course design and he has confided to Carr that when his career comes to an end it is to this he will turn. 'Designing golf courses is one thing that I like very much. I think it's fantastic to go to one place and to see a piece of land that is nothing, and in one year you see a golf course. And to play there and to enjoy it and to give the chance to other people to have so much fun in the future, is something very special and I enjoy it very much. It's a pity that I cannot put as much time into it as I would like because I still like more the competition, but it's fantastic.'

Meanwhile, after all these years, IMG are still trying to recruit Ballesteros. 'We're trying,' admits John Simpson of IMG. 'You know, he's got his whole team around him at the moment. He knows what we can do and I think he's very complimentary about us, but it's all down to what he wants and what he perceives he wants . . . I never really got to know [Ed Barner]. He was always quite distant and you never knew, really, what was going on there. But, obviously, that came to an end and then rather than come with us he went with someone else and then that came to an end. And he's with his brothers and Joe now. So, you know, who knows whether the right decision had been made? All I can say is we could have done a helluva good job for him. And I don't say what job's been done now because I don't know, but I know we'd have done a helluva good job.'

Whether or not Ballesteros has made the right decision in steering clear of IMG remains to be seen, and may not be known until the end of his career, but financially, at least, he has not suffered unduly. His annual off course income, including endorsements, golf design and returns from his clothing, cosmetics and luggage lines, mainly distributed in the Far East, is estimated at around $7 million. On course he has done almost as well. At the end of 1991 he was second only to Greg Norman on the world-wide career money list, with earnings of £8,754,571.

15

Home Fires

Half to forget the wandering and the pain,
Half to remember days that have gone by,
And dream and dream that I am home again!

James Elroy Flecker, 1884–1915

The moment that Ballesteros stepped out of obscurity and into history at Royal Birkdale, shattering the sedate, gentlemanly and unremittingly colourless world of professional golf with his Latin looks, swashbuckling style of play and captivating smile, it was obvious that sport had found itself a hero worthy of romantic fiction. Other players tended to be bland by comparison, both in personality and appearance, and inclined, like Watson and Kite, to wear clothes in muted shades of beige or brown. Ballesteros, on the other hand, was not only tall, dark and handsome, he was also arrogant enough, charming enough, dashing enough and unpredictable enough to have stepped straight from the pages of a *Mills and Boon*. Ed Barner, with his keen eye for star quality, recognized this in an instant. So, too, did the media, whose curiosity about his life off course, which they hoped matched his on-course image, grew in proportion to the spread of his fame. What did he do when he wasn't playing golf? Where did he go in the evenings? Was there a steady girlfriend? Did he, in fact, not date at all? Or did he, they wondered, have a sweetheart waiting faithfully for his return in Pedreña?

But Ballesteros would always just laugh and reply, 'Many, many, many girlfriends.'

When they persisted, their efforts came to nought. No player is more adept than the Spaniard at side-stepping questions, personal or otherwise, with a grin and a self-deprecating quip. Nevertheless, his appeal to women was undeniable. 'Wherever he goes, girls flock around him,' Michael McDonnell wrote in the *Daily Mail*, the week after he won the Open in 1979. 'He enjoys their company but can also be slightly callous sometimes. There is no steady girlfriend. After his romantic interludes, he's impatient to get back with the gang.'

'He was very shy of women,' explains Dudley Doust, who knew something of the man and not the myth. Once Ballesteros had snapped at him: 'Trevino and you and everybody have suggestions for me. I don't know if I should have a holiday. I don't know if I should have girlfriend.'

'After he won the Masters for the first time and he went to California for the Tournament of Champions, Michael Williams and I had dinner with him,' remembers Doust. 'We were talking about women – he was very successful with women, actually. We said: "What do you really think of women?" He said: "The trouble with women is they're very sticky." And Williams and I didn't know what the hell he was talking about, whether they clung to you, or whether their skins were actually sticky! I think that he meant the second. I think he meant they're a bit sticky! Maybe they sweated when they saw him or something, I don't know. Oh, and then he had that awful stuff in *El Pais* when he was very young, and he said women were second-class citizens.'

In the course of that particular polemic, which appeared in the Madrid newspaper in 1980, Ballesteros remarked to the Spanish journalist conducting the interview: 'You women want equality but you'll never get it because women are inferior to men in all sorts of ways – physically, intellectually and morally. There are exceptions, but on the whole women are inferior to men.' What is sad is that although he himself was still fairly socially immature at that age and more starkly black and white in his thinking than he has become, his attitude was typical of his background and also of Spanish society at the time when he was growing up. One doubts very much has changed.

Ballesteros's 'romantic interludes', as McDonnell called them, were indeed fleeting. So much so that he can only recall having one steady relationship in his youth. 'I was sixteen and dating one of the local girls in the village. I went to play in a tournament where, I remember, I thought of her most of the time, but when I came home she left me for no reason. After that, there was no-one until Carmen because I was absorbed by the game.' No-one, that is, unless you count Liz Hoad, the sister of former European Tour professional, Paul. Readers of a certain tabloid newspaper were later regaled with an account of her alleged brief encounter with Ballesteros.

Some time before the unhappy day when young Severiano was dropped by the merciless village girl, *destino* had occasioned his father be hired as a periodic caretaker of the house of the Botins, one of Spain's richest families. When the Botins were out of town, it was the duty of Ballesteros Snr to ensure that vandals did not ransack their Pedreña home before they returned. As the months passed and the families became better acquainted, Severiano, who by then was fifteen years old and in the Spanish Under 15 team, began giving lessons to Emilio Botin Jnr, son of the man whose house his father cared for, as well as his children. One of these children – the sister of Carmen, his future wife – had what is described by Collet as 'not a romance but a close friendship of the sort' with Ballesteros. Carmen was still only a child.

'Carmen received her first golf lessons from me,' recalls Ballesteros proudly. 'Then she went to study in Switzerland and later in England, where I met her in 1981 when I won my first World Match Play Championship at Wentworth. That is when we fell in love and we've been together since.'

Carmen is the quiet, dark-haired, dark-eyed daughter of Emilio Botin Jnr, president of the Bank of Santander and one of the wealthiest men in Spain. According to *Forbes* magazine in America (quoted by *Golf Digest* in October 1988), Banco Santander 'is the only major Spanish bank still controlled by a single family. The Botins' visible stake is only some 5 per cent. But knowledgeable sources say affiliated Botin entities bring the total to 25 per cent, worth around $1.5 billion at current market prices.' Money not being an obstacle, Botin Jnr decided that his daughter should have a classical English and American education. Thus, she was sent to St Mary's in Ascot, Berkshire, the same convent attended by Princess Caroline of Monaco, and to Brown University in New York, where she graduated in 1987 with a bachelor's degree in organizational behaviour.

Carmen and Ballesteros began seeing one another intermittently in 1981 and by 1983 were dating as regularly as they could hope to, given that he spent half his season in Europe and she spent a good deal of time in the United States. The next summer there were rumours of their impending marriage, but at the Open Ballesteros joked, 'She won't have me,' and hinted that it was because Carmen herself felt she was not old enough. There is, after all, a nine-year age difference between them. However, it was generally believed – and still is – that her father was reluctant to allow them to marry because of the humble circumstances of Ballesteros's birth, and for that reason it pleased the tabloids greatly to cast him as the villain of the piece in a Romeo-and-Juliet-type romance – the autocratic father who would stop at nothing to prevent his precious daughter from marrying the son of a peasant farmer. This saga went on for years and much innocent pleasure was derived from it, as the following piece by Peter Dobereiner (*Golf World*, April 1988) shows:

In our popular press, whose salacious obsession with secrets of the boudoir totally eclipses any notional interest in sport, Ballesteros is presented as the victim of unrequited love. Romeo Ballesteros, son of a poor dirt farmer from the wrong side of the tracks, sighs beneath the balcony of Juliet (Carmen Botin, actually, daughter of the high-born and wealthy president of the Bank of Santander, near Seve's hometown of Pedreña).

'See how she leans her cheek upon her hand: O! that I were a glove upon that hand, that I might touch that cheek.'

Juliet demonstrates that her expensive education at St Mary's and Brown University in Rhode Island has not been wasted by responding: 'O, Romeo, Romeo! wherefore art thou Romeo?'

The plot now thickens. In his office at the bank, father Botin studies the statement of Romeo's account. Each figure is followed by a seemingly endless row of zeroes, like the wheels of freight trains rolling across La Mancha bearing treasures to his vaults. An eminently suitable son-in-law, he concludes.

'But mother Botin, the blue blood of the Capulets rising in her gorge, has a proper scorn for money, especially new money. You can, she asserts with vigour, take the boy out of the caddie shack, but you can't take the caddie shack out of the boy. I will never permit the most fragrant flower of the Capulets to be united with a Montague.

The speculation increased as the years passed and the promised wedding failed to materialize, despite the fact that Ballesteros, Carmen and Botin Jnr were frequently to be seen together and in the friendliest of circumstances. In May 1987, for example, Ballesteros shot a record-breaking eight under par 64 at the Spanish Open at Las Brisas, delighting his prospective father-in-law, a twelve handicapper, with whom he was playing in the pro-am. Nevertheless, the repeated postponement of Carmen and Ballesteros's marriage began to be held up more and more as one of the major causes of the Spaniard's lack of inspiration on the golf course. At the Open in 1988 Carmen told the press: 'Seve's private life is private. His golf is separate.' But she added, 'We will be getting married pretty soon, but not just yet.'

On Friday, 25 November 1988, Severiano Ballesteros and Carmen Botin were at last married. Only their immediate families were invited. 'Otherwise,' explains Collet, 'there would have been literally hundreds of people there. They're related to hundreds and hundreds of people. They were married in Santander but they led everyone to believe it would be at Carmen's grandfather's other house, out in another village. They let it out and they said, "This is a big secret, don't tell anybody," knowing full well that it would get around and it would seem like an authentic secret and so everybody would be flocking out there on that day. And that's precisely what happened. They didn't tell me because they know that if somebody calls and asks me questions, I won't say I don't know if I do know. I'll say, "I do know but I can't tell you," and that would just make them angrier. So they just preferred not to tell me anything. They also planned it for three days after Seve came back from Japan (the Dunlop Phoenix), and the honeymoon was going to be in the Caribbean. Nobody in their wildest dreams would believe that after coming all that way he would then get married and go on another trip, because it's just so unlike Seve it's unbelievable. So I didn't believe any of the rumours. They told his mother the day before the wedding.

'I found out the morning of the wedding it was happening,' continues Collet. 'One of our secretaries went downstairs to buy a newspaper and heard over the radio: "Seve Ballesteros has just been seen coming out of a church in his wedding attire and they're driving off now . . ." His brother Baldomero hadn't come to work and Manuel was still at La Manga Club at that time, so he wasn't there. I thought, "Well, it wouldn't surprise me if it's true." And sure enough, minutes later it was all confirmed.'

In this way, Ballesteros and Carmen had the private wedding they wished for. No photographers were allowed, and the only pictures that resulted from it were informal ones taken by a member of the family with a small camera. Sadly, the couple took the roll of film with them to the Caribbean and had it processed there, whereupon an unscrupulous person in the photo-lab made extra copies and despatched them to a news agency, which duly had them published around the world. The photographs were unflattering and of a poor quality and, to make matters worse, the news agency captioned them incorrectly so that the names of the people who appeared in them were wrong.

'It was just a complete disaster,' recalls Collet, pitying Ballesteros, whose efforts to keep his wedding day sacred and away from the prying eyes of press and public had all been in vain. 'It caused a big scandal.'

Ballesteros has always been an intensely private man. Ever since those first lonely and difficult days on Tour in 1974, after which Manuel had advised him to go home until he recovered his spirits and his game, Pedreña has been his refuge, the place where he goes to heal himself when the pressures of fame get too much for him.

'When I go home and when I stay in Pedreña, my village, it's probably the only place that I feel a normal person,' he says. 'My friends, they see me as a normal person, they don't see me as a superstar. They respect me, I respect them and I feel very happy and very comfortable. I can do a lot of things and the people are not on my shoulder, which sometimes happens when I'm on the Tour – which is part of success but it's tough. And I feel extremely happy there.'

Years ago, when he was still very conscious that he had to be seen to be a resident of Monaco, he told *Hello* magazine that he derived as much pleasure from being there as he did from being in Spain. 'There are only two places in the world where I feel at home. One is my home in Monte Carlo where I can walk around the streets without anybody talking to me. Anywhere else, what always happens is someone comes up to you and says: "Hey, Seve, I saw you on television. Why did you miss the fifteenth hole?" and so on. That doesn't happen in Monte Carlo. Carmen and I spent all yesterday afternoon shopping and didn't get disturbed once. The second place is Pedreña. There I find the same peace and quiet as in Monte Carlo. To me, the people in Pedreña haven't changed since my youth. They accept me for what I am. Even though I now live in Monte Carlo, I still belong in this village. When I'm home we play cards together, go clay [pigeon] shooting or just sit in the bar and watch a football game on television, like the old times, and that makes me really happy. Anywhere else, you're looked at through different eyes when you achieve fame or have a lot of money in your account.'

As soon as all four Ballesteros brothers were professionals, and were either attached to golf clubs or on Tour, their parents retired, drew on their state pensions and were taken care of by their sons. Severiano then built a luxurious villa only an iron shot away from Real Club de Golf de Pedreña, complete with swimming pool, gymnasium, tennis courts, practice bunker and putting green, There, in the winter months and during his mid-season weeks off, when most players are resting, drinking beer and growing idle, Ballesteros puts himself through a rigorous training schedule. Beginning at eight o'clock in the morning, he spends an hour doing callisthenic-type exercises, lifting weights, stretching and working out on special machines designed to ease his back problems; eats breakfast; goes down to the golf club and either plays eighteen holes or hits two or three hundred balls; practises chipping, putting and bunker shots for a couple of hours; goes home for lunch; returns to the golf club and either plays or practises for the remainder of the afternoon.

'I practise every day,' says Ballesteros, 'including Saturday. On Sunday I play only in the morning until one o'clock, because on Sundays at the golf clubs there are many people and it's difficult.'

In between the Spaniard somehow finds time to run, play tennis, swim, sail, fish and cycle. He has become progressively more health conscious over the years. Once he smoked up to ten cigarettes a day, drank coffee, the occasional glass of wine and a beer with every evening meal; now he never smokes, rarely drinks even decaffeinated coffee, has shandy instead of beer and seldom imbibes wine. His diet is watched with equal care. Where once he tucked into high cholesterol foods with gay abandon, now he eats more carbohydrates, such as pasta, which give him energy. And when he is preparing for a major, he adheres strictly to a carefully calculated regime of nutrition, exercise, practice and rest.

'His strengths,' says Carr, 'are his desire to work and his passion. People have no idea how much he works, no concept of the amount of hours he puts in. And he does it every day, rain, hail or storm. He'll be up at Santander, it'll be pissing out of the heavens, and he'll be there with his wet suit on hitting balls. All the time. He might get up and ride a bike after that and go and do his weights and his training. He never stops. A Tour event – that's not his work schedule. His work time is at home. So when people say, he's at home resting, he's at home grinding himself out.'

When Ballesteros does want to relax, he watches videos, plays cards with his friends or goes out on his boat. When he feels so utterly overwhelmed by the pressures of success that he just has to escape, he goes hiking in the mountains with his sports psychologist, a man by the name of Caycedo, who is based in Andorra. Dr Caycedo was introduced to Ballesteros by a television presenter in Barcelona whom he dated for a brief period at the start of 1980. He is an expert on *suffrolgia*, a form of positive thinking, and he interviews the Spaniard and prepares cassette tapes for him to listen to on his Walkman.

'I don't know exactly what goes into them,' says Collet, who often roomed with Ballesteros on Tour before he married Carmen, 'but every once in a while I'll know he's locked in the room and he's got his headset on, and we don't disturb him during that period. Then he comes out and everything's fine and he has dinner and plays golf the next day. He doesn't like to talk about it, really.'

'What the doctor says to me is private,' Ballesteros told Doust. 'But it helps me to relax and convinces me I am good.'

'I'll tell you something about Seve,' says Collet. 'When he was a youngster he skipped school a lot, never really was very fond of academics, so anything that required him to do a lot of reading and analysing or writing down figures and stuff he didn't have much of an affinity for, and anything that he could do just with his hands or talking came more naturally to him. One of his friends in the US suggested he play chess. He said, "Oh no, that's for those intellectuals. I don't want to do that." But the guy kept on so he tried it and he said, "I don't like this," and he quit. But his friend just kept on and, I think, let him win once or something and it gave him a little confidence. Finally, he took an interest in it and he started playing. He was a very amateur player. When he started getting better he asked me if I knew how to play, and I played him and soundly thrashed him the first few games. But he was more determined than ever that he was going to beat me because that would prove something, so he kept working on it and I'll be doggone if the last three times we've played he hasn't beat me. He's got pretty good. He's a very aggressive chess player. I can see how that might be a factor in his golf game because it's just attack, attack, attack all the time.'

Like all great competitors Ballesteros loves to watch sport. He is a cycling *aficionado* and follows the progress of the top riders with an enthusiasm matched only by his love of football. Trajectory, his golf design company, sponsors a third-division football club in Santander, which he goes to watch most Sundays when he is in Pedreña. 'They can really play,' says Ballesteros with pride. 'They are leading the league at the moment, so it's very good advertising for my company.' Such is his competitiveness that he even wants his own football team and the teams he supports to be winners. Santander, a second-division club, is another of his favourites, 'but the real one is Barcelona football club. They have been my team since I was very young. At the moment they are second in the Spanish league, but I think they are the best in Europe at the moment.'

The price of Ballesteros's athleticism has been the agony he has suffered with his back, although the origin of his problems is unclear. Doust suggests that it might have been caused by an injury he suffered while boxing as a child. He lost his footing, fell backwards onto his coccyx and limped for a fortnight. On another occasion he strained his back while lifting rocks on his father's farm. But Ballesteros himself feels that it may have been initiated by excessive practice in 1974, the day before the first round of the Under-25's tournament at Pedreña. He hit 700 balls in the cold and rain, and woke the next morning with shooting pains in his back. Desperate to play, he had a series of pain-killing injections, which almost certainly compounded whatever damage he might already have inflicted upon himself, in the same way that professional riders who administer lame horses with cortisone ruin them for life for the sake of a single event.

In 1977, on the advice of Ceballos, Ballesteros went to see an eminent orthopaedic surgeon in Madrid. Dr Carbajosa X-rayed him and discovered a minor injury in the lower back, notably in the fifth vertebrae. He suggested that Ballesteros take a six-month break from the game and sleep on a hard mattress with a board underneath. The mattress was easy enough to arrange; the rest was out of the question. Later that year he paid a visit to the Spanish surgeon who had worked miracles with Trevino's back after the Mexican was struck by lightning. A discal hernia was diagnosed. The surgeon advised him to udergo an operation to fuse the weakened vertebrae. But Ballesteros, terrified of going under the knife, refused, convinced himself that if nothing else it would affect his golf swing.

It was around that time he began his world-wide search for a cure-all in earnest. First, he tried acupuncture and spent several years wearing tiny needles behind his right knee and in his right shoulder. He visited eye specialists after deciding his vision was failing. An ear, nose and throat specialist examined him and suggested surgery for the nasal congestion which caused his persistent cough. He was operated on for the first time in 1980 and has been in and out of hospital for the same reason on several occasions over the last fifteen years.

Initially, the Spaniard used to pour his heart out to the press about these trials and tribulations, telling them of his fears that one day his ailing back might stop him playing. At the Open in 1979, for instance, he confessed that he had spent months sleeping on the floor to ease his suffering. Thomas Boswell quotes him confiding to David Graham: 'Only I will ever know how bad my back has ever been.'

Then, quite suddenly, having been assured by a Californian orthopaedic surgeon that his condition was not career-threatening, he arrived at the conclusion that speaking of his injuries gave others a psychological advantage over him. From that moment on he avoided the issue. 'My back is fine. No problem.' Only his close friends knew of the scores of specialists and alternative healers he continued to visit.

'He's tried everything,' says Collet wryly. 'I don't think it's been as painful as you'd like to believe but it's been constant and uncomfortable. He has no problem in the medical sense. I've been with him through every conceivable discipline that claims to have knowledge about the back that there is. We've been to podiatrists who say that maybe his arch is off or the shoes that he wears bother him, because they say there's a relationship between the stance that you take, your posture and how your spine lines up. We've been to dentists who say that it works from the top to the bottom – if his bite is wrong, theoretically that could cause stress in the neck muscles, the neck would affect the spine and so forth. He's been for therapy. He's had experts on exercise talk to him . . . about doing things that are supposed to keep the alignment nice and straight and reduce stress and strengthen muscles. We've been to high-tech people who claim to know all about orthopaedics and they have just the machine that will strengthen the side of his body which is weak and which is causing the other side to be too strong and pulling the discs out of alignment . . . There's a guy down in Stratford-upon-Avon, Dr Hugo Kitchen, a homeopathic physician, who Seve goes to and who has one of these machines. The machine indicated that Seve's left side was stronger than his right, which means that he actually pulls the club through rather than pushes it and the braking muscles – as the doctor put it – are possibly weaker than the power muscles. He's given him a series of exercises to do to strengthen the other side so that it's symmetrical.'

Collet sighs heavily. 'I've been to regular orthopaedic surgeons with him and they've examined and X-rayed him. There's nothing out of line; he *has* no slipped disc, he *has* no herniated disc . . . I think the problem is one of tension, not a physical disability or a congenital shortcoming. I think he's a perfectly fine specimen. What he does is he puts a lot of stress on himself and of course his back's going to ache. I don't know of a golfer in the world who doesn't have a backache once in a while. A golf swing is completely unnatural.'

On 20 August 1990 Ballesteros's first son was born. A robust, healthy child with huge black eyes, his parents named him Baldomero Javier after Severiano's father. His arrival into the world (though premature) gave rise to the joke: Why did Carmen take so long in labour? Because the baby was demanding appearance money!

Ballesteros has always had a deep affection for small children and animals. Throughout his career they have been drawn to him and he in his turn has been gentle and endlessly patient with them, for they don't invade his privacy or try to steal his soul. So comfortable does he feel with children that when he went to play an exhibition match in Argentina in

1992 it was the most natural thing in the world for him to ask Fernandez if one of his young sons, whom he had met four years previously, could caddie for him, even though he was being accompanied to South America by his cousin who was perfectly willing and able to carry the bag.

'They were like two boys together,' recalls Fernandez smiling. 'Because my son treats him like somebody else like him, and he likes that. So I think he will be a more relaxed person from now on because of his son. He loves children. For such a long time he lived a life, maybe not by himself, but the people around him made him feel that he's the only one. But now he has a son he will not be the only one.'

'You don't know how much you love children until you have your own,' says Ballesteros. 'It is something very special. And it is difficult to leave them. You don't want to miss anything. It is wonderful how quickly they learn and how smart they are. Then they cry when you leave for the airport. It gets harder and harder to go.'

One of the hardest battles that Ballesteros has had to fight in his life is loneliness. As he says, 'It is not normal for the Spanish people to leave the place where you were born for long spells. The philosophy in Spain is to stay close to the family.' The bond between him and his brothers is still very strong – stronger, even, than it was in his childhood – and the long periods he endures away from home in vast, impersonal hotels only serve to accentuate it.

'He's close to each of them in their own way,' observes Collet. 'Manual started the pro Tour before Seve and sort of was his guide and helped him along in the early years. Manuel did a lot of nice things for him, which Seve appreciates, and he has a special place in his heart for him . . . The oldest brother, Baldomero, is, if not the father-figure of the family, he's the one everyone kind of looks to for advice. Seve's very close to him in an emotional way, wanting to have his older brother's approval. It's important to him to know his brother's opinion, and they don't always agree, but one usually convinces the other and then they're in harmony. He likes to have Baldomero involved in a lot of the decisions that he makes. The younger brother, Vicente, is the closest to Seve in age and, I think, is the one Seve feels the closest to socially. He kind of makes him laugh the most. He goes out with Seve once or twice a year (on Tour). Sometimes he caddies, and sometimes he goes to watch his golf swing. Vicente is a very gifted teacher.'

On the European Tour Ballesteros turns to a handful of close friends for support. He trusts few people because, as Fernandez says, 'he doesn't have time to choose the right friends . . . When you get to the position he is, you get more inside yourself because you know those people are talking to you because you're famous or because they want to make business with your money or whatever.'

Nick Price agrees. 'Character-wise, I'd say he's an introvert.'

'When he is with a few people, then he is very friendly and he's a nice guy,' says Jose Maria Olazábal who, along with Fernandez, Piñero, Lyle, Eduardo Romero, Anders Forsbrand and the tall Fijian Vijay Singh, is one of Ballesteros's most faithful friends. They had first met when they played an exhibition match for charity in Santander in 1984 and, recognizing the same qualities of fire, intensity and determination in each other, had formed a lasting friendship. 'Obviously, for me it was very special,' says Olazábal, 'and since then I have a lot of respect for Seve and I reckon he's a good friend of mine . . . But I think that he doesn't like crowds or people in general. Then what he tries to do is just try to avoid all those people, and sometimes it feels like he's not very friendly or a very nice guy. But that's the only reason why he reacts like that. When there is only four or five people he can be very, very friendly.'

'He's changed,' remarks Fernandez. 'He's changed for the better . . . I'm not saying Seve wasn't good before, but he has improved in his social relationships. I mean, he's started to understand how other people feel.'

'He's always been a hero in my eyes,' says Forsbrand. 'He's a wonderful man, absolutely wonderful. A lot of things have been said about him but I think he's one of the best guys out here . . . He's a great golfer and a very warm guy. Very warm heart.'

Marriage and the birth of his children have, to some extent, chased the loneliness bird from Ballesteros's door. He still longs for Pedreña and the sweet hills of home but now at least he has a choice: he doesn't have to be alone if he doesn't want to be. 'It helps a lot when you've finished the day,' says Ballesteros. 'If you've had a good day, you go back to the hotel and you feel very happy, of course. But if you've had a bad day and go into the hotel, you don't feel very well. But once I go into the hotel and I see my wife and I see my little boy, I just forget totally all those bogeys that I make and all the double-bogeys and those things, and it's something that helps a lot.'

But he admitted to *Hello* magazine that although, 'My family, my wife Carmen and our sons are a huge part of my life. The centrepoint was, and always will be, golf.'

'If Carmen confronted you with a choice of golf or family, how would you decide?' asked the reporter.

'I would try to keep on playing,' replied the Spaniard, 'although my family are much more important to me than golf. But I know it wouldn't come to that. Carmen knows I love my job so I would never be confronted with this choice.'

'It is my hope for my sons to be professional golfers,' says Ballesteros now. 'I can make sure they don't make the same mistakes I did. The biggest mistake I made was to start playing professional golf so early. I turned professional when I was only sixteen. I should have started three years later. It was my decision, mainly because I had nothing else to do. I thought I was ready to play and I was. But for me, I think it was a mistake. In one way it was good to have success so quickly, but in another way it meant I was facing things for which I wasn't really prepared. And it took a lot for me to face some of those things. In one way I regret it. I lost all my growing up years. I haven't lived a normal life.'

16

Hard Day's Night

The least thing upset him on the links. He missed short putts
because of the uproar of butterflies in adjoining meadows.

P.G. Wodehouse, *The Clicking of Cuthbert*

Sunday, 17 June 1990, US Open, Medinah. At first glance,
nothing was amiss. The club flowed back as fluidly and beautifully as ever, a sharp crack rang out, and then the crowd,
tense with excitement, surged forward with one movement
under the bright summer sky. Ballesteros, club in hand, eyes
on the green, proceeded after them up the opening hole of
one of America's toughest golf courses in the final round of
the US Open. His proud head was held high, his stride was
determined. Even his name occupied its usual place on the
leaderboard. It was not until he played his second shot and
then his third that it became obvious that something was
horribly, perhaps irremediably, wrong. It was there in the
hesitancy of his club selection, in the tentativeness of his
putting, in the uneasiness with which he examined each
stage of his oft-repeated practice swings, in his deeply fur-
rowed brow, in the agitated clearing of his throat and in the
hopeful but unmistakably desperate way in which he watched
the fluctuations of scores. With Ballesteros, body language has
always spoken more eloquently than words.

Three days earlier the Spaniard had commenced his bid

for the title he has always longed for. When he made two birdies in the first three holes, an expression approaching cheerfulness had appeared on his face and he had momentarily cast off that air of despondency which had hung like a cloud over him all season. Almost as suddenly, however, he had lost control of his driver. From there on in he had hooked wildly from every tee, and it was only his ability as an escape artist that had allowed him to hit sixteen greens in regulation and score 73. The following day his attitude had been one of defiance. It was almost as if he thought that by directing his anger inwardly he could prevent the misery he felt from consuming him. But after nine holes despair was getting the better of him. Goaded by the prospect of missing the cut, he launched himself into his tee shot at the par five tenth and hooked it into a fairway bunker. His recovery shot clattered in amongst the trees. He had 130 yards to the green and no shot. Low-hanging branches blocked all escape routes. Finally, he selected a six-iron and, to the amazement of his audience, hit an exquisite punch shot which never rose above waist-height off the ground, pitched just short of the green, skipped between two bunkers, bounded onto the putting surface and came to a stop 8 inches from the pin.

Inspired, Ballesteros fairly flew home, scoring 32 for a total of 69. Two days later, he was four strokes behind the leaders, Billy Ray Brown and Mike Donald, and in contention for the US Open title. Then he arrived at the par three second. Standing on the tee with a club in his hand and Lake Kadijah yawning at his feet, he did something which he himself would have thought inconceivable in the days when he was young and intense: he lost concentration. Later he confessed, 'My thoughts were everywhere but where they should have been.'

'Ahhh!' moaned the crowd in sympathy as his ball curved out over the water, wrestled briefly with the wind and then cleaved the oily green surface of the lake. They craned forward to gaze into its quivering depths. On the tee it was as if Ballesteros had been hit by a mortal blow. His shoulders sagged forward in utter dejection; the light went from his eyes. 'After that, I just put myself down,' he said miserably, having finished equal thirty-third. 'I was there to win and I hit it in the water. If things are going badly it becomes a kind of routine.'

He sighed. 'Every time I feel things may get better, that I am about to break through and win again, it's like I run into a wall.'

Ballesteros had been on the road to nowhere since the beginning of the new season. Some said that his journey may even have started sooner, for even in 1989 there had been signs that all was not what it should be. His first finish of the season was equal fifty-fourth in the Open de Baleares and, although he had victories in the Madrid Open, the Epson Grand Prix and the European Masters, they were interspersed with a twelfth place tie, a seventy-sixth place tie, a thirty-eighth place tie, a twentieth place tie and two missed cuts. Nobody thought anything of it. Golf is too capricious a game and the golf swing too mysterious a movement for any player to be expected to perform year in and year out at a consistently high level, least of all a player as inspirational as Ballesteros. There are just too many intangibles involved. And at the outset of the 1990 season, everything seemed to be much the same as usual. He was equal third in Dubai, equal fourteenth in the Mediterranean Open and then won the Open de Baleares in a play-off. What could be more normal than that? Ballesteros himself agreed. 'My game is back,' he said cheerfully. 'It was the best I've felt on a golf course in six or seven months.'

The first indication of the nightmare that was to come occurred a fortnight later at the Nestlé Invitational in Bay Hill in Florida; Ballesteros took nine at one hole and missed the cut. It was the second worst score of his career. His worst had been the eleven he had notched up in the Spanish Open at La Manga in 1974 when he was seventeen years old. Nevertheless, he finished third the very next week in the Houston Open and all seemed to be well again. Which it was if you looked no further than the record book. What the results didn't show was that while the Spaniard had had three birdies in the first eight holes and picked up another trio at the eleventh, thirteenth and sixteenth to be tied for the lead going into the closing holes, he had also clipped the trees with his approach shot on the seventeenth to drop a shot and lose the tournament. Afterwards, he claimed there had been mud on the ball.

At the Masters he seemed disgruntled and generally out of humour, but no-one would have described his form as bad. He shot 74, 73 in the opening rounds and complained that he had been disadvantaged by his late starting time on the first day, since he was struggling with his putting and by the time he had teed off in the afternoon there were so many spike marks left by the rest of the field that they had only accentuated the problem. He three-putted both the sixteenth and eighteenth holes as a consequence. His fine scores of 68 and 71 on the last two days, which helped him to joint seventh place, were all that was needed to convince him that *destino* had, once again, withheld what was rightfully his. 'Overall it was not too bad, but decidedly not what I was looking for.'

The trouble was that each time Ballesteros returned to Augusta he was reminded of the promise he had made to his father, reminded too of the manner in which he had broken it and therefore confronted with proof that he was not invincible. In 1990 he went fishing for a week afterwards to try to overcome his disappointment and banish the vile image of that four-iron shot splashing down into the pond. It had not, as he thought, been exorcized when he won the Open in 1988. At Lytham he had said confidently: 'Now I can forget about hitting into the water at Augusta . . . and remember instead how I played today.' But at that time he had no experience of how one shot, one split second of lost concentration, could cause years of devastation. He found he could no more shrug it off than Nicklaus had been able to after Watson chipped in to beat him at the penultimate hole of the 1982 US Open at Pebble Beach; or Hubert Green had been able to after missing that 3-foot putt for victory at Augusta in 1978; or, most remarkably of all, Jacklin had been able to after Trevino had chipped at the eleventh hour to snatch victory from him at Muirfield in the 1972 Open.

But, in a way, the knowledge that someone else had been responsible for his failures at Augusta might have alleviated Ballesteros's suffering. As it was, he had no-one to blame but himself. He set off to Puerto de Hierro for the Madrid Open, tired and unrefreshed. It did him no good at all to learn that one of his companies had become embroiled in a storm of controversy. It transpired that Olazábal was refusing to play in the Spanish Open the following week because Amen Corner had rejected his demand for a £24,000 appearance fee. Instead he had been offered £36,000 to play in the Spanish Open in 1990 and 1991 as well as in the 1991 Open de Baleares. Nothing could have been more reasonable since only major champions and past winners of the Order of Merit are entitled to appearance money and Olazábal didn't meet either criterion. He didn't see it that way, though.

Essentially, the dispute was between Carr and Sergio Gomez, Olazábal's manager. Ballesteros insisted that he had nothing to do with the negotiations, but was embarrassed nonetheless. He reiterated what he had said a hundred times during the appearance money war of 1981 – namely, that no player should be allowed to ask for a fee although they should be entitled to accept it if offered.

With that, he went out onto the golf course, where his problems started in earnest. The news had only just broken that Carmen was pregnant and the Spanish paparazzi, guessing she would be following his match, had arrived at Puerto de Hierro *en masse*. Wholly uneducated in golf etiquette and devoid of the commonest forms of courtesy or human decency, they swarmed over the fairways like rats, creating havoc wherever they went. After two hours, Carmen couldn't stand it anymore and fled in tears. Ballesteros had just had to step away from the ball at the short seventeenth (his eighth) because of all the scuffling and clicking and he had fluffed his chip, chipped again, missed the putt and taken a double bogey five. When he reached the ninth hole he appeared to be in a towering rage. His drive hooked obstinately away and finished halfway up a bank on the left side of the fairway. He clambered up after it, balanced precariously on the steep face, smashed at the ball and had to take hasty evasive action as it came back at him like a bullet off a pine tree and vanished under a small bush. This he destroyed with a furious lunge, sending his ball straight into another tree, which luckily deflected it onto a place from where it was possible to reach the green. Squealing tyres announced his departure.

The next day, wrapped up as much against the prying eyes of the press as against the Arctic wind blowing off the snow-capped mountains of Madrid, the defending champion added a 70 to his 76 and missed the cut.

It was now that the idea that Ballesteros had fallen into a deep slump really began to take root in people's minds. Previously, it had just been considered a spell of bad form. After that, it was only a matter of time before the smallest gesture and most ordinary stroke was taken as evidence that he was no longer the player he had once been.

The Spaniard, for his part, was unable to hide his despondency. At the Spanish Open he was tense and distracted and kept up a muttered stream of invective between shots. Wright plodded at his side, listening but not hearing. 'Keep out of his way,' he warned journalists when he came off the course. 'He's ready to explode.'

Ballesteros had more on his mind than the state of his game, the antics of the paparazzi or his differences with Olazábal – which by now had been resolved. Olazábal had appeared at the tournament on the first practice day and said quietly: 'We are good friends and I would do anything for him. When he asked me to play on Monday, I said yes straight away.' Ballesteros's most pressing concern was the outcome of the campaign to bring the 1993 Ryder Cup to Madrid's Club de Campo, the Spanish Open venue. He regarded it as his own personal crusade and had devoted a considerable amount of time and energy to it – even going so far as to lead a Spanish delegation to the PGA in February. He had also dwelt long and hard on the opposition he was likely to encounter. Consequently, when he walked into the press centre after the first round of the tournament, having shot 74 and taken nearly five hours to do it in, he had worked himself into a state of rare fanaticism.

He sat on the podium and glowered, his body rigid with temper. Shortly before his arrival Faldo, immaculately groomed and on top of his game, had breezed into the press centre and, on being asked which of the favoured Ryder Cup courses – Club de Campo, Royal Birkdale or Portmarnock in Dublin – he considered most suitable, had replied that he thought Birkdale would give the Europeans the best chance of victory.

When Ballesteros was informed of this he was beside himself with rage.

'Why should we play in England, why?' he cried passionately, eyes blazing. 'Why should we play in Ireland, why? Spanish players have done enough for European golf. We *must* have the Ryder Cup in Spain. I'm not saying I won't play if it doesn't come here, but remember one thing: I would be disappointed. I would lose a little bit of my desire for the Ryder Cup.'

Order took wing; chaos reigned. Spanish translations were hurled back and forth.

'People should remember that, without the European players, there probably would be no Ryder Cup,' said Ballesteros coldly when peace had broken out. 'The future of the European Tour is in Spain . . . Golf here needs the push the Ryder Cup would provide. It would be the best thing for the game as a whole. It is what Samuel Ryder would have wanted if he were alive today. To wait until 1997 would be too late.'

Then he added darkly, 'I feel I have played a part in the success of the Ryder Cup. This is the first time I have asked for anything.'

There is no question that Ballesteros's tactics, not only at that particular press conference but also at every opportunity that came his way over the next few months, were tantamount to emotional blackmail. But it's important to realize that there was nothing selfish about his motives. He wasn't doing it to glorify the name of Severiano Ballesteros. He was trying to achieve, sooner rather than later, the same dream he had been committed to ever since he became famous enough to make any impression at all on the powers that be – that of bringing golf to every village in Spain.

'I've been fighting for a long time to build more golf courses for the Spanish people,' Ballesteros told *Today's Golfer*. 'But the people with power do not understand how important golf is.'

'You have a situation in Madrid where there's 6,500,000 people and a bus driver can't go and play golf,' explains Carr. 'There's only one place he can go and that's Club de Campo at £25 a round . . . There's 70,000 rounds played over Club de Campo every year. There's 20,000 members at one club and two other clubs have 6,000 members each . . . And that's basically what he's saying . . . "Let's build some golf courses." Because for the man in the street, it's still in the classification of élitist. And that's not what he wants.'

'Sadly, because golf is such an élitist game in Spain, I don't think Seve will find that his terrific world presence over the last fifteen years has had the impact on Spanish golf that it should have had,' observes Jacklin. 'Sad, because it's not a game for the people in Spain, it's a game for the hierarchy. I know how disappointed Seve was when he didn't get those municipal courses off the mark, and I think he had fallouts with the mayor up in his home town . . . It's very difficult. I think golf in Spain is run by such a small circle of people that they're the only ones he's getting the recognition from.'

'I have met many liars in politics,' says Ballesteros bitterly. 'I particularly remember one of the mayors at one of the villages where I built a golf course, who promised me he would build a driving range for the village and two years later he forgot what he had told me and repeated the same promise. These people are unbelievable . . . I would not like to be in politics . . . Politicians are only interested in their own positions. For them, it is much easier to build a football stadium. They get more votes. Golf to them has the image of being a very élitist sport.'

In May Ballesteros came to Britain for the Benson and Hedges International. He had narrowly escaped missing the cut at the Spanish Open and though he eventually finished joint sixth was becoming increasingly anxious about the state of his game. His performance at St Mellion gave him good cause for alarm. He scored 68, 77, 73, 76 and finished forty-first. Olazábal won. The only bright spot in the week was the statement by Ryder Cup captain Bernard Gallacher, to the effect that the Tour had recommended that the event be held at Club de Campo in 1993. 'To play the match in Spain would be a particular tribute to Seve Ballesteros for all he has done in Europe, and we think that to leave it until 1997 would be too late since there is a possibility that by then Seve would no longer be an automatic choice.'

On 24 May 1990, at the PGA Championship at Wentworth, it was confirmed that the Ryder Cup would *not* be going to Club de Campo or anywhere else in Spain in 1993. It would be going back to the monstrously over-hyped, over-rated, pseudo-American Belfry. It was understood that Lord Derby, who eventually resigned over the matter, had had the casting vote. At home in Pedreña, Ballesteros was distraught. He issued a statement to say that he was 'very disillusioned' with the decision and that his 'motivation would not be the same.'

This caused an immediate uproar. Relations between the European Tour and the PGA were already strained to breaking point and further animosity would result in a revolution.

'I was bitterly disappointed that the 'ninety-three match did not go to Spain,' says Schofield now. 'There was no good reason for it not happening. Tony Jacklin was a hundred per cent correct. You can't go on taking – a third of the team was Spanish in 1985 – and not giving. There is a good side to it. The 1997 match will go to Spain. I don't think anybody knows [where]. Severiano, I think, is hopeful of doing his own sort of Muirfield Village. I've seen his site. It's superb. Its location is good. It's very close to Puerto de Hierro and Club de Campo, so it's got reasonable access to Madrid . . . If we did make an error, and it's always easier in hindsight, then it was tying the bid to one golf course. It wasn't just Spain, it was Club de Campo, and obviously a lot of people, including leading players, were not certain that Club de Campo was the right venue.'

'There are two main reasons for playing the Ryder Cup,' said Ballesteros months later. 'One is for the competition between the Americans and the Europeans. The other is to use the Ryder Cup for the benefit of the game – to make the game bigger all over the world. And the only way to do that is to take it to places that need help. Golf in Britain and

Ireland is already developed. The next step is Spain, because Spain is playing a big role not only in the Ryder Cup but also on the European Tour. Also, I always felt that to take the Ryder Cup to Spain in 1993 would have been a reward for myself – *agradecimiento*, we say in Spain. I feel that it was an opportunity to say: "Hey, we feel that Seve has done a lot for the European Tour, we feel Seve has done a lot for European golf. We feel golf in Spain needs a lift." '

This rational statement only came later, however, and the whole incident was threatening to escalate out of control when it was diffused, suddenly and unexpectedly, by Olazábal. In response to Ballesteros's comments about the possibility of him losing his motivation and interest in the Ryder Cup, he simply said calmly and with a maturity far beyond his years: 'Well, he had to say that, didn't he? When he gets on the golf course I know he will give a hundred and ten per cent. He wants to kill everyone. He won't need any motivation.'

Wednesday, 18 July 1990, Open Championship, St Andrews. Six years after the sun had set on one of the most glorious battles the game has ever seen, Ballesteros, its conquering hero, pulled up a chair on the interview platform and beamed at the world's press. He was the picture of health and happiness. Recent weeks spent fishing, practising, cycling and watching the Tour de France on television had relaxed him, and he looked more at peace with himself than he had at any other time during that strife-torn year.

'It's always nice to be back at the place where I have so many good memories,' said Ballesteros, eyes sparkling with pleasure. The previous evening he had run round at the R&A dinner like a small boy, merrily collecting autographs from fifteen past champions. 'I must say, to win the Open is something special, but to win at St Andrews, that's something very few people have the chance to do and I'm fortunate to be one of them. If I had to pick one of my three Open Championships, I would definitely say this is the one. It's very special.'

'How is your game compared to how it was coming into the Open at Royal Lytham?'

'Well, it's much the same as it was in 1984, and the same

as it was in 1988. It's true that it's not been very good, but there's still half a year to go and anything can happen.'

'But what's the matter with your game?' a reporter demanded.

The smile left Ballesteros's face. 'There's nothing the matter with my game,' he said curtly, 'there's nothing the matter with my swing. It's just a matter of confidence.'

An American reporter waved his pen in the air. 'Your swing change,' he asked, 'is it complete?'

Ballesteros's mood changed as suddenly as a shadow slides over the sun. 'People keep talking about my swing change,' he snapped. 'Why should I change my swing when I've been the best player for ten years?'

The European press cast covert glances at one another. Was this the same man who had shown them calloused hands only two months before, which he said were the result of hitting three thousand balls at Pedreña while he tried to implement the third swing change of his career? Was this the same Seve Ballesteros who had told them at the Italian Open: 'I decided it was time to make big changes and I've spent hours with my brothers Vicente and Baldomero looking at videos and films of my major victories to see what I was doing. When I first started golf I swung the club too upright and kind of tilted at the ball. I made corrections and went too far and began swinging too flat. The result of that was hitting a very bad pull-hook under pressure, and that has been a killer for me.'

And after admitting it was that shot that had cost him victory at the 1986 Masters as well as at the 1989 Ryder Cup, where he had hit his approach shot into the water at the eighteenth to lose his singles match against Paul Azinger, he added: 'I've felt uncomfortable with my swing the last couple of years, and my brothers and I have been working on the way I pick up the club and take it back. They are major changes but I think they are necessary.'

By the time he reached Monte Carlo in June he was no longer speaking of swing changes but was experimenting instead with different putters. The Ping that had won him more than sixty tournaments world-wide and had ensured he became, earlier in the season, the first European golfer to pass the £2,000,000 mark in earnings, had been tossed aside like a broken umbrella. A few days later it was plucked out of the wastepaper basket and set to work again. The new putter had failed to bring about the miraculous recovery he was hoping for.

All of these things had, it seemed, slipped Ballesteros's mind. He also had amnesia where David Leadbetter was concerned. Previously, the most natural player in the world insisted: '[My brothers] are the only ones that know my swing because they saw me grow up. Everybody else, they don't know my swing . . . To teach someone that plays good golf is very difficult unless you know their swing.' But at the Western Open in the US, he sought the advice of the man who had helped make Faldo great. Afterwards, Leadbetter commented: 'He needed someone to talk to about what he's working on. It was just a case of listening.'

As the year went on and Ballesteros sank deeper and deeper into the mire, he began clutching at straws. Leadbetter was required to do more than just listen. 'Seve has always had to guard against going left,' he said. 'Even when he won the Open at Lytham in 1979, you could see he was fighting to hold the club on line. When he won the Open there in 1988 he hadn't been playing well for some time, but once he won that he was off and winning again. With him, it may just come down to confidence, but I don't really think he's played really well for four years. Seve still has a young man's swing, and it's hard for his body to cope with the power it generates. He has a perfect grip, a perfect set-up and wonderful rhythm, but he does tend to hit the ball while off balance, leading towards a reverse-C position in his follow-through.'

In *The Sunday Times* he added: 'He's swinging as he was at twenty, relying on his hands and arms to control the club. In his heyday his short game pulled him through. It is not as good as it used to be. Now he needs to hit more fairways and greens.'

'Seve should just tee it up and let it fly,' was Jacklin's opinion. 'My advice to him is to ignore everyone. There's only one guy that made him great and that's him.'

Faldo thought that Ballesteros's excessive leg action put

strain on his back, causing him pain. 'He still has a very good backswing but he loses it on the downswing. He needs to slow down his aggressive leg action. He's contorting himself. He should be trying to hit the ball with very little bending of the spine.'

But, for now, Ballesteros wasn't having any of it. 'I think my swing has been good to me so far,' he said with a scowl. 'It's just confidence.' And he stalked off to practise.

In the second round of the Open, on a cool, changeable day, Doust went out with Manuel and old Dr Campuzano to watch Ballesteros play. They strolled across the links, buffeted by the fresh wind. After the first round the Spaniard had been full of smiles. He had scored a one under par 71, which could, he insisted, have been a 69, had it not been for the double-bogey he took at the Road Hole. Now his face had taken on that familiar I'd-rather-be-wrestling-alligators expression. He had worn it all season. He grimaced, he sighed, he looked out to sea, he complained of his sufferings to Vicente.

His elder brother, with whom he had never won so much as an egg-cup, was temporarily taking the place of Wright; the Englishman and Ballesteros had parted company at the US Open. Wright insisted that it was a mutual and completely amicable separation. So, indeed, did the Spaniard. The caddie grapevine had it that the Englishman secured car and clothing contracts on the strength of his position as caddie to Ballesteros, and that those, as far as his boss was concerned, were the final nails in the coffin of their relationship. My own opinion is that Ballesteros was looking for a scapegoat to take the blame for his inadequacies and that Wright was as convenient as any. Fernandez had managed to secure him a reprieve but could not persuade Ballesteros to allow him to work at the Open; hence, Vicente.

Out on the gloomy links, the Spaniard chalked up another bogey.

'*Que Paso?*' asked the good doctor. What's wrong?

'His problem is in his head,' replied Manuel. 'He listens to too many people.'

'Does he listen to you?' Doust wanted to know.

'No,' said Manuel. 'I don't tell him anything. He doesn't listen to me.'

Manuel, like everybody else, had his own theory as to why his brother had come crashing down so ignominiously from the pinnacle of his profession. 'Men are like motor cars. They show signs of breaking down at 100,000 miles. Seve has gone farther. He's gone 200,000.'

Fernandez agrees. 'I kept telling him for many years that he was playing too many tournaments and travelling too much.' He feels that because Ballesteros puts so much pressure on himself on the golf course he suffers far more stress than most players do. 'In one year he won on every continent, but under his contracts he had already committed himself so he had to do it. And I told him: "Sooner or later, you're going to pay for it." And I think it took longer than I expected. I think I thought it would affect him six or seven years before.'

'He's much older than his age in that he's been playing a long time,' Miller told John Hopkins. 'He's got to learn to pace himself. He should wash this season down the drain, go home and set a new game plan. He should take six months off because he's losing his freshness.'

Inevitably, there was speculation about the effect on Ballesteros's game of married life – fuelled by his insistence that something was destroying his concentration on the golf course and his refusal to say what it was. 'We always used to say if they get married they're no good for a year,' says Musgrove sardonically. 'That was one of our old caddie theories. Big change in your outlook. Especially if you've got to be single-minded to be at the top and all of a sudden you've got somebody else to think of.'

But Roddy Carr was convinced that he was just finding fame and its accompanying pressures harder to deal with. 'He gets unmercifully harassed – not by the professional journalists on the Tour – but by everybody all the time. He's unmercifully harassed *all* the time. Can't go to the toilet, can't go and have a meal, can't go to the golf course, can't go and have an hour's practice. That's the price he pays . . . I mean, if you listen to a question that an unqualified Spanish writer

302

would ask, it's pathetic. You know, sneaking into his private life and stuff like that. He's a very private person, Seve, and he wants it that way and he's entitled to that. He's had horrific encounters that nobody would ever know about with the press – following him and this and that. That's all part of the harassment factor.'

All of these things, together with his court battles with Barner and UMI which did not actually come to an end until 25 April 1990, undoubtedly took their toll, but only Manuel, walking beside Doust and Dr Campuzano at St Andrews and watching his brother take a double bogey seven from a bunker at the fourteenth for an eventual 74 and another missed cut, touched on what the real reason for Ballesteros's decline might be. 'He's not as keen on his golf as when he was a boy,' he told his companions. 'If it snowed, I can tell you, he would no longer practise in the snow.'

In March 1990, the day before winning the Open de Baleares, his only victory all season, Ballesteros observed that 'some people want to become champions and when they become a champion – once they have that and all the tension and all the pressure that comes with it – they cannot take it any more. So they escape from it. That's why they come down.'

By the autumn it was beginning to seem as if he himself had fallen victim to that very syndrome. At the US PGA Championship at Shoal Creek he had shot a second round 83 – his worst round in fifteen years of major championship competition and the highest score he had recorded since the opening day of the French Open in 1979 – which included nine bogeys and one triple bogey. Added to his first round 77, it left him nine strokes shy of the cut. It was the fourth time he had failed to qualify in eight appearances in America.

From Birmingham, Alabama, Ballesteros flew to Birmingham, England, where he sat behind a microphone in the press centre at the English Open looking as persecuted as a man can look, out of chains. He refused to discuss the US PGA, his golf game, his personal life or anything related in any way at all to his career. Everything except the weather was taboo.

'Apart from the concentration problem, are you happy with the way you are playing?' asked a reporter once we had explored the outer limits of meteorological conversation.

'I say-a that I just don't want to talk about that,' said Ballesteros miserably.

His unhappiness was remarked upon.

'*Unhappy?*' echoed Ballesteros, as though he were the most cheerful man in the universe. 'I'm not unhappy. I'm just not happy with the way things are going for me in golfing matters.'

'His intensity to win is like a drug, you know,' explains Carr. 'And when he's not winning, he's not happy. He was born to win. If he's not happy, that's the reason he's not happy; it's nothing to do with the fact that he's in a bad humour, or he's a bad guy, or he's angry, or whatever. He just hates losing, which is an ingredient of the great players in all sports. People who hate losing are great champions. So all it is, is an expression of his hatred of losing. Nothing else. So that part of him was misunderstood when he was going through that period. He was just angry at not winning.'

'The problem is that I don't have the same degree of concentration that I used to have on the course,' Ballesteros confided to Robert Green. 'I have trouble keeping it up for eighteen holes. I now get distracted very quickly and very easily; my mind wanders off on to other things – like a movie I've seen or what I'm doing for dinner – and that never used to happen before. My concentration goes so I make some bogeys, and then I lose my confidence. Then I start to hit more bad shots, and then I can never get my concentration or confidence back. The longer the round goes on, the worse things seem to get.'

At The Belfry things degenerated to the extent where, in the last five holes of the English Open, he missed a 2-foot putt and took a bogey six to lose the lead and ultimately the tournament. The following week he demanded an appearance fee of approximately $100,000, plus travel and accommodation expenses, to play in the German Open. On being refused it (only because the sponsors were experimenting in doing away with appearance money by claiming they had put it into the prize fund), he stayed at home in Pedreña, where Carmen gave birth to their first child. A month later, he appeared at the Lancome Trophy looking completely rejuvenated. It transpired that the joys of fatherhood were only partially responsible for this change of heart; he had also just beaten Manuel in a small local event in Spain and won £200.

'More important than that,' said the Spaniard with a grin, 'I scored 71 and 66.'

When the tournament ended, the smile had gone from his face. A visit to the pond on the eighteenth had cost him a double bogey, and victory, once again, had been denied him.

These were among the darkest days of Ballesteros's life. At the World Match Play at Wentworth in October, an event which he had dominated between 1981 and 1985 with his fearlessness, genius and flair, he was twice humiliated: not only did he suffer the indignity of being unseeded for the first time in fifteen consecutive starts, he was also beaten 8 and 6 by Irishman Ronan Rafferty.

Ballesteros was devastated. Later, when that traumatic period was over, he told Guy Hodgson: 'I was very aware that the golf I played was not that of Severiano Ballesteros. I felt as if it was not me out there, as if there was a devil inside me.'

Looking at Ballesteros in his match against Rafferty, fretting and frowning, agonizing over club selection, hunching his shoulders and biting his nails, it was hard to doubt his words.

'That's what happens to you when you're in a slump,' said Faldo sympathetically. 'Things just don't go for you and after a while your shoulders start to ache with all the weight you seem to be carrying. You just want to lie down and scream, "Give us a break, please!" '

When the season ended Ballesteros was seventh on the World Rankings and eighteenth on the European Order of Merit with earnings of £167,674. In three seasons he had missed five cuts in Europe, one more than he had missed in the preceding twelve years.

'My advice to Seve is to disappear for two or three months, get the swing right, work everything out,' commented Faldo. 'He's got nothing to prove any more.'

'He hasn't got the yips,' Miller told Hopkins. 'He hasn't lost his nerve. He still wants to play. Golf is a game of misses. Seve was the best at recovering from them.'

One morning Ballesteros, dejected, apathetic and a shadow of his former self, looked in the mirror and said to himself: 'Well, Seve, you have to do something to come back and be like you're supposed to be.'

'And the only thing I did was work harder,' he remembers. 'And this is the key.'

17

After the Storm

We can secure other people's approval, if we do right and try hard; but our own is worth a hundred of it, and no way has been found out of securing that.

Mark Twain, *Following the Equator*

Monday, 27 May 1991, PGA Championship, Virginia Water. Excitement swept through the Wentworth gallery like fire through a cane field. They poured down the seventeenth like an army of butterflies, past the last of the carefully screened mansions of celebrities and royalty, past the towering trees that separate green from tee, and then out onto the final hole where they formed a ragged and lively line along the fairway. Ballesteros came behind them, tense and absorbed. All afternoon he had courted danger without a qualm, thrilling the crowd with his great drives, bold escapes and touch and ingenuity around the greens – almost as he had in his youth. But at the sixteenth his audacity had caught up with him. He drove into the gallery and took bogey there, then blocked his drive into a grove of trees on the seventeenth, took two to reach the green and three more to get down, missing from 4 feet.

Now he felt nervousness take a firm grip on his heart. He had gone to pieces too often in this situation over the past year not to approach it with some trepidation. A fortnight earlier, he had scored a course record 63 to lead the Spanish Open by five strokes after the first round, but had followed it with rounds of 70 (including a four-putt at the eighteenth), 67 and 75, which allowed Eduardo Romero to catch him and force a play-off. The smiling Argentinian had triumphed after seven gruelling holes at Club de Campo. 'I had joy and sorrow today,' said Romero afterwards. 'Joy, because I won an important tournament. And sorrow, because I've beaten my friend and hero.'

Ballesteros looked along the wide, graceful curve of Wentworth's eighteenth fairway and made a conscious effort to force the image of that particular loss out of his head. He needed a birdie to catch Colin Montgomerie on 271, seventeen under par.

'Seve,' he said to himself, 'you can't lose all the time. Something good must happen to you.'

A few moments later it had. His approach shot flirted with a greenside bunker, but it landed safely and he chipped to 7 feet. 'I think if I had missed the putt on the last hole, that would have damaged my confidence,' he said later, 'because until the last three holes the tournament was in my hands.'

As evening began to cast long shadows across the West Course, the Spaniard and Montgomerie made their way to the 471-yard, par four first hole for the play-off, the vibrant crowd rushing ahead of them. Ballesteros, breathing deeply to try to settle his nerves, smashed his drive from the tee. Then a minor miracle occurred. As the ball hooked away towards rough, trees and possible disaster, it collided with a parked golf cart. Ballesteros watched it spring into the light rough and felt his heart lift. It was a long time since fortune had smiled upon him. When he reached his ball it was lying on a slight slope, some 220 yards from the pin. He took a five-iron from the bag and, summoning every ounce of will-power he possessed, struck it smoothly into the cross-wind with an easy, rhythmic swing. It soared over the shallow valley that crosses the fairway, pitched onto the green and finished 3 feet from the pin. It was an awe-inspiring stroke.

'Given the situation, it was one of the best shots I've ever hit,' said Ballesteros afterwards. Montgomerie had no reply to it. He did, nevertheless, fight valiantly to the bitter end, hitting an exquisite chip and run to within inches of the hole before watching the Spaniard sink the putt for his first European victory in more than fourteen months.

The king was back and in full possession of his gifts.

When the 1990 season had drawn to a close, Ballesteros had reached the stage where victory was hardly in his reckoning. He had fought so long and so hard for so little reward, that he had grown weary and pessimistic. All through the year dark clouds had ridden across his skies and menaced him with their terrifying clashes. Caught up in this 'thunderstorm', as he described it, he had been swept along, hurled about and finally dashed upon the rocks of an ailing career and left for dead. There he had lain for several months, shell-shocked and weak – no longer capable of struggling. After a while, he had hauled himself to his feet and done what was required of him. He had punished himself with gruelling work-outs and marathon bicycle rides and runs. He had worked himself to a standstill on the practice range. And he had cut a sorry figure on Spanish television in December, explaining to viewers with much clearing of his throat that he had not been sufficiently prepared for the season, that his schedule had been wrong and that he had changed clubs and they hadn't worked.

In February 1991 he had won a Skins game in the Canary Islands, and his confidence had begun to seep slowly back. But in the first week of March, the terrible pattern of 1990 had repeated itself. On practice days at the Doral Ryder Open in Florida, at the club where he had once been touring pro, Ballesteros had been very wild, even hitting a spectator. Gambling establishments had put him at 50–1, last in their list of favourites to win the tournament. He had justified their estimate by shooting 75, 78 and crashing out of the event, failing to qualify for the weekend by ten strokes. Next, he had returned to Europe to play the Open de Baleares, where he was defending champion. He confessed that he was 'in bad health, low in confidence and fighting a hook,' and proceeded to compile rounds of 73, 75, 78, 68 to finish equal thirty-third. The following week, he fumbled a one-handed tap-in from 6 inches to miss the cut by a stroke at the Catalan Open.

By then the idea that the king had lost his crown – that he would never ever be as great as he had once been – had become well and truly entrenched in public opinion. The media reminisced nostalgically about his glory days, the players talked of him in the past tense, and across Europe people described the man who had once been the most charismatic and exciting player since Palmer, as 'ordinary'. There was no more damning a word.

Then, in the first week of May 1991, while steeling himself for a play-off and the possibility of losing yet another tournament, Ballesteros did what no-one – least of all himself – was expecting: he holed a 25-foot birdie putt to win the Y120,000,000 Chunichi Crowns tournament at Nagoya Golf Club in Japan by a stroke from Australian Roger Mackay. It was his sixty-first victory, and his first for fourteen months; ultimately it marked a turning point in his career. Four things may have been responsible for it. One was the intensive coaching sessions he had had with Leadbetter at the Dunlop Open the previous week, from which it emerged that he should be trying to restrict the hip turn on his backswing; another was the metal woods he had begun using for the first time in his life ('I call it mental not metal because everybody thinks they can win more using it'); the third was his new Maxfli Tad Moore putter, which he had changed to after using a Ping Anser nearly all his professional life; and the fourth was the appointment of Billy Foster, his new caddie.

After Wright and he had parted by mutual agreement in August 1990, Ballesteros had not, as was expected of him as a top player, hired a regular replacement immediately. Instead he had played out the season with a succession of sundry bag-carriers, among whom were a twenty-one-year-old hotel receptionist named Miguel Betrissey, who helped him finish tied twenty-first at the European Masters in Crans-sur-Sierre, and a local boy named Jonathan at the Epson Grand Prix. This last was considered so extraordinary that it triggered a discussion on how important a role he thought his caddie played in his success.

'Well,' said Ballesteros, 'I can give you a good example.

At the French Open four years ago, my cousin was caddying for me for the first time, and for the first time he was walking on the golf course. He didn't know anything about golf. And I won and I shot 62, the course record. It shows something there.' He laughed, pleased to have made his point. 'But it's good to have a regular caddie,' he added graciously, 'because it's always good to have someone where you have confidence, and especially to talk to on the golf course. But the caddie in my case doesn't help very much. Not really.'

He was asked what he demanded from the men who carried his bag.

'Basically, what I want from a caddie is to stay quiet, having the right yardage, being there on time and keeping up with me on the golf course. Some of them, they walk way behind.'

'In a critical self-analysis,' asked one reporter, 'would you say that you are an easy man or a hard man to caddie for? I'm thinking back to the Nick de Paul days when you had one or two harsh words with him.'

Ballesteros refused to allow himself to be riled. 'Well,' he replied, 'I was hard on Nick a few times because he was wrong a few times with the yardage. And I mean, once you're a professional and you charge so much money for you, you should be a hundred per cent right.'

'But would you say you are a difficult man to work for?'

'I think I'm very fair. Sometimes I get upset when they make a mistake, but that happens to everybody. I'm fair, I would say.'

The questions went on and on. Eventually, Ballesteros grew tired of them. 'The caddie's . . . never been my problem,' he snapped. 'I don't really worry about that. I work with good caddies and I work with caddies that never know anything about the game, and I really don't care about that. I think I can do all by myself. The only thing that a caddie does is they save you time.'

Oddly enough, it was at the German Masters the very next week that Ballesteros approached Gordon Brand Jnr's twenty-four-year-old caddie, Billy Foster, about working for him. Foster is a lithe, athletic Yorkshireman with a pleasant

311

easygoing manner and a ready smile. He is also thoroughly reliable and professional and, at the time the Spaniard spoke to him, had spent three years working for South African Hugh Baiocchi and five years with Brand Jnr. His aim was to retire at the end of the 1990 season, 'get a decent job at home and play a bit of golf myself [he is a four handicapper].' To this end, he had already handed in his notice. Ballesteros told him he was too young to quit caddying, and offered him a job the following season. Foster knew he'd be a fool to turn it down, so he gave the Spaniard his address and told him with a grin: 'If you want to bring me out of retirement, I'll come back next year.' A few weeks later, a letter of confirmation came. He was to start at the Doral Ryder Open.

'I was very, very nervous,' says Foster, recalling their first tournament together. 'I was sort of sat by the locker room with Pete Coleman and Pete says, "Oh, you'll be all right," and I'm sort of shitting myself, you know. And a few footsteps come behind me and Pete says, "Oh, he's here," and I'm sort of – "this is him, the Great Man!" Turned round and he had a big smile on his face, and he said: "How ya doing, mate?" And straight away I felt a bit more at ease. Went out to practise and had a real good talk with him and felt as though I got to know him a little bit.'

Foster's impression of Ballesteros before he started working for him was that he was 'a bit intimidating. He's sort of like one of the best players there's ever been, and to be out in his company, you feel a bit dwarfed. In golfing terms he's royalty, isn't he? So I mean, you feel six inches tall. But once you get to know him, he's just another human being. He's a super bloke . . . I find him funny . . . He's a kind bloke. I think we get on so well because I might be a bit different. I'm very much down to earth with him, you know. A bit abrupt, really. He ain't used to that. It's all, "How are you, Seve?" this and "How are you, Seve?" that. I go up and say, "Now then, kid, how ya doing?" I guess it's a bit different.'

But whether the sea-change in Ballesteros's career was due to the unique, almost brotherly relationship he formed with Foster, Leadbetter's coaching, his new putter or his metal woods, it manifested itself in Japan with that 25-foot birdie putt.

'When you hole a putt like that your confidence comes back,' said Ballesteros with relief. 'I also had no three-putts throughout the tournament. That is very important. Winning broke the barrier that was in front of me.'

Four days after winning the PGA Championship at Wentworth, Ballesteros came into the Dunhill Masters press tent at Woburn looking irrepressibly cheerful and wearing, for reasons known only to himself, two hats: a tweed cap was pulled down over his hair, a blue Paddington Bear hat was perched at a jaunty angle on top of it. To complete the effect, he had on a scarlet shirt and a maroon sweater. There had been great hopes for an improvement in his dress sense when he married, but thus far Carmen has failed to exert her influence (if indeed she has any).

'You've been playing very well these last couple of weeks,' remarked a reporter. 'Can you remember the last time you were in this kind of form?'

'Yes,' replied Ballesteros with a grin. 'The two weeks before that.'

The previous day he had had an incredible nine birdies (and three bogeys) for a first round score of 66. His previous personal best was eleven. 'I can't remember when that was,' he remarked consideringly, adding wickedly: 'When I was a better player!'

'Is it like Christmas, playing well?'

'Things are going well,' admitted Ballesteros carefully, reluctant to count his chickens, 'but golf is the kind of game where today you are playing well, but tomorrow you grip the club and things feel completely different. So you have to always be humble.'

'Where did that tweed hat come from?'

'It came from Scotland,' said Ballesteros, who had just had seven birdies in the second round for a second consecutive 66 and was leading the field by four strokes. 'Scottish hat.' He winked and tapped the top of the press officer's balding head. 'This one would cover you a little bit,' he suggested teasingly.

'Why do you think you're playing so well, Seve?'

'My attitude is very good on the golf course. I'm very

positive. I'm playing very steady and I'm not making any mistakes out there. I think I've played the last month nearly as good as I can play. I feel that I have a lot of fun out there and the good thing about it is that when I wake up in the morning I'm looking forward to going out to play. There's times when you're making bogeys when you're just trying to survive out there . . . I was waking up in the morning and for me to go onto the golf course was like a pain in the head. And now I can't wait to come to the golf course and play because I feel comfortable.'

'During the time you felt bad about playing, did you stop practising?'

'I promise you last year I was practising more than ever,' said Ballesteros sincerely. 'I tell you what, this game is not easy. There's a lot of frustration when things aren't going your way. It's not as easy as some people may think . . . It might look the other way but I'm a very humble person, and you need to be like that in this game. Golf, sometimes it becomes very tough, so you've got to be humble and you've got to walk with both feet on the ground.'

He said he felt that putting, more than anything, had been the key to the dramatic change in his fortunes. Three-putting the first play-off hole in 1987 (US Masters) had drained him of his confidence, but when he holed that long putt in the Chunichi Crowns tournament 'a lot of my confidence came back.'

'Why didn't you change your putter before?' someone queried.

'I did try very hard to change from Ping putters to other putters, but always it was hard for me. This putter was easier than all the others.'

'Did you pay for it?' the reporter asked slyly.

The Spaniard looked at him in amazement. 'You think I must pay for it?' he demanded, half incredulous, half amused. 'How many putters do you think they are going to sell now?'

No doubt about it, Ballesteros was back. Gone was the morose and sulky Spaniard of 1990, the black moods, the great man at odds with the universal press conferences, the 'Why me?' grimaces on the golf course. In their place was the old piratical grin, the irresistible charm and the gentle, rather wry sense of humour that makes him so human and so likeable. On the golf course, too, he was a new man. Drama and light-hearted adventure surrounded every one of his rounds, as he lashed from the tee, prowled about wearing theatrical expressions of anguish in the bushes, and conjured up wonderful little chip shots and recoveries. It was no surprise that great crowds flocked to Woburn to relive the past – to see Severiano Ballesteros play golf again the way he had done when he first won their hearts. And to the casual observer, he really did. It was only when you looked closer that you could detect a hint of caution and a kind of frailty that had never been there when he was young and dauntless.

But these did not detract in any way from the shot-making skills that have always made watching him such joy, and that were shown to the fullest advantage in the closing stages of the Dunhill Masters. After three rounds of the tournament Ballesteros had had a seven-stroke advantage, and might have led by two more had not Eamonn Darcy eagled the eighteenth on the third day. These strokes he squandered on a bogey at the second in the final round, a double bogey at the third and another bogey at the fourteenth. Nevertheless, he still had a four-shot lead when he stood on the fifteenth tee on that bleak and rainy afternoon. Then he proceeded to hook his drive deep into a forest, where it came to a halt only a whisker from out of bounds.

Foster followed him worriedly into the trees. 'He had no shot,' he recalls. 'I'm thinking, "Chip out up t' fairway." Then he said, "Just pull the stakes out up there" – about a hundred yards up in t' trees. So I've gone up and pulled them out and I've looked and thought: "The only gap I can see over there is about two feet." And he pulled a one-iron out the bag and sort of hit it left of this tree and slicing. I'm stood over the other side of the fairway. And about a hundred yards up the fairway this ball's appeared, and it's somehow raced across the fairway and gone into the greenside trap. Up and down. Par. Yeah, nice one, Sev.'

One bogey and two pars later, Ballesteros won his second tournament in seven days by three strokes.

When Foster had first picked up Ballesteros's bag at Doral he, like most other people, had had a very good idea of what the Spaniard was capable of. Yet after three months of working for him, he had still not ceased to be astounded at the creativity and genius of his recoveries. 'Some of the shots he played were just miraculous. Unbelievable. Not many other guys would come close to even attempting them, and he'd pull them off. The imagination and the feel of some of them was scary.' One example was a shot Ballesteros had played at a par five in Japan, after he had hooked his drive and then had a flyer out of the rough into a dark and impenetrable forest. From where he stood, the only chink of daylight was a 3-foot gap about 20 yards ahead of him, which was partially blocked by a stanchion that held up one of the trees. The most realistic exit route was behind him.

'I'm thinking, "Well, there's just no shot," ' recalls Foster. '"Get out backwards and make a six if we can." And he says, "Have you got a yardage?" And I'm thinking, "A *yardage*? What do you want a yardage for?" I sort of walked over there and got a couple of numbers and said, "You've got 220 yards to the front of the green." He said, "Give me a two-iron." I've given him a two-iron and I've walked a hundred yards to the other side of the fairway and I'm thinking, "Oh, Jesus Christ! This is an eight or a nine, this. If it hits the tree, it's just staying in there all day." At the time he was more or less leading the tournament. And he's hit this two-iron out of the trees and he's somehow managed to get out through this gap and he's come out, and then there's a fifty-foot tree in the middle of t' fairway – it goes over that and soaring onto the green. I'm on the other side of the fairway, just laughing my head off. I couldn't believe it. He comes out of the trees, big grin on his face. I said to him, "Paul Daniels couldn't have played that shot!" He just laughed. He made par there as well.'

Just how extraordinary Ballesteros's gift is for envisaging shots which are, in theory, inconceivable, can be measured by the fact that other professionals – the most cynical and

316

demanding observers of golf in the world – go out in their hundreds to see him play.

'I don't watch golf,' insists David Feherty. 'I don't watch golf at all. The Ryder Cup is the first golf that I've actually gone out and watched in fifteen years. But I would go and watch him. He has the most incredible imagination for the game. You know, if you can visualize it, you can do it; and he has the power to visualize the most extraordinary things.'

'I think he's got great charisma as a player,' remarks Mark James. 'You know, when Seve steps on the tee you get the feeling that something might happen and few players can arouse that sentiment in fellow players.'

'I remember seeing two things that really just stunned me about Seve,' says Tony Johnstone, a talented and excitable Zimbabwean. 'One was at the Scandinavian Open in 1980. It was my first year on Tour and I was travelling with a South African guy by the name of David Stratton. We'd played early and we went out to watch Seve. On the fourth hole he hooked his second shot with a three-wood and buried it under the lip of the bunker. But it had gone into the *earth* – not the sand – into the earth lip. The whole ball was in the ground. You could only see the ball from inside the bunker. And he stood there and we thought, "Oh, well, that's an unplayable. He's got to take a drop." Well, he went through every club in his bag except the woods, and he eventually decided on a putter. He turned his Ping putter on its toe, took a swing at it, and took a piece of ground out the size of a brick. I mean, it was just not the sort of shot you could have ever practised. It just came to him. An inspirational shot. With the toe of his Ping, he just smashed at it; the ball came out at a hundred miles an hour, ran up the face of the bunker, hopped out, rolled down to about ten feet and he holed it for a birdie. I walked in. I couldn't handle it. I thought, "Well, that's it. What am I doing out here?"

'The second time was at Chepstow a few years ago,' continues Johnstone. 'It was late evening and he was down at the chipping green with Manuel, his brother, and he was just hitting trick shots. He was hitting balls with a seven-iron, standing at right-angles to the green with the face wide open

317

and just catching the ball on the toe. And they were almost going at right angles to him, but high and soft and landing on the green and spinning backwards. It was unbelievable. At one stage he was aiming straight at the restaurant. I mean, if he had made a mistake it was going to end up in some guy's soup at four hundred miles an hour . . . Then he started stamping the ball into the ground and hitting shots. You know, it's against the bounds of science, but he was hitting shots with a ball that was entirely, one hundred per cent underground. He was hitting these shots and getting them to come out high and soft and land and then run three or four feet. I mean, it can't be done. It *can't* be done. But he was doing it. I sat there and watched him do it. I could stand there for fifty years and I couldn't ever make that happen. And he did it time and time again. A high, soft lob with a buried ball. Don't know how he did it. Don't want to know.'

Until Collet took over his management and virtually eliminated his company outings and golf days, Ballesteros's clinics were legendary. No player in the world could equal him as a trick-shot artist. The day after he won the Open at St Andrews in 1984, he was on his knees at the Old Course – after only three hours sleep – hitting 200-yard drives before fifty open-mouthed businessmen. Later, he was taken by helicopter to The Belfry where, having amusingly impersonated Trevino, Nicklaus and Palmer, he put on a breathtaking display of trick shots. The touch and ball-skill he showed during such performances were as much proof of his greatness as anything he did on the golf course.

'I've watched great players all my life and I think he's as gifted a player as I've ever seen,' enthuses American Chip Beck, who has encountered Ballesteros in full flight at the US Open, the Ryder Cup and the World Match Play. 'He's got the natural physique. He's tall, he's got long arms, long legs, and that really is something that's God-given . . . You put a golf swing on top of that physique and they're tough to beat.'

'He has that Sam Snead talent,' says Crenshaw enviously. 'Sam Snead just absolutely looks like: Here is *the* golfer. This is *the* way you're supposed to look. This is *the* way you're supposed to play. And there's almost no weaknesses in their

318

game. Bobby Jones had that kind of talent. Gifted is probably a better word in Seve's case. He's got a wonderful physique. He has long arms and he has wonderful hands. He's got this tremendous heart and the brains that go with it. He's also a player that's never been satisfied with what he's done. Ever. But still he has to be proud of what he's done.'

Ballesteros had every reason to be proud of himself in 1991. In the fifteen events he played between the Dunlop International Open in April and the European Masters in September, he won three times and was only twice out of the top ten. His scoring average was 68.65. He was third in the Dunlop in Japan, second in the Spanish Open, equal fifth in the Buick Open, equal tenth in Monte Carlo, equal eighth in the Scottish Open, equal ninth in the Open, second in the Scandinavian Masters and he tied for third place at the European Open and in Crans-sur-Sierre. He only had two disastrous tournaments – the US Open in June and the US PGA Championship in August.

His success could not be put down to any one particular factor. Rather it was due to a dozen small things, all of which combined to make him more positive and confident on the course. Regular supervision from his coach, for instance, helped a great deal. Leadbetter felt he had 'a couple of big flaws. I tightened up his swing. It was weak and sloppy; it had lost all its torque. He's still off line with some shots but before he was short, too. I also got him to open his stance a little when he was putting.'

As the season went on and Ballesteros's form held and he continued to play with his old fire and enthusiasm, he became philosophical about past misfortunes and could explain more lucidly what had happened to him in 1990. 'Everyone suffers a slump,' he told the *Independent*. 'Nicklaus did, Watson, everyone. Why should Ballesteros be the exception? Maybe it's a bit surprising it didn't happen sooner. I've had fifteen years of travelling, expectation, pressure. Also, I didn't play enough competitive golf. I'd be in one or two tournaments and then have a week off. It was stupid. I was trying to stay fresh but all I did was leave myself without time to find rhythm, to get sharp. I've learned the lesson. There are so many good players in Europe and America that you can't afford to stay away from tournament play too long. If you do, no matter how good you are or how big the reputation, you will suffer . . . I had lots of negative thoughts. I knew I would win again, it was not a question of if but when, but I was not certain that I'd be as good as I had been before.'

He added that he felt he had begun to improve during the Masters where his joint twenty-second place hadn't reflected how well he had played. 'This is a strange game. You make some putts and the confidence comes back. The more confident you are, the more putts go in. It's a circle. It's why golf is so fascinating.'

Altogether, Ballesteros was a far more relaxed, amiable person throughout that season than he had been in years. On the golf course, he smiled more and brooded less. Off it, he lowered his guard and became more approachable, and his willingness to help other players and to participate more in Tour life and in the good-natured banter of the practice range earned him new respect from his colleagues.

'I never really got to talk to him until a few years ago,' says David Feherty. 'I mean, now we can sit and have a conversation. In those days, it was like talking to God . . . I think he has the qualities that can be confused for a lot of things. To be very, very good and to dominate in this game, you have to have an exceptionally high opinion of yourself. You have to have that. You know, that's a prerequisite. And that's often confused for arrogance or conceit. There were times when I might have thought he was that way, but having played with him in the Ryder Cup [1991], we saw the human side of him much more. He was a tremendous influence on all of us that week. You saw the vulnerable side of him. He was willing to open up and say, "You are going to feel that way, we all feel that way. Don't let it worry you." '

'He was pretty much like Nick Faldo for a long, long time,' comments Mark James. 'Very guarded, almost secretive. No-one really knew him much. It's only the last probably two or three Ryder Cups that quite a lot of the players have got to know him at all . . . He's pretty much like Faldo. I'd say they're very similar personalities.'

'Trevino, many years ago, lived like a hermit almost,' remembers Sandy Lyle. 'He'd give his all on the golf course and he'd give autographs, but when he was away from the golf course he got to the stage where he'd lock himself away in the room. Seve's a bit like that in some ways – just to get a bit of peace and quiet.'

'I don't think he's the type of guy that you would ever get to know,' says Scotsman Stephen McAllister. 'I mean, I've played with him a couple of times, spoken to him a couple of times, you know, we've had a bit of a crack, a few jokes – that sort of thing. But I don't think I would ever get to know him. I don't think he wants anybody to get to know him. I respect that. A lot of guys get upset by that, because they think, Christ, one minute I'm speaking to him, the next minute he's ignoring me . . . I think these guys have got to distance themselves from people. I mean, none of the top ten in Europe are guys who have loads of friends on Tour. Woosie's probably the only one . . . Woosie's different because he's more a sort of one-of-the-boys personality. Seve and Langer and these sort of people are more private – and they've got to be. You can't be chums with everyone.'

'I don't really rate him – as a bloke,' says Australian Wayne (Radar) Riley with a scowl. 'I don't think he's got any time for any other people. I don't think he's got any time for our young players. I think he just walks straight by you in the locker room without even saying hallo to you. I think he's rude. I think he's arrogant. That's probably what makes him so good. But I don't think he's a good bloke.' With that, he rushed over to Jay Townsend, a quiet, intelligent American. 'Do you think that Seve is a friendly person?' he demanded.

'I think he's a lot more friendly now than he was,' replied Townsend, taken aback.

'You could walk into the locker room and I'd go, "G'day, Jay," and you'd go, "G'day, Wayne." But whatever mood he's in, he's got the idea that he doesn't have to say hallo to you, and he won't. I don't like that.'

'I don't know,' says Townsend doubtfully. 'I think he's a lot better. When I played with him in 'eighty-five/'eighty-six, he'd never say anything or make eye-contact with anybody. Even on

the range. Now he'll hit balls on the range and converse . . .
I mean, I just notice a night and day difference in Seve . . . I
think he's much more friendly. Much more than Faldo. He'll
make eye-contact and won't even nod or anything . . . I think
he's much more friendly.'

'Oh, yeah,' says Riley sarcastically. 'But that's not hard,
is it? Friendlier than Faldo? I mean, shit!'

'I'm talking about how he's much more friendly than
he used to be,' Townsend tells him drily. ' 'Course, nobody
wants to talk to you, Radar.'

'I never used to like him, but I do now,' says Malcolm
Mackenzie. 'He never used to talk to anybody. But he does
now. He talks to everybody now. He'll talk to rookies now,
which he never used to. And if he sees a good swing on a
rookie he'll go over and he'll say, "You swing good, hey."
So he's helping youngsters, which is good.'

Tony Johnstone agrees with Townsend. 'A few years
ago he went a bit sort of hostile towards everybody, really. I
think the demands on him were too great. But I think he's a
great person. He's always friendly to everyone, he always has
a nice word. He gets wrapped up in his game, but that's why
he's the best.'

When the season came to an end Ballesteros was, indisputably,
the best. He had overcome Nick Price in the final of the World
Match Play to equal Gary Player's record of five titles; he was
the No. 1 player in Europe, and had won the Vardon Trophy
for a record sixth time with earnings of £744,236, and he was
fourth on the World Rankings. 'The key in golf is consistency,'
he said – 'to make the putts and be good under pressure. That
is the key . . . And you've got to have a big heart. It is more
important to have a big heart than a great swing.'

One incident in particular illustrates how much Ballesteros
was enjoying the game again. It took place on a summer's
evening after the final round of the Scottish Open. The
Tour caravan had already moved on to Birkdale for the
Open Championship, and only a handful of players remained
at Gleneagles. Mark Roe, who was one of them, took his
sand-wedge and putter and wandered out to the putting green

beside the hotel. In the tranquil dusk, he chipped balls to his heart's content. After a time, he looked up and saw a tall figure coming eagerly across the green towards him. It was the Spaniard.

'Do you want to have a game?' he asked Roe.

'With pleasure,' replied the young Englishman with a smile.

'Right,' said Ballesteros, taking charge. 'We'll play for £1.'

They played on as twilight closed in, the Spaniard winning the first nine holes, Roe winning the next, and so on.

'That hour that I spent with him is something that I'll always treasure,' says Roe. 'It was wonderful . . . It was like being out there with a friend. And the banter was lovely. You know, he was trying to wind me up as much as I was trying to wind him up. He was at ease . . . And it's just a side of him that ninety-nine per cent of people would never get to see. It was almost like being out there with somebody who was sixteen years of age, you know, and you were kids and you were chipping around as juniors. It was a lovely side of him to see . . . He's just such a warm human being. Such a fun person to be around . . . We played until it went pitch black, then we had to finish because we couldn't see the flags. But even when it had gone pitch black, as we walked up the hill towards the hotel, he still dropped two balls down and turned round and said, "Here, I'll show you a little shot." And I marvelled at his enthusiasm, I really did . . . I think all that really matters to Seve, and all that has ever mattered, is the game of golf. And I think that's why he's been so great. I regularly argue with people who say that he's money-orientated. I'd like to think that's not true. I'd like to think Seve was as great as he was because he loved the game.'

At the end of the evening, Ballesteros was £3 up. He departed in the best of all possible moods, and Roe did not have the chance to play with him again until they were drawn together at the European Open at Sunningdale in September the following year. He walked onto the first tee, waited for the starter to announce the players' names, then turned to the Spaniard and wished him luck. Ballesteros returned the favour. 'Shall we play for the £3 that I won at Gleneagles?' he asked the astounded Roe.

A year and two months after the Scottish Open, when the 'thunderstorm' had once again descended upon Ballesteros, the memory of that one perfect hour on the putting green provided a welcome light for him at the end of an increasingly hard day's night.

18

Head to Head

If you're a winner, you've got to be as hard as nails. The softest thing about you's got to be your teeth. And I learnt that playing in the States. I learnt very early on, that you've got to be single-minded and determined and tough. Very tough.

Tony Jacklin, *Jacklin Speaks*

The loyalties of the gallery were clearly divided. They looked from the old maestro to the young Master and back again with growing consternation; but in the end it was Arnold Palmer, for he was the certain victor, to whom they accorded a hero's welcome as he walked down Wentworth's eighteenth fairway.

He acknowledged them with a wave of one great paw, his nut-brown face wreathed in smiles. At nearly fifty-four, it was almost more than he could have hoped for – to cross swords with this Spanish magician in the first round of the 1983 World Match Play and come out on top. 'I'm looking forward to it,' he had told the press on the eve of the tournament. I don't have many more matches like this coming up, matches which have this kind of value or distinction. Heck, I'm a grandfather. I've got a daughter older than he is.'

Thus far it had been an excellent match. Apart from a brief spell at the fourth and fifth holes, where Ballesteros had birdied to go to one up, Palmer had been in control the entire way. The only slightly disconcerting thing was that he had missed putts to win holes on the thirteenth and fifteenth and had failed to match the Spaniard's birdie on the par five seventeenth, which meant that he was one ahead when he teed off the last instead of two. He cast a glance at his opponent, who was prowling up and down, considering the lie of the land. Palmer turned away to prepare for his own shot. What did it matter, anyway? The match was won.

Ballesteros did not share Palmer's mood of buoyancy and optimism. Having defied doctor's orders to play in the event in the first place (he had a particularly virulent dose of flu), he now felt fury at the chances he'd let slip, and a kind of ruthless determination to be the victor at all costs. Victory, however, required an eagle and, after fading his drive and clipping the trees with his second shot to finish 50 yards short of the pin, it seemed an unlikely prospect. Still, he had everything to gain by trying. He addressed the ball and whipped it away with an easy, rhythmic swing. Up it went in a graceful arc and then down, down, down, a couple of bounces and into the hole.

'Oh, shit!' said Palmer distinctly and with feeling.

Ballesteros, his face alive with joy, just stood on the fairway and let the applause wash over him. The match went to extra holes and he won with a birdie at the twenty-first.

In years to come, when the finest players of this era have become the legends of the last, literature will show that while some have won more major championships than Ballesteros and others have earned more money, none apart from Gary Player have been his equal in head-to-head competition. That is because few men have been quite as obsessed with victory. No player revels more than he in the psychological warfare that is match-play; no-one is as adept at the freak shot, the unexpected twist, at the long climb back from the point of no return; and no-one thrives more on the thrill of the chase, the bloody clash and the moment of reckoning.

From the very first time that Ballesteros, aged eight, dropped a pebble on the ground and challenged all comers to strike it further and more skilfully than he, he has been consumed by the desire to be the best. Throughout his career it has goaded

326

him, gnawed away at him and driven him to perform feats almost beyond comprehension. And it is this quality, more than anything else, that has made him the champion that he is. 'Wherever he goes to play or whatever he's playing for, he *wants* to win and he *tries* to win,' says Fernandez. 'For example, in Argentina (exhibition tournament, March 1992), we played for nothing. He got appearance money, of course. He played for nothing but he wanted to win as much as if it were for a million dollars. And that's what makes him great. Because wherever he goes he wants to win and he works hard to win. Even in practice rounds, whenever we play for a coffee or a drink, he tries his heart out. When he's on the golf course, it's business. Which you don't see in other players.'

'Great competitor, *great* competitor!' says Trevino with a laugh. 'Oh my God, he hates to lose. I don't care if you're shooting marbles or playing pool or throwing darts, he wants to win. That's good. That's good in a person. I don't have it in anything else [other than golf]. Seve has it in *everything* else, whether it's a foot-race or what. If he's sitting with you in a room playing cards, he wants to win.'

Peter Dobereiner once said that in all his years he had never met another human being with Ballesteros's competitive drive; 'winning is his whole life and it does not matter whether it is on the golf course or playing shove half-penny, or arguing whether Maradona is the best footballer in Spain.' In 1983 he offered two fine examples of this. The first incident occurred during the Italian Open. He was sitting on the steps of his hotel, waiting for a courtesy car and playing with a plastic toy in the form of a miniature race-track. You wound it up, twiddled a knob and attempted to steer a car safely through a series of chicanes. Each collision was recorded in a small window. If you completed the course without touching an obstacle the symbol of a crown appeared in the window.

'Ballesteros,' recalled Dobereiner, 'strolled out and said: "Let me try." I would have said that it was impossible to get anywhere with the thing without resting it on a firm surface but he held it in the palm of his left hand and started twiddling. "Shit!" He rewound and tried again. The car arrived. "Shit!" He sat in the back, absorbed by this new challenge. The twenty-minute journey through the hilly Tuscany countryside with an Italian at the wheel, was not exactly tranquil. Ballesteros was totally absorbed by the toy. His all-purpose expletive preceded each of about fifty rewindings. As we drew into the driveway of the Ugolino club he tossed the toy at me, along with a grin of satisfaction. The crown was in the window.

'Later in the year, at the Scandinavian Open, he was staying at the home of the sponsor and he was introduced to the game of pool. He was partnered with a good player, in opposition to two moderate ones. For his first few attempts he made a bridge for the cue with his left hand held about a foot off the surface of the table. They were playing for token bets and Ballesteros's side lost constantly, although he quickly picked up the rules and basic technique. "We double the bets," he announced. Ballesteros took charge of the team. He commanded his more experienced partner which ball to hit, which pocket to select, how hard to strike. He chided him for leaving the cue ball out of position. They played on and on, doubling the bets. Ballesteros ran out of small change. He went to his bedroom and returned with more money. Double up again. At last Ballesteros and his partner won a frame. Ballesteros picked up his winnings, representing a profit of a few pence on the evening, and announced: "I have to play golf tomorrow. Good night." '

Musgrove had a similar experience. 'They said to me one night, "He's playing pool and he's lost three times." I said: "Well, he can't lose anymore because there's only three cues." '

In 1984, at the time the feud between Ballesteros and Langer was at its height, a friendly soccer match between the Spanish players and the Rest of the World was arranged after the Spanish Open at El Saler. The Spaniard captained his national team, and the German was at the helm of the foreigners. Stories of Ballesteros's aggression on the pitch that day, his monopolization of the ball, and his absolute determination to win, are part and parcel of Tour lore. The final score was 2–2, and post-match celebrations included Ballesteros being thrown into the swimming pool.

It is this yearning for battle that has made Ballesteros one of the greatest match-players of all time. His tenacity, fearlessness and ability to haul himself back time and time again from the abyss of self-destruction have brought him five World Match Play titles – an achievement matched only by Player – and his exploits in them are legendary.

In 1982, for instance, the year after his first World Match Play victory, he met Lyle in the final at Wentworth. He had already beaten Bobby Clampett 2 and 1 in the second round and Lanny Wadkins 3 and 1 in the semi-finals; but that was nothing when compared to the big Scot's incredible comeback against Faldo after being six down going into lunch, or his vanquishing of Floyd and Kite. Nevertheless, it was the Spaniard who first gained the upper hand when they went out together on the last day. He was three up after eighteen holes and retained his advantage until the fourteenth (or thirty-second) where Lyle won the hole with a birdie two. It was a wild and stormy day. Rain teemed down unpleasantly as they trudged home, but Lyle's valiant struggles earned him the fifteenth and sixteenth holes and the match was level after thirty-six holes.

They splashed to the first play-off hole in the dying afternoon. Lyle hit a booming drive up the centre of the fairway; Ballesteros pulled his into the left rough. They marched purposefully from the tee. The Spaniard's recovery was remarkable, a three-wood smashed to 30 feet. Lyle had reached the back of the green with a one-iron and was less than half that distance from the pin. They waited while the water-logged green was squeegeed, for there were four or five puddles on Ballesteros's line. When the putting surface was almost clear, he replaced his ball, studied the borrow and, without further ado, sank the putt.

'That's just Seve,' says Lyle admiringly. He missed his own putt to lose the match. 'You can expect that.'

'I've seen him pull off some of the darnedest shots I've ever seen in my life,' says Ben Crenshaw, whose weakness has always been his reverence for great players. He lost by a hole to Ballesteros in 1981 and then crashed to a 9 & 8 defeat in the semi-finals in 1984. 'In the '81 World Match Play final he hit two of the greatest shots I've ever seen. He hit it left in the trees on the twelfth – the par five. He was forty yards into the trees. I was on the right side of the fairway and I could see these people go in and watch him try to play the shot. There was a little lane. He was right up against the tree. He had no stance and he had to take the club and play it backwards. I think he took a three or four-iron. I saw him in there and he was taking these great big swings. And he hit this ball and it went off and hooked up the fairway and went forward about 170 yards. I was dumbfounded. So were the people watching. And then in the afternoon he hit a one-iron second shot on number three. He was just over the ball and almost ready to hit when the wind came right up a lot harder. And he merely put the ball a little bit further back in his stance and he hit this shot about four feet from the hole. His instinct is incredible.

What's he like to play match-play against? Oh, God! Oh, he's extremely formidable because, you know, he's never in trouble. You say, "How the heck am I going to win a hole from this guy?" I had a very good chance to beat him that day in the finals. It was very close. Neither of us were two up. It was always one up, one down, one up, one down. It was a very good match. But he pulled it out. I don't think he was playing his best either. He's a very tough match-player.'

'Oh, in his day he was evil,' says Faldo laughing. 'In a nice sense,' he adds quickly. 'It didn't matter where he hit it, he was always going to be in the hole. And if you gave him half a chance he'd be chipping in and he'd be holing ninety-footers and doing this and doing that. In the early days I did find him intimidating, yes. In the early days, you know, in match-play, you'd think: "How the hell am I going to beat this guy?" Even when he's out the hole he's in the hole. And it wasn't until '89 that I beat him [semi-finals, 6 & 5] – when his swing wasn't good. I actually beat him on the fact that I knew his swing wasn't right. I thought, he's got a fault, keep the pressure on. And it worked.'

'I played against him in the World Match Play,' remembers Watson with a wry smile. 'He beat me pretty soundly there [5 & 4, 2nd round, 1977]. In match-play he's just like he is in medal-play. He's very intense on the golf course. I think that describes Seve. He's very intense. I think because of his intensity sometimes things bother him more than they should.'

'He's pretty hard,' says Langer shortly. 'He's very competitive. He certainly doesn't talk very much. He doesn't very often say good shot – unless you do something outstanding. Things like that, you know, which are different from other players.'

The *Oxford Dictionary* defines the word gamesmanship as: 'The art of winning contests by upsetting the confidence of one's opponent.' When Langer described Ballesteros as 'intimidating', it was this that he was taken to mean. Consequently, there was a great furore because golf is a game of honour and integrity and gamesmanship is a cardinal sin. But how does one define gamesmanship more specifically? Is gamesmanship practising your putting within your playing partner's field of vision when he is trying to concentrate on his own stroke? – which is what Langer accused Ballesteros of doing. Is it making contemptuous remarks about the inferior quality and flight of an opponent's ball on the first tee of a tournament? Or is it simply coughing when you shouldn't be coughing at all?

'I think a lot of the things that people say about him are uncalled for because I've never found him to be a bad sport or to have any other kind of gamesmanship or anything,' says Nick Price, who played against Ballesteros in the 1991 World Match Play final only a month after coughing, among other things, had caused a row at Kiawah Island. 'I think he's the kind of person that if perhaps you do throw up the gloves he might throw them back at you. But I've never done that. And if he'd done that [practised his putting], I would have told him. I don't think he ever does anything like that on purpose. I might be wrong.'

The Spaniard and the amiable Zimbabwean met at Wentworth in the final, after the former had overcome Fred Couples and Billy Andrade and the latter Steven Richardson, Ian Baker-Finch and Faldo. Both men were at the top of their games; both were looking forward to the fight. 'On the first tee, I said to Nick, "Let's have another Lytham,"' recalls Ballesteros. 'Then when he birdied three of the first four holes, I thought: "Shit, he must be really mad at me." But he managed to claw his way back and by the fifteenth he had squared the match. Two holes previously, however, at which point Price was still one up, a curious incident had taken place. Ballesteros had been standing on the fairway eating a piece of fruitcake while he waited for the Zimbabwean to play his approach shot and, just as Price had initiated his backswing, a crumb had gone down the wrong way and he choked. Price's ball veered off into a bunker.

'First of all, to be totally honest with you, I don't think it affected my shot at all,' admits Price, who eventually lost 3 & 2. 'Because once I'm committed to hit the ball I go ahead and hit it. I looked around and . . . his eyes were glassy. So I knew he'd coughed. I knew that it wasn't a put on. And I suppose with what I'd heard had been going on in the Ryder Cup – some of the American guys had been saying that Seve had this little cough that he put on – I had kind of looked for it the first five or six holes, but it never came out. I didn't know because match-play is a little different sometimes. And he said to me then: "Replay your shot." ' (The referee informed him that that was impossible under the rules of the game.) 'And I said, "Oh, no, I can't do that." And then when I walked up to the green, I hit it in the bunker. He was on the back of the green and he said: "Let's take a half and go." I sort of thought about it for a second and then I said, "No, let's just play. It's fine." And we played the hole out and halved it anyway. But I think that pretty much summed up how we felt about one another. It was like, the guy who played the best golf was going to win that day. And that's why I enjoyed it so much.'

'What's he like to play match-play against?' echoes Mark McNulty, Price's compatriot. 'Obviously, he wants to win. That's intimidating enough. Any great golfer, they can make themselves intimidating if they want to. Gary [Player] could be more intimidating than Seve ever was. But they're in the same mould, put it that way.'

'I enjoy playing with him,' says Australian Rodger Davis,

one of the few men to have comprehensively beaten Ballesteros at match-play. 'I like watching some of the stuff he does – as a pro. I now try not to let him get to me. And he's not trying to, you know. He's not doing it on purpose. It's just his natural way . . . I think he's good to play with. I s'pose some guys out here believe that he stands in the wrong position when you're putting. You know, because he's so intent on his own game and he practises his putting swing or he's swinging his full swing and working on his hips or whatever . . . In my opinion, he doesn't realize he's doing it, although a lot of guys are now pulling him up. I think on the odd occasion he's put a few players off – I think Howard Clark was one of them – by practising putting in the wrong position. But it hasn't happened to me . . .

'He [used to] give off that aura that he was going to win and you had to try and stop that somehow in your mind,' continues Davis. 'The way I did it when I played him in the World Match Play and I beat him seven and six [2nd round, 1986] – admittedly, I had to play really well to do it – was that, if I watched him and watched his body language, I felt a little intimidated. So I didn't watch him. You know, I just watched about ten yards in front of him, right, and when the ball took off through that ten yards I watched where it went – just in case he did hit one off line so I could help him find it, right. But that just stopped me looking at him. And he actually said to me after the match, he did notice that I wasn't looking at him.

'And maybe that got to him a little bit.'

27 September 1987, Muirfield Village, Columbus, Ohio. Red and blue stripes bobbed nautically on a sea of swirling colour. Once or twice an arm had tried to wave a European flag, but it had fallen back helplessly when a roar went up and the tide of spectators moved on to the next fairway. The patriotism of the Americans went unrewarded. On the leaderboard the numbers changed: Europe 13½, US 11½.

How different this Ryder Cup was from all those that had gone before it. How frenzied and how electric. Ballesteros who, through his commitment and presence, had done more than any other player to help generate this fervour, felt the difference, and was uplifted by it. He had known since the fifteenth hole, where he had holed an 8-foot putt to stay two up in his match against Strange, that the fate of Samuel Ryder's trophy was in his hands. Europe might have retained it but they still needed a point to win it. He quickened his stride and hardened his resolve. Once he had said: 'If you ever feel sorry for somebody on a golf course, you better go home. If you don't kill them, they'll kill you.' He had meant it, too. Now, as they walked up the seventeenth fairway, there was a merciless glint in his eyes, and Strange would not have been human if he hadn't felt afraid when he saw it. The end, assuredly, was near.

In the Ryder Cup competition, all of the skills which have made Ballesteros the world's greatest match-player are heightened and sharpened to an astonishing degree. When he committed himself to the matches he committed himself absolutely; and it is his passion, his enthusiasm and his achievements, combined with Jacklin's own talent and industry as captain and the sudden revival of American interest in the matches, that has made the Ryder Cup one of the most extraordinary sporting spectacles on earth. He fought his heart out for a European victory in 1983. He cried when they only drew. And when the European team convened at The Belfry in 1985, he and Jacklin whipped them into a state of rare euphoria, convincing them that not only were they no longer the underdogs in world golf but that they, if anything, were the dominant players.

'We built on the experience of 1983 and we were *sure* that we were going to win in 'eighty-five,' recalls Jacklin. 'I would never have said that to a press person before because you're always apprehensive and you put more pressure on yourself by saying it, but Seve and I were the backbone of the team, Langer and Faldo (we didn't get the performance out of Faldo in 'eighty-five, he was going through a divorce), we made it happen, nevertheless. We were very sure and very confident and that was a step to winning in 'eighty-seven again. It all evolved very quickly but it all evolved from applying ourselves positively to each area that needed attention.'

'I think if [Seve] hadn't come along it would have been a different story,' says Ken Brown positively. 'He was the catalyst that made it all happen.'

In 1985 Ballesteros, paired with Piñero after his original partner, Jose Rivero, 'lost his driving' in practice, led the Europeans to battle in the first day's foursomes. Their opponents, Strange and Mark O'Meara, were four down after six holes but clawed their way back to be two down after nine. Ballesteros then drove the green on the tenth for birdie to return to three up, and the Europeans won 2 & 1 on the seventeenth. In the afternoon the Spaniards won again, beating US Open Champion Andy North and Peter Jacobsen 2 & 1 after Ballesteros squared the match with a birdie on the fifth, drove to 8 feet at the tenth, almost holing the putt for an eagle two, and pitched to 3 feet at the seventeenth. The rest of the European team had struggled in the foursomes and when play was over the Americans led 4½ to 3½.

When Sunday came, there had been a drastic reversal of fortune. Europe led by two points. Ballesteros and Piñero had lost 3 & 2 in the second day's fourballs to O'Meara and Lanny Wadkins, but administered a crushing defeat to Craig Stadler and Hal Sutton 5 & 4 in the foursomes. In the singles matches on the last day the Spaniard, splendid in red, found himself three down with five to play against Kite. With a supreme effort, he sank a huge putt from the back of the fourteenth green to win a hole, followed it with wonderful birdies at the fifteenth and seventeenth, and was still furious with himself when his putt for a win slipped past the cup on the eighteenth and all he could manage was a half. It was incredible golf. The overall score at that point was: Europe 13½ – US 8½. Then North, tall, slim and out of form, hit his drive to the last into the water. Sam Torrance, his rival, burst into tears of joy and, upon reaching the green amid scenes of great jubilation, sank the putt that won the Ryder Cup for Europe for the first time since 1957.

Ballesteros was almost overcome with emotion. 'I feel like I won another British Open,' he said. 'It was fantastic. Tremendous.'

There is no doubt that during the Ryder Cup Ballesteros

reaches down very deep inside himself and produces something – whether it is desire or genius – that is almost magical in its potency. 'He's unbelievable,' says David Feherty, who witnessed his efforts with incredulity at the 1991 Ryder Cup. 'It's almost like there's a force-field around him. He gets this aura of invincibility.'

'Well, he has a sort of tunnel-vision,' agrees Mark James, 'and at the Ryder Cup he channels that into the performance he can get out of the team as a whole, whereas someone like Faldo would tunnel it into his own personal performance. Seve is very much on top of everything that's happening in the team. Faldo isn't. And it does give the players a boost to know that Seve is there and there's every chance he'll perform very well because he does tend to play well in the Ryder Cup, specially with Olazábal.'

'I think the change is that he is instilling in eleven others what's in him,' says Schofield. 'Manuel Piñero will tell you that in 1985 he felt that it would be totally unthinkable for him, playing with Seve, to lose a foursomes or a fourball. That was his feeling, that it would actually be impossible.'

'I think Seve's always a fantastic player to play with,' responds Piñero. 'He's a great inspiration. The only problem with playing with Seve is, in a way, you need to have a very strong character. He's so brilliant and he puts everything into it – he puts so much into the match that you can feel it yourself – that if you don't have your confidence a hundred per cent, his attitude can put you down. You can sort of get an inferiority complex. I've played with him a few times and he's the best partner in the world because he gives help and you can feel he is there. You feel he can beat anybody. Doesn't matter if he plays badly, he can still win the match . . . But to play with him as a partner you need to have a lot of confidence in yourself . . . When you play with Seve, the problem is his level is so high. He's exceptional.'

'I think that's probably right,' says Jacklin. 'I mean, I put Rivero with him one year and I changed and put Piñero with him. I think he's all right with Piñero and he's certainly all right with Olazábal. There's a camaraderie there and a mutual respect. I think other individuals find it difficult to marry up to Seve's standards. They feel inferior, you see. But he's no more difficult to partner than anybody else.'

In Jose Maria Olazábal, Ballesteros found the perfect partner. To watch them at work in the Ryder Cup is to see team-work at its most harmonious and the game of golf played as exquisitely as it ever can be. They are in perfect unison at all times, and yet they still manage to inspire one another to greater efforts.

'I really do enjoy playing with him in the Ryder Cup,' says Olazábal, 'and I think the reason why is maybe because of that first match we played when I was an amateur. I feel comfortable with him since then. I think that was a special thing for me. I always try hard when I play with him. We understand each other very, very well, that's the most important thing . . . He's not individualistic at all when it comes to team events and that, I think, is a point on his side. It's very difficult to get a great player who can be a great player and a great member in a team.'

In 1987, Olazábal's Ryder Cup début, they won three of their four matches together. They met the daunting partnership of Payne Stewart and Larry Nelson, who had played nine Ryder Cup matches over the years and won every one of them, in the first day's foursomes and beat them by a hole. In the fourballs, against Curtis Strange and Tom Kite, they put on one of the most amazing displays of golf in Ryder Cup history. Ballesteros began by chipping in from 40 feet for a winning birdie at the first, and went on to make five more, including a 45-footer to win the tenth and a 72-footer to win the seventeenth and end the match 2 & 1. 'Did I watch Ballesteros?' a despondent Jack Nicklaus, the American captain, said afterwards. 'Unfortunately, yes. He not only played his own ball, he played Olazábal's ball as well. He played beautifully.' The following day the Spaniards overcame Ben Crenshaw and Tom Kite by a hole in the second day's foursomes, but lost 2 & 1 to Hal Sutton and Larry Mize in the fourballs.

'It just seems like he goes into a different gear,' says Crenshaw, recalling his match against Ballesteros and being unable to prevent a note of awe creeping into his tone. 'He wants it so badly, and the spirit of the matches is so high, and I think he enjoys that arena. Certain players just relish it and somebody like Seve just elevates his game. It actually helps his game and it's wonderful. Some people, it frightens them and they have to go into the week and hopefully they're playing well. But, I think, no matter how Seve's playing, it charges him up to the point where he will be playing well. And I think he knows that.'

Ballesteros, marching down the seventeenth hole at Muirfield Village, flanked by that roaring ocean of red, white and blue, certainly did know it. His tee shot had been fluid and strong, while Strange's had been poor and his approach had run through the green. Ballesteros's second shot flew straight for the heart of the green. He strode after it, head held high, the cheers of the European supporters ringing in his ears. Then he sank the putt to halve the hole and win the match and thus had the honour of guaranteeing the first European victory on American soil.

A more fitting end could not have been scripted in literature. 'I played well today,' he said. 'This was my day.'

'One of the things that I do remember,' says Jacklin, 'is that, after all the ceremonies and our victory dinner, I got all the players – they were all exhausted – to make this three-mile trip to take the trophy to where our supporters were. And I'll never forget walking into that hotel. It was frightening. I mean, the noise and the cheers and the sheer joy of everybody. I said, "Just give two minutes of your lives to these people." And when it came to it, I was the only one who stayed two minutes because I just had to get out. I had to get straight in my mind what had happened that day. And I went to Seve and I said, "You know, you can go now." And he said, "I'm very happy here. I'm very comfortable." And I was the one that just scooted off and had a quiet whisky and contemplated the week.'

By 1989 the Ryder Cup was a phenomenon, though nothing compared to what it became two years later and what it will become in the future. The chemistry between Ballesteros and Jacklin, brothers-in-arms – bound by circumstances and a mutual desire to destroy the smug complacency of the

Americans and prove once again that the Europeans reigned supreme, was almost tangible.

'They want to win at all costs,' comments Ken Brown, 'within the rules of the game.'

Thus do we return to the finest line of all, that which divides competitiveness at its most extreme from gamesmanship. In 1989 Ballesteros played Paul Azinger, one of America's most powerful players and determined players, in the singles matches. Europe led 9–7 going into the last day, and they were the first pair out. 'That's a tremendous responsibility,' says Ballesteros, who had volunteered to play in the lead match after Ian Woosnam told Jacklin that he didn't want to, 'because if you lose it's difficult for the team but if you win it's great for the team.'

The pressure both players were under manifested itself at the second hole. 'I hit the ball a little thin and the grooves on my sand-wedge cut it badly,' recalls Ballesteros. 'I asked [Paul] if I could take it out of play and he said: "Seve, I don't think this ball is in bad shape." It was a ridiculous thing to argue about. So I called the referee, and he said he thought the ball was still playable. So I putted – no big deal. But if it was the other way around, I would say change the ball if you want to. I mean, what advantage is that?'

But Musgrove insists, somewhat cynically, that Azinger had 'already been told that Seve might do something like that', which is why he suggested calling a referee. 'And [the referee] says the same,' continues Musgrove. ' "You can't change your ball, it isn't cut." Which Seve knows anyway. So with that he turns to Azinger and he says: "OK, if that's the way you want it, it's all right with me." He can be all indignant then, you see, because he's made it look to the crowd as if Azinger's getting at him.'

When they reached the fifteenth hole, the match was level. While Ballesteros hit a fine drive and second shot, Azinger drove into the trees, was short of the green in two, over the back fringe for three and chipped in for a winning birdie. They halved the sixteenth and Ballesteros holed from 8 feet at the next to keep the match alive.

By now most of the twenty-thousand strong crowd at The

Belfry were out of control and excitement was at fever-pitch. Great roars rang through the air as the fate of Europe hung in the balance, and everywhere people rushed, swerving, running and leaping down the fairways. Jacklin weaved his way among them, crouched low in his buggy like a military commander, his dark glasses flashing. The atmosphere at The Belfry was thick and intoxicating. It went to your head like strong wine and made you almost dizzy with exhilaration. I stayed close to the European Tour players who were following Ballesteros's match, hoping they would be the last to be crushed in the event of a stampede. We watched the Spaniard and the American tee off, and Azinger's ball plummet like a stone into the water. We stifled our joy as Ballesteros, tall and strong, strode up to his own ball, which was just through the fairway, not far from where we sat. Across the water, partially obscured by trees and bushes, we could see Azinger and the referee walking up and down and gesticulating. Then the most extraordinary thing happened. The spectators were cleared, the rules official stood back and Azinger hit a huge third shot, which carried the water easily and finished in a bunker beside the green.

Ballesteros's expression never altered but it was clear that he was shaken. It was unlikely Azinger would make anything worse than a five, which meant that the Spaniard needed a four to halve the match. He handed his four-iron to Wright and took out a three. Then he clipped the ball thinly from its tight lie, and watched thunderstruck as the ball described a low curve into the water. It was Augusta revisited. The gallery were stunned; Ballesteros was enraged. 'It didn't come out the way I thought,' he said.

'I must say,' continued the Spaniard, 'that I was very surprised that Paul Azinger was the only player out of the whole Ryder Cup team who was able to get to the green. That's the only thing I still think about. Why? I didn't put too much attention to what he was doing. He was trying to drop his ball and I was concentrating on my shot, but looking back I have the feeling that something was wrong. But that's history.' At the time he just stormed to the water's edge, peered angrily into its depths and muttered under his breath in Spanish. Then he pulled himself together, selected a club

340

and played his pitch shot. It finished nearly 20 feet away from the pin, on the top tier of the green. Ballesteros lost his temper. Wright had given him the wrong yardage. For several seconds he heaped a torrent of awful abuse on the luckless caddie's head. Then he gathered himself once again, carefully studied the line of his putt and holed it. Azinger splashed out the sand to 5 feet, holed out and won the match.

At the end of the day both teams had 14 points. Europe had retained the Ryder Cup but not won it.

In the aftermath, the anti-climax was horrible. The high which accompanies the anticipation of victory was banished in an instant and, like a punctured balloon, the collective mood of the Europeans came crashing to earth. I stood at the hotel bar, feeling so depressed I was almost in tears, while the roar of conversation and clinking glasses rose to a crescendo around me and a couple of magazine journalists analysed and critiqued the day's play – as if what had happened could ever really be explained and as if anyone such as they could ever understand it.

All of a sudden the bar went quiet. I felt a hand touch my shoulder and turned round. Ballesteros was standing there in the dim and smoky light.

'There you are,' he said, almost as if he had been expecting to find me there.

I was speechless with surprise. 'Well played, Seve,' I managed to say. 'You were great.'

I'll never forget the expression that crossed his face as long as I live. He was almost grief-stricken. His dark eyes were so unutterably sad that it was terrible to look into them.

'We should have won,' he said. 'We should have won.'

Then he was gone and I was crying and everyone in the bar was looking on in amazement.

Trevino is of the opinion that, day in and day out, Paul Azinger is the only American player who is a match for Ballesteros. It was fortuitous, therefore, that Azinger and Chip Beck confronted Ballesteros and Olazábal in the first day's foursomes and fourballs at the 1991 Ryder Cup at Kiawah Island. And it is interesting to note that, by strange coincidence, both of the Americans had had almost identical experiences with Ballesteros in major championships prior to the event. In the case of Azinger, it took place in June 1988 in the final round of the US Open – the one where the Spaniard finished third and might have won if it hadn't been for a 75 in the second round and bad luck in the last.

'Seve hit his drive out of bounds on the first hole and got off to a bad start,' recalled the American in an interview with Jerry Tarde, 'I was playing great, five under on the front nine, right in contention. Instead of being quiet and disgusted with his own game, Seve was very encouraging to me when he didn't have to be. He kept rooting me on. On the fifteenth hole, he said, "Make one more birdie and you will win." I did birdie 16, but then there was a long wait at 17 and I bogeyed there. He said to me on the eighteenth tee, "That was very unlucky for you to wait that long, but you can still do it. Birdie this hole. Think birdie, birdie, birdie, birdie." He wanted to drill it into my head. I didn't win, but I'll never forget the way he treated me. When I'm forty years old and playing with some rookie kid in contention, I hope I treat him the same way.

'He's the world's best,' Azinger added to Tarde. 'Nobody's close. Absolutely the best.'

Beck – who has gone down in history for commenting mournfully, after he had been brutally thrashed by Ballesteros in the 1989 World Match Play (9 & 8, 2nd round), 'Every good man is tested in the crucible of humiliation' – had a similar thing happen to him at Shinnecock Hills in the 1986 US Open. There, too, the Spaniard had had an opportunity for victory but had been unusually slow in pursuing it.

'My first true experience of Seve was when I played with him on the Sunday of the US Open when Raymond Floyd won,' remembers Beck. 'I finished second. I was playing very slowly that day and yet I felt really wonderful and I was playing well and things were falling into place for me . . . But I remember on the last hole, he said, "Come on, Chip. If you can birdie the last hole, you'll be the Open Champion." It was extraordinary. And I really admired him for that. It takes a great champion to do that . . . I hit it very close and I almost birdied the last hole.'

Now, however, they were all at the Ryder Cup – the so-called War by the Shore – and relations were no longer so amicable. Azinger and Beck were three up on Ballesteros and Olazábal after nine holes in the foursomes when two things happened. To begin with, when Beck teed off on the seventh hole Ballesteros noticed that the American had changed from a 100 compression ball to a 90 compression ball, thereby contravening the one-ball rule which had been specifically agreed at the teams' rules meeting and in any case is in daily operation on the US and European Tours. Ballesteros did not call the referee immediately. He and Olazábal debated what to do and, having discussed the matter with their caddies, agreed on the way to the tenth tee that if they were going to win, they should win fairly and on ability alone rather than because the Americans had been penalized.

They say that the road to hell is paved with good intentions. Bernard Gallacher, the European captain, was summoned to the tenth tee, where he spoke at length to officials. An unpleasant row ensued. Ballesteros had walked over and looked at Beck's ball on the ninth hole, but had said nothing to either of the Americans before sending for Gallacher.

'That was their mistake,' says Beck. 'I think they were afraid of upsetting us by declaring something that wasn't right.' He confesses to changing his ball on the seventh tee but says that that was the only time it had happened. 'I was just thinking of Paul [who had to play the approach shot]. I said, "Paul, I don't think you can get there. I might as well play your ball." Not thinking, you know. I don't think there's that big a difference [between the two balls], personally, but mentally, I think there's as big a difference as anything. If you get more compression on the ball, you get more spin on it. But that's part of human nature, making mistakes. And that's what it was . . . And, obviously, anything in match-play that's not declared at the time, on completion of the hole or before the hole is completed and the score is marked down, is over and done with. So I was very happy about that. Because I felt we got away with something there. I thought: "Hey, that's great. We made a mistake and got away with it. We're lucky." I felt fortunate, really. I wasn't bothered by it. I don't think they were very happy about it. I think they were hoping that we'd get penalized a hole or two.'

On the tenth tee, the Americans had admitted that the ball had been changed. 'We made a mistake,' said Azinger sullenly, 'but we certainly weren't cheating.'

'We don't say that, Paul,' Ballesteros told him. 'It has nothing to do with cheating. Cheating and breaking the rules are two different things.'

After about fifteen minutes they continued their match, and the Spaniards won 2 & 1 and then beat them with the same score in the afternoon fourballs.

Meanwhile, the Americans had grown increasingly irritated by Ballesteros's persistent cough. 'Well, it was very disappointing for me,' says Beck, who was disturbed by it during the morning foursomes, 'because it seemed like all the coughing and everything was catching me . . . I told Paul, "It's bothering me. I just want you to watch it and if it continues, we'll say something." But I didn't really want them to know it was bothering me. So I just mentioned it to the official after the ninth hole to make sure everything was on the up and up. And he was the one that reported it and did all the other things that made all the commotion. Paul Azinger and I never said a word. I just politely asked him [the official], "Joe, just check [whether or not they were coughing] and let me know if I'm just imagining things." Because I didn't want to be that way. And after the round he came up to me and said, yes, they were. And I reported to Bernard Gallacher that the coughing was going on. Do I think it was deliberate? Little bit of both. When you have a cold, it's difficult to control it, but it's the nature of the game *to* control it. You either have to control it or just move away. Stay out of the game. That's the way I play, anyway.'

At the end of the day Azinger caused still greater controversy by declaring Ballesteros to be: 'the king of gamesmanship.'

It was not until the Volvo Masters, in the last week of October, that the subject came up again (Europe had lost the Ryder Cup 13½–14½, despite the fact that the two Spaniards had contributed eight points on their own). Ballesteros, responding to Dave Stockton's comments to the

British press a few days earlier, that he had tried to keep Azinger and Ballesteros apart during the matches 'because Seve coughs and splutters a lot' and because Azinger felt that he only did it on American backswings, brought it up and said vehemently 'Azinger said it happened once [the change of ball], but we know it happened three times. At first he denied it completely, then he changed his statement. I don't think for a minute he and Chip Beck were trying to cheat. They just didn't know the rule. Azinger is a great player, but he hasn't won a major tournament and I think he was trying to be a hero for his team. The American team were eleven nice guys and Paul Azinger.'

Ballesteros denied that he had tried to put the Americans off by coughing. 'I did nothing like that at Kiawah Island.' But Olazábal conceded that the Spaniard did cough on the course. 'I was coughing, too. We were not very well that week. But he was coughing when nobody was hitting shots. The fact is, they changed balls and they admitted it. Then they lost the match and now they're complaining about Seve coughing. That's rubbish. Azinger should not be saying anything when it is he and Beck who broke the rules. He should keep his mouth shut.'

The Spaniard said that the bad feeling between himself and Azinger stemmed from the incident at The Belfry in 1989. 'He got a wrong drop. He knows it and he knows that I know it.'

But as Ballesteros himself admits, 'Above all, these things show how much everyone wants to win.' Many things are said in the heat of the battle, few of them are meant. There is no question that Ballesteros lives for victory on the golf course, whether he is playing in a pro-am in Tokyo or in the Ryder Cup at Kiawah Island. But that is what makes him great, and it is the positive effects of his desire, his genius and his charisma that have helped make the game and, more especially, the Ryder Cup, what it is today. In five Ryder Cups he has won or halved twenty-one of his twenty-five matches.

'Oh, he plays with such passion and conviction,' agrees Jacklin. 'I mean, he's been fantastic. He's made things happen out there in Ryder Cup confrontation in individual matches that couldn't happen – just because of his commitment. He just *believes* . . . I've seen it all through my life with individuals like Seve. I've seen it with Gary Player. I've done it myself on occasion. You can turn things around for yourself. There's a determination in some people that won't go away, and other people recognize it and they stand aside when they see it. I think Seve's done it on numerous occasions. I mean, in Ryder Cup conflict he's turned matches around, he's chipped in; he's done things in tournaments – against Arnold Palmer in the World Match Play, he chipped in at the last hole. He hit a shot out of the bunker on the eighteenth in 1983 against Fuzzy Zoeller that you couldn't hit. It was an impossible shot. But he did it. And he hit through the green on the eighteenth in two when nobody else got within sixty yards of it at West Palm Beach in the '83 matches. Superhuman things, you know. When you get rolling and the adrenalin gets going and you're excited, you get carried away with your own determination. It's a peculiar thing but really great players all do it at certain times. They're concentrated yet totally relaxed about making it happen, and then it's almost like they have a premonition that they can do it. And it's a wonderful thing to see.'

19

The Road Less Travelled

To be a champion you have to live for what you do. For golf or football or any sport, you have to think and you have to live all the time for that, otherwise it's impossible to be a champion. And you must like it.

Severiano Ballesteros, Spain, March 1990

Eighteen years after his first harrowing days as a tournament professional, Ballesteros strode out onto the sun-speckled range at the Emirates Golf Club in Dubai, on his way to practise. It was still early but already the sky was a deep sapphire blue and the air was close and warm. Caddies strolled about swinging practice ball baskets, players gossiped, warmed up or conferred with their coaches, and a small bottleneck of admirers gathered behind the Spaniard. He acknowledged them with a smile and a genial remark. Once it would have been a folly equivalent to entering a cage of hungry lions to approach Ballesteros while he was working on his golf game, but the inexorable march of time has mellowed him, just as it does everyone else, and now it seems as if he sometimes welcomes distractions for they take him out of himself.

The years have wrought many changes in the man who, for nearly a decade, was the best player in the world. No longer does he glory so much in his own strength and ability, the way he did at Royal Birkdale in 1976; no longer does he hit the ball with such back-wrenching force that he is almost carried after it and has to balance himself with a sort of high twirling follow-through; no longer does he have an unruly mop of jet-black hair, cheap golf shoes or Johnny Miller flares; and no longer do his dark eyes shine with laughter and with fire. Instead he wears the finest designer clothing, has neat, carefully cropped hair and strikes the ball with a stylish, elegant swing, perfectly on plane. Indeed, his whole aspect reflects the rites of passage he has undergone as faithfully as a mirror. Once he was wild, carefree, arrogant, colourful and filled with *joie de vivre*; now he has learnt patience through suffering and humility through insecurity.

Ballesteros waited while Billy Foster tipped practice balls onto the emerald grass, and then hit them crisply out towards the palm trees on the horizon. He was preparing for the Desert Classic, the second event of the season. The Emirates Club, where it is held, is literally an oasis in the desert, complete with flamingoes, fountains, brilliant beds of flowers and a great marble clubhouse in the style of a Bedouin tent.

'Still looking for Joe Collet?' he said enquiringly, when I walked over. He grinned. 'Joe is in church. He's preparing for the next life.'

'We should all be doing that,' I remarked philosophically.

'Do you believe there is another life?' he asked.

'Yes. Do you?'

'I don't know, but it must be good because no-one ever comes back from there!'

'Do you think there is, though?'

Ballesteros laughed, white teeth flashing in his dark face. 'I will write you a letter from there and let you know.'

He rapped his club smartly against his shoe and resumed practising, propelling fifteen of the most perfect golf shots imaginable into the distance. Peter Smith, a talented Scottish player, but one who has never won a tournament in Europe, ventured closer, his face enraptured.

'There's something wrong,' Ballesteros told him. 'What do you think it is?'

Smith was taken aback. 'I don't know,' he said, embarrassed. 'I haven't given a lesson in three years and I've never taught anyone at your level.'

But the Spaniard insisted and so Smith found himself giving a lesson to a man who, in the eyes of most professional golfers, has one of the finest and most exquisitely natural swings in the game and who, until 1990, had been almost entirely self-taught. The next day somebody else was in Smith's shoes.

On the practice range Ballesteros's concerns about his swing seemed unfounded; on the golf course, less so. He had been working to perfect a right-to-left tee shot, which he felt was the key to conquering Augusta's par fives, and he was caught somewhere between the two swings. Still, he was purposeful and confident and thus survived the consequences of his waywardness to score 66, 67 in the opening rounds and lead by a stroke from Anders Forsbrand. He had the advantage of being match-fit, as they say in professional sport. Where most players had taken a long winter lay-off and were rusty and out of condition, Ballesteros had had a mere three weeks – one of the shortest breaks ever in his career – between the World Championship in Jamaica and the Asian Classic in Bangkok, during which time he had practised and ridden his bike assiduously. It was all part of his decision to 'play more golf in order to keep up with the competition. You've got to work harder to stay at the same level. Ten years ago there were about fifteen players capable of winning championships. Now there are between thirty-five and forty.'

For the first time in his life he had announced his intention of becoming the No. 1 player on the Sony World Rankings, a system devised and operated by IMG. Previously, he had not been enamoured with it; besides which, he had always felt in his heart that, regardless of who was at the top of the rankings, he was the world's greatest player. Now he appeared to require proof of that. As Collet said, 'For him to feel secure that he has the recognition as being No. 1 he needs to achieve that in the rankings, which is symbolic to him of how he is actually doing.'

Essentially, Ballesteros's schedule for the season has always been divided into quarters and geared around major championships. For instance, once he has decided which events he should enter before the Masters in April, his performance at Augusta will more or less dictate his schedule from then until the US Open in June. He alters his preparation for the majors constantly. Some years his strategy has been to compete the week before; others he has deemed it better to rest. For a while he thought that a fine performance in a major would guarantee him a high finish in an ordinary event the following week; now, as a general rule, he takes a break. But in Dubai he told journalists that he thought inadequate preparation was responsible for his recent failures at Augusta – his manager and Manuel having persuaded him that was the case.

'I firmly believe that he's taken too much time off in the winter in the past and therefore it's been difficult to get going in time,' said Collet. 'And we've had talks about this. His brother, Manuel, strongly feels that way and has been even more outspoken than I have. This year, he's trying an experiment. We convinced him to play in Jamaica just before Christmas, and also to start in Thailand. Now that cuts about four weeks out of this period that he normally sits around and gains weight and gets lazy and melancholy. I said to him, "If you want to be a peak performer, you've got to make a sacrifice. The sacrifice has to be that you've got to maintain your skill level a little bit higher than you have in the past . . ." And the proof is in the pudding: he's leading the tournament.'

On Sunday, 9 February, Ballesteros won the Desert Classic, holing a 10-foot birdie putt on the second hole of a play-off to defeat Ronan Rafferty. It was eloquent testimony to his mental strength. In the third round of the tournament, after snap-hooking his tee shot to within 4 feet of out of bounds, he had told Foster: 'It's not working. We've got to rethink our ideas and play with what we've got.' But his golf game was capricious and unreliable and, having arrived at the thirteenth to find himself two strokes behind, it had taken a supreme effort of will for him to single-putt each of the remaining holes to tie Rafferty on 272, sixteen under par. The Desert Classic was his fiftieth title in Europe and his eighty-seventh world-wide since that first triumph in the Spanish Under-25's tournament in 1974.

'Ballesteros has always been the best in the world,' Rafferty conceded graciously.

'My determination is to go all the way to the end of the century,' said the Spaniard. 'One thing I'm very proud of is that I'm a great competitor. To win when you are playing great is easy, but to be confident when you are not is something different and something great.'

The following week he finished twenty-fifth at the Turespana Masters in Spain, after rounds of 78, 69, 73, 70, to become the first player to win more than £3 million in prize money on the European Tour.

In March Ballesteros teed up in the Open de Baleares. He had recently returned from an exhibition match in South America and seemed tired and uncommonly depressed. Only will-power drove him on. Asked what motivated him to keep practising so hard and striving so resolutely to be the best season after season after season, he replied: 'Well one thing is very important. Discipline is the key in life for many things. You need discipline; you have to take care of yourself; you have to sleep eight hours every day; and you have to practise. I go to the driving range many times when I don't feel like it. I tell you the truth: I've just come from Argentina, and the way I feel at the moment the best thing for me would be to go to the hotel – my boy is there – and I would like to be there and play with my boy. But do you know what I'm going to do? I'm going to the driving range now because I know that tomorrow is a big day and I want to be ready. That's my profession.'

After three rounds of the tournament he was a stroke off the lead, but his mood remained unchanged. He insisted, with a half-hearted attempt at his old mocking humour, that he was 'playing for second place'. Then he admitted that he was struggling once again to keep focused on the golf course. 'I really have a problem concentrating today. Sometimes you find it more difficult than on other days. I'm playing quite well but there are a lot of players here this week and they're all against me. It's not very easy to win. I've played well for three rounds and I should be leading right now. But if the ball doesn't go in, you just have to be patient.'

Patience proved an essential virtue since, with four holes to play, Jesper Parnevik, the twenty-seven-year-old son of a Swedish television personality, was leading by three strokes and Ballesteros was out of the running. That's when pressure brought its influence to bear. Parnevik dropped three strokes in the remaining holes and found himself in confrontation with the Spaniard in a sudden-death play-off. Six times they toiled up Santa Ponsa's steep 460-yard par four eighteenth, until eventually, an hour and a half after they had set off, Ballesteros sank a 4-foot putt for victory. By then he was panic-stricken about his travel arrangements to Pedreña and, having signed his card, sprinted across the car park to a waiting courtesy car and was whisked away.

Later, the golf writers followed him along the same dangerous grey highway to the airport. When we arrived, Ballesteros was pacing up and down by the ticket counter, looking utterly crushed and dejected. Anyone less like the jubilant winner of a six hole play-off would have been hard to imagine. Carmen was 20 or 30 yards away, standing rather lamely on the concourse. It transpired that, although she had left the course ahead of him and had reached the check-in desk a full fifteen minutes before the plane took off, the Spanish airline they were travelling to Santander with had refused to hold the flight.

'British Airways, they wait for me, Concorde, they wait for me, but *Iberia*?' said Ballesteros bitterly. 'Iberia, they can't wait.' And he cleared his throat miserably as he reflected on the cruel irony of it all. 'We come here at 150 kilometres an hour, risking the life,' he added, his hands describing the heart-stopping journey. He folded his arms and looked glumly over at Carmen.

We stood around and mulled this over. 'But surely winning the tournament was worth missing your flight?' said one journalist, voicing what everyone else was thinking.

Silence. Ballesteros stared morosely at the floor.

'*Surely* you'd rather win the tournament and miss your flight?' There was a note of amazed disbelief in the journalist's voice.

'That is something else altogether,' said Ballesteros cryptically, without meeting anybody's eyes.

Jack Nicklaus was walking down the fairway at Royal Lytham during the 1988 Open Championship, when he was confronted by a large pool of rainwater, the result of Saturday's flooding. He skirted it carefully, causing David J. Russell to remark with a smile, 'I thought you could walk on water.'

'That was a long time ago,' replied Nicklaus wryly.

Ballesteros had reached the same stage. Gone were the days when he would march boldly over or through any hazard that golf or life presented him with. Now, like those men in insurance advertisements, he always carried an umbrella – even when the sun was shining. And he always walked around puddles.

Little more than a year had gone by since he had emerged from his last slump and already he was in the doldrums again. It was hard to know why. Even he was at a loss to explain these great depressions on the graph of his career and only repeated the refrain of 1990, with one or two variations. His principal difficulties then had been confidence and concentration. 'I had lots of negative thoughts,' he said. 'I knew I would win again – it was not a question of if but when – but I was not certain that I would be as good as I had been before.' Now he began to talk of a lack of desire, although essentially they are all the same thing. 'The desire is still there but perhaps not as much as before,' he confessed. 'When the desire and enthusiasm goes down, the concentration becomes more difficult. I still like to win but maybe not as much as when I first started. But that's natural; it happens to everyone as they get older.'

To the *European* he added: 'Desire comes and goes like weather.'

The enormity of the cloud Ballesteros was under was illustrated at Augusta, where he opened with a 75 and followed it with an unbelievable 81 in the final round. Before the event he had been in tears as he vowed: 'In 1992 I want to win the Masters for [my father].' The agony he went through after it was terrible. For months he had rehearsed for Augusta, changed his swing for Augusta, dreamt of Augusta and convinced himself that he could win at Augusta for his father, and all he had succeeded in doing was wrenching once more at the knife buried in his heart.

Jacobs was unsympathetic. 'He's hugely gifted,' he said, 'but, you see, one of the lessons of golf is that you must never pack it in. I can't believe that he took 81 without thinking, "Oh, to hell with this." The score doesn't half mount up quickly if you ever think, "Well, bugger it." I can't believe that he didn't get a bit disgruntled.'

Heartsore and travel-weary, and at as low an ebb as he had been in the worst moments of his first season on Tour or during 1981 or 1990, Ballesteros trailed along to the PGA Championship in May, where he was defending champion. The previous week he had been further demoralized by a joint thirty-fourth place finish in the Spanish Open, but the sight of Wentworth's Burma Road course – which he loves because he feels it is similar in style and character to his home course in Pedreña – and an evening spent watching his beloved Barcelona win the European Cup from the second row of the Royal Box at Wembley, temporarily revived his enthusiasm. 'If I am going to get my game back then this is the place to do it,' he said hopefully, adding that he had won seven times in twenty-eight starts at Wentworth. 'I always play the course well. If I score well in the first round then I will pick up confidence and anything can happen. I always feel good when I play here.'

But when the subject of his poor form arose, he lapsed back into his sombre state and mumbled that his confidence wasn't very high. 'Mentally, I feel very tired. Why, I don't know. I don't have much desire to play. It could be that I have played too much in the last year. I kept going, playing thirty-two tournaments in 1991, compared to my normal average of twenty-seven over the last ten years, but I am looking at taking at least three months off this winter.'

Two days later he failed to qualify. Sandy Lyle, who had been paired with him in the first two rounds, described him as subdued. 'I've never seen him so down. He could have been somewhere on Mars. He wasn't with it. He wasn't there at all.'

Lyle's explanation for Ballesteros's fall from grace was that he had dominated European golf for so long that he had had his nose pushed out of joint when Faldo replaced him at its pinnacle. Faldo, who had spent the early part of his career 'hoping there was going to be some competitive rivalry' between himself and the Spaniard, 'but he was so good then', felt that Lyle was probably right. 'It's the difference between your tail up and your tail down, isn't it? When your tail's up in this game you're blitzing it and trying to blast through everybody and, you know, right now my tail's up and his tail's down.'

There was no doubting the truth of that statement. Faldo, even before he won the Open at Muirfield in July and then finished joint second in the US PGA Championship, was the undisputed world No. 1, while Ballesteros had followed his Wentworth nightmare with a joint seventeenth place, a tie for twenty-seventh place, a tie for forty-second place and two more missed cuts, to be lying twenty-first on the Order of Merit by August. None of this caused him as much pain as his performances in the majors, the only standards he had ever measured himself by. He shot 79 in the last round of the US Open at Pebble Beach to finish out of the top twenty, he missed the cut in the Open and, most damningly of all, he withdrew from the US PGA Championship, despite the fact that he had previously been very critical when other Europeans had done the same, and that his non-attendance of golf's fourth major had been one of the main issues in his fight against Barner. In a faxed letter to the PGA of America, Manuel wrote on his behalf: 'Please withdraw my brother, Seve Ballesteros, from this year's PGA Championship, the reason being that Seve is having some back trouble [brought on by three missed cuts in five tournaments] and he feels he won't be able to play up to his usual standard.'

The strange thing was that, although Ballesteros looked increasingly tormented on the golf course, he didn't walk around like a bear with a sore head off it. If anything he became a kinder, more compassionate person in inverse proportion to the decline of his game. Technically, he clutched with ever more desperation at the tiniest straws. He asked advice indiscriminately from almost any player he laid eyes on; rookies, journeymen or coaches, they were all the same to him. In Monte Carlo, having spent two hours working with Forsbrand on the practice range, he walked into the palace courtyard in his dinner jacket, tapped the tall Swede on the shoulder and there, before the startled eyes of Prince Rainier and his guests, proceeded to demonstrate the advance he had made with his swing since Forsbrand had last inspected it.

Forsbrand didn't mind in the least. 'I enjoy spending time with him. He wants to listen and hear my view of everything, and I think it's in every player's interests to listen to different people. You trust certain people and you don't trust some other people.'

'He asks different people, but he doesn't listen too much,' insisted Piñero. 'He goes his own way.'

Eduardo Romero found the whole thing slightly alarming. He, like Player, felt that the Spaniard should be spending more time working out problems for himself and less time compounding them by over-analysis. 'I play many practice rounds before the tournament with him,' he explained, 'and when he hit the ball perfect he say, "Well, I want to hit it with a fade now." I say, "Seve, why? It's a perfect shot." "No, but I want to try it with fade." And then he miss and miss and miss.'

Ballesteros was honest enough to admit it was true. 'Sometimes you try to change things for the better and your game ends up getting worse. Then you go back to your own style and that doesn't work either. You lose both ways.'

Jacobs didn't believe that Ballesteros's sudden propensity to change his swing on a whim was anything new. 'Seve's a bit like Jack Nicklaus. Seve walks onto a practice ground and decides how he's going to play that day . . . He's hugely gifted – a touch player to a degree. In other words, he can play extraordinary shots but in terms of repeat, repeat, repeat . . . But those are the balances, aren't they? He's more gifted, in my view, than anybody who's going to become a mechanical player.'

Ballesteros's answer to the confidence crisis he was suffering was the same as it always had been: he escaped to Pedreña and

356

the warm bosom of his family. But now he had the added joy of seeing his tiny son, whom he had presented with a plastic club and who could already wield it so well that he managed, before the eyes of several astonished Tour players, to loft the ball from a tee eight consecutive times without once missing. His wife and child and his precious dogs gave him a great deal of pleasure. He had adjusted to married life and it had helped to fill a small corner of the void which has always existed in him when he is not playing golf. Once Trevino told him: 'If you don't take up a hobby pretty soon, you're going to drive yourself crazy.' But no matter how many interests Ballesteros took up, no matter how passionately he pursued his cycling, his fishing or his football, the emptiness remained.

'One thing that was always hard for Seve . . . was that his life revolved around golf,' says Miller. 'I always knew that my children were much more important than my golf, where a lot of golfers are not that way. So when I played bad, it was like, "Oh, what the heck, I've still got a good wife and kids, that's more important." That was my fallback. And I had a lot of hobbies. I was passionate about fishing and racing cars and working on my ranch, and Seve basically didn't have any hobbies. His passion lies in golf. So his life, his happiness, revolved around golf. Period. I was never that way. That was my weakness, too. My weakness was that I wasn't passionate about golf after my big years. I lost my desire a little bit, and I felt like, well, I climbed that mountain, that was cool. Let's try something else.'

But Miller was aided considerably by his faith, whereas Ballesteros is a non-practising Catholic. 'Seve's basic philosophy is: Christian approach to life, don't do anything that you wouldn't like done to you, be honest in your dealings,' says Collet. 'He went to the baptism of his son. He goes to weddings and funerals and things like that, but it's difficult for him because he's very involved in his professional career.' Nevertheless, he feels strongly that the Spaniard 'needs to have some sort of personal philosophy, and that includes a hobby – something more than winning golf tournaments, than fulfilling obligations, than being a good father. He needs something in his socio-religious background . . . I think there could have been times when he was down where, if he had something else to look to that would pick him up, that would help. Like doing something for somebody else who was even more down than he was. And lately he's understood some of that. He's been more active with charity work and doing exhibitions and things that have a charitable purpose. He seems more attracted to those than he is to some that just pay him a lot of money . . . because it makes him happy to see how much things mean to people. It makes him feel good.'

The extent to which Ballesteros has come to realize the vacuum there is in his life apart from golf, was shown when he spent nearly two hours during the 1992 season talking to born-again Christian, Bernhard Langer, about religion. 'He doesn't believe, but he doesn't not believe,' says Langer. 'He's searching.'

But for the moment Ballesteros was far too preoccupied with the deterioration of his golf game to spend time dwelling on anything aside from swing theory. His appearances on the European Tour were few and far between and distinctly uninspired when they came. 'I have no feeling for the game,' he confessed to a reporter in August, after spending several weeks in Pedreña watching the Olympic Games on television. 'You could play better than me. I don't know what is wrong. When I lose confidence I begin to change things . . . and I create a lot of confusion in my mind and every round is a mystery. When you get into that state you need a catalyst. Once you start making putts, for example, your confidence comes back and that affects the rest of your game. You win and that gives you more confidence. That's exactly what happened to me last year.'

'Well, physically he's got problems,' said Faldo. 'Obviously, he's suffering with his back right now and I know he has for a long time. And it's tough on top players when you've been good and you go backwards, because you know that all the work that you're doing is just to get back to where you were. That's the hardest thing for us. You don't want to go down.'

But the bottom line was that Ballesteros had no desire to play, and nothing and nobody could arouse it in him.

Nicklaus understood the feeling well. 'I have a hard time getting inspired,' he admitted. 'I just don't have the belief in myself that I had. And Seve is saying the same thing. He says he doesn't get inspired, but maybe you use that as a pacifying thing to yourself. You say, "Well, if I don't try real hard, then I can't be a failure." You know what I mean? He wants to, but can't. I went through that stage in the early Eighties where I really had the desire but I didn't have the desire, and I didn't want to work at it, yet I wanted to work at it, and I always had a built-in excuse for myself. Not that I wanted to use it, but I always had it. That's mentally what it does to you.'

After missing the cut in the Open and the Scandinavian Masters, the Spaniard took a month off to recoup. Even an offer in the region of £40,000 to play in the English Open failed to rouse his enthusiasm. Appearance money doesn't exist anymore, of course, but in the words of Tony Jacklin: 'We all know what that means.' Then he played in the European Masters in Switzerland the week his wife gave birth to a second baby boy (8.15 p.m. on 3 September), named Miguel and weighing 8.5lb. Asked if he intended to withdraw from the tournament and fly home, he simply said: 'I'm here to play golf.' He finished joint thirtieth, went straight to England for the European Open and, if he had not failed to qualify, would not have seen his new son until ten days after he was born.

Manuel Ballesteros was under no illusions about his brother's decline. 'Seve's problem is in his mind,' he said frankly. 'The more he thinks, the worse he gets.'

'I used to think he was the best player in the world,' says Romero, who has hero-worshipped the Spaniard for as long as he can remember. 'But not now. Now he's not confident. I don't know why. Golf is a very strange game, you know. Very strange. And Seve lose the concentration. He told me, "I can't hit the ball. When I hit it I don't know·where it will go – go right, go left." It's incredible . . . Unbelievable . . . But I think Seve will come back. He's practising now, I speak with him two weeks ago and he say, "I'm doing a lot of work." But it's not practice. The problem is mental. He's not confident. He say, "My head is not for golf now." I think if Seve wants come back, he can. But he has to want to, that's the problem.'

'I'm a great subscriber to the belief that people have a finite amount of bottle,' observes Doust. 'And I think that he's run out of his bottle. If he's in the forefront of a challenge now he'll back off. I don't think he likes pressure any more. And he put himself under *so* much pressure always, year in and year out, round in and round out. Finally, he's run out. There's a reservoir of that kind of strength that everyone has . . . and I think that he's exhausted his . . . You saw him last year in the Open, coming down the last fairway – I've never seen him behave this way – sort of waving to the crowd in a way that he was relieved that it was over. When he missed that short putt on the third green and that really was the end of his charge, you could see – or we Ballesteros watchers thought we could see, and he may have not recognized it himself – he was glad. You can't go into the kitchen always, and you can't keep going into the kitchen.'

As the season wore on and nothing halted the Spaniard's downward slide, Doust's theory began to seem like a realistic probability. After brief appearances at the Piaget Open and the German Masters, where he played his way shakily to joint third and joint twelfth place finishes, followed by an even shorter visit to the World Match Play, where he lost by two holes to Jeff Sluman, he quit for the year, whereupon a statement was issued to the effect that he had developed an allergy to house dust and was having to undergo treatment for it. When the season ended he was tenth on the World Rankings and twenty-eighth on the Order of Merit – his worst placing since 1974, the year he turned professional. Then, however, he had not had two victories to disguise the depths he had plumbed.

So ordinary did Ballesteros appear as he bowed out of the World Match Play at Wentworth, that for a moment it crossed our minds that we might have been mistaken about him all along, that the flame which burned so brightly in him had not been an eternal one, but a flickering candle which had been snuffed out by one too many gales. Herbert Warren

Wind was convinced that this was the case. In May 1980 he had written in the *New Yorker*: 'He is something else, this young Spaniard, and all things being equal he has an excellent chance of becoming one of the most authentically great golfers of all time.' But at the Masters in 1991 he said disparagingly: 'I think we may have overrated Seve. He wasn't a great player, finally.'

Sometimes a man's life can seem like a river, shaped by outside influences from its source to the sea. Here's where it was a powerful stream, rushing gloriously and relentlessly over anything in its path; here's where it became a raging torrent, headstrong and irrational; here's where it was diverted from the straight and narrow by heavy storms; and here's where the years of drought reduced it to a trickle.

It was Severiano Ballesteros's *destino* to be born a farmer's son in a small village in northern Spain, to have three older brothers who were professional golfers and to be spoiled, adored and endlessly encouraged as he learned the game, yet at the same time be forbidden to play at the golf course he loved because of his social status, and thus be denied the perfect happiness which might have tempered his desire. It was his destiny, too, to be influenced by the presence of his huge indomitable father, who taught him how to be tough, independent and resolute and how to triumph in the face of all adversity.

When he left home at sixteen to become a tournament professional, he was confident, fiery and wilful but also emotional, kind-hearted and passionately in love with the game. Protected by Manuel and by his loyal friends, Piñero and Chino Fernandez, he survived the trials and tribulations of those early days and began to live up to his incredible promise. In July 1976 he exploded onto the world stage at Royal Birkdale and experienced, for the first time, fame and adulation and that 'sweet, sweet' high that accompanies attainment of lifelong dreams. Three years later, when he won the Open at Royal Lytham, he knew what it was to have everything – to be handsome, wealthy and gifted beyond his wildest dreams; to have women, journalists, officials and sponsors falling at his feet; and to have the power to say that black is white and be believed. In 1980 he soared to even greater heights with his triumph in the Masters and he dominated the European Tour and anywhere else he played. He began to find that not everyone appreciated his talent. The Americans called him 'lucky', and Peter Thomson, president of the Australian PGA described him as 'a prima donna with an inflated ego and exaggerated opinion of his own importance.'

The criticism and fury engendered by his missed tee-off time at the US Open in 1980 was like a dash of cold water in his face. He grew rebellious, and the desire to vanquish his opponents on and off the course burned so fiercely in his heart that it threatened to consume him. Money and victory became his twin obsessions. Misguided by Barner and confused by his own instinctive hatred of being controlled by people in positions of power, he withdrew his membership of the European Tour, and learnt what it is to be an outcast. The appearance-money battle won, he returned proudly to Europe, only to discover that he had been spurned by the Ryder Cup committee. Nevertheless, he resumed his position at the pinnacle of European golf, and once more was worshipped and fêted by ministers and royalty. By the end of 1983 he was the best player in the world. He was struggling to win Carmen's hand, to have the rules rewritten to accommodate him on the US Tour and to persuade his government to build golf courses for the people. He was moody and volatile as often as he was sunny and good-humoured. Warren Wind commentated that: 'There seems to be a streak of capriciousness in Ballesteros. Almost as though he had risen to stardom too suddenly and had trouble adjusting to the realities of the world.'

Throughout these years of triumph and disaster he was bold, brilliant and a virtual magician on the golf course but, though lonely and weighed down by the pressures of fame, was essentially happy off it. Then in 1986 he lost his father, who had been his greatest friend and moral support. And after promising him as he lay dying that he would win the Masters for him, and then coming within three holes of keeping that promise, he hit the four-iron shot into the water to break it. For the first time in his life he knew tragedy and heartache, and for the first time in his life he learnt fear. But he picked himself up and he fought back because he convinced himself that the green jacket would be his the following year. The blow he suffered when he three-putted the first extra hole to open the door to Larry Mize almost finished him. But in 1988 at Royal Lytham, he flew to his greatest victory. Scarcely had he time to savour that when he found himself at war again with Ed Barner, just as he had done with the European Tour and with Deane Beman, and came off second best. He lost confidence in his invincibility as a person and his indestructibility as a golfer. He no longer believed he could hit a ball anywhere on the golf course and still win. The slump of 1990 carried him to lows he had never experienced before. He rose gloriously to the heights once again the following year, and then found himself suffering such depression and devastation in 1992 that he might have been forgiven for crying, like Thomas Hardy's Eustacia Vye: 'I was capable of much but I have been injured and blighted and crushed by things beyond my control.'

If Severiano Ballesteros was anyone other than who he is, if he wasn't the most gifted, most inspired, most loved player of the modern era, we might doubt that he could ever be as great as he has been. If he wasn't so fiery, so charming, so kind, so generous and so utterly human, we might forget who he is and how much he has done for the game, and how many times he has brought tears to our eyes with his genius and his heart. There is no player in European golf to whom he has not been a hero; there are few members of any gallery at any tournament anywhere in the world who wouldn't prefer to watch Ballesteros on a bad day than all the other great stars combined on their best, and there are few people in tournament golf whom he has not touched with some small gesture or word. All of his career has been a series of great peaks and troughs – genius does not manifest itself to order – and from every depression he has emerged to scale still greater heights. Among the top players, there are few who do not believe that Ballesteros will rise again and be greater even than before.

'I've always thought that Seve is the most gifted player that has ever been born,' enthuses Tony Johnstone. 'Definitely.

I don't think there's anything more awe-inspiring than Seve when he's in full flight . . . I'd like about two per cent of his talent . . . He's going to win plenty more majors. Plenty more.'

'He has to be extremely proud of what he's accomplished,' says Ben Crenshaw. 'He's a very proud man. *Extremely* proud. He has an incredible determination about him. I'm sure his wife and baby are giving him lots of enjoyment and who knows what that's meant to his life. I know that he knows he can achieve a lot more . . . and I'm sure that's frustrating to him at times because everyone knows that he's always had more ability than five or six people the game's ever seen. His talent is that unique. There are not many people that come along like Seve. They just don't. He's very special.'

'I think we all lose our way technically and I think Seve's lost his way technically, that's all,' observes Mark James. 'I think the desire is still there. Someone like Seve doesn't lose the desire and he doesn't lose the talent. But, on the other hand, if he goes on playing very badly for too long, then he will lose the desire. But certainly, if he starts swinging it better within the next two years, he'll be off and running again and I can see him having more majors in him. I think he needs to swing it a bit better, it's as simple as that.'

'I think he would be my greatest player of all time, because I didn't get the opportunity to see Nicklaus and I didn't get the opportunity to see Hogan,' says David Feherty. 'We might have seen the best of him but he'll certainly be that good again. He's got too monumental a talent not to be. Getting married and having children and having a wife and all this sort of thing, that's an immense change . . . He'll win majors again, that's for sure.'

'To me, he is the most talented player I've ever seen,' says Piñero. 'And through my career I've been lucky enough to play with all the best players of the 'seventies and 'eighties. I've played with Nicklaus, Gary Player, Johnny Miller, Tom Watson, Raymond Floyd and Lee Trevino, and Seve is the most talented player of all of them. I know Nicklaus has won more tournaments and he is the best performer. But I don't think that Nicklaus needs the talent of Seve because he was born a steady player and Seve, he's a genius. He's not a machine, he's a genius. To me, he's No. 1.'

'He's got such a terrific inherent talent and he's got a desire to succeed above all else – to be the best – that certainly has sustained him for sixteen years,' says Jacklin. 'You know, one wonders how much longer he can go on. And that's what happens with every champion. Each champion has his time and it depends on how much his priorities in life change . . . how long he's going to sustain the standard . . . I would suspect he's had the best part of his career. He's had sixteen years near the top. The early part of that was a learning process and the subsequent part of it was maintaining a standard that is very high. It would be my guess, as the years pass slowly by, that his direction will change to some degree. I think he will always play golf. I think he will play seniors' golf, probably, but I think other priorities will come into his life that mean he won't be going just as hard at it as he's had to in the past. He's got a family now and other things will begin to take priority and all of a sudden he'll wake up one day and say, "Hell, is life all about just going round on aeroplanes, playing tournament golf, or am I going to enjoy some other aspects of it?"

'But he's certainly in the top five of all-time greats. The others are all debatable. They go from Vardon to Nicklaus to Jones to Hogan to Snead to Nelson. All a player can do is try to be the best of his time. Seve was certainly that.'

For his own part, Ballesteros has dreams of winning another five majors or a Grand Slam of titles, and of winning the US Masters for his father. His love for the game he has graced with his brilliance and humanity is unquenched to this day, and the spirit of golf still lives in him.

'My ambition is to play as much as I can and to keep that passion for the game and that passion for competition. Because, of course, when I play bad I get a lot of frustration on the golf course, like everybody, but when I play good I have so much fun and so much pleasure that there's no money in the world that can buy that. And this is what I want. I want to keep that for as long as I can.'

20

Conflicts and Interests

When a tree falls down a lot of people want to take a cut out of it. My feeling is that this is what's happening. I have only one way to go and that's to reach the top again. Then I'll have my power back.

Seve Ballesteros on his trials, 1994

It was a measure of Ballesteros's continuing influence and his fiendish ability to stage-manage a situation that, minutes after entering the press centre to discuss the 66 with which he had finished eighth in the Spanish Open, he had reduced the listening journalists to a shocked, scandalized silence. A small smile, somewhere between sympathy and satisfaction, tugged at the corner of his mouth. 'Excuse me?' one was tempted to burst out. 'Say that again.'

It was May 1994, one week after the Spaniard's triumphant return to the winner's rostrum at the Benson and Hedges International at St Mellion in Cornwall, and Ballesteros had just alleged – with a breathtaking degree of casualness and calculated intent – that he had been offered a $1 million bribe to help ensure that the 1997 Ryder Cup went to Valderrama in Spain.

'The offer did not actually specify that figure, but that was what it amounted to,' he reported. 'I have a letter at home which tells me I would get a percentage of the green fees and the sales of the building plots. It has nothing to do with the work I did in redesigning the seventeenth hole there, because I did that for nothing.' He glowered at the room. 'I don't like to be bought,' he said proudly. 'I have my principles.'

The Spanish press contingent came noisily to life. Who, precisely, was he accusing? they demanded. When and where did he receive the letter? But Ballesteros was coy. He would say only that although he knew for a fact that the technical commission had advised the Ryder Cup committee that Jaime Ortiz Patino's exclusive Sotogrande club did not have the minimum necessary facilities to host such a big infrastructure, Bernard Gallacher had told him that the committee was strongly in favour of taking the match there.

He paused for effect. 'So one has to ask if those gentlemen on the Ryder Cup committee have received similar offers to the one I received,' he said piously.

For Severiano Ballesteros, struggling to retain some dignity, the journey from purgatory to top form had been a rougher ride than even his worst fears might have led him to suppose. He had begun the 1993 season with a brief, promising burst of form, finishing equal third in Dubai. The following week, he missed the cut in the Asian Classic and entered free-fall, producing a set of statistics that would have been hard to believe in his rookie year on tour, let alone his sixteenth: five missed cuts, two top tens and a series of embarrassing finishes, including a tie for thirty-fourth in Morocco, thirty-seventh in the Spanish Open, fiftieth in the Scottish Open, twenty-seventh in the Open, seventieth in the Scandinavian Masters and twenty-first in the German Open.

None of these results had any discernible effect on Gallacher, the Ryder Cup captain. On the contrary; in July, he took pressure off the Spaniard by informing him that he was guaranteed a wild card and, less than a month later, he presented one to Olazábal. 'Seve and Olazábal have formed the most outstanding partnership in the history of the Ryder Cup,' he said. 'I don't believe there is a partnership in the world which looks forward to stepping on the tee with them.'

It was a contentious decision. On the one hand, there was no denying that Ballesteros was playing some of the worst golf of his career, but on the other, his psychological impact on the team was crucial. Among both players and public, there was an almost superstitious faith in the ability of Ballesteros and Olazábal – a kind of blind confidence in the power of chemistry over form – to combine to devastating effect in matchplay. Besides which, a Ryder Cup without Ballesteros's passion and fury was unthinkable.

On Friday 26 September, Sam Torrance launched the opening drive at the Belfry, and almost immediately things began to go wrong. In the process of hitting his shot, the Scotsman wrenched at an already painful ingrown toenail, and by the ninth hole he could hardly walk. On the mist-wreathed fairways, he and Mark James soon surrendered to the formidable partnership of Lanny Wadkins and Corey Pavin, and the Spaniards were dispatched 2 and 1 by Tom Kite and Davis Love III.

In the afternoon fourballs, where the US team are traditionally stronger, the Europeans edged ahead by a point, largely due to the inspired début of Peter Baker and the resurgence of Ballesteros and Olazábal. Gallacher's hopes rose. Torrance had been sidelined, effectively reducing the Europeans to eleven men, but the backbone of the team was still working well. Further encouragement was provided by Faldo and Montgomerie, Langer and Woosnam and Seve and Jose Maria in the foursomes matches on Saturday morning, and Gallacher, the 'consensus captain', was reviewing the situation with optimism when he received a radio summons from Ballesteros shortly before lunch.

Tension formed a hard knot in Gallacher's stomach. He departed at speed for the fourteenth, where he arrived to find the Spaniards two up over Kite and Love. Ballesteros had missed the green right and was standing beside his ball, his face shadowed and anxious. He hurried over to Gallacher. Swallowing his pride, he begged the European captain not to send him out in the afternoon. He felt that he had let Olazábal down.

Gallacher was astounded. Later, he recalled that Ballesteros had appealed to him to replace him with someone else in order to allow him the time to go and work on the practice ground. 'And despite speaking to Seve for several minutes, trying to persuade him that that might be the wrong thing to do, I felt that Seve, who always likes to lead from the front, who's never shirked a battle, especially that week, who loves the Ryder Cup, knowing how important it is to Seve, I felt I owed it to him to agree to his request. As it turned out, he couldn't find his game. He started well at the beginning of the week, his game was quite good when he came, and it deteriorated as the week went on, and by the time the singles came he was quite distressed. And I personally wouldn't put Seve on the course when he felt like that. In actual fact, I even put Seve well down the list in the pairings for the singles to try and keep him out of the spotlight, because I've got so much respect for Seve, and I've never heard Seve ever, *ever* say to anyone that he didn't want to play.'

For the European team, it was a crippling blow, made worse by the absence of Torrance and the withdrawal of Langer with a sore back from the afternoon fourballs. As if that wasn't enough, on Friday night, Baker's baby daughter was rushed to hospital with suspected meningitis. Europe led by a point going into the singles but the momentum had gone. Even before Ballesteros began with four bogeys in his match against Jim Gallagher Junior, the Ryder Cup was slipping, painfully and irredeemably, from the European's grasp. When Langer was beaten by Kite, James by Payne Stewart and Barry Lane, who had been three up with five holes to play, lost to Chip Beck, the die was cast. The only way out was Costantino Rocca, who was one up over Love with two holes to play. When he bogeyed both, crumbling under the terrible pressure, the US team won the match 15–13.

'Nobody can blame Costantino,' said Ballesteros, who was sent by Gallacher to comfort the devastated Rocca in the locker room and ended up doing most of the crying himself. 'I felt very sad for him and I feel bad about myself. You can blame me. I played very badly. I tried my best, but it was not to be. I'm sorry.'

To all intents and purposes, Ballesteros's season was over. Bruised and lonely, he attempted to work out his frustrations on the practice ground, watched over by an ever increasing procession of teachers and gurus. 'He's a difficult pupil in the sense that he can be strong willed, very, very proud and makes you prove to him that what you're telling him is correct,' commented Simon Holmes, a former Leadbetter assistant, whose tousled, sleepy presence followed the world-weary philosophizing of Bob Torrance and the blunt contributions of Manuel Piñero. 'What I've been telling him is that what he feels he does and what he actually does are not the same thing.'

In the end, it only mattered what Ballesteros felt. Holmes went the way of all the other well-meaning advisers, and Ballesteros struggled on, finishing a career worst forty-second on the money list. It was the first time he had ever failed to win a tournament in a season. For such a proud man, these statistics must have cut to the bone, but *destino* had not done with him yet. At the World Match Play, an event he had won five times, he suffered the ultimate humiliation when he was beaten 7 and 6 by David Frost in the first round.

Afterwards, he sat in the interview room with his head in his hands and tears in his eyes. 'I don't know what to do any more,' he mumbled helplessly, and there was something in his demeanour, in his sad grey features and the slump of his shoulders that suggested he had reached the end of the road. He refused to deny that he was thinking of giving up the game. 'I don't know what's wrong,' he said miserably. 'I've tried everything. Nothing works.'

And with that, he quit for the year, leaving us shocked and silent, our hearts aching.

A sharp breeze tugged at the green and gold grasses of the Montecastillo course and accompanied Ballesteros into the clubhouse. Heads turned, mouths dropped open. Necks craned to follow his progress down the corridor. It was an impressive entrance under any circumstances; against the backdrop of 1993 it made for compelling viewing. For the best part of two months, Ballesteros had been endeavouring to strengthen the muscles in his ailing back at the Desert Institute of Physical Therapy in Scottsdale, Arizona, spending more than five hours a day stretching, running, cycling and pushing weights, and the result was a tanned, chiselled physique and a military haircut, set off to perfection by a red shirt and toothpaste smile. 'I have had to rededicate myself,' Ballesteros said. 'I have a lot of pride and it's been damaged.'

He was reluctant to admit that the World Match Play may have seen him at the lowest ebb of his career, although he conceded, 'I was very low.'

'You gave us the impression you were thinking of quitting the game.'

'Quit! What? The *game*?' Ballesteros smiled widely. 'No, no, I might have quit for a year, but not for ever. I'm only thirty-six. I'm just a kid.'

As far as he was concerned, his 'physical problems' – namely, the degeneration in his spine, had been a decisive factor in his bad results the previous season. 'Since 1977 my back has been an important handicap, and lately it has been worse. I have not been able to sleep for the pain. I have been to chiropractors and witches and they haven't helped me.'

However, it transpired that his back was the least of his concerns. The dramatic improvement in his overall fitness, coupled with the steady rehabilitation of his game had brought back his old fighting spirit, and shifted his focus to larger issues and new battlefields. Asked about the terrible trials of the previous season, he told the Spanish newspaper *El Pais* that the past two years had done him good. 'I have become stronger mentally and have confirmed what I already knew, that I have a few friends, many acquaintances and very many enemies – many more than I thought I had.'

There was little doubt to whom he referred. There was only one item on Ballesteros's agenda and that was the 1997 Ryder Cup venue, and he had made up his mind that the only truly suitable venue for the matches was Novo Sancti Petri, the course he himself had designed near Cadiz. It was a safe bet that anyone who opposed him was considered an arch-enemy. The Spanish Golf Federation was at the top of the list.

'The federation has always been a cancer,' Ballesteros said sourly, 'although that sounds very harsh. Their job has been to maintain a social circle. It seems incredible to me that these people who have done nothing for golf are arm-wrestling with me when it is I who have brought the Ryder Cup here. When we got the cup in Spain nobody called me, nobody congratulated me and nobody asked me for my opinion. It is very possible that if I hadn't played in the 1983 match, the Ryder Cup would not be what it is now. It is possible that the event would have disappeared altogether. It is bad that I have to say so, but I have to because no-one else does. The federation say they have to remain neutral, but the obvious thing would be to consult various people and present a united candidate. Now we are all in a fight to see who wins.'

The following day, Jack Nicklaus, who, as the designer of Montecastillo, one of seven candidates bidding to host the matches, was leading that course's campaign, announced that he in his turn planned to do everything in his power to bring the Ryder Cup to Jerez.

In retrospect, it is not hard to see why Ballesteros, anticipating war and believing himself friendless, should, in the spring of 1994, find himself being shadowed around St Mellion by a mop-headed figure in a white rain-jacket, making copious notes on a dollar bill.

At Christmas, 'Mad Mac' O'Grady, a former tour player and long-standing friend of Ballesteros, had telephoned him to say that he had just completed a ten-year scientific study of the golf swing. These researches had resulted in five 250-page volumes known as MORAD (Mankind's Objective Research and Development). Twenty pages alone had been devoted to the shot Ballesteros hit into the water at Augusta in 1986, and O'Grady had called to ask for his old pal's input and to see how his game was going. One thing led to another, and before the Spaniard knew what had hit him, he was driving out into the desert near Palm Springs, California with a box of old Seve photographs, which he proceeded to bury while Mac said a prayer. Mac then told him to cleanse himself by cutting his hair and stood him in a bunker and made him hit three-irons.

'Mac is a very good player,' Ballesteros said of the American. 'He probably strikes the ball better than anyone else. He has only one problem – he cannot focus on what he's doing. He's too friendly with people. He has a great heart, but a lot of people misunderstand him.'

If O'Grady was perceived as an eccentric, it was because he cultivated the image. 'I'm not nearly so bingo-bango-bongo as people think I am,' he would tell people. On another occasion, he said, 'Right now, I'm going through a catatonic, neurosomatic disorder. I'm in a total emotional upheaval.' In April, at Augusta, he held an impromptu press conference on the lawn in front of the clubhouse, informing reporters that he had adopted a neuro-scientific approach to Ballesteros's swing. The Spaniard had, he said, already incorporated thirty-eight of the forty changes he had recommended into his game. Ballesteros himself had declined to give details about their relationship, but O'Grady had no such scruples. He was in the midst of explaining that most teachers were 'sycophants looking for a passport to legitimacy', and that Leadbetter had been charging Seve $500 an hour, while he, O'Grady, was helping him free, when his pupil came storming over. He was plainly furious.

'Mac, where have you been?' he cried. 'I've been waiting an hour and a half on the practice ground.'

He stomped off without waiting for a reply. O'Grady shuffled his feet in embarrassment. 'Did you see the look of commitment and dedication in Seve's eyes?' he asked his startled audience.

Mentally, Ballesteros was still very fragile, but his confidence was returning by degrees. At the Players Championship, where he missed the cut by a shot, he had sat in the locker room and talked about his achievements as a young prodigy and all they had meant to him. 'I just feel that in life everything went OK for me, but everyone has to pay their dues and it looks like I'm paying them now. This is probably what's happening. Because I really feel that my game is there and it's coming along. So it's just a matter of being patient and waiting for my time. My time will come back, I'm sure of it.'

In May, Ballesteros teed up at the Benson and Hedges International at St Mellion, still reeling from a double blow. The previous week, he had finished 138th in a field of 139 and now, to add insult to injury, the USGA had snubbed him by not inviting him to the US Open.

'The tournament belongs to them but my feeling is that I'm part of the history of that tournament and I think it's very unfair,' Ballesteros complained. To his mind, his record and the fact that he had played in every US Open since 1977 meant that he should have got a place ahead of Arnold Palmer. He could attempt to qualify, but he hadn't had to pre-qualify for an event since the Portuguese and Spanish Opens in 1974 and he didn't see why he should do so now. 'In Portugal I finished last in the qualifying because I shot eighty-nine. I took fifty-six on the back nine. My sponsor, Dr Cesar Campuzano, told me, "Don't worry, you're still the best in the world."'

For the umpteenth time in his career, Ballesteros went out to play feeling persecuted, his most dangerous frame of mind. On the windswept, tightly contoured course, he shot 69, 70 to lead by a stroke at the halfway stage from Gary Orr and two from Paul McGinley. He began the third round by rolling in a 40-footer at the first, a 7-footer at the second and a 30-footer at the third, eventually shooting 72 to lie a stroke behind Orr at the end of the day on 211. Afterwards, he talked of how, just eight weeks earlier, his caddie Billy Foster had begged him to walk in on the twenty-seventh hole in Majorca, telling him, 'I can't bear to see you suffer like this.' Ballesteros had put a hand on his shoulder and said, 'Billy, we are professionals. We must keep going. I never quit.'

In the final round, an ecstatic, hopeful crowd watched Ballesteros grind out fifteen hard-won pars, and willed him on as he drove into unexplored territory at the sixteenth, chopped a seven-iron back onto the fairway, hit an indifferent wedge to 15 feet and holed the birdie putt. When he hit his approach at the seventeenth to 3 feet, the tournament was won, and the roar of acclaim that greeted Ballesteros's towering shot to the last, reverberated around the links as the crowd broke through the ropes and swamped their tearful hero and his police escort.

'It was difficult,' admitted Ballesteros, whose victory by three strokes from Nick Faldo was his first in twenty-six months. He dedicated the tournament to Foster and O'Grady. 'I have not been in a winning position for so long. I was nervous all the way, tense, tight. You know, there are nerves to compete, nerves to make the cut, nerves to finish in the top ten and nerves to win. I know all of them.'

As he had predicted, Ballesteros had restored his power. Now he used his newfound confidence to lend zest and determination to his twin objectives: to force the USGA to eat humble pie and offer him an invite, and to take the Ryder Cup to Novo Sancti Petri. His first move was to attack Valderrama and the Ryder Cup committee with bribery and corruption allegations at the Spanish Open, the week after his victory at St Mellion.

David Huish, a member of the Ryder Cup committee, was outraged. 'If Seve said that to my face I'd punch him on the nose,' he said angrily. 'I can't believe it. If he's suggesting that members of the committee have been offered inducements I'd take it all the way to the courts. It would be like winning the pools.'

If there was one thing more intriguing than Ballesteros's insinuations and the splutterings of the Ryder Cup committee, then it was Jaime Patino's response to them – pure astonishment. In an interview with the *Guardian*, Valderrama's owner openly admitted that, in April 1993, one month before it was announced that Spain would host the 1997 event, he had decided to seek the support of Ballesteros, who, coincidentally, had redesigned the seventeenth hole and refused to accept a fee. Patino had written to him offering him a percentage of Valderrama's green fees as compensation for the work on the seventeenth hole and 'for your . . . agreement to support our candidacy for the Ryder Cup and in particular if you are prepared to publicly communicate your support to the press and the PGA executives at the Volvo PGA at Wentworth on 28 May 1993.' The green fees alone were guaranteed to net Ballesteros at least £675,000. Nonetheless, Patino claims that he didn't consider the letter a bribe because the Spaniard had not yet been appointed a member of the Ryder Cup committee.

'I felt honestly that, knowing politics in Spain, it could become very nasty, as it did in the end, and that I could avoid all this nonsense. I knew that we had the best course and if we had Seve on my side there would be no opposition. You want Jack Nicklaus on your team you give him $2 million. There's nothing wrong with making someone a business proposal.'

Initially, Ballesteros seemed to be of a similar mind. On 22 June 1993, he replied, thanking Patino for the 'very kind offer to collaborate in your project', and asking for time to consider the offer. He signed the letter with *un fuerte abrazo,* a big hug. By the end of July, Patino had heard no more, and he wrote back to Ballesteros, explaining that he would withdraw the offer on 30 September if no further communication was forthcoming. On 12 October, a letter arrived on Patino's desk, in which Ballesteros said that he had received similar offers from other Spanish clubs and was still unwilling to commit himself to any particular one. He concluded, 'I thank you from the bottom of my heart for the interest you have always shown in me personally.' Patino heard nothing more until the following year, when Ballesteros's bribery allegations appeared in the papers.

On 26 May, Ballesteros came into the press centre after a rain-soaked practice round at Wentworth, clutching a white scroll etched with pink handwriting. He had already dealt with the US Open invite drama – 'If I have to go and pre-qualify, I'll do that. I've filled in the form. You know me, I'm humble. I'll go there by boat, rowing, if I have to' – and now he was responding to the announcement that the Ryder Cup would, after all, be going to Valderrama. There will be no questions, only answers,' Ballesteros said with a sly grin, and unrolled his script. 'My heartfelt best wishes are extended to Valderrama and Mr Patino for winning the right to be the hosts in 1997,' he began. 'Mr Patino has worked long and hard to stage this prestigious event and I'm sure every one of the *American* team will enjoy Valderrama.'

He extended his congratulations to the Ryder Cup committee and said that he had served golf for twenty years and would continue to do so. 'I know that all the other clubs who were hoping to be selected are greatly disappointed. I wanted Novo Sancti Petri but life sometimes is not so sweet. We do not always get what we want.'

He added that he had written his statement the previous week. 'I knew who was going to win so it was easy to write. I was one hundred per cent right.'

As loser's speeches go, it was a masterpiece, a subtle interweaving of graciousness, diplomacy and barbed comment. To cap it all, when Ballesteros walked out of the interview room the following day, Patino was standing in his path. Another man might have given his victorious opponent a curt nod or a cold handshake, but Ballesteros went rushing over to the little Bolivian and embraced him in a huge bear-hug. To this day, Patino is still bemused by the whole saga. 'When I saw him at Wentworth he grabbed me and gave me a big hug and said, "You were too strong for me," as if nothing had happened. He had a smile from ear to ear. I don't understand how he went off the deep end.'

21

To Valderrama

When a true genius appears in the world, you may know him by this
sign, that the dunces are all in confederacy against him.

Jonathan Swift, *Thoughts on Various Subjects*

With hindsight, it is possible to trace the beginning of
Ballesteros's decline as a major contender to the day after his
victory in the 1988 Open, when the energy and time he
expended on conflicts began to grow in inverse proportion to
the periods he played his best golf. By the mid-Nineties, they
dominated his life.

Once, comparing the personalities of Ballesteros and his
brilliant Ryder Cup partner Olazábal, Sergio Gomez, the
latter's manager, described Seve as 'naturally aggressive. In
life, he tries to make room for himself with his elbows. That's
what we say in Spain about someone who's always pushing
ahead and trying to be one step further than the others . . .
You will never see Jose pushing his arguments or pushing a
situation to the boundaries. Seve's always on the edge of being
impolite, and being so harsh with everyone that everyone is
shocked. When Seve's not happy, he always threatens, "I will
lose interest in the Ryder Cup, I will play on the US Tour, I
will go to Japan where everybody loves me."

'For instance, with the Ryder Cup course. Seve pushed the
situation to the absolute limit: "I won't be captain, I don't

know if I will play again in Spain." Jose, from the beginning, was favouring Valderrama. But not publicly, because he didn't want to be in that situation. He went to Ken Schofield and he went to George O'Grady and he said, "Don't be stupid, the only place we can play is Valderrama." He came to that decision because he said, "Where can the Ryder Cup work? Valderrama. Why? Because Jaime Patino will make it work."'

Ballesteros survived the Ryder Cup venue drama unscathed, going on to win the German Masters in a play-off from Ernie Els and Jose Olazábal later that season, and then beginning the 1995 season with victory in the Spanish Open in May, but by June his back problems had escalated and his game had gone into tailspin. If Seve has one defect, it is that he overweights the short-term solution,' said Joe Collet, with whom Ballesteros has now split (Roddy Carr has taken over his management). 'He always wants a panacea, a quick fix. That has hurt him with building his game.'

Significantly, he had parted with Billy Foster and fallen out with O'Grady soon after the Masters. Then, within a week or two of the US Open, he had engaged in a fresh struggle with Joey Jones, Foster's wholesome, efficient replacement.

Ballesteros had taken Jones, one of the most professional and reliable caddies on the tour for a trial outing at the Benson and Hedges International. When that went well, he asked the young Liverpudlian to work for him full time. Jones was reluctant. After years of caddying for players of the calibre of Ronan Rafferty, he had opened a highly successful hamburger business, Caddyshack Catering, on the European circuit, and, with a family to support and a mortgage to pay, he was not about to give it up. Ballesteros won him over. According to Jones, he guaranteed him a year's employment and agreed to pay him £400 a week plus 7 per cent for a place or win (the average in Europe is £350 a week with 5 per cent for a place and 10 for a win).

The first sign that all would not be roses came the very next week, when Ballesteros won the Spanish Open and, out of the £92,000 winner's cheque, presented Jones with just £4,000. He had subtracted Spanish withholding tax, a PGA levy and Spanish VAT. Most players pay for some or all of their caddie's hotel and travel expenses, Jones received nothing. Five weeks later, Ballesteros phoned him at home and announced that he was dispensing with his services and taking on a Japanese professional who had worked with Mad Mac. 'He wanted to kill two birds with one stone,' said Jones, who issued Ballesteros with a £15,000 writ on the Friday of the 1996 Benson and Hedges International at the Oxfordshire after receiving just £400 redundancy pay. 'Most players on tour have a coach and a caddie, but Seve's so tight, it's unbelievable. He'd fallen out with Mac O'Grady over money because Mac billed him for a tournament, and this guy had worked for Mac so Seve thought it would help his game if he caddied for him. But where does that leave me? I've got a wife and two kids, and it took me five weeks to find another job. That's the reason I'm suing.'

Ballesteros was furious. 'I am a little disappointed,' he said. 'I was nice to him. I respect caddies and treat them well. I had no written contract and the matter has been passed to my solicitor. That's all I have to say.'

At the time of writing, Ballesteros was attempting to have the case heard in Bilbao, Spain, while Jones was doing his best to keep it in England. Earlier in the season, he had confronted Ballesteros at a tournament in Spain, and claims that Ballesteros initially denied that he had promised to keep him on for the season 'no matter what', but later admitted, 'Well, maybe I did.' Jones recalled, 'He then said, "Maybe I'll take you to Spain." I wasn't sure whether he meant on holiday. I thought, I don't want a holiday, I want the money . . . He knows what he said to me. He knows he let me down. And he knows I'm right.'

Foster remained as loyal as ever. 'He's a hard man to caddie for, but he's great in the same breath,' he said.

Then came the final day of the Ryder Cup at Oak Hill. When Ballesteros arrived in Rochester, New York, he was, to say the least, playing poorly. As Dobereiner pointed out: 'O'Grady tried to flatten Seve's swing into a Hoganesque plane. At the Ryder Cup, Seve was in the transitional stage when his old swing was going out of commission and the Hogan model had not yet begun to bed down.'

As a consequence, Ballesteros hit three fairways in three matches, and might have lost every match had he not part-nered David Gilford on the first day and coached him to victory. 'David Gilford had the best caddie of all time,' Foster said later. But even Gilford couldn't help him on the second day, and he and the Englishman lost their fourballs match against Jay Haas and Phil Mickelson because Seve could not see the wood for the trees.

In the singles, Ballesteros met Tom Lehman, the gifted Mid-westerner, whose calm, gracious manner belies his toughness as a competitor. The American was one up when he and the Spaniard reached the twelfth hole. Both men had birdie putts, and Lehman rolled his to within inches of the cup and then holed out without waiting for Ballesteros to give him per-mission to do so. Ballesteros promptly objected, provoking loud jeers from the partisan crowd. He informed Lehman that he had putted out of turn, and, citing Rule 10-1c, requested that he replace his ball and mark it.

It was un unpleasant moment. Everything Lehman had ever heard about Ballesteros's reputation for ruthlessness, gamesmanship and ability to work miracles in matchplay came back to haunt him, and he summoned the official, J. R. Carpenter, and asked for his opinion. To the disbelief of the gallery, who greeted the news with hostile cries, Carpenter told him that Ballesteros was quite correct. Lehman replaced his ball and Ballesteros missed his birdie putt, at which point he magnanimously conceded Lehman's tap-in.

In years to come, when history shines a light on Ballesteros's legend, that singles match – with all its hooks and slices, controversy and impossible recoveries, will hold its own among the major victories and impressive feats, regardless of the fact that he lost. No man ever fought with more courage, or played with more heart, with so few tools. Awestruck, Lehman said he felt privileged to have witnessed it, and Ballesteros's team-mates, watched the board with incredulity, drew inspiration from it and achieved a miracle of their own: the Europeans, underdogs from the start, won the Ryder Cup on US soil.

'He has the best charisma in the world,' Costantino Rocca,

the Italian, said. 'It's not important whether he plays good or not, it's his charisma and his effect on the team.'

'It was the most amazing effort I've ever seen in my life,' recalled Ken Brown, who commented on the match for Sky. 'Lehman was playing as well as you could possibly play, hitting the middle of every fairway and green. Seve was playing just as badly as you can play. He really didn't know where the ball was going. Yet after nine holes, Seve was just one down and you still had the feeling that if just one chink appeared in Lehman's armour Seve would have pounced and won the match.'

Foster, who saw the match on television, could not get over Ballesteros's audacious escapes. 'I'd go so far as to say that we wouldn't have won it if he hadn't been there,' Foster said. 'His inspiration pulled them through. Watching him playing Lehman, I was just laughing. I thought it was fantastic the way he just hung on and fought like a tiger. It gave the rest of the team confidence because they knew how badly he was playing and he was still fighting and it encouraged them to do the same.'

'He's always incredible,' said Sam Torrance admiringly. 'He's probably the best team man who's ever lived. He's got so much heart and soul and he gives so much. The fact that he held Lehman for so long, even though he was hitting it off the golf course, had a filter-down effect that helped the rest of us.'

'He's got so much pride,' someone said.

Torrance laughed. 'Pride or hate?' he asked.

When the Ryder Cup ended, Ballesteros announced that he would be taking a five-month sabbatical, an unprecedented interruption in the career of a great player. In spite of his contribution to the team's morale, the devastation of his game had left him saddened and dispirited. His fellow players thought more highly of him than ever. On Friday 15 December, they sent Ken Schofield, executive director of the European Tour, to meet him at Garfunkels restaurant in London's Heathrow airport and ask if he would captain the Ryder Cup team when the matches went to Spain in September 1997.

'I said to him, "Do you want to do it on the committee's terms, because you might not want to?"' Schofield recalled. 'We knew he wanted more than two wild cards, but there is a feeling that, although both teams want to win the Ryder Cup, there is something above that which is that every player should have the right to try and qualify.'

One month later, Schofield went to see Ballesteros at his home in Santander, where he officially agreed to captain the European team. He stipulated that he wanted the right, should he qualify automatically, to drop himself if he didn't feel he was playing well enough. Manuel Piñero would, in all probability, help him, but he didn't plan to nominate an official deputy until July, if at all.

'I remember asking him, "Can you handle defeat?"' Schofield said, 'And he replied, "The fact that I am captain is no guarantee that we will win."'

Five months after his abrupt, depressing departure, Ballesteros was back with a new set of Cobra clubs and the same erratic game. His first shot of the season was a blocked drive at the Moroccan Open, and his scores, 78–79, reflected more of the same. Bernhard Langer's suggestion, that he change swings if only to alleviate the pressure on his spine, fell on deaf ears, and Ballesteros withdrew from The Players Championship in March with a bad back and a familiar refrain.

'I have no confidence,' Ballesteros repeated yet again. 'Confidence is everything.'

But there was more to it than that. Once Ballesteros was obsessed with nothing but the game, with the ultimate recovery, the most ingenious, floating chip or the most belief-beggaring birdie, but marriage and three children had changed all that. His golf had suffered as a consequence, but he had become a more complete person, a more compassionate person. 'I'm scared of what is happening in our world,' he told Derek Lawrenson of the *Sunday Telegraph*. 'Maybe it is since having kids, I don't know. I used to drive a car fast and now I drive it slow. I look at the flowers on the trees at this course in January and I think, That never used to happen. Why are we having nuclear tests? This is what happens when you get older. You see the world through more cautious eyes.

'It is the same with my golf. The first time I went in the trees I saw only the green and how I could put the ball on it. Now I see the branches and the roots and the trunk. Experience can be a marvellous asset but it can be bad, too.'

When Lawrenson asked him how much his back had contributed to his results in recent times, he came close to losing his temper. 'People don't realize how sensitive the mind is. The more I'm asked about my back, the more pain I feel . . . One of the things that is killing the superstars and why no player dominates any more is that there is pressure all the time. There is no release from it. I remember going to England when I first started and you could go into the lounge after a round and have a cup of tea. You can't do that any more. Don't get me wrong, it's not a bad thing. It means the game is popular, which is good. But it does make it difficult – all the demands on your time, all the questions, the lack of space.

'People use my back as an excuse to say I'm finished. It's a very easy thing to say, isn't it? You can be a great champion for fifteen years, you have one bad year and that's it, you can't play any more because of your back. It's the same as my cough: I wish there was a miracle cure but there isn't. Every morning I wake up with this itch at the back of my throat. Even changes of temperature cause me to cough. When I'm on the course I never stop coughing. Azinger thought I was trying to put him off all those years ago, but it wasn't the case at all.'

But by the time Ballesteros arrived at the Masters in April, he was playing some of the most inconsistent golf of his life. 'It's very painful when you have to talk all the time about these things,' Ballesteros told Jaime Diaz of *Sports Illustrated* when Diaz asked him what he felt was causing his problems. 'It's not easy – why this, why that, and what are you going to do and why don't you do this. It drives you crazy. It's not good because the mind is very powerful, and everything is negative, negative, negative.'

It didn't help that every player, coach and caddie in Christendom had an opinion on the subject. 'It's shocking to see how much Seve has deteriorated,' David Leadbetter said. 'At the top of his swing, Seve's clubface is shut. From that position, he cannot release the club properly and the inevitable result is that he either snaps the ball left or blocks it to the right.'

Curtis Strange: 'We all struggle at times but I have never seen a player of Seve's calibre hit the kind of shots he was hitting at the Ryder Cup.'

'Even at his best I always thought Seve was living on the edge,' said Lanny Wadkins, who captained the US Ryder Cup team. 'He erased a lot of mistakes with his short game. I equate Seve with Crenshaw, but Ben would have his straight-hitting periods. Trying to play from crooked drives can wear on you.'

Even O'Grady gave his two cents' worth. 'When it comes to competition, Seve burns like a nuclear reactor. But he became unhappy because he started letting winning majors mean everything. He got so disappointed that he stopped loving the game. He has to turn that reactor loose on the process of becoming a great golfer again. If he does, there's no doubt he can play as well as Norman. In fact, in a street fight, I'd take Seve.'

On being informed of these observations, Ballesteros scowled. 'My message to the teachers and everyone else who has been writing me letters is that I know a little bit about this game,' he said darkly.

In June, the US Open rolled around again and this time Ballesteros was not invited and did not, as he had in 1994, manage to play his way into the tournament. In Germany, he commented, 'I have had two chances of winning the US Open in the past but I have never enjoyed that tournament. I won't miss going there this year. Sure, it's a major, but it's not a good tournament because eighty per cent of the game in the US Open is about hitting the fairways. It takes away the skill factor. Everyone wants to compete in the US Open but then when they get there they all hope the week will finish quickly.'

Asked whether there was a possibility of a last-minute invitation, Ballesteros responded, 'No chance. The Americans only invite Americans. Everyone knows that.'

A month later, the inspiration he had been hoping would revisit him during the Open at Royal Lytham, the scene of his comeback victory in 1988, had vanished in a puff of smoke. 'I've been lucky to win the opens in such good style,' he said before the event. Nobody gave them to me, nobody threw them away.' Then he confessed quietly, 'But I don't mind if somebody gives it away in the next few years.'

In October, Ballesteros returned to the milky columns, sun-dappled courtyard and emerald fairways of the course he had fought so hard to better in the struggle for the 1997 Ryder Cup. In every respect, he had been as good as his word. In the two years since the match had been awarded to Valderrama, he had done nothing but work positively towards ensuring that the event would be a success, and since being appointed captain, he had been personally involved in every decision from uniforms to locker rooms. In 1994, he had commented that it was impossible, in this day and age, to be both player and captain, but he seemed to have forgotten that, and Schofield, among others, encouraged him to believe that his biggest contribution could come on the course. 'In the case of Seve, we are dealing with genius and his best inspiration would be playing. He is, unquestionably, Europe's Arnold Palmer.'

On the practice ground at the Volvo Masters, a group of caddies joked that Ballesteros's national pride meant that it would be more than the European team's lives were worth to lose the Ryder Cup in Spain. 'He'll bring back capital punishment,' one laughed.

On the surface, Ballesteros maintained a sardonic, confident façade, wittily responding to the news that Tom Kite, the American captain with whom he had crossed swords in a Madrid tournament two weeks earlier, had visited Valderrama. 'I like to hear that he likes the course. At Oak Hill, the Americans liked the golf course very much and they lost. I'm happy he likes it.'

He also exchanged words with Colin Montgomerie, who was the European Order of Merit winner for the fourth time running. Montgomerie had made the fatal mistake of criticizing Ballesteros's redesign of the pivotal seventeenth hole. 'He's a great player but he's not a course designer,' Montgomerie said.

George O'Grady, deputy executive director of the tour, could not believe his ears. 'We have a situation where the Ryder Cup captain, who designed the seventeenth hole, regards it as one of the best in the world, and Europe's Number One thinks it's one of the worst in the world. And they are diametrically opposed.'

Ballesteros was unconcerned. 'Monty never likes anything,' he said with a grin. 'The seventeenth is the most spectacular hole on the golf course. It's a tremendous hole – beautiful views, good for spectators, good for matchplay. When did you last see Monty happy?'

But he was only now beginning to realize what he had taken on. Eleven months remained before he captained Europe in the Ryder Cup, and already the pressure was proving almost unbearable. In a radio interview, he said the job was becoming a 'nightmare'. Later, he insisted that he hadn't meant 'nightmare' as such. 'There is so much talk about the Ryder Cup that I am dreaming about it at night,' he said after shooting a 76 for a 13 over par total of 226 in the third round. I can't talk about the Ryder Cup every five minutes. My job is to have a good team, but people are asking me when the road outside will be finished and how many people will be coming.'

He reiterated what he had said earlier in the season, which was that he would not be making an exception for players like Nick Faldo when it came to wild cards, particularly if they didn't make a concerted effort to qualify. Faldo had responded by drawing attention to Ballesteros's habit of changing his mind. 'Throughout last year Seve was saying he should have four picks instead of two, and now he has done a 180-degree turn.'

'No-one has a guarantee,' Ballesteros said. 'I will not be picking any wild cards before the last qualifying event.' He had, he claimed, asked for his quota of wild cards to be increased from two to four and been rebuffed. 'I still believe it's a mistake,' he said.

Schofield insisted that two wild cards were sufficient. 'If the European Tour can't keep enough of its players to compete in the Ryder Cup, there shouldn't be a Ryder Cup.'

At the end of the day, the only thing that mattered was that Ballesteros, the bravest and most inspirational player the Ryder Cup has ever seen, retained his ability to thrill with his courage and his humanity and the diamond-bright shards of his game. 'At his best, his explosively aggressive long game, combined with a touch as tender as a lover's caress, was a perfect expression of his personality,' Dobereiner recalled, and Foster agreed.

'He's got more talent than anyone in the world, even now. That's why I've got so much respect for him. To me, his career is like that of a world championship boxer. He's taken so many blows, so much punishment over the years, that it's getting harder and harder to pull himself up off the canvas. But there's no reason why he can't bounce back.'

In *Golf Digest*, Jerry Tarde once estimated that there had been ten golfing genius's since the Second World War: Snead, Nicklaus, Locke, Casper, Trevino, Crenshaw, Babe Zaharias, Mickey Wright and Nancy Lopez. 'Which brings us to the last golfing genius, the youngest of them all, and the one America never recognized – Seve Ballesteros. He, as much as any of the above, had the primal characteristic of genius. He could light his own fire.'

In his heart, Ballesteros knew that nobody but he could light that fire again. 'I was not wrong, was I, when I said that only once or twice does a man get to play so well?' he observed quietly. 'I knew at the time that I had reached some sort of peak, that it was a round of golf that I would think fondly about for the rest of my life. I remember saying that I hoped there would be another as good, but there hasn't been. Now I think it will probably remain the best round I play. I hope to be proved wrong.'

Index

The word 'Open' in this index refers to the British Open